Global M

Global Marketing

Douglas Lamont

First published 1996

Blackwell Publishers, Inc.
238 Main Street
Cambridge, Massachusetts 02142

Blackwell Publishers Ltd.
108 Cowley Road
Oxford OX4 1JF
UK

Library of Congress Cataloging-in-Publication Data
Lamont. Douglas F.
    Global marketing / by Douglas Lamont.
       p.   cm.
    Includes bibliographical references and index.
    ISBN 1-55786-493-4. - - ISBN 1-55786-829-8 (pbk)
    1. Export marketing.   I. Title.
HF1416.L36 1995
658.8'48 - - dc20

                        95-11202
                        CIP

British Library Cataloguing in Publication Data
A CIP catalogue record for this book is available from the British Library.

Commissioning Editor: Rolf Janke
Production Manager: Jan Leahy
Text Design: Benchmark Productions
Typeset by Benchmark Productions

Typeset in Bodoni on 11 pt. by Benchmark Productions, Inc.
Printed in the United States of America

This book is printed on acid-free paper

The book is dedicated to my father, Felix Michael, who died and to my grandsons, Michael Joseph and Brandon Anthony, who were born during the preparation of the manuscript.

Let the torch pass to a new generation.

Table of Contents

Part 3. Positioning Global Brands   216

7. Marketing Teamwork   218

foreword

I am pleased to see the publication of Douglas Lamont's new book on Global Marketing. His book represents a fresh and original exposition of the issues in marketing goods and services in global markets. He presents a framework which synthesizes both traditional analysis (country risk and company tactical marketing mix decision making) and nontraditional analysis (political, technological, cultural, and marketing strategy factors).

The book analyzes and discusses some of the most contemporary challenges facing today's global marketers: How to position Mexico within NAFTA? How to grow European market segments within France, Germany, and other countries? How to sell in Japan? How to discern future markets within China? How to assess risk in various countries?

The analysis takes place in connection with several major global industries including telecommunications, cable TV, multimedia, and logistics. At the same time, the book emphasizes the need for localizing marketing content and practice. Professor Lamont shows how companies in such industries as retailing, automobiles and computer software must manage appropriate cultural signals in planning their advertising, pricing, sales force, and value marketing. Throughout, there is an emphasis on how companies as learning organizations must position their global brands through teamwork, marketing strategy, new product development, and channel management.

Chapters 14 and 15 provide a cogent vision of the environment that international marketers face today. These chapters serve to tie the whole book together and could be profitably read both at the beginning and at the end of the course.

Professor Lamont is to be commended not only for presenting an excellent analysis of current international marketing strategies but for proposing and applying a comprehensive framework that will serve readers well in coping with the complex issues facing international marketers.

Philip Kotler
S.C. Johnson & Son Distinguished Professor of International Marketing
J. L. Kellogg Graduate School of Management, Northwestern University

preface

During the many years teaching international marketing, it became clear that neither an export-import or a global focus explained what is going on today in the world. Old 'isms fled the world scene with the fall of the Berlin Wall. Newer ones (such as, free trade, the market economy, and yes enterprise capitalism) grabbed hold of the world's economic future and would not let go.

Countries as diverse as Mexico and China were unhappy with their economy lot. They had a desire for change. They took action. Mexico joined NAFTA. China created markets with socialist characteristics. Most of the third world joined in this dash towards exports, open markets, and private capital investment.

This book attempts to capture the spirit of the times. The mid-1990s is a period of great change in the world. Either the poorer countries will combine their talents and resources with foreign capital to join the global economy, or they will be left behind. The fall back position is not another 'ism, but a retreat to long periods of poverty among even those who thought they finally had their feet planted in the middle class.

Global Marketing shows how to assess risk among countries and markets, position products globally, and tailor marketing services nation-by-nation.

The book is guide for marketers who want to sell their products throughout the world. Most of the suggestions made in the book come from many years consulting for corporate clients both at home and abroad.

Each chapter in *Global Marketing* features a unique three-scan model – *environmental, competitive, and marketing* – that provides a consistent framework for analyzing the tremendous variety of global marketing problems. By using one model to determine the similarities and differences of different situations (i.e., Mexico in NAFTA and Finland in the European Union), students get a clearer understanding of how to devise a marketing strategy that works across markets while taking regional differences into account.

The comprehensive *Instructor's Manual* to accompany *Global Marketing* was written by Van R. Wood, Professor of Marketing and Philip Morris Chair in International Business at Virginia Commonwealth University. It contains chapter outlines, lecture notes, test questions and answers, and transparency masters. The test questions for each chapter include true/false, multiple choice, concept oriented matching, and short answer essay questions. The answers for the test questions also reference the page number where the correct answer is discussed in the text.

Who to thank? I thank my clients, of course. Without their concrete problems you could not read about the solutions in this book. I also thank my colleagues at the Kellogg Graduate School of Management of Northwestern University, especially Phil Kotler who gave me many insights about international marketing. Thanks to my students who listened to many different approaches to global marketing, and to my family and friends and who suffered through my absence while I wrote the book.

Thanks to Rolf Janke, the editor at Blackwell, who had faith in the project and nursed it along when we had some rough spots in the road. Also thanks to other folks at Blackwell: Richard Burton and Mary Riso. Then there are the reviewers of the manuscript:

John H. Antil
University of Delaware

Jeffrey Fadiman
San Jose State University

John D. Furniss
Pace University

Joby John
Bentley College

C. Boyd Johnson
Central Washington University

James E. Littlefield
Virginia Polytechnic Institute and State University

Cyril M. Logar
West Virginia University

Joseph C. Miller
Indiana University

Richard Oliver
Vanderbilt University

Charles Pahud de Mortanges
University of Limburg, Netherlands

Thomas G. Ponzurick
West Virginia University

Gillian Rice
Thunderbird—The American Graduate School of International Management

Van R. Wood
Virginia Commonwealth University

Finally, thanks to the librarians at the American Marketing Association. Without their ideas and professional insights this book would be less than it is. To everyone, thanks.

My father passed away in March 1994. He lived only to see one of his two great-grandsons be born. My father was a great man who left me with a legacy: love learning, go the extra mile, and help the next generation cope with the future. This book is dedicated to all students who must get ready for a tomorrow that is still unwritten. *Global Marketing* provides all of us with crucial signposts for the future.

Douglas Lamont
Chicago, Illinois

Part One

Introduction

Chapter Format

Introduction

Framing Qualitative Ideas

Framing Corporate Culture

Understanding the Work of Global Marketers

Traditional Global Marketing

Traditional Contexts for Global Marketing

Learning About Marketing Fundamentals

Nontraditional Global Marketing

Nontraditional Contexts for Global Marketing

Learning about Emerging Marketing Principles

Comprehensive Global Marketing

Inclusive Contexts for Global Marketing

Learning About Integrating Marketing Ideas

Conclusions

Learning Objectives

After reading this chapter, you should be able to:

- Discuss the concept of global marketing within the international economy

- Outline the use of frames of reference in summarizing the fundamentals and emerging principles of global marketing

- Explain the importance of country risk, firm-specific 4Ps analysis, national marketing decisions, political frame, technological frame, cultural frame, and marketing management frame to global marketing

Marketing Frames of Reference

chapter 1

Introduction

Sometime during 1994, while contemplating Mexico's future, I learned something about the principle of cultural context, something other social science scholars call framing.[1] We bring different frameworks of understanding to the same words. Let me relate the following country-risk incident at a 1994 meeting of the Bankers Association of Foreign Trade.

"What's Mexican risk?" a banker asked.

"Now that the [presidential] election is over, it's a 'hot' country. Mexico is growing again, perhaps 5 to 6 percent in '95," I responded.

"No, no. Should I buy Mexican treasuries? The rate?" she demanded.

"Yes, it's 300 to 350 basis points above US treasuries," I replied.

Scholars and business people know that meaning depends more on the context and relationships of words than on definitions in textbooks. I was operating in one frame while the banker was operating in another frame. I was thinking about the traditional meaning of country risk in economics and international marketing while the banker in the audience was thinking about risk in financial terms, her investments, her returns.

The simultaneous existence of such different frames can have disparate business consequences. I give advice about the big picture—for example, Mexico is a "hot" country for foreign direct investments. The banker puts her clients' money to work. I am judged over the long term while she gets compliments or criticisms quarter by quarter. My original answer would have labeled me unresponsive to my audience and helped affix the epitaph "it's academic" to my speech. Giving due credence to a different frame lifted me to a level of providing sound professional advice.

Framing Qualitative Ideas

Country risk stands for something. It expresses content. For example, political risk is an expression linked with elections, assassinations, military governments, and restoration of leaders. These connections are arbitrary. Political risk is also an idiom linked with balance of payments deficits, currency devaluations, lack of profit repatriation, and failures to service sovereign and commercial debt; sometimes, this content of political risk is called economic risk (Exhibit 1-1). We interpret risk based on the current content of information, the changed circumstances of this information, and validation given these qualitative ideas by those who use the information.[2]

Country risk is more than the political risk of political scientists. For about 20 years country risk has included the economic risk of economists. For about 10 years country risk has included the cultural risk of marketers and other social scientists. Today, country risk is beginning to include the demographic risk of social scientists, and even the financial risk of bankers. These pieces of qualitative and quantitative information have been validated as useful country risk data by their users. Therefore, we have a new country risk paradigm, context, or frame of reference for global marketing.

This process of framing gives us rules to help us understand the meaning of global marketing events. We have traditional or primary contexts of global marketing, and we have nontraditional or emerging contexts of global marketing. Both together help us organize global marketing experience. Everything has meaning, and each frame fits together in part or whole with all other frames. Thus the task for marketers is to use all this qualitative information to find markets, sell products, and make money throughout the world.

Exhibit 1-1.
Emerging-Market Indicators

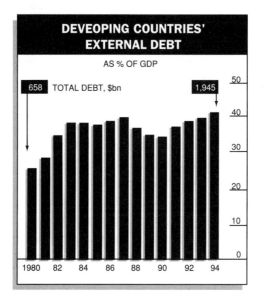

Courtesy of The Economist

Framing Corporate Culture

Here's how business people respond to new challenges overseas.[3] Each group has its own personality and nurtures its own culture: exporting, international marketing, and global marketing.

Exporting stands for something. It expresses an idea–namely, selling goods across international boundaries (Exhibit 1-2). It includes specific tasks: responding to orders, filling out customs documents, arranging for ocean or air freight and insurance, obtaining nonrecourse letters of credit, and factoring or forfeiting receivables. Exporters (and importers), ocean carriers and freight managers, and trade finance bankers share values, perceptions, and symbols about their foreign trade culture.

International marketing stands for something, too. It expresses an idea–namely, finding sales opportunities and selling goods across international boundaries. It includes specific tasks: researching foreign markets, finding overseas distributors, purchasing comprehensive logistics services, and working with others to minimize international financial costs. International sales and marketing personnel share some values with exporters and freight managers, and share other symbols with internal international finance and external trade finance managers. Theirs is an international marketing culture in which some groups are specialists in sales to Canada, Mexico and Latin America, Europe, eastern Europe and Russia, the Middle East and North Africa, India and South Asia, southeast Asia, East Asia, China, Korea, and Japan.

Global marketing also stands for something. It expresses an idea–namely, encouraging research initiatives to find new markets, segments, and niches; developing buying and selling opportunities; and marketing goods across international boundaries. It includes specific tasks: organizing a worldwide marketing effort, researching domestic and foreign markets, finding overseas partners, purchasing comprehensive support services, and managing the costs of international transactions. Global marketing executives share some values with international marketing personnel and with exporters, and share other symbols with global business executives and bankers. Theirs is a global marketing culture in which the world is their battle-

Exhibit 1-2.
Foreign Buyers of Fresh Eggs From the U.S.

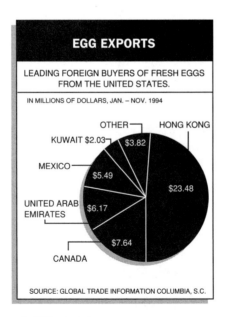

Courtesy of the Journal of Commerce

ground. Global marketers look for "hot" countries in which to invest, sell goods, and build market share.

Understanding the Work of Global Marketers

Global marketers share a common language of business. Some of it includes the traditional frames of reference about global marketing. However, year by year the language of global business includes many nontraditional frames of reference about global marketing. In the next few pages, this division between fundamentals and emerging principles will be outlined in detail. With this discussion we will have a good picture about the important work of global marketers in today's global economy.

Let's simply conclude here that global marketing is developing a new personality separate and distinct from exporting and international marketing. This new corporate culture will become readily apparent in chapter 2 when we talk about organizing marketing experience from the point of view of country risk, firm-specific 4Ps analysis, and national marketing decisions. The subsequent chapters give details, case examples, and learning exercises about global marketing for the latter part of the 20th century.

Traditional Global Marketing

Global marketing exists within several primary frames of reference. These traditional cues are the central elements of exporting, international marketing, and global marketing. They are the basic corporate culture of exporters and importers, international sales personnel, and multinational business executives. These fundamentals organize the experience of international marketers throughout the world.

Here is a short list of the traditional contexts for global marketing:

- *Country risk frame*: economic data, cultural information, and political insights

- *Firm-specific 4Ps analysis frame*: competitive analysis, product positioning, place or channel management, promotion marketing, price-driven costs, prices and revenues, and customer-oriented selling

- *National marketing decisions frame*: opportunities, analysis, strategy

All the key ideas listed in Exhibit 1-3 will be outlined in chapter 2 and explained in detail in chapters 3-15.

Exhibit 1-3.
Traditional Contexts for Global Marketing

Country Risk

Economic data

Economic growth

Disposable personal income

Balance of payments

Foreign exchange

Cultural information

National preference for local or foreign products

Power distance

Individualism versus collectivism

Middle-class lifestyle

Political insights

Privatization

Deregulation

Liberalization

Markets with socialist characteristics

Firm-Specific 4Ps Analysis

Competitive analysis

Imperfect information

Future predictions

Product positioning

Product-development life cycle

Pre-entry and post-entry product line quality

Place or channel management

Promotion marketing

Images

Brand loyalty

Direct selling

Dominant expectations

Local traditions

Price-driven costs

Offer large price savings on bundled items

Add nonprice savings on bundle

Offer smaller price savings on individual items

Anticipate moves of competitors

Continued on next page

Exhibit 1-3. *Continued from previous page*

Prices and revenues

   Higher price points

   Price targets

   Discounts off list prices

   Additional revenue

   After-tax returns on capital invested

Customer-oriented selling

   Quality concerns of customers

   After-market services

   Credibility of sales approach

   Ability to keep promises

   Value added per employee

   Savvy partners

National Marketing Decisions

Opportunities

   "Hot" country analysis

   Industry analysis

Analysis

   Who uses the product?

   How to increase market share?

   How to provide value?

   What customer signals show changes in local markets?

Strategy

   Which alternatives, and where?

   Which products, and for whom?

   Who are our customers?

   What is our value added?

   Can we do better than our competitors?

   Do we have a competitive strategy?

   Should we find better competitors?

   Are competitive forces changing in our favor?

   Is the environment conducive to our products?

Learning About Marketing Fundamentals

Traditional global marketing is about three essential ideas: country risk, firm-specific 4Ps analysis, and national marketing decisions.

Global marketers use economic data, cultural information, and political insights to rank countries by the risk involved for foreign investors in local manufacturing plants, transportation services, and financial instruments. Everyone calls this *country risk analysis.*

Marketers also do an expanded 4Ps analysis. They study their competition and then apply product, place, promotion, and price strategies to marketing goods across the globe. Strategy-minded business executives prefer to call this *competitive analysis*, and sales and marketing managers prefer the universally known term, *4Ps.*

Moreover, global marketers make national marketing decisions. Although they think globally about marketing, they must act locally to sell goods and services. Marketers weigh the risks and opportunities open to them in new markets. Then they analyze who uses competing products. Finally, they develop appropriate marketing strategies to carry them out. Marketing executives use one or more of the following terms to refer to these national marketing decisions: teamwork, marketing strategy, positioning, brand marketing, relationship marketing, and value marketing, among others.

Nontraditional Global Marketing

Global marketing also exists within several new frames of reference. These transformed cues are the central elements of an expanded view of export, international, and global marketing. They too are a part of the corporate cultural of exporters and importers, international sales personnel, and multinational business executives. These principles also organize the experience of international marketers throughout the world. In short, global marketers are reframing or transforming global marketing because they face nontraditional situations, questions, and problems. Here is short list of the nontraditional contexts of global marketing:

- *Political frame*: reinventing nation-states, free trade regimes

- *Technological frame*: decision making under uncertainty; multi-markets across technologies, industries, and nation-states; information technologies

- *Cultural frame*: demographic analysis, national character, youth and young adult culture, universality-of-freedom lifestyle, contingency perspective, walking-around research

- *Marketing management frame*: segmentation, positioning, and tailoring decisions; learning curve; institutional framework of market transactions; product diffusion; signaling game; category errors; imagined differences; measurable results; value-focused thinking

All the key ideas listed in Exhibit 1-4 will be outlined in chapter 2 and explained in detail in chapters 3-15.

Learning About Emerging Marketing Principles

Nontraditional global marketing is about the political, technological, cultural, and marketing management frames of reference. These, along with the fundamentals of traditional marketing, are brought together in the environmental, competitive, and marketing scans (see chapters 2-15). The latter outline a new set of conventions about global marketing. They also bring into global marketing analysis new information from economics, sociology, demography, and other social sciences about the meaning of things to marketers. Moreover, the importance of understanding national character, the contingency perspective, and value-focused thinking goes right to the heart of global marketing–namely, success means making sales and earning profits overseas.

Comprehensive Global Marketing

Let's summarize the argument so far.

New country risk ideas include the following: an analysis of economic data about implementing free trade and reinventing nation-states; a review of cultural information embracing national character and trends in cross-border consumption; and scrutiny of political insights about different approaches to government's involvement in the market. These ideas are explained in the section on researching international markets. The concepts are applied in the country risk cases on Mexico, Europe, Japan, and China in chapters 3-6, and in the country risk cases on South America, eastern Europe, the Middle East and North Africa, southeast and South Asia, and sub-Saharan Africa in chapter 15.

New techniques for 4Ps analysis encompass the following: an industry or competitive analysis done through the eyes of a business strategist who

Exhibit 1-4.
Nontraditional Contexts for Global Marketing

Political Frame

Reinventing nation-states

Economic change through public policy

Governing the market

Capitalist development nation-states

Regulatory nation-states

Markets with socialist characteristics

Free trade regimes

Scale economies

Larger home markets

Lower final prices

Long-term planning horizon

Technological Frame

Decision making under uncertainty

Multimarkets across technologies, industries, and nation-states

Information technologies

Contractual supply management

EDI logistics

Interactive advertising

Demand and price-drive cost strategies

Customer-oriented sales behavior

Value-focused thinking

Cultural Frame

Demographic analysis

Age-period cohort groups

Disconnection between younger and older age groups

Local and global trend setters

Similar market segments across national boundaries

National character

Second culture: global, largely American lifestyle

Cultural bilingualism

Self-referencing criteria and material success

Continued on next page

Exhibit 1-4. *Continued from previous page*

Youth and young adult culture
  Preference for global lifestyle
  Preference for Euro-American future
  Rebellion and conformity
  Disorder and achievement Hedonism and work
  Way of life
  Influence of families
  Routine purchases among family members
  Family formation
Universality-of-freedom lifestyle
Contingency perspective
  Standardization (minimum differentiation)
  Adaptation (maximum differentiation)
Walking-around research
  Period eye
  Consumer attributes unobservable
  Humbling feedback
  Clumsy vetting of new consumers

Marketing Management Frame
Segmentation, positioning, and tailoring decisions
Learning curve
Institutional framework of market transactions
  Govern the market
  Industry analysis
Product diffusion
  Discontinuous change
  Six-sigma question: What do I get?
Signaling game
Category errors
  Immature market growing
  Marketing vision
  Durable lifestyle
  Nondurable purchases
  Spanning boundaries
  Adapt to unanticipated needs

Continued on next page

Exhibit 1-4. *Continued from previous page*

Imagined differences
   Difference not in brand itself
   Difference in mind of customers
   Emotional values
   Paradigm shifts
Measurable results
   Add value
   Multiply information
   Cost-per-sale
   Set outsize targets
   Futures budget
   Cross-border partnerships
   Quality-product-price relationships
Value-focused thinking
   What is the context of a decision?
   What is the object of the decision?
   What is the impact of the decision?
   What are the enduring set of guiding principles?

helps marketers carry out teamwork, span intra-firm boundaries, and prepare an effective marketing strategy. These new management insights affect the positioning of products, middle men, and advertising agencies; the segmentation of prices and markets; and the tailoring of marketing efforts throughout all local markets in the world. These terms are defined in the section on positioning global brands. The concepts are applied in the wired and wireless telecommunications, multimedia, and EDI logistics cases in chapters 7–10.

New approaches to national marketing decisions contain the following: signals from promotion, prices, sales behavior, and value-added per employee; value-focused thinking; and value marketing. These new ideas also help marketers develop an effective marketing strategy about tailoring marketing efforts throughout the world. These terms are defined in the section on signaling national information. The concepts are applied in advertising agencies, supermarkets, megamalls, computer software, and automobile cases in chapters 11–14.

All the key ideas listed in Exhibit 1-5 will be outlined in chapter 2 and explained in detail in chapters 3-15.

Exhibit 1-5.
Inclusive Contexts for Global Marketing

Country Risk (A)
Reinventing nation-states, free trade regimes
Political insights, economic data
Political Frame

Country Risk (B)
Walking-around research, contingency perspective
Demographic analysis, national character, youth culture
Universality-of-freedom lifestyle
Cultural information
Cultural Frame

Firm-Specific 4Ps Analysis
Institutional framework of market transactions
Competitive analysis
Segmentation, positioning, and tailoring decisions
Learning curve, product diffusion
Signaling game
Category errors, imagined differences, measurable results
Product positioning
Place or channel management
Promotion marketing
Price-driven costs, prices, and revenues
Customer-oriented selling, value-focused thinking
Marketing Management Frame

National Marketing Decisions
Decision making under uncertainty
Multimarkets across technologies, industries, and nation-states
Information technologies
Opportunities, analysis, strategy
Technological Frame

Learning About Integrating Marketing Ideas

The best marketing strategy comes from a complete understanding of all possible relationships between fundamentals and emerging marketing principles. This gives us a comprehensive approach to global marketing. Nevertheless, segmentation, positioning, and targeting offerings remain the single most important work of sales persons, manufacturers representatives, exporters, international sales personnel, and global marketing managers. They ask crucial marketing questions: How do I apply value-focused thinking, and what do I get? This means marketers must use unconventional thinking about integrating nontraditional ideas into traditional frames of reference for global marketing. In this way, global marketers expand demand in Mexico, Europe, Japan, China, and the rest of the world.

Conclusions

In summary, both traditional and nontraditional frames of reference are crucial to understanding the reach of global marketing in the world economy.

Let's return to our initial three learning objectives.

1. Discuss the concept of global marketing within the international economy.

    You should have a first impression of global marketing and the work of global marketers. As you read chapters 1 and 2, you should master the major ideas in the exhibits. As you read chapters 3–6, you should master the new ideas about country risk and how they fit into the political and cultural frames of reference for global marketing. Also, as you read chapters 7–10, you should learn the new techniques of 4Ps analysis and how they fit into the marketing management frame of reference for global marketing. Moreover, as you read chapters 11–14, you should grasp the new approaches to national marketing decisions and how they fit into the technological frame of reference for global marketing.

2. Outline the use of frames of reference in summarizing the fundamentals and emerging principles of global marketing.

    You should begin committing to memory the details of all the frames of reference. In chapter 2, these traditional and nontraditional concepts are more fully explained through text and cases. In chapters 3–6, these ideas are transformed into tools for doing walking-around research in Mexico, Europe, Japan, and China. In chapters 7-10, these impressions become your checklist for doing more formal research about positioning global brands, especially in wired and wireless telecommunications, multimedia, and logistics EDI. In chapters 11-14, the resulting hard data become your tools for signaling important national information about the work of global marketers in advertising agencies, food retailing, computer software, and automobiles.

3. Explain the importance of country risk, firm-specific 4Ps analysis, national marketing decisions, political frame, technological frame, cultural frame, and marketing management frame to global marketing.

You should be aware that a comprehensive concept of global marketing is only beginning to unfold in these first few pages of the textbook. Throughout chapters 2-14 we work on creating inclusive contexts for global marketing. In chapter 15, we summarize what we have learned and apply it to the probable "hot" countries for investments in the latter part of the 20th century. If these countries do become meccas for exports and foreign investments, then the global marketing methodology developed in this book has met its first test-namely, theory becomes applied research and these become successful cases in the ever-unfolding drama of the international economy.

Notes

1. Frame analysis (or frames, contexts, situations) and the activity of reframing or transforming concepts comes from the following published work:

   Erving Goffman, *Frame Analysis: An Essay on the Organization of Experience* (Cambridge, MA: Harvard University Press, 1974).

   John O'Neill, "A Preface to Frame Analysis," *Human Studies* 4:4 (October–December 1981): 359-364.

   P. L. Manning and Betsy Cullum-Swan, "Semiotics and Framing: Examples," *Semiotica* 3/4 (1992): 239-257.

   Mary Chayko, "What Is Real in the Age of Virtual Reality? 'Reframing' Frame Analysis for a Technological World," *Symbolic Interaction* 16:2 (Summer 1993): 171-181.

2. Manning and Cullum-Swan, op cit.

3. Lise Boily, "On the Semiosis of Corporate Culture," *Semiotica* 93:1/2 (1993): 5-31.

Chapter Format

Introduction

Country Risk Questions

Environmental Scan

Initial Analysis of Marketing Opportunities

Clues to Capturing Customers

The Firm-Specific Assignment

Competitive Scan

Estimates of Market Potential

Similar Market Segments Worldwide

National Marketing Decisions

Marketing Scan

Strategies for Increasing Marketing Effectiveness

Marketing Implementation

Inclusive Contexts for Global Marketing

Conclusions

Cases: Telecommunications, Discount Retailing, Automobiles

Learning Objectives

After reading this chapter, you should be able to:

- Discuss traditional and nontraditional contexts of global marketing opportunities within the international economy

- Outline the use of the environmental, competitive, and marketing scans in global marketing research

- Explain the importance of national character, product life cycle, market contingencies, relationship marketing, and value-focused thinking to global marketing strategy

Organizing Marketing Experience

chapter 2

Introduction

Marketers manage final demand by researching international markets (chapters 3-6), positioning global brands (chapters 7-10), and signaling detailed national information (chapters 11-14). Here are emerging principles for studying global marketing.

Scanning Global Markets

Scanning the environment. In 1994, the ability of Mexico and China to deliver an increasing number of middle-class customers to American and Japanese marketers stood as a model of success for poorer Latin American and Asian nations. Notwithstanding the current higher level of country risk in 1995, marketing executives foresee higher levels of imitation and rapid rates of product diffusion as Mexico and China accept more American, Japanese, and global products in their lifestyles. Successful marketers learn how to deal with these different situations in Latin America and East Asia.

21

Scanning the competition. Foreign direct investments come in many ways because marketers react differently to the country risk associated with a particular country. After entry, all worry about the continuation of favorable economic policies. In the final analysis, marketing executives err when they choose to go too slowly into "hot" countries, such as Mexico and China. Marketers make sales by paying close attention to age, income, sex, and other demographic variables. Most youth participate in both their national culture and the global, largely American entertainment culture. Today, marketing executives do their 4Ps analysis in terms of this cultural bilingualism.

Scanning marketing. Global marketing exists within several primary frames of reference. *Traditional concepts* are as follows: country risk frame, firm-specific 4Ps analysis frame, and national marketing decisions frame. Moreover, marketers are reframing or transforming global marketing because they face nontraditional situations, questions, and problems. These *emerging principles* are as follows: political frame, technological frame, cultural frame, and marketing management frame.

Both traditional and nontraditional frames of reference are crucial to understanding the reach of global marketing in the world economy.

Governing the Market

First, let's look at the political frame. Japan matters. It promotes economic change through public policy. Its bureaucrats seek to govern the markets of consumer-friendly technologies. Japan is a capitalist development nation-state in competition with the free trade capitalist, regulatory nation-states of North America and Europe. The Japanese approach toward governing the market is deemed an appropriate model by government, business, and society in East Asia.

Success in governing the market leads to decreased country risk as foreign firms are better able to compare the value of incentive packages among competing governments. For example, the capitalist development nation-states of East Asia have lower country risk than the capitalist regulatory countries of Latin America. Yet Mexico within NAFTA has a lower country risk than Chile outside NAFTA, and both have lower risks than Brazil. Finally, both East Asia and Latin America have lower country risks than the nation-states of eastern Europe, Russia, Central Asia, South Asia, and Africa.

Global marketing is about choosing where to invest money, time, and talent to build up market share; see Exhibit 2-1. Northern Mexico, the European

Exhibit 2-1.
"Hot" Countries for Foreign Direct Investment

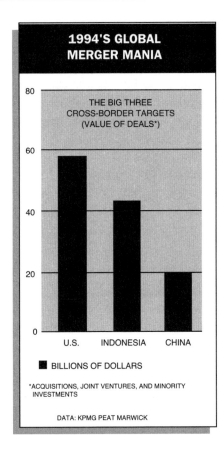

1994'S GLOBAL MERGER MANIA

THE BIG THREE
CROSS-BORDER TARGETS
(VALUE OF DEALS*)

■ BILLIONS OF DOLLARS

*ACQUISITIONS, JOINT VENTURES, AND MINORITY INVESTMENTS

DATA: KPMG PEAT MARWICK

Reprinted from February 13, 1995 issue of Business Week by special permission, copyright © 1995 by McGraw-Hill, Inc.

Union, Japan, and southern and coastal China are all good bets to make money in the future. Time will tell how well local governments price incentives to deflect the entry of foreign firms into the national markets of other countries. That's the bottom line of governing the market within global marketing.

Marketing Decisions Under Uncertainty

Second, let's study the technological frame. New technology is simply out-pacing the development of a coherent management strategy, performance-based teamwork, and relationship marketing. This is most evident in the emergence of multimarkets for computer-based wired and wireless telecommunications and

multimedia services, but it's expected to come about in retailing, food marketing, automobiles, and many other industries. Hence, marketers struggle with
speeding up the product-development life cycle and with implementing EDI
logistics, interactive advertising, price-driven cost strategies, customer-oriented
sales force behavior, and value-focused thinking. Marketing executives want to
answer the crucial six-sigma question first asked by Peter Drucker: What do I
get? Marketers call the dispensing of information about demand and price-driven cost strategies, the sharing of information about pre-entry and post-entry
product-line quality, and the application of faithful national economic, cultural,
and political risk information a *signaling game*.

Hunting for Consumers

Third, let's examine the cultural frame. Some global consumers (e.g.,
Mexicans who live American lifestyles; committed Europeans among
younger age-period cohort groups; and accomplished North Atlantic, trans-
Pacific, and East Asian overseas Chinese peoples) know about quality-product-price relationships from their previous purchase decisions in more
mature American, European, and Japanese markets. Over time, the prices of
high-quality local products fall. Their absolute decline is the greatest for local
goods whose cost is most sensitive to an end of tariffs under free trade and
the subsequent import of comparable goods from trading partners within
NAFTA and the European Union, or among competitors from East Asia.

A second culture exists worldwide. It's the global, largely American fast food,
entertainment, sports, and business culture. Stir into that pot traditional
Mexican and Latin American sensibilities, plus European and North Atlantic
ideas about age-period cohort groups. Then fast forward to Japanese convictions and overseas Chinese judgments about America's freedom lifestyle.

Unfortunately, many marketers are guilty of clumsy vetting when they do cultural research, particularly on Japan. They fail to situate Japan in its historical
context-a closed society, a rapid race for industrialization, and a quick study
of American material success. The Japanese share an emotional degree of intimacy attached to goods made by other Japanese, even those that are copy-
cat versions of the American youth-oriented culture.

Segmentation, Positioning, and Tailoring Decisions

Finally, let's look closely at the marketing management frame. Marketers have
difficulty predicting consumer choices as tastes (or unobservable attributes)

become more heterogeneous. Even though marketing executives offer standardized products, consumers impose differentiation of their own based on attributes unknown to marketers. Moreover, customers must pay a transaction cost to obtain tailored products and logistics services. Value creation takes place within a set of regional trading institutions created by nation-states to serve their own nationalist economies, the competitive position of their firms, and the marketing needs of their consumers.

Organizing Global Marketing Experience

The simultaneous existence of traditional and nontraditional marketing contexts has social and business consequences, which brings us back to the three basic divisions of this book on global marketing: researching international markets, positioning global brands, and signaling national information. Giving due recognition to the fundamentals and emerging principles of global marketing spares us from returning to older contexts (such as exporting, importing, or foreign trade, or the international marketing of American firms) that have less meaning to the real nature of global marketing at the end of the 20th century.

Let's do two things in this chapter. First, we will discuss how marketers place global marketing within traditional and nontraditional marketing contexts. Then we will apply this frame analysis to how marketing teams create, organize, and carry out effective global marketing strategy worldwide.

Country Risk Questions

Marketers manage final demand by researching international markets. Here's how fundamentals and emerging principles are combined into an analysis of global marketing opportunities. See Exhibit 2-2.

Traditional Frame Analysis

For example, NAFTA offers marketing executives a long-term planning horizon during which more Mexicans come to enjoy the lifestyle of other North Americans. Today, marketing executives rate Japan (i.e., its country risk) as equal to the United States and Europe, and less speculative than Mexico and China. Notwithstanding this analysis, explosive economic growth is occurring throughout northern Mexico and southern and coastal China. Marketers say these are "hot" countries. Let's see why.

Exhibit 2-2.
Country Risk Analysis: The Environmental Scan

Traditional Frame Analysis for Global Marketing

Country Risk

Use starting of free trade as data for long-term planning

Reinvent nation-states through economic reforms

Study trends in cross-border consumption within free-trade areas

Find similar market segments

Firm-Specific 4Ps Analysis

Competitive possibilities

Product positioning

Channel management

Promotion marketing

Pricing signals

Customer-oriented selling creates value marketing

National Marketing Decisions and Marketing Opportunities

Pay attention to impact of national character

Collect both hard and soft information

Recognize the import of the contingency perspective

Build up market share through standardization and adaptation

Promote relationship marketing

Nontraditional Frame Analysis for Global Marketing

Political Context

Promote economic change through public policy

Compete for investments among nation-states

Reduce country risk by governing the market

Technological Context

Outpace marketing management reforms

Dispense information on demand and price-driven costs

Share information about product-line quality

Apply faithful country risk information

Cultural Context

Accept marketing values of second culture worldwide

Try to avoid clumsy vetting of local cultures

Recognize most consumer attributes are unobservable

Continued on next page

Exhibit 2-2. *Continued from previous page*

Marketing Management Context

Work on new marketing strategies for free-trade regimes

Implement segmentation, positioning, and tailoring decisions

Nontraditional Frame Analysis

Value creation is about configuring offerings made by firms to customers. Offerings are shaped by the following:

- The institutional political context of market transactions (aka governing the market, public policy, or country risk)

- The technological context of product positioning, interactive channel management, aggressive approach to promotion and advertising, and price-driven cost strategies

- The cultural context of reconfiguring marketing strategies, shifting responsibilities for final products and services, and providing a wide selection of value creation activities based on the real needs of customers within "hot" nation-states

- The marketing management context of customer-oriented teamwork, relationship selling and marketing behavior, and value-focused thinking on a grand scale

This reinvention of public policy, the 4Ps strategy, customer-oriented selling behavior, and value-focused management thinking are at the heart of effective relationship marketing.

Environmental Scan

Marketers employ environmental scans within three different traditional contexts for global marketing. They also add cues from new information about global marketing. Let's emphasize the fundamentals, add some of the emerging principles, and summarize their joint contribution to global marketing.

Country Risk

Marketing executives try to understand how governments reinvent nation-states through substantial economic reforms, for example, privatization in

Mexico, liberalization in the European Union, and markets with socialist characteristics in China.

They also study trends in demographic data to see what these show about cross-border consumption within free trade areas. For example, committed Europeans tend to be young adults or "Yeppies" (young European professionals), fashion trend setters, and transcontinental business executives.

Moreover, marketers try to find similar market segments across the North Atlantic and the Pacific regions of the world. There's money to be made in Japan—that is, if one knows how to go about studying young working males, office ladies (or secretaries), working executive women, and cross-over market segments in Japan. The same can be said about China and other markets in East Asia.

Finally, successful executives place global marketing within the context of political reforms. China is pushing a gradualist approach that experiments with limited overseas Chinese-style changes in the southern and coastal provinces before trying them throughout the rest of the country.

Firm-Specific 4Ps Analysis

For firms within the telecommunications services industry, many competitive possibilities are simply unknown, some present imperfect information, and only a few offer assurance about the future. Marketers find it difficult to predict the future. Moreover, to get from telephones to telecommunications, then to telecomputers, and now to multimedia requires major revisions in the way marketers look at the future. They must span technological boundaries and leave themselves open to exploiting the ambiguities of soft information about alternative futures.

Product positioning. Successful telecom executives develop a habit of teamwork in preparing a 4Ps-based marketing strategy for the following product market segments:

- Basic telephones for older persons

- Enhanced telephones for middle-agers

- Online telecomputers for young adults

- Telecom services for rich persons

Between now and the end of the decade, the focus of all telecom firms must switch to the last two product market segments.

Channel management. A new services marketing category is emerging from the underworld of computer hacking, the *demi-monde* of virtual reality, and the universe of logistics EDI, and their digital convergence with wired and wireless telephone, microwave, and satellite technologies. Because the telecom services (multimedia, logistics EDI) industry is relatively new, marketers must prepare themselves for a wide array of new and different industry, market, and cultural possibilities.

National Marketing Opportunities

Marketing executives measure their success by adding local promotion campaigns in the advertising of global brands, by pushing for price-driven cost data, by struggling to gain customer loyalty throughout the world, and by being sure all these changes lead to more value added per employee.

Promotion marketing. Do ads interpret current images? Do brands convey dominant expectations and conventions? Will customers buy products based on advertising global brands? Today's advertising signals tell us to combine global commitment with local vision and to make promotion appeals compatible with international and national lifestyles. Messages must use local traditions and symbols of each country to enhance national demand. This is the contingency approach to promotion and advertising.

Price signals. Are prices based on costs? Or do prices reflect quality or image, or both? Will customers buy products based on a bundled price strategy? Do firms always anticipate the strategies of competitors? Should firms target prices as the basis for customer choice?

The difference between observable and unobservable attributes exists in pricing when customers make decisions about brand choices. Even under the condition of sufficient customer heterogeneity, the unobservable attributes direct our attention to minimum differentiation in product positioning. When some customers prefer to buy standardized products from sellers with higher prices, price competition is taking place in which the unobservable attributes are more important than the observable attributes.

Peter Drucker insists marketing executives develop a price-driven cost strategy based on observable attributes so that market share is never lost. He also suggests pricing new products two or three years down the learning curve so that they are much lower initially than all their competitors. He also recommends that marketers answer the six-sigma question: "What do I get?" from product positioning, channel management, promotion marketing, and segmented price signals.

Selling and value marketing. How does the sales force deliver a high-quality product line? What does this behavior mean in terms of customer satisfaction and loyalty? Do customer-oriented selling practices increase profitability?

What is the value added per employee? What do I get in terms of additional revenue? What is the financial impact of quality improvements? An increase in sales? More pretax revenues? Higher after-tax returns on capital invested? What is the return on assets? There's money to be made in customer loyalty, expectations, and customer satisfaction. They are best attained through horizontal or team-managed corporations, which are going through discontinuous change and where effort to make changes is on a grand scale.

Initial Analysis of Marketing Opportunities

Successful marketers ask the following marketing questions: Who uses the product? How to increase market share? How to provide value? What customer signals show changes in local markets? With answers to these questions, marketing executives know rates of product diffusion for *Pepe* jeans, *Zanussi* white-line appliances, *Sensor* razors, and *Vaseline Intensive Care* lotion among Parisians and Germans (east and west), and within the eternal cultures of Provence, the Mezzogiorno, and County Cork. Let's strengthen these national marketing opportunities with additional nontraditional information.

National Character

For example, national character plays the crucial role in determining whether local or foreign products are accepted within Japan. To speed up the rate of product diffusion within Japan, marketers search for useful fragments of cultural information (such as dressing samurai warriors in baseball uniforms) that give the products an alluring appeal among Japanese youth. By pretesting *Coke*, *McDonald's*, and *Avon* products among overseas Chinese, these goods are more easily accepted by mainland Chinese.

"Soft" Information

However, trend is not destiny in goods without a past, but with an expectant future. This is especially true in the telecom services industry. We don't know which type of wireless service (cellular, digital GSM, specialized mobile radio, or direct broadcasting satellites) or which set of telecom alliances will prevail. All are substitutes for one another, and consumers pay an opportunity cost if they make the wrong decisions.

But trend may be destiny in the video games industry. First, remember the sweeping technological revolution that moved successive groups of adults to become users of computers. Second, recognize the growing passion of governments to privatize the telecom services industries. Third, recall the disconnection between those who came of age before and after computers. All three are "soft" information for the environmental scans. They tell us the following: the early adopters of multimedia are teenage boys who become young working adult men, husbands, and fathers, and entrepreneurs in the computer-based telecom services industry.

Market Share

Japanese firms built up market share among the vidkids. They followed Drucker's advice: Set up a price-driven cost strategy to capture market share; premium prices must reflect higher value-added extensions to the product line; management negotiates prices that closely resemble the real economic and business conditions of local markets. Japanese firms asked the six-sigma question: What do I get? And then they added more questions: When do I get it? Why must I wait so long? Can't you do something to speed up delivery? What can I do? Their sales force personnel who built up relationship selling with customers answered all these six-sigma questions.

Relationship Marketing

Is there a commitment to change on a grand scale among governments, firms, suppliers, and customers? Is their movement toward predictable change? Do the sum of sales made to customers show gains in values important to them (e.g., lower retail prices, public access networks for interactive connectivity, and a high-quality product line)? Is the sum of alliances, partnerships, joint ventures, and wholly owned investments made with existing or new partners from traditional and nontraditional competitors, suppliers, and customers good for future business?

Clues to Capturing Customers

If their marketing plans are well executed, marketers cut through most of this cross-cultural confusion. For Mexico marketers promote cultural bilingualism–that is, a traditional ethnocentric Mexico intermixed with a global, largely American lifestyle. They bring order to unfolding events under NAFTA, reinvent Mexico's free-trade future, and grow its middle-class market.

For eastern Europe, marketing executives must pay attention to national character, power distance, traditional self-referencing criteria, low incomes, high unemployment, and many other demographic difficulties. Again, marketers call this cultural bilingualism—that is, a western, largely German and American gloss with eastern thinking about marketing practices.

Marketing within Japan builds on national character, collectivism, material success, and Japanese-only self-referencing criteria. Although Japan is different, cultural bilingualism does exist—that is, a largely American gloss with Japanese thinking about marketing practices.

Once we move from Europe and the United States to East Asia we know intuitively that we must alter our promotion and advertising images to mesh with the local cultural values predominant in Japan, China, and southeast Asia. This, too, confirms the need for a contingency perspective when dealing with global promotion and advertising.

Summary: Scanning the Environment

In 1994, the ability of Mexico and China to deliver an increasing number of middle-class customers to American and Japanese marketers stood as a model of success for poorer Latin American and Asian nations. Notwithstanding the current higher level of country risk in 1995, marketing executives foresee greater imitation and rapid rates of product diffusion as Mexico and China accept more American, Japanese, and global products in their lifestyles. Successful marketers learn how to deal with these different situations in Latin America and East Asia.

The Firm-Specific Assignment

Marketers manage final demand by positioning global products. Here's how emerging cultural principles enhance an analysis of global marketing opportunities. See Exhibit 2-3.

Freedom Lifestyle

For example, *Levi's* or *Pepe* jeans, *Benetton* sportswear, and *Nike* sport shoes fit neatly into the global, largely American consumer culture. This is the freedom lifestyle, the second-culture for the youth of the world. Let's see how this lifestyle is working itself out in Europe and Japan.

Exhibit 2-3.
Firm-Specific 4Ps Analysis: The Competitive Scan

Traditional Frame Analysis for Global Marketing
Country risk
Study privatization and deregulation of PTOs
Negotiate incentives for foreign direct investments
Firm-Specific 4Ps Analysis
Product positioning of telephones, computers, and multimedia
Channel management of EDI logistics
Integrated promotion and interactive advertising
Price-driven cost strategies
Selling through quality, after-market services, and relationships
National Marketing Decisions and Marketing Research
Who uses the product?
How to increase market share
How to provide value
What customer signals show changes in the local market?

Nontraditional Frame Analysis for Global Marketing
Cultural Context
Accept universality-of-freedom lifestyle
Pay attention to age-period cohort groups
Avoid humbling feedback
Try to avoid clumsy vetting of demographic information
Note teenage boys (or vidkids) are tomorrow's computer experts
Marketing Management Context
Be careful in defining a new or changing industry
Avoid category errors
Add value by multiplying bits of information
Study cross-border mergers, acquisitions, and partnerships
What will be the long-term use of interactive multimedia?
How will marketing teams span managerial boundaries?
How will teams create unstructured marketing decisions?

Continued on next page

Exhibit 2-3. *Continued from previous page*

Technological Context

Forget wired or landlines telephone connections

Stress wireless, cellular, or satellite connections today

Look to interactive multimedia connections for the future

How will consumers adapt multimedia for unanticipated needs?

Political Frame

Gain scale economies

Tie production to cross-border continental market segments

Get down the learning curve

Practice value-focused thinking and value marketing

Age-Period Cohort Groups

Today, marketers declare younger French and Germans dedicated Europeans or Euro-Americans. The North Atlantic youth culture is a collective work of the imagination whose making never ends. This is an important cultural frame for global marketing.

What does it mean to grow up in the 1990s and be a part of the youngest age-period cohort group? In France, youth are the family's primary influence in the purchase of food, clothes, cosmetics, TVs, sound systems, computers, cars, and holidays. Unlike their counterparts in the United States, the French and other European young adults live at home until about age 25. Nevertheless, they have a preference for Europe over individual countries. Moreover, and this is especially important to marketers, the young carry this preference for Europe forward when they marry, form families, and buy their own furniture, white-line appliances, and TVs.

Lifestyles

Modern European youth culture offers rebellion and conformity, disorder and achievement, and hedonism and meaningful work. Youth fashion is a way of life. The youth want to be themselves by showing a product's trademark to their friends. They also want to be different within their own tribe. Since the youth of France believe in the meaning underlying the trademark rather than the trademark itself, they expect fashion to give them a way of life suitable to carry them forward into the future. This is the subculture that is going mainstream in France–and in Europe.

The values and expectations of French, Finnish, and Turkish youth, seemingly so far apart in economy and cultural background, appear to be converging, brought together by America's entertainment industry. The values of American culture that most attract young people include respect for the individual and his or her freedom of choice. Absorption of American values via TV culture is a major source of sociocultural change around the globe.

"Humbling" Feedback

Euro-American trendsetters face resistance from traditional, rural, ethnocentric French and Germans. American Yuppies brave protests from European Yeppies. National character is still more important to Yeppies than the global, largely American consumer culture.

Many marketers are guilty of clumsy vetting when they do demographic research on Europe. They have failed to situate the European Union in its historical context–a reaction to two World Wars, the looming threat of the former Soviet Union, and the American view of what Europe should be until the eastern countries are reconnected to Western Europe. To avoid "humbling" feedback, marketers must pay attention to the real national differences among French, Germans, British, and Italians.

Cultural Insights

Today, marketers consider younger Japanese consumers as both Japanese and accomplished trans-Pacific people; see Exhibit 2-4. Young working male adults purchase *Levi's* jeans, *Nike* sports shoes, and leather jackets for their weekend, leisure time. Working women travel throughout the Pacific to buy luxury goods more cheaply than at home. These routine purchasing activities fit neatly into the global, largely American consumer culture, adapted to Japanese pursuits of recreation, leisure, and play. As we approach the new century, the Japanese youth culture is a collective work of the imagination just beginning because their parents still prefer more traditional lifestyles.

Is the new Japanese consumer fantastic, unfathomed, secretive, odd, and enigmatic? Is this new consumer Different with a capital D? Or is this new Japanese consumer different with a small d, similar to the difference one finds in Mexico or Europe? To avoid "humbling" feedback, US marketers must pay attention to the real national differences between Americans and Japanese. Marketers must also recognize that Japanese consumers are changing

Exhibit 2-4.
What the Japanese Buy

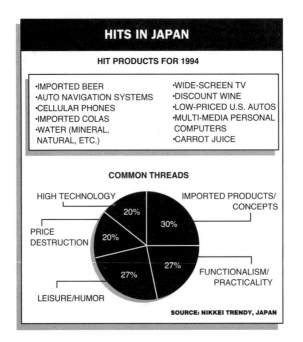

Courtesy of the Journal of Commerce, January 6, 1995

with other groups in the world, but they are changing at a much slower pace than are the Europeans.

Competitive Scan

Marketers employ competitive scans within an industry-analysis context for global marketing. Here's how emerging marketing management principles enhance an analysis of global marketing opportunities.

Category Errors

Within the computer-based telecom services industry, traditional contexts exist for wired telephones and have been replicated for wireless or cellular telephones. That's a classic category error in marketing. Today, digital-based multimedia that comes into homes and businesses through wired and wireless telephone lines is an emerging new marketing category. The value added is in the use and multiplication of bits of information rather than in the transmission of data by traditional telephone and cable TV companies. Let's see how this important change in the telecom services industry is working out throughout the world.

Immature Market

Mexican customers want better telephone service today, not tomorrow, and international business customers are among the drivers of the telecommunications revolution within Mexico. Telecommunications deregulation is going forward within Mexico no matter the pain it might cause Teléfonos de Mexico, the recently privatized Mexican telephone monopoly. Telmex must give the partnerships formed by Bell Atlantic and MCI with Mexican firms equal access to the existing wired long-distance network. This development is a product of NAFTA.

Marketing Vision

Many telecom alliances (such as Bell Atlantic and MCI in Mexico, AT&T with cellular partners in the United States and around the world, and the Baby Bells and the state-owned PTOs in Europe) are positioning wireless interactive connectivity for voice, data, and video traffic. This is just the beginning of an immature market growing, prospering, and seeking new ways to become mature.

Interactive wireless services pose a competitive threat to both wired telephone and cable TV firms. Today, customers with high incomes are already buying video servers for their PCs. Young adult customers who are the vidkids of the 1990s' computer revolution are not far behind. This is a fast-changing industry that needs marketing vision from its managers.

Unanticipated Needs

Throughout the world, teenage boys are precommitted to Japanese video games and they are ready to make interactive multimedia games a part of their durable lifestyle. Yet differences do exist among these customers. American boys prefer more bloodthirsty games. Japanese young adult men prefer less violent games and role-playing games with some subtlety and complexity. Excessive violence is not popular in Germany.

In the minds of young women and upscale families, interactive amusements still are a nondurable part of their routine purchasing behavior. When these products become similar to TV entertainment, many middle-age customers will give their precommitment to firms offering interactive videos on games, foreign travel, home shopping, sports statistics, and new fashion items.

We are in the midst of creating a new marketing category. The products are similar and typical. They share common features. Moreover, these products serve as props for some culturally defined purpose–that is, for families to be entertained together. Thus the boundary for this new category is based on usage for entertainment, transactions, communications, and information.

Unfortunately, we don't know two crucial pieces of information: After initial market entry, how will consumers adapt interactive multimedia products for their own unanticipated needs? What will be the long-term usages of interactive multimedia? Until we know answers to these contingency questions we cannot forecast accurate sales numbers for the product-development life cycle of interactive multimedia products.

Imagined Differences

Both Europeans and Americans suspect most advertising does not work in getting more sales for new products. A successful telecom advertisement must create an imagined difference–that is, a difference that does not necessarily reside in the brand itself, but lodges in the customer's mind. Yet advertising conveys emotional values, most of them tied to national cultures. Marketers err when they mistake paradigm shifts in the United States for trends in Europe, East Asia, and Latin America.

Measurable Results

If we apply integrated marketing solutions to interactive multimedia and other parts of the emerging telecom services industry, we can obtain measurable results. Our promotion creativity will give us bottom-line results, such as the cost-per-sale of each ad or direct marketing piece. Even when we cannot forecast entry, growth, maturity, and decline in the product life cycle, we may wish to determine larger-than-life goals and then use them in a futures budget.

If we decide to export, we should not fall into the trap of most American, Canadian, and British exporters. They think about pricing new products after they resolve their product, place, and promotion strategies. Moreover, UK exporters are more prone to give richer discounts off list prices than are American and Canadian exporters. On the other hand, German exporters prefer to match price and quality for their customers abroad. Given the high value added of their export products, the Germans are not willing to give more than minimal discounts–and then only to their most valuable clients. Japanese exporters price according to transactions. Their goals are to increase market share and capture higher price points. Price discounts are part of an overall pricing strategy to gain access to local distribution channels in Europe and the United States.

Price-Driven Costs

According to Peter Drucker, price targets and higher price points are more important than costs, profit margins, and streams of future revenues. If products are priced correctly, then production costs, the export marketing sales effort, and all international costs are covered, and the firm makes money, too. This is Drucker's price-driven cost strategy and a crucial frame for global marketing, especially in the telecom services industry.

Marketing Strategy

Although the telecom services industry is alive wherever affluent consumers live, it is premature to think of a global telecommunications industry. The deregulation concerns of the United States are different from the privatization efforts of Mexico. Governments seek the best of both worlds–modern forms of connectivity for their citizens without giving up control over cash flow and culture to outside, foreign interests. All the telecom service firms cooperate with government because traditional managers prefer known risks over the uncertainty and ambiguity of the future.

Will the telecom service companies find ways to offer value-added services within NAFTA and the EU, and throughout East Asia and the rest of the world? Many firms are using "juice" teams, executives who play ambiguous roles, associates who span boundaries, groups that make unstructured marketing decisions, and a corporate culture for collective managerial decision making. All the telecom service companies need better managerial decision making in an era of governing the market through privatization and subsequent deregulation. The answers lie not in technology, but in how the firms put together their nonroutine partnerships for marketing telecom services to business and household customers throughout the world.

Estimates of Market Potential

Successful marketers ask the following national marketing questions: Who uses the product? How to increase market share? How to provide value?

What customer signals show changes in the local market? Mexico is a good place to do walking-around research. Go to the large retail stores and observe what Mexicans buy. They prefer very large family sizes–sizes never seen in US retail stores. Wal-Mart and others know the benefits of matching size with quality and bundled pricing. Wal-Mart initiated a merchandising revolution in Mexico similar to what it had done in the United States. This development is a product of NAFTA.

As more fashion, film, and music cross national boundaries and become European, cross the North Atlantic and become Euro-American, and cross the Pacific and become Ameri-Asian, the media broadcast the universality of the global, largely American consumer culture. Careful marketing research shows the achievement of making products seem less strange in Japan when they are familiar in Europe and a part of ourselves in the United States.

Framing the Research Problem for Consumer Goods

Today, a great deal of marketing research done in Japan concerns the following questions:

- Is the self-expression found in juniors the birth of a youth culture?

- Are these juniors more collectivist than their counterparts in Europe or the United States?

- Do juniors (similar to their parents) harmonize their individual, in-dependent self-expression within the whole of Japanese society?

Although some things are changing within Japan, many parts of the youth culture from Europe and the United States are not appropriate in marketing goods within Japan.

Moreover, China's huge internal market is a mirage. Here's what we know. Consumption patterns in Hong Kong spill over into imitation purchases within the Guangzhou region of southern China, but the richer patterns of consumption among the overseas Chinese do not affect purchasing behavior among poorer mainland Chinese. Product diffusion occurs slowly on the mainland, faster in Hong Kong, and even more quickly among the overseas Chinese who live in Taiwan, Thailand, and Singapore. None of these Chinese groups choose a lifestyle imported from Japan, Europe, or the United States. All marketing effort within China must recognize that mainland Chinese are mostly ethnocentrists who favor traditional consumption habits. Marketers will find customer markets in China, but they will have to work at translating these into sales.

Framing the Research Problem for Services

In China, build brand loyalty. Employ direct selling. Team up with savvy partners. Carve a tiny luxury niche. Overcome the lure of the billion-buyer market. Look for opinion leaders. Get the numbers right. Estimates of market potential within China must be tempered with a realistic plan for paying back foreign investors. Otherwise, the Chinese market is indeed a mirage for foreign telecom service firms.

Customers in Europe and the United States want the expertise of sales personnel, their knowledge of other suppliers and competitors, and their personal insights about whether the deal is a good value over the long run. Sales personnel have three ways to build customer loyalty, improve their performance, and get the greatest payback possible. First, address the quality concerns of customers; second, make after-market service dependable; third, improve the credibility of the sales approach.

In Japan, customers expect products and services to be of the highest quality and to perform as anticipated. The most important issue for Japanese customers is that sales personnel keep their promises. These Japanese "salarymen" will build long-term relationships and eventually sell new telecom services, such as multimedia, Internet, and direct satellite transmissions.

Similar Market Segments Worldwide

If value-focused thinking is done well, marketers reinvent older industries and turn them into something new and different for today's global consumers.

For example, within the US automobile industry, location decisions about assembly operations are made by executives from the auto companies and their suppliers, and by Mexican bureaucrats who offer incentives for foreign investments to lure them away from Korea and southeast Asia. Their collective marketing strategy under NAFTA is to choose the optimal site within North America and Mexico for the manufacture of a full range of cars, trucks, and parts. Plants located in Mexico gain scale economies as their costs of production are tied to a larger North American home market, continental market segments for small cars, and lower final prices to Mexican customers.

Ford's Mexican-made cars are world cars because all the major systems and components are identical to those found in the United States and Europe. This distinction is the result of joint efforts by engineers, designers, manufacturing experts, and suppliers—Ford's launch team. They are Ford's firm-specific answers to the uncertainties found in the microeconomic policies of the NAFTA and EU countries.

Ford made these investments to improve its international competitiveness. Ford wanted to get down the learning curve before its competitors, and it wanted to do so on a grand scale. Thus, Ford committed its senior management to reengineering, benchmarking, and value marketing, and forced its worldwide supplier network and its Japanese partner, Mazda, to join in the rush to become more competitive.

Summary: Scanning the Competition

Foreign direct investments come in many ways because marketers react differently to the country risk associated with a particular country. After entry, all worry about the continuation of favorable economic policies. In the final analysis, marketing executives err when they choose to go too slowly into "hot" countries, such as Mexico and China. Marketers make sales by paying close attention to age, income, sex, and other demographic variables. Most youth participate in both their national culture and the global, largely American entertainment culture. Today, marketing executives do their 4Ps analysis in terms of this cultural bilingualism.

National Marketing Decisions

Marketers manage final demand by signaling detailed national information; see Exhibit 2-5. For example, US firms see Mexico as an export opportunity for nut-inserted abrasive discs, an investment opening for discount retailing and automobiles, and a national market for telecommunications partnerships. Japanese firms view China as a growing market for cosmetics, personal care products, consumer electronics, TV productions, cellular phones, credit cards, and many other goods and services. These two "hot" countries are examples of the possibilities of global marketing within the international economy.

Exhibit 2-5.
National Marketing Decisions: The Marketing Scan

Traditional Frame Analysis for Global Marketing
Country Risk
Construct clusters of purchasing behavior

Compare individualism versus power distance

Examine imitation purchases

Pay attention to self-referencing criteria

Use a product diffusion model

Stress national character and cultural distance

Firm-Specific 4Ps Analysis and Product Positioning Strategies
Capture first-mover advantage

Import products on a timely basis

Provide technologically superior goods

Adapt products to country's unique cultural identity

Compare new imports with existing products

Pay attention to product diffusion within nation-states

Firm-Specific 4Ps Analysis and Price Segmentation Strategies
Research customers' view of price-quality relationship

Entry: Bundle prices to obtain high profits

Growth: Offer higher prices to get increased market share

Maturity: Discount prices to avoid brand switching

Decline: Permit lower price points to maintain revenue

National Marketing Decisions and Marketing Strategy
Apply standardization, adaptation, or contingency perspective

Target customers, segment by lifestyles, select observable groups

Pursue relationship marketing with alliances

Answer the six-sigma question: What do I get?

Promote relationship marketing

Implement effective sales force behavior

Make good value marketing decisions

Continued on next page

Exhibit 2-5. *Continued from previous page*

Nontraditional Frame Analysis for Global Marketing
Marketing Management Frame and Value-Focused Thinking

What is the context of a decision?

What is the object of the decision?

What is the direction of preference or impact of the decision?

Combine strategic and means objectives

Identify potential decision opportunities

Develop an enduring set of guiding principles

Copyright © Douglas F. Lamont. All rights reserved.

Marketing Scan

Marketers employ marketing scans within both traditional and nontraditional contexts for global marketing.

Country Risk and National Character

Hollywood says Mexico's national culture is converging with the popular culture of the United States. This general conclusion does not help marketers target their products to Mexican consumers. No signals are given to marketing executives about what is really Mexican and what is really American.

Here's how marketers assemble national marketing signals through walking-around research:

1. Construct clusters of purchasing behavior.

2. Compare individualism versus power distance.

3. Examine imitation purchases.

4. Pay attention to self-referencing criteria.

5. Use a product diffusion model.

These marketing research techniques help marketers determine the collective image of a country or assess why a people's national character is similar to or different from others.

Sometimes cultural distance between two countries is small. Hence, most American products sell well in the UK and vice versa. At other times, cultural distance is large. Many US products don't do well in Japan. They lack symbolic importance as gifts, fail to meet quality tests demanded by Japanese in their routine purchasing behavior, or do not fit within the collective memory of Japanese society. On the other hand, many Japanese goods do well in the United States because they match the needs of American consumers.

Although the Chinese buy both Japanese and American products, the Chinese prefer their own goods because they fit similar to a glove over their national character. The Chinese also invest with their family, friends, and coworkers to avoid the market ambiguities preferred by Americans, English, and other Europeans. Moreover, these two attributes of national character are common among mainland Chinese and between them and the overseas Chinese who live outside of China. Western marketers often overlook this important marketing fact.

Product Positioning and Marketing Management

When foreign products are imported on a timely basis, are technologically superior to locally made goods, and are adapted to a country's unique cultural identity, they capture first-mover advantage during the entry phase of the product life cycle. If these new imports compare favorably with existing products (or focal option), they enjoy a rapid product diffusion during the growth phase of the product-development life cycle.

Price Segmentation and Marketing Management

Price plays a crucial role in the adoption of innovations. Diffusion success depends on customers' view of the price-quality relationship during the different phases of the product life cycle. Here are four stylized situations:

- Bundle products and price, and obtain high profits during the entry phase

- Offer better quality with higher price points, and get increased market share during the growth phase

- Discount prices to avoid brand switching from nonloyal customers during the maturity phase

- Permit lower price points to maintain revenue from loyal customers during decline phase

A mixed bundling pricing strategy is more profitable than other selling alternatives. Sellers must offer buyers savings on both individual and bundled items, but a larger proportion of the savings must be offered on the bundle rather than on individual items. Consumers first are looking for price savings on the bundle, then nonprice savings on the bundle (i.e., after-market support), and almost as an afterthought they are looking for price savings on the individual items, too.

Trying to change consumer values about products, brands, and prices is almost impossible once the product-development life cycle moves from the growth to maturity stages. The diffusion of products across many price segments leads consumers to accept certain price points as the crucial indicator of price-quality relationships. These don't change once the product is well established in the marketplace.

Strategies for Increasing Marketing Effectiveness

Here is a sample list of questions for executives to use in developing a marketing strategy for all countries:

1. Which alternatives, and where?

2. Which products, and for whom?

3. Who are our customers, and do they exist across borders?

4. What is our added value, and can we do it better than our competitors?

5. Do we have a competitive marketing strategy for ourselves and for our partners?

6. Are our competitors worthy of our interest, or should we find better competitors?

7. What is the makeup of our industry, and are the competitive forces changing in our favor?

8. Is the overseas environment conducive to our products, technologies, and marketing efforts?

Marketing executives prepare a marketing strategy based on standardization (or minimum differentiation), adaptation (maximum differentiation), or an in-between situation called the contingency perspective. The last is the place in which nontraditional cues are crucial to preparing a successful global marketing strategy. We do "walking-around" marketing research to be sure we have the best information possible to make crucial national and global marketing decisions.

Market Contingencies and Product Positioning

The task for marketers is to invest in customers and reduce the uncertainty over unobservable attributes. The former must determine which customers to target, then segment them by lifestyles, and finally place them into groups with observable traits. Moreover, marketing executives must use unconventional thinking to uncover those demographic reference groups that help find long-term customers.

For example, in the quest for first-mover advantage, all multimedia competitors are looking for partners and investors from the telephone, cable TV, computer, publishing, and entertainment industries. Together they are trying to define a new industry, one based on the value added in using bits of information. These partners-competitors-investors, together with customers, are in the process of deciding how the new industry will combine hardware standardization, software adaptation, and marketing mix differentiation in price, promotion, and place strategies. This is their contingency perspective.

Today, marketers are expanding final demand by convincing affluent teenage vidkids and their parents to augment use of video games with new forms of interactive multimedia. Nintendo dominates the video games category because it has adapted its games to suit both Japanese and American cultural tastes. More is required in terms of software development, new hardware, and online connections. Nintendo games are no longer unique in the minds of customers. Nintendo must customize its games so that users can change their interactive multimedia to suit their own entertainment preferences. This is a positioning strategy for multimedia video game products within global markets.

Marketing Implementation

Globalization, standardization, minimum differentiation, least-common denominator approach, and not-invented-here syndrome: these describe a global path pocked with the ruts of language and cultural differences. Here are several crucial marketing signals: "think global, act local"; target global consumers carefully in all countries; keep costs to a minimum because lost business is expensive; and tie strategy to new ways to carry out business abroad.

Relationship Marketing

Clearly, cross-border alliances, joint ventures, and partnerships are the up-and-coming way business leaders choose to participate in the global marketplace. Partners go into alliances to open new markets, gain new skills, and share fixed costs. Their bargaining over rights and responsibilities commits the participating firms to a long-term economic relationship in which all partners deal with the competitive changes in an industry worldwide. The crucial asset is the quality of the partner relationships.

Do the partners trust one another? Do their joint customers trust them to provide a high-quality product line? Does everyone involved trust all salespersons to behave in a manner consistent with the long-term interests of customers? Do all the past, present, and future interactions match performance with customer expectations? Do customers gain satisfaction from the partners, their sales force, their products and services, and all other aspects of the selling relationship?

Sales Force Behavior

Sales and marketing teams, sales force behavior, and salespersons' effectiveness all promote customer loyalty, effectiveness, and satisfaction. These are all forms of personal selling–one-on-one cold calls, status reports, and the "close" on the sale. Segmentation, positioning, and targeting offerings remain an art of salespersons, manufacturers' representatives, and other commissioned sales agents. The sales force still is the eyes and ears of the firm.

Global selling is closely bound to national culture. Therefore, the sales force must always ask the crucial six-sigma question: What do I get?

Value Marketing Decisions

Here are the decision opportunities open to the senior management at Ford, Nissan, BMW, Honda, Mercedes-Benz, and other auto firms as they set marketing strategy.

What is the context of a decision? For Ford, BMW, and Mercedes-Benz the context of their individual decisions is the restructuring of the auto industry worldwide. For Nissan and Honda the context of their individual decisions is Japan's long-term recession and the appreciation of the yen vis-à-vis the US dollar.

What is the object of the decision? Again, for the first three auto companies the object of their individual decisions is manufacturing capacity in North America and Europe. For Nissan the object of its individual decisions is its financial losses in the UK and Spain. For Honda the object of its individual decision is finding another low-cost way to participate in the European auto market.

What is the direction of preference or impact of the decision? Finally, Ford wants to build a world car for both Europe and North America. It's leading the auto industry.

BMW needs small cars and utility vehicles in its product line for the North Atlantic area. It wants to avoid using its high-quality brand name on Rover cars.

Mercedes-Benz prefers cars and trucks with local content. It wants to use its high-quality brand name for its new smaller cars.

Nissan needs cars that meet customer needs in Japan, the United States, and Europe; it must stop its slide in sales revenues or face substantial shrinkage in cash flow.

Honda wants to replicate its American success in Europe, but without paying the huge investment costs required of a crucial player in Europe.

Decision opportunities. All these are strategic objectives of the auto firms. These objectives provide fundamental guidance for senior management. Then add means objectives; for example, BMW cuts prices in the United States to maintain market share against luxury imports from Japan. Finally, combine strategic and means objectives to produce potential decision opportunities. After deciding to go ahead with increasing manufacturing capacity in North America and cutting prices in the United States, BMW negotiates with the state of South Carolina to build a new plant there.

Value-focused thinking. Such thinking helps in three ways: to recognize and identify decision opportunities, to create better alternatives for decision problems, and to develop an enduring set of guiding principles for the firm. Get going on Mexico, Brazil, and Latin America. Get going on East Asia, and especially China. Get going on the Czech Republic, Hungary, and eastern Europe. Get going on Turkey and the Middle East. (Chapter 15 gives details.) That's the order of the day for all world-class car makers.

Summary: Scanning Marketing

Global marketing exists within several primary frames of reference. These traditional concepts are as follows:

- *Country risk frame*: economic data, cultural information, and political insights

- *Firm-specific 4Ps analysis frame*: competitive analysis, product positioning, place or channel management, promotion marketing, price-driven costs, prices and revenues, and customer-oriented selling

- *National marketing decisions frame*: opportunities, analysis, strategy

Marketers are reframing or transforming global marketing because they face nontraditional situations, questions, and problems. These are as follows:

- *Political frame*: reinventing nation-states, free trade regimes

- *Technological frame*: decision making under uncertainty; multi-markets across technologies, industries, and nation-states; information technologies

- *Cultural frame*: demographic analysis, national character, youth and young adult culture, universality-of-freedom lifestyle, contingency perspective, walking-around research

- *Marketing management frame*: segmenting, positioning, and tailoring decisions; learning curve; institutional framework of market transactions; product diffusion; signaling game; category errors; imagined differences; measurable results; value-focused thinking

Both traditional and nontraditional frames of reference are crucial to understanding the reach of global marketing in the world economy.

Conclusions

Global marketing is carried out within traditional and nontraditional situations in the world economy. The primary contexts of global marketing include country risk, firm-specific 4Ps analysis, and national marketing decisions; see Exhibit 2-6. Moreover, marketers are reframing global marketing to include governing the market, technological change, attributes of a second culture, team-based managerial change, application of industry analysis to category marketing, and value-focused thinking.

Let's return to our initial three learning objectives.

1. Discuss traditional and nontraditional contexts of global marketing opportunities within the international economy.

   You should have a clear perception of global marketing and the work of global marketers. As you read this chapter, you should be mastering the

Exhibit 2-6.
Inclusive Contexts for Global Marketing

Country Risk (A)

Reinventing nation-states under free trade

Long-term planning horizons

   NAFTA for Mexico

   EU for western and eastern Europe

   East Asian economic consensus for Southeast Asia

Mexico and China as "hot" countries for investors

Political Frame

Country Risk (B)

Walking-around research

National character as first culture

   Ethnocentrist and nonenthnocentrist Mexicans

   Committed European "Yeppies"

   Japanese young working males, office ladies (or secretaries),
      working executive women

   Overseas Chinese and mainland Chinese

Global, largely American lifestyle as second culture

Demographic analysis

   Freedom lifestyle

   Age-period cohort groups, collective work of imagination

   Socio-economic change through TV culture, clumsy vetting

Marketing research

   Self-expression and clusters of purchasing behavior

   Collectivism versus individualism and imitation buys

   Harmonization and self-referencing criteria

   Product diffusion

Cultural Frame

Firm-Specific 4Ps Analysis

Unknown competitive possibilities

   Ambiguities of soft information, alternative futures

   New computer services marketing category

Value creation

   Configuring offerings

Continued on next page

Exhibit 2-6. *Continued from previous page*

Value-added through multiplication of bits of information

Boundaries of new marketing category

Adapt products based on unanticipated needs

Reinventing industries

Site location and public policy

Scale economies and economic policy

Continental market segments and free-trade policy

Lower final prices, get down learning curve

Positioning products and distribution services

Promotion marketing conveys emotional values

Price-driven costs, higher price points, bundled prices

Marketing Management Frame

National Marketing Decisions

Decision making under uncertainty

Contingency perspective

Opportunity costs, "soft" information

Observable attributes, price-driven cost strategy

Market share

Institutional framework of multimedia market transactions

Transmission of data by telephone and cable TV firms

Privatization and joint venture partnerships

Growing an immature market through vidkids

Routine purchasing behavior from young adult males

Nondurable goods for middle-age customers

Marketing strategy

"Juice" teams play ambiguous roles, span boundaries

First-mover advantage

Hardware standardization (minimum differentiation)

Software adaptation (maximum differentiation)

Contingency perspective in price, promotion, and place

Customer-oriented selling, value-focused thinking

Think global, act local

Technological Frame

major ideas in the scans and exhibits about country risk, firm-specific 4Ps analysis, and national marketing decisions. We introduced two important country risk concepts (reinventing nation-states under free trade and the shaping of national character by traditional ethno-centrism and popular foreign entertainment or cultural bilingualism). Also we offered additional insights in firm-specific 4Ps analysis, such as value creation by introducing a new marketing category and reinvent-ing industries by the joint work of public policy, and positioning, seg-mentation, and tailoring strategies. Moreover, we presented clear choices about national marketing decisions (e.g., opportunity costs ver-sus market share, selecting transmission of data versus value added through multiplication of bits of information, and standardization and adaptation versus the contingency perspective). All these efforts are required to be successful in national and global markets.

2. Outline the use of the environmental, competitive, and marketing scans in global marketing research.

You should begin committing to memory the details of the scans and exhibits. These help you do some preliminary analysis of four crucial markets. In chapters 3-6, ideas and concepts are transformed into case studies of Mexico within NAFTA, the European Union, Japan, and main-land China. In chapters 7-10, these scans and exhibits help you review the performance of the telecommunications, multimedia, and logistics EDI industries. In chapters 11-14, the three scans help you evaluate new global marketing values and attitudes emerging in advertising agen-cies, food marketing, computer software, and automobiles.

3. Explain the importance of national character, product life cycle, market contingencies, relationship marketing, and value-focused thinking to global marketing strategy.

You should be aware that national character affects product, place, pro-motion, and place strategies. You should be able to use the contingency perspective to enhance the chances of success of global marketing throughout the world.

Making global marketing a triumph is the work of global marketing executives.

Part Two

Researching International Markets

Chapter Format

Introduction

Country Risk Questions

Environmental Scan: Economic Reforms

Initial Analysis of Marketing Opportunities

Clues to Capturing Customers

The Firm-Specific Assignment

Competitive Scan: Foreign Direct Investments

Estimates of Market Potential

Similar Market Segments Worldwide

National Marketing Decisions

Marketing Scan: Product Diffusion

Strategies for Increasing Marketing Effectiveness

Marketing Implementation

Conclusions

Cases: Ford, Wal-Mart, Teléfonos de Mexico

Learning Objectives

After reading this chapter, you should be able to:

- Discuss the need for predictability in macro- and microeconomic policies to carry out successful country risk analyses

- Outline alternative firm-specific strategies for marketers who are making foreign direct investments

- Explain the importance of product diffusion decisions during the product-development life cycle

Country Analysis

chapter 3

Introduction

Marketers manage final demand by researching international markets. In this section, we
look at Mexico, Europe, Japan, and China
(chapters 3–6), and in chapter 15 we study
Latin America, eastern Europe, the rest of East
Asia, the Middle East, and sub-Saharan Africa.
Let's begin our analysis of global marketing.

Scanning Global Markets

Environmental scan: economic reforms.
Until the devaluation of the Mexican peso in
late 1994, Mexico's economic reforms stand
as a model of success for other Latin American
countries. Its ingredients include privatization, deregulation, monetary reform, price sta-
bilization, foreign investment, free trade with
its largest trading partner, and sink-or-swim
competition for domestic firms. Although
large Mexican-owned firms are improving
productivity, small and medium-sized
Mexican-owned firms are having trouble finding capital to buy new technology and
improve the performance of their workers.

Notwithstanding social unrest, Mexico has reinvented itself for foreign marketing executives. That's the meaning of NAFTA.

Competitive scan: foreign direct investments. Foreign direct investments come in many ways because individual firms react differently to the country risk associated with a particular country. Ford, GM, and Nissan made wholly owned investments in Mexico; Wal-Mart, Price Costco, Bell Atlantic, and MCI preferred equity joint ventures with Mexican partners. After entry into Mexico, all firms worry about the continuation of favorable macroeconomic policies (such as a stable Mexican peso) and microeconomic policies (such as deregulation, privatization, and liberalization). In the final analysis, marketers err when they choose to go too slowly into Mexico because NAFTA is forcing all competitors to become world-class firms.

Marketing scan: product diffusion. American partners bring a knowledge of sophisticated marketing research techniques (e.g., clusters, diffusion, and imitation), and Mexican partners contribute their intimate sense of individualism and power distance within Mexico. Both contributions are needed to carry out the entry phase of the product-development life cycle and to make successful product diffusion decisions under the new rules of NAFTA.

Traditional Contexts for Global Marketing

Exhibit 3-1 lists the traditional contexts for global marketing in the case of Mexico within NAFTA. We examine economic reforms, foreign direct investments, and walking-around research. The first two signal dramatic change in how the Mexican government deals with its domestic economy, and in how global marketers evaluate their chances for competitive success in Mexico. The third cue tells us that reputable quantitative data and qualitative information are more difficult to obtain in Mexico, and we must use other research approaches to determine the size of the market and our potential market share. The case of Mexico within NAFTA is a prototype for other countries in Latin America. (See chapter 15.)

Nontraditional Contexts for Global Marketing

Exhibit 3-2 lists the nontraditional contexts for global marketing in Mexico. We examine reinventing nation-states, decision making under NAFTA uncertainty, cultural bilingualism, and regional analysis. The first two flag a transformed political and economic environment for the Mexican government,

Exhibit 3-1.
Traditional Contexts for Global Marketing

Country Risk
Macroeconomic reforms

Reduce sovereign debt

End deficit financing and curb hyperinflation

Mini-devaluations and float of peso in terms of US dollar

Microeconomic reforms

Privatization of state-owned firms

Deregulation of state- and privately owned firms

Liberalization of trade and investment rules

Strengthen competition for domestic firms

Restructure commercial debt

Political reforms

Firm-Specific 4Ps Analysis
Organizationally based decision making under NAFTA uncertainty

Exporting, international marketing, global marketing

Foreign direct investments

Equity and contractual joint ventures

Distribution and licensing agreements

Relationship marketing
Teamwork

"Juice" or new idea teams

Location decisions

Scale economies

Supplier partners

Segmentation, positioning, tailoring decisions

Product-development life cycle

Product diffusion: country and time effects

National Marketing Decisions: Cultural Context (A)
Culturally based decision making under uncertainty
Socio-cultural information

Total population: 90 million

Distribution of income (triangle)

Disposable personal income

900,000 are rich

Continued on next page

Exhibit 3-1. *Continued from previous page*

US view: 8 million middle-class consumers

Mexican view: Add another 12 million middle-class consumers

70 million are poor

Chiapas is Mexico

National Marketing Decisions: Research Tasks (B)

Walking-around research

Cluster (convergent and divergent) purchasing power

Product diffusion: country and time effects

Coefficient of imitation

Individualism versus power distance

Self-referencing criteria

Cross-country similarities and differences

CETSCALE: Ethnocentrists and nonethnocentrists

Who uses the product?

Self-referencing criteria

Emulate lifestyle of North Americans

Emerging middle-class way of life

How to increase market share?

Local producers

Foreign suppliers

Foreign-owned firms producing products locally

Profitability

Disposable personal income

How to provide value?

Define value

Price, customer service, quality, timeliness

Distinctive packaging, faster distribution

Imported products meet expectations about value

What customer signals show changes in local markets?

Foreign ideas seeping into social fabric

Pop trends, cross-border intellectual currents

Get ahead of foreign competitors

and for Mexican and foreign business executives. The last two pay attention to the demographic differences inherent in national character, social class mobility, and regional location of customers. Again, the case of Mexico within NAFTA is a prototype for the emerging countries of Latin America, Asia, and Africa. (See chapter 15.)

Governing the market. First, let's look at the political frame. Over the last 10 years, Mexico reinvented its status within the global economy. In 1987, Mexico joined the General Agreement on Tariffs and Trade (GATT). Then, in 1994, in a dramatic reversal of fortune, Mexico became a founding member of the North American Free Trade Agreement (NAFTA). Finally, the Organization for Economic Cooperation and Development (OECD), a club of the 24 richest countries in the world, confirmed Mexico's importance as a crucial international market by inviting the country to join in 1995, ahead of South Korea, Hungary, Poland, and the Czech Republic. These external awards confirm Mexico as a country on the move for marketers.

During the post-World War II era, the world's most important industrialized countries pushed for the reduction of import tariffs on manufactured goods. These taxes on world trade went down from 40 percent to 5 percent *ad valorem* (the declared value of the imported goods). GATT's effort at reducing tariffs is a great free-trade success story for Europe, the United States, Canada, and Japan.

Unfortunately, for almost 35 years, Mexico pursued opposite programs: high tariffs to protect national industries, reduction in imports to build up locally owned industries (i.e., *import substitution*), national content rules for foreign direct investment, and the state's take-over of key sectors of the economy (e.g., oil, telecommunications, and the banks). Mexico did not want to be a member of GATT nor was it eligible to join the free-trade club of nation-states.

The debt crisis of the 1980s forced Mexico to change course. It cut tariffs, privatized 80 percent of the national economy, ended subsidies for private firms, and opened up all sectors of the national economy to foreign investment. Mexico learned what others had learned before: Countries prosper more when they pool their economic sovereignty over tariffs, foreign investments, and national industrial policy, and when they force national industries to compete within the global economy. Today, Mexico is so sure of itself that it has joined the United States and Canada as founding members of NAFTA.

Exhibit 3-2.
Nontraditional Contexts for Global Marketing

Political Frame

Pool economic sovereignty with the U.S.

Reinvent nation-state within international economy

General Agreement on Tariffs and Trade (GATT)

North American Free Trade Agreement (NAFTA)

Organization for Economic Cooperation and Development (OECD)

Reinvent nation-state within NAFTA

Promote border industry program

15-year transition period (or long-term planning horizon)

End import substitution and national content rules

End import tariffs on manufactured goods

Curtail state ownership of key industries

Create common market in agricultural goods

Provide national treatment for banks and manufacturing firms

Offer transparent national rules

Restructure national industries to compete in global economy

Technological Frame

Decision making under NAFTA uncertainty

Multimarkets across nation-states, technologies, industries

Produce for domestic and export markets to earn foreign exchange

Information technologies

Cultural Frame

Demographic analysis

Cultural bilingualism

Nonethnocentrists and ethnocentrists

North American and traditional lifestyles

Second-cultural and national lifestyles

National character

Social classes: rich, upper middle class, poor

Regional analysis

Northern Mexico is more nonethnocentric

Central Mexico is more ethnocentric

Southern Mexico is more traditional

Continued on next page

Exhibit 3-2. *Continued from previous page*

Marketing Management Frame

Competitive analysis

Industry analysis

Increase in domestic demand

Rise in export demand

Enhance scale economies

Foreign direct investment

Larger home market

National treatment

Pool manufacturing, build distribution capacity

Segmentation, positioning, and tailoring decisions

Marketing decisions under uncertainty. Second, let's study the technological frame. Since 1965, Canada and the United States have had a free-trade pact in new cars and auto parts. Neither country charged tariffs against the import of GM, Ford, and Chrysler cars assembled in either country. In 1989, the two countries set up the US–Canada Free Trade Agreement (FTA) with the expectation that over a transition period of 10 years no tariffs would impede the movement of goods, some services, and most investments across the common border. In 1994, both the Auto Pact and the FTA became a part of a larger framework called NAFTA as Mexico began its 15-year transition period toward free trade with the United States and Canada.

NAFTA free trade means *no tariffs* for goods manufactured within one country and exported to other member countries. After the 15-year transition period, NAFTA sets up a *common market* in agricultural products (such as sugar, fruits, and vegetables). However, if imported goods do *injury* to local firms, the host country can impose short-term, higher *snapback tariffs* for up to 18 months so that injured firms can make changes in their competitive strategy. Free trade permits citizens of one country to receive *national treatment* in other member countries. Thus nonnationals can render financial services, provide telecommunication connections, and carry out direct investments (except in Mexican oil and certain cultural industries within Canada). Free trade requires member governments to be more *transparent* about their national rules for protecting the environment, enforcing collective bargaining, and enhancing democratic freedoms.

Hunting for customers. Third, let's examine the cultural frame. NAFTA creates a larger home market for all North American business firms. US-based firms export to and invest in Mexico through alliances, partnerships, joint ventures, and wholly owned subsidiaries. These American- and Japanese-owned firms receive national treatment in Mexico, and Mexican- and Canadian-owned firms receive national treatment in the United States. All these firms review pertinent economic, cultural, and political information about Mexico and then decide whether to locate in northern, central, or southern Mexico. Auto and auto parts, telecommunications, retailing, and food processing: these industries will grow the fastest in Mexico because of NAFTA.

Segmentation, positioning, and tailoring decisions. Finally, let's look at the marketing management frame. Marketers have more difficulty predicting Mexican consumer choices as tastes range from traditional to North American. Even though marketing executives offer standardized US products, Mexican consumers impose differentiation of their own based on cultural attributes unknown to global marketers–for example, the use of Bart Simpson rather than a burro as the piñata at the birthday parties of Mexican children. Value creation takes place within NAFTA, by the competitive analysis of Mexican and American firms, and through purchase decisions by Mexican consumers.

Organizing global marketing experience. The simultaneous existence of these four different contexts forces marketers to research Mexican markets carefully, to position some global brands in Mexico, and to watch for different national signals from northern, central, and southern Mexico. Let's do two things in this chapter. First, we will discuss the use of NAFTA to enhance Mexican trade opportunities with the United States Then we will apply this country analysis to how marketing teams make decisions about exports to and investments in Mexico.

Country Risk Questions

Marketers manage final demand by researching international markets, such as Mexico, a country of 90 million people.[1] (See Exhibit 3-3.) About 1 percent of the population is very wealthy and can buy anything the world offers. An additional 8 percent is truly part of North America's middle class–effective consumers with sufficient disposable income to buy a wide range of the world's goods and services. Another 12 percent has some

Exhibit 3-3.
Country Risk Analysis: Mexico
The Environmental Scan

Traditional Frame Analysis for Global Marketing
Country Risk and Political Reforms
Recognize the impact of political reform

Assess country risk of market-opening measures

Pool economic sovereignty over foreign trade: GATT and OECD

Country Risk and Economic Reforms
Reduce inflation to single digits

Maintain stable national currency

Eliminate deficit financing

Increase support for social welfare programs

Privatize telecommunications and banking

Deregulate airlines, trucking firms, and ports

Continue government control over oil

Improve productivity of nationally owned firms

Nontraditional Frame Analysis for Global Marketing
Political Context under NAFTA
Zero *ad valorem* tariffs for manufactured goods

Foreign investments for consumer and industrial goods

Common market for agricultural goods

National treatment for automobile firms

Transparency for the environment

National content for textiles

North American content for automobiles

15-year transition period

Cultural Context and Bilingualism
Compare nonethnocentrist and ethnocentrist Mexicans

Pay attention to North American and traditional lifestyles

Anticipate impact of global and second-culture lifestyles

Cultural Context and Regional Analysis
Northern Mexico is more nonethnocentric

Central Mexico is more ethnocentric

Southern Mexico is more traditional

Marketing Management Context and Marketing Opportunities
Pool manufacturing between northern Mexico and the United States

Build distribution capacity within central Mexico

End social unrest within southern Mexico

disposable income to buy a limited range of goods at discounted prices, and they expect NAFTA to do what Mexico by itself has not been able to do: enhance their standard of living and make them a part of North America's middle class. The remainder of the Mexican population, about 70 percent, lives in rural poverty, scraping by in the informal economy of the cities, and outside Mexico's middle class.

NAFTA offers marketing executives a long-term planning horizon (a transition period of 15 years) in which more Mexicans enjoy the lifestyle of other North Americans. NAFTA also changes the perceptions of marketers about the uncertainties of Mexican government macroeconomic policies toward American exports and foreign direct investments.[2] Today, marketing executives rate Mexico within NAFTA (i.e., its country risk) as more predictable than other Latin American countries and China, but still more speculative than Canada, Europe, and Japan.

Marketing audit. Even as more Mexicans prosper under NAFTA, most Mexicans will remain poor for the rest of the decade. Mexico within NAFTA offers marketers a long-term planning horizon. Therefore, the Mexican consumer market is small and growing each year, but it does not encompass the total 90 million Mexicans, who are often quoted in the press as the market for nondurable and durable consumer goods. More on these details later.

Understanding Regional Mexico

Mexico is a country of regions. Northern Mexico is tied closely in culture and economics to California, the American Southwest, and Texas. Although large numbers of Mexicans live at the border, this is a recent phenomenon spurred by the 30-year binational border industry programs. The programs will be phased out under NAFTA. New foreign investments will be directed toward regional manufacturing centers further inland within northern Mexico (e.g., Monterrey, Potosi, and other towns along the Pan American highway.)

Central Mexico is less closely integrated into North America because its cities are tied to Mexico's history of Indian, Spanish, and Mexican rule and foreign conquests by the French and the Americans. Central Mexico includes Mexico City, the center of Mexican government, banking, manufacturing, and art and entertainment. These Mexicans have a hugh pent-up demand for modern goods and services, many of which come from the United States.

Southern Mexico has a largely indigenous native Mayan and other Indian populations who do not speak Spanish, resist change, belong to Central America, and thus remain outside modern Mexico. Most of our country analysis is about researching northern and central Mexico, positioning global brands within modern Mexico, and signaling national information about traditional Mexico.

Environmental Scan: Economic Reforms

During the last 10 years, Mexico has been forcing its economy through a savage restructuring and essentially reinventing itself to be a founding member of NAFTA. Mexico insists its business firms sink or swim, compete against the best foreign firms, or go out of business. Today, Mexico is the newest convert to the principles of free trade.

Interpreting Economic Reforms

Since 1982, when the first of four right-of-center presidents was chosen by Mexico's ruling party, the PRI (or Institutional Revolutionary Party), to get Mexico out of its debt crisis, Adam Smith has been in favor in Mexico City. The Mexican president's task was to reduce the role of government in business, expand the money supply on a noninflationary basis, and make the country an alternative to East Asia for investments by US, European, and Japanese firms. Here is a short list of the Mexican government's successes and failures.[3]

Privatization Since 1983, the Mexican government has sold 80 percent of the 1,155 companies it used to run for about US $21 billion.[4] The cost: over 400,000 jobs lost, social unrest, closed sugar mills, nearly bankrupt shipyards, still sluggish telephone service, and sky-high rates of interest from the recently privatized banks. The Mexican government no longer wants to shape business strategy, make manufacturing investments, and set final prices.

Macroeconomic Policies The annual rate of inflation fell from 157 percent in 1987 (or *hyperinflation*) to 8 percent in 1993. Yet Mexico still has high real interest rates, an unsustainable current account deficit in its balance of payments, and at the end of 1994 a devalued national currency. Foreign capital inflows amounted to US $25 billion in 1993 and US $30 billion in 1994, both records. Nevertheless, in the last six months of 1993 and in 1994, gross domestic product (GDP) actually shrank. The end result: Not enough jobs were created to employ the one million new workers entering the work force annually. Worst of all, double-digit inflation and negative economic growth are back for 1995.

Microeconomic Policies The big Mexican manufacturing companies (Grupo Industrial Alfa and DESC Fomento, for example) have been improving their productivity, up 19 percent between 1990 and 1992. However, many medium-sized and smaller companies have been unable to scrap their out-of-date equipment and technology fast enough. For example, CYTESA makes woven straps for bags and suitcases, but Samsonite has had to reject 7 out of 20 shipments because quality was too low and defects were too high.[5]

Moreover, noncompetitive Mexican firms cannot pay for new capital goods from current sales. Their customers now prefer imports from the United States rather than equivalent goods made in Mexico. In 1994, each unit of foreign investment in Mexico pulled in 1.8 units of imports (far higher than the 1.1 figure of Chile).[6] Thus, not enough free cash exists in 1995 to improve manufacturing productivity among most Mexican-owned firms.

Trade Liberalization Lorenzo Servitje, the billionaire president of Bimbo, Mexico's bread maker, offers this insight: The free trade policy favoring NAFTA "has not taken into consideration that restructuring must be a gradual process, and has failed to appreciate the limitations of our economic structure."[7] Now that relative prices have changed worldwide, Mexican textiles, leather goods, and petrochemicals are stuck with the wrong technology. Only those sectors whose productivity compares favorably with that of the United States are being modernized, made more efficient, and attracting more foreign direct investment–namely, autos, auto parts, retailing, food processing, and glass.

No doubt Adam Smith is proud of what Carlos Salinas Gotari, the Mexican president from 1988 to 1994, achieved in privatization, deregulation, monetary policy, and foreign trade. Northern Mexico is fast being integrated with the rest of North America as a place for producing a wide range of manufactured goods for Mexican and American markets. Central Mexico seeks to make these same changes, but it is burdened with both rural and urban poor who have not done as well under the Salinas reforms. Southern Mexico is still overwhelmed by its landless rural poor and its indigenous, non-Spanish-speaking population.

Paying Attention to Cultural Signals

The uprising in the southern Mexican state of Chiapas on January 1, 1994 (the day NAFTA began) surprised some Mexicans and almost all foreigners (see Exhibit 3-4). No one in New York's Wall Street knew about Mexico's secret guerrilla war in the border areas with Guatemala. After all, most investment bankers come to Mexico City for meetings at the newly privatized Mexican banks, then fly off to their meetings with business executives at their factories somewhere in central or northern Mexico. All the foreign bankers could do in the short run was to hold off upgrading Mexican debt from speculative to investment quality.

Social Unrest Among the Chiapas Indians   Here's what American bankers don't know about southern Mexico. The "descendants of the Mayans are now dirt-poor, with high illiteracy rates, and lie at the bottom on an ugly caste system, in which ascendance depends on the percentage of European blood."[8] Chiapas is really Guatemala with native Indians in rebellion against landowners and the central government.

According to the Chiapas Indians, the Mexican government's sweeping changes in land-tenure law add up to a sellout of the indigenous rural poor. This remote government in Mexico City, together with politically well-connected feudal landowners and village bosses, abolished the common (or *ejido*) land and permitted it to be sold to large landowners for their cattle ranches. Moreover, the guerrillas in Chiapas, the labor protestors in Sonora (which has a common border with Arizona in the United States), and many urban poor demonstrators all want their lot in life improved today, not tomorrow. "Chiapas is Mexico" is the graffiti of guerrilla sympathizers within Mexico City.

Throughout its history, Mexico has been torn between the magnetic attraction of the past and the call of the future.[9] Many in central and northern Mexico have embraced a NAFTA future. Some in southern Mexico prefer the indigenous remote past, while others want more investments in roads, electricity, oil, timber, and everything else in Mexico's antipoverty program. The latter want the government to run a budget deficit, restart the payment of corn subsidies based on output, print more money, and restart inflation. Theirs is a cultural clash with the ruling PRI bureaucracy and its business allies in Mexico City.

Reading the Political News

Mexico's economic reforms follow the model set by the East Asian countries. It is a modified form of free trade, not quite American, a little more European (see chapter 4), but a great deal more in line with the practices of Japan, Singapore, Malaysia, and China (see chapters 5 and 6).

For example, the United States protects uncompetitive domestic industries through administrative dust-ups with foreign firms over loss of sales (or *injury*) because of low prices (or *dumping*); it also guarantees market access to foreign firms from NAFTA partners, Israel, and the Caribbean countries. The European Union expands market access by adding new members to its single integrated common market, and it forces them to be more transparent in their dealings with firms from all of Europe.

The East Asian countries insist government and domestic firms agree on the economic agenda for the future: keep the national economy stable, choose winners among business firms, invest in high-technology industries, protect domestic markets from imports, export products, and keep social peace.

Mexico and the other Latin American countries want to prosper in ways similar to those of the East Asian countries, but they want something the East Asians don't have: guaranteed, unimpeded access to the US market. This is the reason why Mexico, Chile, and others want to join NAFTA.

Govern the Market The Mexican government governs the market by making choices about privatization, deregulation, and investments. It gives the privatized Teléfonos de Mexico (itself a joint venture of Grupo Carso, Southwestern Bell, and France Telecom) seven years of monopoly on wire connections throughout the country. Yet the government permits other combinations of Mexicans and foreigners to offer competitive wireless, cellular, and satellite services (see chapters 7 and 8). Also it encourages the government-owned national railroads and Union Pacific Railroad to lay fiber-optic lines from the United States to central Mexico. The Mexican government intervenes in the market to set macroeconomic direction and offers guidelines for microeconomic decisions. Salinas's decision to go into NAFTA is an important example of how the government governs the market in Mexico.

Political Reform After the assassination of the PRI presidential candidate in early 1994, the incumbent PRI president, Carlos Salinas Gotari, chose as his successor Ernesto Zedillo, a man of the Mexican north, educated in the

United States, and the architect of Salinas's economic reforms. Zedillo won a relatively clean election, became president, dealt with the peso crisis, and instituted political reforms to end social unrest within central and southern Mexico.

Initial Analysis of Market Opportunities

Large American, Japanese, and European firms pursue a foreign direct investment strategy of Mexico first in Latin America. Salinas's economic reforms and Mexico's entry into NAFTA put Mexico near the top of the charts when marketing executives make business forecasts about "hot" countries. Nevertheless, international capital is highly mobile, and it will move away from Mexico if the PRI presidents are unable to find quick solutions to the peso crisis and to the social unrest in southern Mexico.

Asking Research Questions

Let's assume continued economic reforms, major additional political reforms, and substantial new social reforms - that is, assume Mexico's country risk is more predictable than that of other countries in Latin America. Now let's shift the focus of our risk analysis to the uncertainty perceptions of firms and their business executives. Here are several appropriate firm-specific marketing questions:

Who uses the product? Does the self-referencing criteria (SRC) used by Mexicans include emulating the lifestyle of Americans? How do Mexicans incorporate American products into their emerging middle-class way of life?

How to increase market share? Are there local Mexican producers? Are there foreign suppliers? Are foreign-owned firms producing goods locally? What market share makes the products profitable? Which Mexicans have sufficient disposable income to be effective consumers?

How to provide value? How do Mexicans define value? Is value based on price, customer service, quality, or timeliness? Do the products need distinctive packaging, faster distribution, and improved advertising? Must imported products be changed to meet new expectations about value?

What customer signals show changes in the local market? Are foreign ideas seeping into the social fabric of Mexico? What are the changes in pop trends, lifestyles, and cross-border intellectual currents? Is it possible for Mexican firms to get ahead of American competitors?

Obtaining Socio-Cultural Information

Most countries provide macroeconomic data, but they lack good microeconomic and market segmentation data. Many of the questions raised above cannot be answered with the usual detail preferred by Americans, Europeans, and Japanese. Unfortunately, marketers are able to provide only rough estimates about demand, market segments, positioning products, and market share. These are the realities of marketing research in Mexico.

Clues to Capturing Customers

Marketing cultivates market niches. When they are a sufficient size, marketing intervenes to create long-lasting market segments. By modest fertilization and selective pruning of the world's goods and services, marketing produces similar market segments from country to country. If done well, marketing cuts through confusion, brings order to unfolding events, reinvents the future, and grows the market.

Defining National Character

"Hollywood manufactures 80 percent of the world's supernatural,"[10] concludes the American writer of Mexican immigrant parents, Richard Rodriguez. He says Hollywood defines Mexico as America's stereotypical exotic *Other*, legitimizing the movie villain, Pancho Villa, or the animated Disney character sleeping under a sombrero. Hollywood made everything connected with Mexico happen off-stage, as if Mexico's cultural participation in North America is not only excused, but excised.

Today, Hollywood is making everything connected with Mexico happen center stage, as if Mexico's cultural participation in North America is not only in demand, but ready for exploitation. This shift in Hollywood perception hints at the impact of the global, largely American popular culture on Mexican consumer decisions, such as preferences for autos, cellular telephones, discount retail stores, movies, NFL football, and hamburgers.

Sensing Cultural Bilingualism

Sports, food, and business color the language of the popular culture. According to the Norwegian media researcher Helge Ronning:

This "global, largely American popular culture is becoming every-one's second culture. It doesn't necessarily supplant local tradi-tions, but it does activate a certain cultural bilingualism. People . ..acquire a second cultural membership, switching with ease from local news to the American Oscar ceremonies, and back again ...

"As the British sociologist Jeremy Tunstall has observed, by the time [television programs, magazines, sports, music, and comedy] leave our shores, much American popular culture has been pretested in a large internal market that incorporates elements of foreign tastes."[11]

Hence, foreign marketers must keep up their alliances with American exec-utives because marketing success in the United States does indicate success in Mexico.

Summary: Scanning Economic Reforms

Until the devaluation of the Mexican peso in late 1994, Mexico's economic reforms stood as a model of success for other Latin American countries. Its ingredients include privatization, deregulation, monetary reform, price sta-bilization, foreign investment, free trade with its largest trading partner, and sink-or-swim competition for domestic firms. Although large Mexican-owned firms are improving productivity, small and medium-sized Mexican-owned firms are having trouble finding capital to buy new technology and improve the performance of their workers. Notwithstanding its current social unrest, Mexico has reinvented itself in the eyes of foreign marketing executives. That's the meaning of NAFTA.

The Firm-Specific Assignment

Marketers manage final demand by positioning global products in Mexico; see Exhibit 3-5. NAFTA offers marketing executives a long-term planning horizon (i.e., a transition of 15 years) for investments throughout North America. NAFTA also changes the perceptions of marketers about firm-specific uncertainties on privatization, deregulation, foreign direct invest-ments, national taxation, and business-labor relations. Today, marketing exec-utives rate Mexico within NAFTA (i.e., its investment- or firm-specific risk) as equal to that found in East Asia, and more predictable than that found in Latin America or in eastern Europe. Let's look at three case studies: Ford, Wal-Mart, and Teléfonos de Mexico.

Exhibit 3-5.
Firm-Specific Analysis: Mexico
The Competitive Scan

Traditional Frame Analysis for Global Marketing
Firm-Specific 4Ps Analysis and Relationship Marketing

Deregulate all Mexican businesses

Encourage informal partnerships, co-marketing alliances

Approve equity joint ventures

Reinvent Mexican firms as North American competitors

National Marketing Decisions and Marketing Research

Who uses the product?

How to increase market share?

How to provide value?

What customer signals show changes in the local market?

Nontraditional Frame Analysis for Global Marketing
Marketing Management Context and Industry Analysis
Automotive: Ford

Drop Mexican national content rules

Take advantage of increase in domestic demand

Build on rise in export demand for small cars and light trucks

Enhance scale economies

Produce common models and parts for world car

Shift production to the north

Twin manufacturing plants

Pool design activities

Discount retailing: Wal-Mart

End Mexican tariffs on consumer goods

Go into equity joint ventures with local partners

Do walking-around marketing research

Undersell traditional retail stores

Modernize merchandise presentation

Act as wholesalers to family-owned retail shops

Provide spare parts and services to customers

Telecommunications: Teléfonos de Mexico

Privatize Mexican telephone service

Give private firm a monopoly for 6 years

Invest in digital and fiber-optic communications

Encourage equity joint ventures to establish wireless networks

Offer incentives for satellite and radio pager services

Mix telephone and credit services

Understanding Industry Analysis

The demand for new automotive vehicles is rising throughout North America. Older cars must be replaced in the United States and Canada, and some Mexicans have both the income and the desire to be auto owners, too. Moreover, in 1993, foreign demand for American- and Canadian-made new vehicles rose to 500,000, and these cars and trucks are being exported to Europe, Asia, and Latin America. Another half-million vehicles will be exported by 1997, some of which will come from operations in Mexico.[12]

The increase in the volume of automobile production for export means the use of two assembly plants (one each in Mexico and the United States) employing 5,000 workers, plus more than 50,000 additional jobs at OEM supplier companies in the three NAFTA countries.[13] At the same time, American and Japanese car makers in Mexico are going after more export volumes; the national railroad of Mexico, a government-owned firm, together with its American partner, Union Pacific, is improving roadbeds, bridges, tunnels, classification yards, and unitized trains to facilitate shipments from the auto plants of Ford at Hermosillo and of GM at Ramos Arizpe to Mexican and American ports. TMM, a privately owned Mexican ocean carrier, is working with Nissan to be sure Japanese-made engines and drive trains arrive at the firm's plant at Aguascalientes and finished cars move back through Mexican ports for sale in Latin America (see chapter 10).

Despite the tariffs imposed on cars of North American origin in Europe, Latin America, and East Asia, Ford cars sell at comparable prices with locally manufactured cars. This is possible because Ford uses about half as much labor to build cars as do European and Japanese vehicle manufacturers. Ford can thank its Japanese partner, Mazda, which helped build the new plant in Mexico, for success in assembling a cost-efficient car.

Competitive Scan: Foreign Direct Investments

Under the Salinas presidency from 1988 to 1994, Mexico pushed the auto industry to redeploy resources away from Mexico City, Toluca, and Puebla (all in central Mexico) to northern Mexico. Moreover, the government began reducing its national content requirement for Mexican-origin cars; at its high point, autos sold in Mexico had to have 75 percent Mexican content (that is, on a value-added basis). Because foreign assemblers were hard pressed to meet this requirement, they specialized in short production runs for a limited number of models, resulting in higher prices for Mexican consumers.

Today, most foreign auto firms have integrated their Mexican operations with their US and Canadian plants, and now they meet the NAFTA content rule–62.5 percent of the autos or trucks must be manufactured somewhere in North America. With manufacturing productivity equivalent in both the United States and Mexico, but with labor costs lower in Mexico, many more cars are assembled in Mexico for sale in the United States and for export outside North America.

Pooling Manufacturing

Let's look closely at the economic ties that bind northern Mexico and Texas. For example, the transshipment of goods within the Mex-Tex region–50 percent of all binational foreign trade crosses the border at Laredo, Texas–plays the crucial role in supplying US-sourced OEM auto parts for auto assembly in Mexico. The plants of Mexican-based GM, Nissan, and Ford cars have twin counterparts in Texas, Tennessee, and Michigan.

These Mexican and US assembly plants share models, parts, truck and rail services, and distribution facilities. During the design phase, executives from the auto companies and their suppliers make location decisions (see chapter 7). These "juice" or new idea teams now have the option of choosing the optimal site within North America and Mexico for the manufacture of a full range of cars, trucks, and parts. This is an example of marketing strategy (see chapter 8). Moreover, the Mexican plants gain scale economies (see chapter 10) as their costs of production are tied to a larger North American home market, trinational market segments for small cars and light trucks, and lower final prices to Mexican customers.

Improving Productivity

In 1987, in an effort to compete against Japanese transplants in the United States, Ford began assembling Mazdas disguised as Mercurys in Hermosillo, Mexico and shipping them to California. They were cheap and had Japanese quality. Moreover, manufacturing productivity at Hermosillo was equivalent to that of the Ford and Mazda plants in Dearborn and Flat Rock, Michigan. The Hermosillo plant started a trend with the GM plant in Ramos Arizpe and the Nissan plant in Aguascalientes. In terms of manufacturing productivity and zero-defects quality, all three outperform their twin plants in the United States.

Now big changes are really on their way for the Mexican automotive industry. NAFTA is causing manufacturers to shift manufacture of light trucks and smaller cars from South Korea and southeast Asia to Mexico. Consequently, Mexico is going to increase its vehicle production by the year 2000 to 600,000 a year, 60% of which would be exported to the United States and Canada, and outside North America. NAFTA is also forcing Mexican auto parts companies to become subcontractors to bigger parts makers from the United States. If the former don't go into these alliances, they will be forced to find a niche in the less exacting spare-parts market or go out of business.[14]

Mexico is definitely coming of age in manufacturing, and northern Mexico is becoming a part of the American industrial belt. The Mex-Tex region is one of the boom areas of the world. Central Mexico also is joining in this boom as the American transplant companies reengineer their suburban Mexico City plants to assemble a new line of compact cars. Many firm-specific uncertainties about Mexico have been minimized by NAFTA.

Pooling Design

Ford cars assembled in Mexico have the same engines and drive trains as those found in the United States, Europe, and Japan. The Hermosillo plant was built by Mazda for Ford because Mazda, Ford's Japanese partner, knew more about building smaller cars than did Ford. Today, from Dearborn, Ford manages a consolidated international design operation.[15] Ford believes global design is the wave of the future for automobile manufacturers.

Cultural differences. On the other hand, both GM and Nissan think the cultural gaps are too large among customers around the world.[16] Hence, GM decided not to fully automate its Ramos Arizpe plant with numerical control machines, and Nissan decided to produce Sentras in Aguascalientes only for sale within Mexico and for export to Latin America.

Devaluation crisis. In 1995, Nissan begins exporting 20,000 Sentras from Mexico to the United States, and Chrysler considers exporting all its Mexican output (160,000 units of RAMs and Cirrus) to the United States. The devaluation of the peso makes cars produced in Mexico too expensive to sell within Mexico.

Global design. Ford accepts this criticism. It did restyle the body of North American models to satisfy American consumer tastes that are different from those in Europe. It made these changes only after market-testing the design; for example, the trunk space was enlarged to suit North American preferences. Today, Ford's world car (the Mondeo in Europe and the Contour in the United States) is being assembled in the Cuautitlan plant just outside Mexico City because Ford has no more capacity in its Kansas City plant in the United States. Thus Ford's central Mexican operations also join Ford's movement toward the world car.

Ford says these models are world cars because all the major systems and components–the engine, the transmission, the suspension, the body frame, the electronic systems, even the seats and tooling–are identical.[17] These worldwide manufacturing efforts help Ford absorb upward and downward variations in demand from different regions. These efforts are the results of work by engineers, designers, manufacturing experts, and suppliers–Ford's "juice" or launch team (see chapter 7). They are Ford's firm-specific answers to the uncertainties found in the microeconomic policies of the countries of NAFTA, the European Union, and of East Asia.

Estimates of Market Potential

When the Mexican government ended tariffs on most US-sourced consumer goods, it opened Mexico up to the big American retail discounters Wal-Mart and Price Costco, which formed equity joint ventures with Mexican partners CIFRA and Comercial Mexicana, respectively. These new retail partnerships began underselling the department stores (Sears, Liverpool), specialty shops (for clothing and computers), and the street vendors, kiosk operators, and other members of the informal economy.[18] These two alliances also act as wholesalers to many smaller, family-owned stores that sell all types of merchandise. Moreover, through the two discounters, Mexicans obtain the quality, spare parts, service, and warranties that were not available from the informal economy of Mexico.

Sam's Clubs in Mexico trade under the name Club Aurrera, a well-known supermarket chain owned by CIFRA. In 1994, the Polanco Club Aurrera, which is located in an affluent neighborhood of Mexico City, sold more per square meter than the most successful Sam's Club in the United States.[19] Knowledgeable Mexican shoppers find prices at Club Aurrera in Mexico higher than those at Sam's Club in the United States (see chapter 12).

Before devaluation, Liverpool, Mexico's up-market retail chain, had a joint venture to build 100 K-mart stores in Mexico; Gigante, Mexico's second-largest retailer, had a joint venture with Fleming, the largest US wholesaler.

All the American partners provide their Mexican partners with the skills to build a national distribution system within Mexico. Even Sears, which has been in Mexico since 1947, completely overhauled itself within Mexico and is now catering to the top 10 percent of the Mexican consumer market. "Tell me a success story" is Sears's new motto for customer service within Mexico.[20]

Doing Walking-Around Marketing Research

Here is a quick way to observe the new Mexican market, segment by segment. Go to any large discount supermarket (such as Comercial Mexicana) and observe crowds of Mexican mothers buying 24-pack and larger family sizes of detergents and toilet paper, sizes never seen in US supermarkets. They know the benefits from matching size with quality and bundled pricing (chapter 12).

Or watch Mexican teenage women spot Gloria Trevi (Mexico's Madonna) on the cover of a magazine and make an impulse purchase while they wait with their mothers in the checkout lines. Similar to the United States, MTV-*Olé* stars sell magazines when their pictures appear on the cover and their stories appear inside with even more photos. Also, these teenage magazines must have stories about hair, facial, and body care that promote the sex appeal of Mexican teenage women. Market segmentation is clearly at work in Mexico, too.

Framing the Research Problem

Sam Walton acted on a hunch when he looked at the pros and cons of going into Mexico with his discount clubs. Before Mr. Sam made his first trip to Mexico, he noticed many Mexicans driving to the United States to buy goods at Wal-Mart stores. Their purchases amounted to more than 60 percent of sales at the stores near the border. Then, on his first trip to Mexico, Mr. Sam saw Mexicans buying local goods at higher prices and lower quality than he offered Americans at his Sam's Clubs. Moreover, he saw that local Mexican retailers poorly arrange merchandise, for example putting clothing next to household appliances. Mr. Sam knew that Wal-Mart was way ahead in displaying products, locating aisles to take advantage of customer traffic, and providing a fun environment for shopping.

Wal-Mart went into a joint venture because CIFRA had more knowledge about the extension of credit in Mexico. Mexico lacks established agencies that can instantly check credit records. Sam's Clubs/Club Aurrera, Price

Costco/Comercial Mexicana, and other American-Mexican retail partnerships want to dominate one market segment in Mexico–11 million upperincome customers. Over time, they also want to control another 20 million middle-income customers. Together, these are the Mexicans who had disposable income to shop in either Mexico or the United States before the devaluation.

Without a great deal of formal research and with a lot of walking-around research, Mr. Sam initiated a retailing revolution within Mexico. "Mexicans spend $450 [per person] a year–four times more than Japanese consumers–buying American products."[21] Today, the Club Aurrera and Comercial Mexicana are monuments to his foresight about modern Mexico within NAFTA.

Similar Market Segments Worldwide

When Mexico privatized the government-owned telephone firm, Teléfonos de Mexico (or Telmex), in 1990, it gave the new owners a six-year monopoly on landlines or wire connections. In the first year of operations as a privatized firm, "Telmex racked up US $2.3 billion in profits on revenues of US $5.4 billion."[22] This money is to be used to spiff up the telephone network (a US $30 billion task!), and brace it for future foreign competition.

Even after several years of private management by Grupo Carso, Southwestern Bell, and France Telecom, Telmex still charges excessively high rates for home and office hookups, international dial-tone service, and global outsourcing (see chapters 7 and 8). It also can take over a year to be hooked up to the landlines, and when phones fail it takes a very long time for them to come back into service. Moreover, directory service is still a luxury within Mexico. These telecom problems are endemic throughout Latin America and eastern Europe because a great deal of the system is still on analog or pulse rather than digital fiber-optic communications.

Doing Competitive Analysis

Already, other telecom firms are looking forward to 1996 when Telmex loses its monopoly over local phone and long-distance service. For example, in 1994, Bell Atlantic took over 42 percent of a Mexican cellular company, Grupo Iusacell, with only 135,000 customers in Mexico. About 23 million Mexicans want cellular service, but only 20 percent (about 4.6 million) can afford the price of cellular telephones.[23] Thus, after a decade of business within Mexico, cellular service reaches less than 1 percent of its potential customers within Mexico, compared to 4 percent within the United States. Iusacell itself only has a 38-percent share of the Mexico City and suburban cellular market, suggesting a slow-moving company more like Telmex than Bell Atlantic. Today, Telmex has twice as many cellular subscribers, and it can do business throughout the whole country.

MCI Communications went into a joint venture with Banamex, Mexico's largest financial group, to promote an alternative long-distance service. "For leverage, the partners will use Banamex's hugh market position (110,000 large business customers and two million retail banking clients) to lure converts to their services. And MCI can tap into the Banamex private microwave and satellite network through which clients electronically transfer funds and use automated teller machines."[24] The MCI/Banamex deal offers corporations the convenience of one-stop shopping for both telecommunications and credit services.

Telmex must give Bell Atlantic and MCI equal access to the Telmex's long-distance network, and the Mexican government must give both partnerships licenses to compete directly with Telmex. These are firm-specific uncertainties faced by the telecom alliances. Telecommunications deregulation is going forward within Mexico no matter what pain it might cause Telmex. What is clear is this: Mexican customers want better telephone service today, not tomorrow, and international business customers are among the drivers of the telecommunications revolution within Mexico. This, too, is a product of NAFTA.

Summary: Scanning Foreign Direct Investments

Foreign direct investments come in many ways because individual firms react differently to the country risk associated with a particular country. Ford, GM, and Nissan made wholly owned investments in Mexico; Wal-Mart, Price Costco, Bell Atlantic, and MCI preferred equity joint ventures with Mexican partners. After entry into Mexico, all firms worry about the continuation of favorable macroeconomic policies (such as a stable Mexican peso) and microeconomic policies (such as deregulation, privatization, and liberalization). In the final analysis, marketers err when they choose to go too slowly into Mexico because NAFTA is forcing all competitors to become world-class firms; see Exhibit 3-6.

Exhibit 3-6.
Cross-Border Trade Under NAFTA

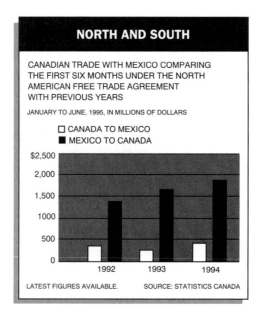

NORTH AND SOUTH

CANADIAN TRADE WITH MEXICO COMPARING
THE FIRST SIX MONTHS UNDER THE NORTH
AMERICAN FREE TRADE AGREEMENT
WITH PREVIOUS YEARS

JANUARY TO JUNE, 1995, IN MILLIONS OF DOLLARS

☐ CANADA TO MEXICO
■ MEXICO TO CANADA

LATEST FIGURES AVAILABLE.   SOURCE: STATISTICS CANADA

Courtesy of the Journal of Commerce

National Marketing Decisions

Marketers manage final demand by signaling detailed national information
about Mexico; see Exhibit 3-7. NAFTA offers marketing executives three
types of business opportunities within Mexico: initial market entry (Wal-
Mart), expansion of the national market (Telmex), and global rationalization
(Ford).[25]

Marketing Scan: Product Diffusion

When Salinas readied Mexico for NAFTA, insightful marketing executives
saw the opportunity for the diffusion of American products in Mexico:[26]

- Thomas Herskowitz obtains exclusive marketing rights in Mexico from
the Dallas franchiser I Can't Believe It's Yogurt Ltd, and sets up 17 shops
through local franchising agreements with Mexican investors

- Underwriters Laboratories, together with the Asociación Nacional de
Normalización y Certificación del Sector Eléctrico, certifies the safety of
electrical products in Mexico

Exhibit 3-7.
National Marketing Analysis: Mexico
The Marketing Scan

Traditional Frame Analysis for Global Marketing
Firm-Specific 4Ps Analysis and Decision Making Under Uncertainty
Gain initial market entry

Create first-mover advantage

Succeed from expansion of national market

Grow through North American rationalization

Firm-Specific 4Ps Analysis and Marketing Strategy
Insist Mexican firms compete within North America

Make managerial decisions under NAFTA uncertainty

Segment markets by region, income, and age groups

Target customers with high-income purchasing power

Tailor marketing decisions for middle-income group

Position global products and brands among affluent consumers

Prepare promotional and advertising campaigns for urban consumers

Carry out bundled pricing for middle-income group

Increase sales force productivity across the board

Set up sales, market share, and profit targets for new products

Carry out value marketing for high-tech goods

National Marketing Decisions and Marketing Forecasts
Continuing trend captures Mexican youth for American lifestyle

Amplifying trend uses aggressive marketing to sell more goods

Doubling trend converts older age-period cohort groups

Nontraditional Frame Analysis for Global Marketing
Cultural Context and Demographic Analysis
Distribute more government money to Mexican poor

Use the triangle as model for income distribution

Divide social classes into rich, upper middle class, and poor

Cluster (convergent and divergent) purchasing power

Determine strength of individualism versus power distance

Measure coefficient of imitation

Understand self-referencing criteria and personal values

Calculate cross-country similarities and differences

Track the diffusion of products and services

Measure country and time effects

Separate consumers into ethnocentrists and nonethnocentrists

- Telmex and GTE permit airplane passengers to place phone calls to people on the ground in Mexico

- Coke buys 30 percent of Femsa, a beer and soft drink bottling company in Mexico

- Anheuser-Busch takes 18 percent of Grupo Modelo, the brewer of Corona, the light golden Mexican beer that became an international success story in the 1980s

- Aetna Life Insurance acquires 30 percent of Seguros Monterrey, a major life and property company in Mexico

- Anchor Abrasives exports nut inserted abrasive discs to Mexico through a contractual distribution alliance with a Mexican firm, Abrasivos Graff

Today, many of these partnerships are making their initial entry into the Mexican market. The potential is there for rapid product diffusion; for many industries within Mexico, this is the entry phase of the product-development life cycle. NAFTA demands quick action today or loss of opportunity in the future. Here are some useful ways to turn quick action into results.

Strategies for Increasing Marketing Effectiveness

Start by imagining Mexico as America. According to the proponents of cultural bilingualism, Mexico's national culture is converging with America's popular culture. Today, Hollywood defines Mexicans as North American, modern, hard-working folks just like their neighbors across the border in the United States. Although this general conclusion has a ring of truth to it, cultural bilingualism does not help marketers target their products to Mexican consumers. No signals are given to marketing executives about what is really Mexican and what is really Mex-Tex, the North American border culture.

Carrying Out More Formal Research

Formal marketing research can be done in Mexico to come up with an answer. However, care must be taken because of the higher chance for human error. Here are some examples.[27]

Imprecise translations. English words do not translate one for one into Spanish. Questions must be phrased to get American concepts about shelf-space and stocking fees across to Mexicans.

Concepts without content. Protestant America focuses on "What I want" or What's in it for me?" On the other hand, Catholic Mexico stresses "What do we want" or "What's in it for my extended family, my closest friends, and my crucial contacts in government?"

Collective responses. Also assume the respondent's self-referencing criteria (SRC) are based on collectivism rather than on individualism, and accept that the answers will be the collective judgment of all concerned in the family.

Too many polite responses. Mexicans are just less willing to talk about personal decisions than are Americans.

Unfamiliarity with research concepts. Some Mexicans are unfamiliar with marketing research techniques, such as structured questionnaires.

The task of marketing executives is to bridge the cultural gap.

The Mexican Sample Reminder: Mexico is not the United States. Mexicans know from birth whether they are rich, upper middle class, or poor.

Income distribution. Most Americans are middle class. In the United States, samples are drawn from the middle class where income, not status, is the reason for inclusion in the research study. Hence, income distribution in the United States looks like a *diamond* with a big bulge in the middle. Income distribution in Mexico looks like a *triangle* with a small pinnacle at the top and a very large bottom area. Samples must be drawn from the proper social group or a selection error occurs in the research.

Social classes. Mexico has a small number of very rich, very powerful, very well-connected families who are the large landowners in Chiapas, at the top of the PRI bureaucracy, and among the new business class. Mexico's middle class was decimated by the debt crisis of the early 1980s. Today, the middle class is growing again, and some are now in the upper middle class with substantial disposable income. Still, many Mexicans are poor, with a large number among the peasant farmers of southern Mexico and the urban poor in central Mexico.

Growing the Market Through Cluster Analysis

Let's start our formal research with what we can observe from a US vantage point. Construct a cluster of purchasing behavior for the Mex-Tex region to show convergence (e.g., in the consumption of snack foods and flavored corn products), and to show divergence (e.g., in the consumption of colored mayonnaise and magazines) between consumers who live in northern Mexico and Texas. Take it one step further. Check to see whether Pepsi Cola's Frito Lay and its Mexican division, Sabritas, or CPC's Best Foods and its Mexican subsidiary care about the Mexican-American border. To them, it's a political division without meaning for marketing *salsa picante* snack foods and flavored corn meal. If disposable income is the same, both northern Mexicans and Texans tend to make similar purchases. This is the tale told by Wal-Mart, CIFRA, and their retail competitors.

Focusing on National Differences

Then compare *individualism* (or the quest for modern material success) versus *power distance* (or the acceptance of traditional hierarchies) within clusters of purchasing behavior among Mexican consumers.[28] Individualism is the strongest in northern Mexico. However, power distance remains a potent force throughout Mexico, but less so in northern Mexico–and is especially weak in the new, bustling Mexican cities along the American border. Therefore, US-origin marketing strategies are most effective in the clusters of border cities between the United States and Mexico, and somewhat less effective in central Mexico.

Applying the Coefficient of Imitation

Follow up with an examination of imitation purchases.[29] Imitators buy foreign products. If they do so within a homogeneous (or high-context) culture, then the transfer of ideas occurs quickly among similar individuals. This marketing research technique helps scan national markets for new customers. Here's how to apply the *coefficient of imitation* to marketing Ford cars in Mexico.

Start by sensing cultural bilingualism in Mexico. Nationalism forces marketers to use different advertising and promotion strategies in communicating about their American-origin products. The hope is that Mexican consumers will adopt these foreign goods because US citizens already use the products.

Add to this the following marketing insight. Successful products in the United States are usually adopted faster in Mexico, especially when Mexican imitators, who are primarily influenced by the number of previous buyers, start making their initial purchases. Call this the *word-of-mouth effect*.

Marketers stimulate demand when they recognize the imitators-market segment as the most important one for new products (e.g., new models of autos
and light trucks and cellular telephones). Then they calculate the coefficient
of imitation to determine real cross-country similarities and differences
between Mexico and the United States. Finally, marketing executives tailor
marketing strategies for this important market segment and apply them
regionally, especially to the border-city clusters within Mexico and the
United States, and to central Mexico and Mexico City.

Using a Diffusion Model

Then track the diffusion of goods and services. This is a marketing research
technique that helps us scan national markets for new customers. Start by
paying attention to *self-referencing criteria* (SRC). Although language, religion, social class, history, and geography are important cultural variables, the
diffusion of new American products among innovators within Mexico occurs
because Mexican cultural models are, day by day, becoming more North
American and less Latin American.

However, among imitators within Mexico, substantial cognitive dissonance
remains between what is truly Mexican and what is global, primarily American.
These differences in SRC between Mexican innovators and imitators causes
leads and lags in the diffusion of American products within Mexico.

Country effect. Let's analyze cross-national differences in the diffusion
process.[30] For example, culture (or the country effect) influences product
diffusion because power distance or individualism, the crucial dimensions in
national differences, bind a good part of society to the past or to the future,
respectively. Where power distance is the dominant culture, the SRC of consumers are tradition, hierarchy, restraints, and no experimentation. Where
individualism is the dominant culture, the SRC of consumers are change,
experimentation, and a quest for the new and the future.

Time effect. Moreover, as products improve and their higher quality becomes
known to imitators, the time between first innovation in the country of origin and wider distribution in other countries is shortened. This is happening
today in telecommunications.

Application to North American Mexico Marketers employ diffusion models within clusters at the US-Mexico border. Here are two types of consumers:

- *Cluster 1.* One group is a small number of innovators who have switched to North American lifestyles and purchasing behavior.

- *Cluster 2.* The other group is a large number of imitators who watch the cumulative purchases of innovators and who are going over in increasing numbers to North American consumption habits.

Therefore, marketing executives should pursue North American marketing strategies within the border-city clusters, large regional urban centers, and in Mexico City. Levels of imitation are high because local culture (or the country effect of individualism) supports duplicating what has already been tried in the United States (or the time effect).

Application to Traditional Mexico   Elsewhere in Mexico, marketers should employ tailored marketing strategies. In the Spanish colonial towns of central Mexico and in southern, largely Indian Mexico, levels of imitation are lower because local culture (the country effect of power distance) favors caution over becoming too American, too tightly integrated with the United States. Those who live in this Mexico chose to remain at home while others migrated to Mexico City, to the border, or to the United States. The former are unwilling to give up their secure attachment to land and family for the possibility of a better, North American future. Marketers find the time effect is a function of the country effect, especially in the refusal of large numbers of Mexicans to give up their history of nationalism for a global, largely American future of cultural bilingualism.

Marketing Implementation

In the United States, marketing executives measure consumer attitudes and preferences as consumers expand their purchase options. In Mexico, when data are available and reliable, marketers prefer to do the same. The problem is the measurement instrument. Besides the human errors of imprecise translations, concepts without content, and too many polite responses, most questionnaires are designed for use in the United States, not Mexico.

Using an Improved Diffusion Model

Therefore, research questionnaires must be designed with Mexican cultural values in mind. Here's how to introduce cross-national psychometric properties when developing a measurement instrument (e.g., the CETSCALE) for two types of Mexican consumers.[31] *Nonethnocentrists* evaluate products more objectively, regardless of the country of origin. In terms of Mexico, nonethnocentrist consumers fancy US habits, such as individualism and globalization. *Ethnocentrists* see their own group as omnipotent and reject culturally dissimilar ideas. These consumers feel that purchasing foreign products is wrong and unpatriotic. In terms of Mexico, ethnocentrist consumers prefer tradition and nationalism, and are power distant toward North American lifestyles.

By dividing Mexican consumers into nonethnocentrists and ethnocentrists, the CETSCALE helps American marketers overcome one major problem in modeling product diffusion. This problem is that the time effect is a function of the country effect, especially in the refusal of large numbers of Mexicans to give up their history of nationalism for a North American future.

A Mexican CETSCALE gives marketers some sense of how quickly non-ethnocentrist Mexican consumers and how slowly ethnocentrist Mexican consumers might become primarily North American in lifestyles and consumption patterns. This one piece of information helps shape future sales and marketing decisions for Ford, Wal-Mart, Telmex, Pepsi Cola, and CPC (see chapters 7-14).

Three forecasts. The "continuing trend" forecast is the easiest to make because things go on as before. The North American lifestyle captures the same number of people in the younger age-period cohort groups.

The "amplifying trend" forecast assumes that Mexican and American firms aggressively market their nondurable and durable goods and that more younger people purchase these goods. This will happen.

The "doubling trend" forecast assumes all firms convert older age-period cohort groups to the North American lifestyle. This is the most likely forecast, especially in northern and central Mexico. With NAFTA in place, product diffusion occurs more rapidly among nonethnocentrists and less rapidly among ethnocentrists; however, power distance, inequality of incomes, and the lack of disposable income retard product diffusion, especially in southern Mexico. This one piece of information should give marketers pause before they think the Mexican national market is similar to those markets in the United States, Europe, and Japan.

Summary: Scanning Product Diffusion

American partners bring a knowledge of sophisticated marketing research techniques (clusters, diffusion, and imitation), and Mexican partners

Exhibit 3-8.
Inclusive Contexts for Global Marketing

Country Risk (A)

Macro and microeconomic reforms

Political reforms

Pool economic sovereignty

    Reinvent nation-state within international economy

    Reinvent nation-state within NAFTA

    Restructure national industries to compete in global economy

Political Frame

Country Risk (B)

Demographic analysis

    Cultural bilingualism

    National character

    Social classes

Regional analysis

Cultural Frame

Firm-Specific 4Ps Analysis

Decision making under NAFTA uncertainty

    Exporting, international marketing, global marketing

    Foreign direct investments

Competitive analysis

Industry analysis

Marketing teamwork

    Segmentation, positioning, tailoring decisions

    Pool manufacturing

    Build distribution capacity

Relationship marketing

Marketing Management Frame

National Marketing Decisions

Socio-cultural information

    Walking-around research

    CETSCALE: Ethnocentrists and nonethnocentrists

Continued on next page

Exhibit 3-8. *Continued from previous page*

Opportunities, analysis, decisions

    Who uses the product?

    How to increase market share?

    How to provide value?

    What customer signals show changes in local markets?

Decision making under NAFTA uncertainty

Multimarkets across nation-states, technologies, industries

Technological Frame

contribute their intimate sense of individualism and power distance within Mexico. Both contributions are needed to carry out the entry phase of the product-development life cycle and to make successful product diffusion decisions under the new rules of NAFTA.

Inclusive Contexts for Global Marketing

Exhibit 3-8 lists the inclusive contexts for global marketing in the case of Mexico within NAFTA. We examine economic reforms in terms of reinventing nation-states and national character in terms of cultural bilingualism. These give us a transformed view of country risk. Also we inspect foreign direct investments in terms of decision making under NAFTA uncertainty. This, too, gives us an altered view of firm-specific 4Ps analysis. Moreover, we carry out walking-around research in terms of socio-cultural information and the opportunities for sales in the three regional economies of Mexico. These results improve our national marketing decisions for Mexico. The case of Mexico within NAFTA is a prototype for Chile, the Mercosur countries, and others in Latin America (see chapter 15).

Conclusions

Global marketing research is carried out at three levels. First, work through good hunches by asking insightful questions (Wal-Mart and CPC Mexico). Then collect all available marketing information (Telmex and Sabritas). Finally, with the help of quantitative methods, use the data to affirm or reject intuitive judgments (Ford and Nissan).

Let's return to our initial three learning objectives.

1. Discuss the need for predictability in macro- and microeconomic policies to carry out successful country risk analyses.

   You should have a clear understanding of the perceptions of marketers about the uncertainties of government macroeconomic policies, and you should be able to make some good decisions about exports to and investments in Mexico. As you read this chapter, you should master the country risk ideas and those from the political and cultural frames. We introduced two important country risk concepts (reinventing nation-states through pooling economic sovereignty and changing national character through cultural bilingualism). We also offered investment choices (such as joint ventures and contractual partnerships) to broaden our concept of firm-specific 4Ps analysis. Moreover, we presented an approach called walking-around research as a means to helping us make better national marketing decisions. All of these tasks are crucial to being successful in Mexico under NAFTA.

2. Outline alternative firm-specific strategies for marketers who are making foreign direct investments.

   You should have be able to explain the firm-specific strategies pursued by marketers to gain market share and become profitable in Mexico. It's clearly decision making under NAFTA uncertainty. You should be able to apply these marketing strategies to the automobile, discount retailing, and telecommunications industries.

3. Explain the importance of product diffusion decisions during the product-development life cycle.

   You should be aware that the diffusion of new American products is taking place much faster today in the new Mexico. You should be able to use both walking-around and formal marketing research to build up market share in Mexico. Nevertheless, prepare for the worst case–that is, negative economic growth in 1995 as a result of the peso devaluation.

Making the NAFTA future happen in Mexico is the work of global marketing executives.

Notes

1. "Mexico: The Revolution Continues," *The Economist*, January 22, 1994, p. 19.

2. Kent D. Miller, "Industry and Country Effects on Managers' Perceptions of Environmental Uncertainties," *Journal of International Business Studies*, 24:4 (Fourth Quarter 1993): 693–714.

3. "Mexico: The Revolution Continues," op cit.

4. Anthony DePalma, "Mexico Unloads State Companies, Pocketing Billions, but Hits Snags," *The New York Times*, October 27, 1993, pp. A1, A6.

5. Geri Smith, "Free Trade Isn't Coming Cheap," *Business Week*, December 6, 1993, pp. 58–59.

6. "Mexico: The Revolution Continues," op cit.

7. Damian Fraser, "No Such Thing as a Free Treaty," *Financial Times*, November 11, 1993, p. 13.

8. Dianne Solis and Craig Torres, "Amid Signs of Spreading Violence, Mexico Asks: When Will It End?" *The Wall Street Journal*, January 10, 1994, p. A10.

9. Enrique Krauze, "New Zapatistas Sully Memory of Their Namesake," *The Wall Street Journal*, January 21, 1994, p. A13.

10. Richard Rodriguez, *Days of Obligation: An Argument with My Mexican Father*, (New York: Viking Penguin, 1992), p. 110.

11. Todd Gitlin, "World Leaders: Mickey, et al.," *The New York Times*, May 3, 1992, Section 2 (Arts & Leisure), pp. 1, 30.

12. Douglas Lavin and Audrey Choi, "Two-Way Traffic: A New Export Power in the Auto Industry, It's North America," *The Wall Street Journal*, October 18, 1993, p. A1.

13. Ibid.

14. "Across the Rio Grande," *The Economist*, October 9, 1993, p. 68. Figures in text (p.75) have been adjusted downward to reflect the impact of the 1994 peso devaluation

15. Julie Edelson Halpert, "One Car, Worldwide, with Strings Pulled from Michigan," *The New York Times*, August 29, 1993, p. F7.

16. Ibid.

17. Richard W. Stevenson, "Ford Sets Its Sights on a 'World Car'," *The New York Times*, September 27, 1993, p. C4.

18. Louis Uchitelle, "US Discounters Invade Mexico," *The New York Times*, March 12, 1993, pp. D1, D2.

19. Damian Fraser, "Retailing Revolution South of the Border," *Financial Times*, January 19, 1993, p. 21.

20. Matt Moffett, "US Firms Yell *Olé* to Future in Mexico," *The Wall Street Journal*, March 8, 1993, pp. B1, B5.

21. Across the Rio Grande," p. 67.

22. "The Deals Are Good, but the Dial Tone Isn't," *Business Week*, April 6, 1992, p. 86.

23. Dennis Kneale, "Bell Atlantic Will Invest $1.04 Billion for 42% of Mexican Cellular Concern," *The Wall Street Journal*, October 12, 1993, p. A3.

24. John J. Keller, "MCI to Hook Up with Mexico's Banacci in Plan to Build Long-Distance Network," *The Wall Street Journal*, January 26, 1994, p. A11.

25. Susan P. Douglas and C. Samuel Craig, "Evolution of Global Marketing Strategy: Scale, Scope and Synergy," *Columbia Journal of World Business* (Fall 1989): 47–58.

26. Matt Moffett, "Heading South: Many U. S. Businesses Entering Mexico Are Small, Entrepreneurial," *The Wall Street Journal*, November 9, 1993, pp. A1, A4. Paul B. Carroll, "U. S., Mexican Firms Announce Wave of Joint Ventures in the Wake of NAFTA," *The Wall Street Journal*, December 21, 1993, p. A7.

27. This has been adapted from how Mayer identifies errors in international marketing research. Charles S. Mayer, "Multinational Market Research," *European Research* 6 (March 1978): 77–83.

28. C. Samuel Craig, Susan P. Douglas, and Andreas Grein, "Patterns of Convergence and Divergence Among Industrialized Nations: 1960–1988," *Journal of International Business Studies* 23:4 (Fourth Quarter 1992): 773–787.

29. Hirokazu Takada and Dipak Jain, "Cross-National Analysis of Diffusion of Consumer Durable Goods in Pacific Rim Countries," *Journal of Marketing* 55:2 (April 1991): 48–54.

30. Ibid.

31. Richard G. Netemeyer, Srinivas Durvasula, and Donald R. Lichtenstein, "A Cross-National Assessment of the Reliability and Validity of the CETSCALE," *Journal of Marketing Research* 28:3 (August 1991): 320–327.

Chapter Format

Introduction

Country Risk Questions

Environmental Scan: Euro-consumers

Initial Analysis of Marketing Opportunities

Clues to Capturing Customers

The Firm-Specific Assignment

Competitive Scan: Age-Period Cohort Groups

Estimates of Market Potential

Similar Market Segments Worldwide

National Marketing Decisions

Marketing Scan: National Character

Strategies for Increasing Marketing Effectiveness

Marketing Implementation

Conclusions

Cases: Benetton, Levi's, Pepe, Nike

Learning Objectives

After reading this chapter, you should be able to:

- Discuss the need for predictability in cross-cultural lifestyles to carry out successful country risk analyses

- Outline the use of age-period cohort analysis in marketing similar products across national boundaries

- Explain the importance of national character to cultural bilingualism, product diffusion, and imitation purchases

Demographic Facts

chapter 4

Introduction

Marketers track final demand by researching international markets. In this chapter, we look at the nation-states of Europe and their collective actions within the European Union. We show how to do formal and walking-around marketing research by asking two crucial questions about Europe: Who are the customers? Where are the customers? In chapter 15, we study the countries of eastern Europe and the Slavic nation-states of the former Soviet Union. Similar to Mexico, good data are hard to find, and we must depend upon informal, walking-around research. Let's extend our analysis of global marketing.

Scanning Global Markets

Environmental scan: Euro-consumers. The European Union's ability to pool economic sovereignty stands as a model of success for other free-trade agreements. Its ingredients include confederation of political institutions, harmonization of commercial laws and trade regulations, and sharing common business experiences among all European peoples. Although large European firms are as global as their American and Japanese counterparts, many find it more difficult to make a success of marketing goods and services in eastern Europe. Notwithstanding the current cultural bilingualism within eastern European countries, marketing executives foresee several cross-cultural clusters emerging among the countries to the east. That's the meaning of EU.

Competitive scan: age-period cohort groups. Marketers make European sales by paying close attention to age, income, sex, and other demographic variables. Living as a part of an age-period cohort group affects purchases for clothes, food, and other consumer goods. Within both Europe and North America, younger age groups are different from older age groups. This disconnection persuades the former to choose jeans, fast foods, and other American-style goods. Notwithstanding the current cultural bilingualism, these youth are Euro-consumers (or Yeppies) with their own cross-cultural preferences in music, entertainment, and sports that differ in detail from those of North American youth. That's the impact of EU.

Marketing scan: national character. US marketers bring an American bias to the use of national character within an age-period cohort analysis. Even though a youth culture exists across Europe, there is no European national character. Clothes personify young adults, peers, and sometimes parents, but they reflect national preferences, too. Telephones personify all persons, and they reflect a global preference for faster communications. For both products, tried and true marketing research concepts, such as diffusion and imitation, need to be applied to ensure an expansion of sales throughout Europe.

Traditional Contexts for Global Marketing

Exhibit 4-1 records the traditional contexts for global marketing in the case of the European Union. We examine microeconomic reforms, decision making under uncertainty, and clumsy vetting of research information. The first two warn global marketers about substantive change in how they must view the new Europe. The third leads them away from making major mistakes in their cultural and demographic analyses of the new Europeans. The case of Europe within the EU hints at what eastern Europe might become when it, too, shares the same cultural context as western Europe.

Nontraditional Contexts for Global Marketing

Exhibit 4-2 chronicles the nontraditional contexts for global marketing in Europe. We examine reinventing nation-states, decision making under EU uncertainty, demographic analysis, and cross-national clusters. The first two

Exhibit 4-1.

Traditional Contexts for Global Marketing

Country Risk

Microeconomic reforms with European Common Market

Political reforms with European Union

Firm-Specific 4Ps Analysis

Decision making under EU uncertainty

Teamwork

Segmentation, positioning, tailoring decisions

    Product-development life cycle

    Product diffusion: country and time effects

National Marketing Decisions: Cultural Context (A)

Socio-cultural issues

    Similarity of economic opportunities

    Pool business experiences

    Standardization of marketing strategies

Individualism, nonethnocentric, pan-European values

    Change

    Experimentation

    Quest for the new and different

Power distance, ethnocentric, traditional national values

    Traditional lifestyle

    Hierarchy

    Restraints

    No experimentation

Uncertainty perceptions about pace and diffusion of change

National Marketing Decisions: Research Tasks (B)

Formal marketing research

    Six cross-cultural clusters across national boundaries

    Self-referencing criteria of language, religion, history

    National character (individualism versus power distance)

    Coefficient of imitation (emphasis on cultural bilingualism)

    Time effect of product diffusion, first-mover advantage

    Country effect of product diffusion, market share estimates

    CETSCALE: Ethnocentrists and nonethnocentrists

Continued on next page

Exhibit 4-1. *Continued from previous page*

Walking-around research
Harmonization of tastes
Preference for individualism
Imitation of trendsetters
Rapid diffusion of high-tech products
Product-development life cycle
Market segments among Euro-consumers

Who uses the product?
SRC of Euro-consumers: cultural bilingualism, individualism
Assimilation of nonnational products into lifestyle
Emerging European way of life
Euro-youth subculture

How to increase market share?
Preference for something new and different
Local versus foreign-sourced products
Social content of brands
Collective feelings among youth
Forget rules of elegance

How to provide value?
Traditions: good links, slower service, higher prices
Standardized marketing strategies and 4Ps analysis
Country effect and the time effect of product diffusion
Offer freedom of choice
Purpose: material success

What customer signals show changes in the local market?
New products and their effect on cultural values
Greater social mobility
Trend is not destiny

Clumsy vetting
Trend is not destiny, resistance, national character
Unforeseen events, microtrends, pan-European segments
Individualism and consumption in rural areas
Humbling feedback

Exhibit 4-2.
Nontraditional Contexts for Global Marketing

Political Frame

Pool economic sovereignty among 15 nation-states

Confederation of political institutions

Harmonization of commercial laws and trade regulations

Similar economic effects

Long-term planning horizon

Share common business experiences

Reinvent nation-state through the European Union (EU)

Coal and steel community

Common Market in agricultural and industrial goods

Single internal market (or 1992)

The European Union (or Maastricht)

Reinvent nation-state within international economy

General Agreement on Tariffs and Trade (GATT)

Organization for Economic Cooperation and Development (OECD)

Technological Frame

Decision making under EU uncertainty

Multimarkets across nation-states, technologies, industries

Information technologies

Cultural Frame: Who Are the Customers? (A)

Demographic analysis

Distribution of ages

Life cycle of age groups

Income and separate housing

Sex and male/female purchases

Family background

Age-period cohort analysis

Much older age groups (became adults before 1950)

Older age groups (became adults before 1968)

Middle-age parents (became adults in 1970s)

Young marrieds (became adults in 1980s)

Teenagers (became adults in 1990s)

Pre-teenagers

Continued on next page

Exhibit 4-2. *Continued from previous page*

Disconnection between older and younger age groups
  Period eye and politics (before and after 1968)
  Period eye and computer-based communications (after 1980)
Cross-cultural lifestyles
  Fashion trendsetters
  Business executives
  English-speaking professionals
Youth culture
  Younger age-period peer groups
  Youth as autonomous decision makers
  Similarities between sexes
  Rebellion through purchase of clothes
  Living with parents
  Risk takers seek personal freedom
  Preference for American goods
Freedom lifestyle
  Teenage children and parents make similar brand decisions
  Friends offer product information
  Rebellion through clothes, cars, and politics
  Preference for European and American goods
Cultural bilingualism
  Nonethnocentrists and ethnocentrists
  North American, pan-European, and traditional lifestyles
  Second-cultural and national lifestyles
  Western Europe versus eastern Europe
National character
  New France versus rural France
  Germany, rural Germany, middle Europe, eastern lands
  Traditionalists (ethnocentrists)
  Euro-consumers (nonethnocentrists or Yeppies)
  North Atlantic and global consumers (nonethnocentrists)
  Cultural distance
  Social classes

Continued on next page

Exhibit 4-2. *Continued from previous page*

Cultural Frame: Where Are the Customers? (B)

Regional analysis

   Northern Europe is more nonethnocentric in urban areas

   Southern Europe is more ethnocentric in rural areas

Cross-cultural, cross-national, multination clusters

   United Kingdom and Ireland

   France, French-speaking Belgium, and Luxembourg

   Portugal and Spain

   Southern Germany, Austria, northern Italy, and Corsica

   Southern Italy, Sicily, Sardinia, and Greece

   Flemish-speaking Belgium, Netherlands, northern Germany,

   Denmark, Norway, Sweden, Finland, and Iceland

Marketing Management Frame

Industry analysis

Decision making under EU uncertainty

   Long-term planning horizon: country risk equals the United States

   Diffusion of sophisticated technology and time effect

   Deregulation of industries and country effect

   Harmonization of macro- and microeconomic policies

   Word-of-mouth effect for imitation purchases

   Real cross-country similarities

Foreign direct investment

Pool manufacturing, build distribution capacity

Segmentation, positioning, and tailoring decisions

signal an altered economic and cultural environment for European, American, and Japanese executives. The third says pay attention to both the similarities and differences inherent in age-period cohort analysis, the youth culture, and national character. The last reminds global marketers to give additional focus to emerging pan-European market segments throughout the 15 nation-states of the EU. The case of Europe within the EU hints at what might be the future of global marketing in eastern Europe.

Governing the market. First, let's look at the political frame. Since the close of World War II, Europe has been reinventing itself as something more than competing small and medium-sized nation-states. From a government alliance of like-minded, government-owned coal and steel industries in the 1950s, to a common market in agricultural and industrial goods for the next 25 years, then to a community of peoples creating a single internal market at the end of 1992, Europe today is a confederal union of mostly autonomous, semi-independent countries, a new sovereign called the European Union.

Marketing decisions under uncertainty. Second, let's study the technological frame. Europe's political and decision-making capital is Brussels. Its multinational commission decides the following: how to implement the single internal market (or 1992); whether to ratify the latest round of the General Agreement on Tariffs and Trade (GATT); and what to do about trade disputes with the United States and Japan. Europe's parliament vets new commission presidents, approves the budget, and admits new members to the EU. Europe's high court interprets the work of both and imposes its decisions about nation-states, business firms, and individual citizens.

On trade matters (such as tariffs, nontariff barriers, and industrial policies), Europe speaks with one voice through its Brussels-based commission in dealing with the United States, Canada, Mexico, and Japan. The EU nation-states are further advanced in pooling their economic sovereignty than are the NAFTA countries, and both are light years ahead of countries in East Asia.

Hence, the EU offers global marketers a clearer picture of what to expect in terms of continent-wide regulation of telecommunications, information, and multimedia technologies (see chapters 7 and 8). This spills out into EU directives about product quality, customs-free logistics services, advertising copy, and discount pricing (see chapters 9–12). The influence of EU's rule-making commission on regulating the introduction and use of multimarket technologies has no counterpart in NAFTA.

Hunting for Euro-consumers. Third, let's examine the cultural frame. The convergence of politics, economics, and culture within Europe is bringing about a similarity of economic efforts, a standardization of marketing strategies, and a pooling of business experiences among the French, Germans, and other Europeans. This coming together of Euro-consumers is an important business opportunity for marketing executives. In addition to the details provided in Exhibits 4-1 and 4-2; here are suggestions, first discussed in chapter 3, about how to increase marketing effectiveness:

1. Grow the market through cross-cultural clusters without regard to national boundaries (e.g., Flemish-speaking Belgium, The Netherlands, northern Germany, Denmark, Norway, Sweden, Finland, and Iceland).[1]

2. Pay attention to the self-referencing criteria (SRC) of language, religion, history, and geography and their impact on social groups (e.g., young people, trendsetters, and business executives).[2]

3. Accept differences in national character, but stress individualism (or the quest for material success) rather than power distance (or the preference for hierarchies).

Exhibit 4-3.
Europe's Dept

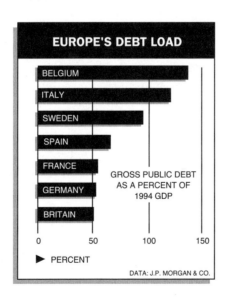

Reprinted from January 30, 1995 issue of Business Week by special permission, copyright © 1995 by McGraw-Hill, Inc.

4. Apply the coefficient of imitation with an emphasis on cultural bilin-gualism (i.e., European and national preferences).

5. Use the time effect of product diffusion (or the time between inno-vation and wider distribution) to capture first-mover advantage across Europe during the growth phase of the product-development life cycle.

6. Exploit the country effect of product diffusion (or the role of non-eth-nocentrists versus ethnocentrists) to estimate market share among urban Europeans who are adopting a European culture versus the rural French and Germans who prefer traditional ways of living.

Segmentation, positioning, and tailoring decisions. Finally, let's look closely at the marketing management frame. Marketers have difficulty predicting local rural and urban consumer choices as tastes become more European. Even though marketing executives offer standardized European products, younger consumers from France to Finland impose differentiation of their own, based on how important sportswear is to subsuming themselves in the western world's freedom lifestyle. Value creation takes place within the EU, through competitive analysis by EU firms, and in the marketing needs of Europeans.

Organizing global marketing experience. The simultaneous existence of these four different situations forces marketers to research European markets carefully, to position most global brands in the EU, and to watch for different signals from Europe's nation-states. Let's do two things in this chapter. First, we will discuss the impact of the EU on the creation of new market segments among the young and old, men and women, and other age-period peer groups. Then we will apply this country analysis to how marketing teams make decisions about selling sportswear to the youth in Europe.

Country Risk Questions

Marketers manage final demand by researching international markets, such as the European Union; see Exhibit 4-4. The EU offers marketing executives a long-term planning horizon. Since they rate the EU's country risk as mini-mal, marketers spend little time monitoring Europe's ability to pool political efforts, economic sovereignty, and cultural experiences. Business people

Exhibit 4-4.
Country Risk Analysis: Europe
The Environmental Scan

Traditional Frame Analysis for Global Marketing
Country Risk and Economic Reforms
Govern the market with directives
Create common internal market
Firm-Specific 4Ps Analysis and Marketing Research
Ask questions
Know rate of product diffusion
Define Euro-youth consumers
National Marketing Decisions and Marketing Opportunities
Know differences between northern and southern Europe
Pay attention to social values of six cross-cultural clusters:
Similarity of economic efforts
Standardization of marketing strategies
Pooling business experiences
Pick up information from walking-around research
Flesh out details on consumer differences with formal research

Nontraditional Frame Analysis for Global Marketing
Cultural Context and Cultural Bilingualism
Devoted nationalists and self-referencing criteria (SRC)
Older age-period peer groups, farmers, government officials
Traditionalists within Europe
Committed Europeans and cross-cultural similarities
Young adults, fashion trendsetters, business executives
New France versus rural France
Germany and cultural bilingualism in eastern lands
Mediterranean cultures
Accomplished North Atlantic People and Redefining Market Segment
Young adults, fashion trendsetters, business executives
English-speaking people
Cultural Context and Demographic Analysis
Pay attention to harmonization of tastes
Recognize preference for individualism
Accept desire to imitate trendsetters

Continued on next page

Exhibit 4-4. *Continued from previous page*

Build market segments through rapid diffusion of products
Establish market share during product-development life cycle
Appreciate the impact of Euro-consumers

pass a bit more time catering to Europe's "potato" and "spaghetti" belts – marketers' terms for consumer preferences in northern and southern Europe. However, marketing executives exhaust a great deal of time dividing the EU into six cross-cultural, cross-national clusters or typical markets for goods and services. These are as follows:

1. The United Kingdom of Great Britain and Northern Ireland, and the Republic of Ireland, a cluster of 60.4 million people

2. French-speaking Belgium, Luxembourg, and France, a cluster of 54.5 million people

3. Portugal and Spain, a cluster of 56.4 million people

4. Southern Germany, Austria, northern Italy, and Corsica, a cluster of 71.5 million people

5. Southern Italy, Sicily, Sardinia, and Greece, a cluster of 31.3 million people

6. Flemish-speaking Belgium, The Netherlands, northern Germany, Denmark, Norway, Sweden, Finland, and Iceland, a cluster of 57.6 million people[3]

Lidwien Jacobs, a product manager at Atag Holdings NV, a diversified Dutch company whose main business is kitchen appliances, fills in important details about Euro-consumers. In her business, she says, Europeans still want 11 ceramic stove tops. "Belgians, who cook in huge pots, require extra-large burners. Germans like oval pots, and burners to fit. Italians boil large pots of water quickly, for pasta. The French need small burners and very low temperatures for simmering sauces and broths."[4] This is Ms. Jacobs's walking-around research.

Mintel, a London-based marketing research firm, confirms these impressions with a formal study of 7,000 Euro-consumers in 8 of 15 EU nation-states. Mintel finds EU's citizens intractable individuals.[5] For example, the French are twice as likely as the average European to sample a new product if they see it being endorsed by a celebrity. Also more than 50 percent of Italians said all forms of advertising played a key role in prompting a purchase versus 31 percent in Spain. Moreover, with more disposable income, 22 percent of the French would increase their spending on meals outside the home versus a mere 6 percent of Italians.

Marketing audit. Today, marketing executives rate the European Union (i.e., its country risk) as equal to the United States and Japan and less speculative than Mexico and China. Even as more Europeans join the EU, the new members from eastern Europe will remain poorer for the rest of the decade. However, the older members from western Europe offer marketers a long-term planning horizon for the sale of consumer goods, industrial products, and services. Therefore, the EU market is large and growing each year, a continental market to rival the United States and Canada. More on these details later.

Environmental Scan: Euro-Consumers

Marketers know for whom they are looking because they have facts and figures about 65,000 European households from ESOMAR, Europe's equivalent to the American Marketing Association. Thanks to ESOMAR's pioneering study on harmonizing European demographics, marketers know how many households in each European country have color TVs, clock radios, VCRs, two cars, home computers, and camcorders.[6] This gives marketing executives an assessment of the standard of living in France, Germany, and many other European countries as well as an insight into the cross-border similarities and differences among Euro-consumers.

Although national differences exist because self-referencing criteria continue to make the French French or the Germans German, the data from ESOMAR's harmonization study show a preference for individualism, a desire to imitate trendsetters, and the rapid diffusion of high-tech products during the product-development life cycle. These data translate easily into market segments for jeans, sweaters, running shoes, and other sportswear goods. Here are several examples.

Assessing Cross-Cultural Similarities

Committed Europeans tend to be young adults, fashion trendsetters, and business executives. Among their contemporaries, they hold similar views about social values, ways of living, and business experiences. Since they are European in outlook, they are equally at home working in France, Germany, Italy, or England. The single internal market (aka 1992) and the Maastricht Treaty on European Union captured their unstinting loyalty to the EU. Over time, these Europeans will form the dominant consumer market within Europe.

Paying Attention to SRC

Today, most Euro-consumers have weak loyalty toward the EU and a stronger loyalty to their nation-state. The French and the Germans are good examples. They share a life together within the EU, but they have two different national cultures.

French National Character Most French are not zealots about the European Union. Parisians and the urban French like the EU because it protects the few remaining farmers, the large state-controlled national industries, and *La Grande Nation*, the Platonic idea of France that wants to be recognized once again as the predominant nation in Europe.

Old France within Europe. The French who voted *non* in the 1992 French referendum on Maastricht "feel cut off from their past . . . so their future makes no sense,"[7] says Jean Raspail, a writer with monarchist views. Those from the provinces, *La France rurale*, "mourn the loss of everything that made them proud to be French."[8] They don't want to give up the Gasçon rooster as their national symbol and the French tricolor as their national flag.

New France within Europe. Jack Lang (the French Minister of Culture) off and on from 1981 to 1993 directed 12,500 French bureaucrats in spending US $2.3 billion (some 29 times more money than that available to the American government) on spreading French culture in the face of an attack from McDonald's hamburgers, Coke, English-language CNN broadcasts, Hollywood films, and American TV sitcoms.[9] All of this is being done as the old France disappears and a new France, whatever it may be, takes its place.

German National Character Most Germans are not extremists about the European Union. The Bundesbank, Germany's central bank, wants to maintain the tie between the strong German mark and the weaker French franc because its high interest-rate policy restrains inflationary pressures throughout the EU. Although the French are more likely to root for the EU and the

Germans are inclined to shout with fervor "Wir sind ein Volk! Schwarz-Rot-Gold!" ("We're all one Folk! Black-red-gold!"),[10] both know that it is Germany and France together that run the EU.

Reunified Germany. In 1990, Peter Schneider, the German political essayist, wrote about the present perspective in *The German Comedy: Scenes of Life After the Wall.*[11]

> *From the perspective of an observer within a reunified Germany rather than from the position of eyewitness within either East or West Germany, Germany is always in* Mitteleuropa – *middle or central Europe, forever tied to the Slavic-German creole (gwara slaska) spoken in Silesia, continually waiting for the zither to give way to Michael Jackson.*

Today's Germany is a trinity of cultures: western, central, and eastern European. They give each other cultural shock – and new ways for France to misunderstand Germany.

Redefining a Marketing Segment

The new Germany offers Parisians avant-garde music, industrial France markets, and the rural French, *Heimat*, home and hearth in the Hansruck. And the new France offers west Germans American rap music but "wholly reconstructed by immigrant Senegalese, whose lyrics and rhythms reflect their own lives and concerns."[12] These are the Yeppies (Young, European, and proud of it!) says *Focus*, a German news magazine, or the Euro-kids, under 30, English-speaking, and "unified more by cultural disposition than national origin,"[13] says Alto, a pan-European advertising agency.

Cross-Cultural Clusters Even though the EU is bringing down trade and economic borders, the French-German political border, which was confirmed once again by the end of World War II, means two national characters within one EU. Moreover, each shares similar social values and common business experiences with neighboring countries.

For example, standardized marketing efforts (e.g., a preference for celebrities in advertising) dominate French-speaking Belgium, France, and Luxembourg, a cross-cultural cluster of 54.5 million people. Similarly, a second set of standardized marketing practices (e.g., a preference for information in advertising) rule Flemish-speaking Belgium, The Netherlands, northern

Germany, Denmark, Norway, Sweden, Finland, and Iceland, a cross-cultural cluster of 57.6 million people. Moreover, a third set of standardized marketing customs (e.g., a preference for home meals and entertainment) govern southern Germany, Austria, northern Italy, and Corsica, a cross-cultural cluster of 71.5 million people.

Starting Over in the European Market

Once marketers understand the relative relationship among the EU, the six cross-cultural clusters, and the nation-states, they will find Euro-consumers strong in number in some countries and weaker in others. The best one can say about the EU is it's heterogeneous, traditional and modern; one-half of the people are against change and the other half are for change.[14] Europe is a mixture of northern and southern, western and eastern Europeans, some of whom are true Euro-consumers.

Initial Analysis of Market Opportunities

Because true Euro-consumers are a minority among all consumers within Europe, marketers must fall back on the tried and true concepts of individualism versus power distance to deepen their understanding of French or German national character. From this observation flows two sets of self-referencing criteria. Individualism means change, experimentation, and a quest for the new and different. Power distance suggests tradition, hierarchy, restraints, and no experimentation.

Asking Research Questions

Let's assume continued pooling of sovereignty among Europe's nation-states – that is, the EU's country risk is very low and predictable. Now let's shift the focus of our risk analysis to the uncertainty perceptions of marketers over the relative strength of cultural bilingualism, national character, and individualism versus power distance. Here are several appropriate firm-specific marketing questions.

Who uses the product? Which Euro-consumers use cultural bilingualism and individualism as their crucial self-referencing criteria? How do the French incorporate non-French products (i.e., the output of cultural bilingualism) into their continuing French way of life? How do the Germans assimilate non-German products into their emerging European way of life?

How to increase market share? Which Euro-products pour into urban and rural France because all French prefer something new and different? Are there local French producers? Are there other European manufacturers? Are American, Japanese, and Korean firms producing locally, and are they able to capture the French desire for change?

How to provide value? How does rural France define value? Is value based on standardized marketing strategies on price, customer service, quality, timeliness, and a willingness to accept experimentation from marketers? Or does rural France define value in terms of tradition – namely, good relationships with rural merchants where slower service, higher prices, and French brand names are preferred? Does the stronger impact of power distance in rural France hinder the rate of product diffusion? Is the country effect more important than the time effect of product diffusion in rural France?

What customer signals show changes in the local market? Are German products seeping into the cultural values of France? Are they viewed positively when they affect urban French preferences for food, clothes, and entertainment? To what extent will these non-French products be accepted in rural France? Will the stronger impact of power distance in rural France slow down the rate of change in the product-development life cycle?

Knowing the Rate of Product Diffusion

The impact of both European and American lifestyles, marketing practices, business experiences, and cross-cultural products is more intrusive today than at any time since the beginning of the EU. Some standardized advertising campaigns push pan-European products (e.g., *Pepe* jeans and *Electrolux/Zanussi* white-line appliances). A few launch pan-North Atlantic products (e.g., *Gillette's Sensor* razor and *Unilever's Ponds* facial cream and *Vaseline Intensive Care*). These marketing efforts target Euro-consumers.

Nevertheless, national character plays the crucial role in determining whether local, pan-European, or pan-North Atlantic products are accepted within the EU. To speed up the rate of product diffusion within rural France, eastern Germany, the Iberian peninsula, southern Italy, and the western counties of Ireland, marketers search for useful fragments of demographic information – such as the eternal culture of Provence, Heimat, Castile and Andalusia, the Mezzogiorno, and County Cork. Then they dress the local culture up when necessary with national and pan-European themes for the Yeppies (young European professionals) or the Euro-youth. Finally, marketers might add the ruffles and flourishes of the global, largely American culture now found in Canada, Mexico, Britain, and elsewhere in the world.

Clues to Capturing Customers

Marketing within Europe builds on cross-cultural clusters. Already, marketers include the four countries seeking admission to the EU (Austria, Norway, Sweden, and Finland) within the clusters of lifestyle information and common business experiences discussed in the previous pages. European marketing executives are bringing order to unfolding events and reinventing the EU's future.

Sensing Cultural Bilingualism

When marketers fast-forward their analysis of European economic integration to the plans for adding three, eight, or more eastern European and Euro-Asian countries to the EU, marketing executives think national character, power distance, traditional self-referencing criteria, low incomes, high unemployment, and many other demographic difficulties. Whereas the EU is western Europe, which has strong ties to North America, eastern Europe is a place with another set of common experiences. Within Europe the eastern countries are different and will remain different for many years to come. Marketers call this cultural bilingualism – that is, a western, largely American gloss with eastern thinking about marketing practices. These executives are unsure of how to bring about change quickly in eastern Europe.

Defining Euro-Youth Consumers

Marketers are most at home with known market segments of the west, for example, the Euro-youth. Because young adults in Finland have more in common with other young people in Greece than they do with their own parents, marketing executives anticipate that young people from the east will become Euro-consumers, too. Today, Finns, Greeks, Poles, and others talk about music from Germany's Fantastischen Vier, or Austria's Falco, or Britain's Right Said Fred.[15] Because similar market segments for this music exist all across Europe, marketing executives can use their knowledge of music marketing in the west to make sales in the east. This is a significant clue to capturing customers throughout western and eastern Europe.

Summary: Scanning Euro-Consumers

The European Union's ability to pool economic sovereignty stands as a model of success for other free-trade agreements. Its ingredients include confederation of political institutions, harmonization of commercial laws and trade regulations, and sharing common business experiences among all European peoples. Although large European firms are as global as their American and Japanese counterparts, many find it more difficult to make a success of marketing goods and services in eastern Europe. Notwithstanding the current cultural bilingualism within eastern European countries, marketing executives foresee several cross-cultural clusters emerging among the countries to the east. That's the meaning of EU.

The Firm-Specific Assignment

Marketers manage final demand by positioning global products within Europe; see Exhibit 4-5. EU offers marketing executives a long-term planning horizon for exports to and sales within Europe. EU also changes the perceptions of marketers about firm-specific uncertainties on economic sovereignty, cultural bilingualism, and Euro-consumption. Today, marketing executives rate EU's firm-specific risk as equal to that found in North America and more predictable than that found in eastern Europe.

Understanding Lifestyle Uncertainties

Right now, Euro-consumers present three lifestyles to marketers:

- Devoted nationalists (French, German, British, or Finnish)

- Committed Europeans

- Accomplished North Atlantic (Euro-American) peoples

Younger age-period cohort groups tend to be committed Europeans or accomplished Euro-Americans. Young adults purchase *Levi's* and *Pepe* jeans, sweat suits, *Nike* sports shoes, and leather jackets. These fit the perception of peer groups about the global, largely American consumer culture – the freedom lifestyle.

Euro-youth buy from the United Colors of Benetton because sweaters and other sportswear impart a European touch to the universality of Western

Exhibit 4-5.
Firm-Specific Analysis: Europe
The Competitive Scan

Traditional Frame Analysis for Global Marketing
Firm-Specific 4Ps Analysis and Marketing Research
Who uses the product: Euro-youth subculture
What do they believe: social content of brands
How do they make purchase decisions: collective feelings
How to increase market share: forget rules of elegance
How to provide value: offer freedom of choice
How to provide value: purpose material success
What customer signals show change: greater social mobility
Realize trend is not destiny

Nontraditional Frame Analysis for Global Marketing
Demographic Analysis and Age-Period Cohort Groups
Youth culture
Younger age-period peer groups
Youth as autonomous decision makers
Friends give product information
Similarities between the sexes
Rebellion through the purchase of clothes
Living with parents versus separate households
Inner-directed risk takers who seek personal freedom
Preference for American and Japanese products
Freedom Lifestyle
Younger and older age-period peer groups
Teenage children and parents make similar brand decisions
Friends and parents offer product information
More dissimilarities between the sexes
Rebellion through clothes, cars, and politics
Living with young adults differs across Europe
Traditionalism in lifestyle choices
Preference for European and American products

consumer culture. To youth, Benetton transcends racial and cultural barriers, gives them timeless themes of fashion and color,[16] and offers them universality within the global village. As we approach the new century, the youth culture remains a collective work of the imagination whose making never ends.

Competitive Scan: Age-Period Cohort Groups

Age, or the distribution of ages within a nation's population, affects the consumption of products. That is the received information.

Knowing About Age-Period Cohort Groups

More useful are impressions about decades. Such prior knowledge systematizes the vision marketers have about an age-period cohort group's sociocultural values and their effect upon consumption. What does it mean to grow up in the 1930s, 1940s, 1950s, or the 1960s and be part of older age-period peer groups? What does it mean to grow up in the 1970s, 1980s, and the 1990s, and be part of younger age-period peer groups?

Even more valuable is side information about the life cycle of age groups, that is, from children and youth through teenagers, young adults, middle-aged, retired, and the sunset years. What does it mean to notice that the per capita consumption of coffee is down and the per capita consumption of soft drinks is up among young adults? Will these trends continue as young adults become middle aged?

Reducing Older Age Groups to a Niche

At some point in time, older people break with younger folks. In the United States, a disconnection is occurring between those who grew up before and after 1968. The former were strongly affected by the Great Depression, World War II, popular luxury (populux) culture, the American empire, and Kennedy's Camelot. These older Americans became adults in the age of the big bands, then the jitterbug, and finally rock and roll; they made the seismic choice to give up radio for television.

Their movies include *Born Yesterday*: conceived in 1950 by George Cukor and for which Judy Holliday won an Oscar and remade in 1993 with Melanie Griffith as the "dumb broad," Billie Dawn, who seems to be unaware of what women have learned over the last 20 years from Oprah Winfrey and Phil Donahue.[17] The character was perfect in the past, but our "period eye" (i.e., our impression of what is proper at the end of the 20th century) tells us she's out of place in today's world.

Another is *Casablanca*, with bad Nazis, nationalistic French prostitutes, sympathetic Vichy police, brave Czech and Norwegian freedom fighters, seedy bazaar merchants, and the American cafe and casino owner who fought against Franco during the Spanish Civil War, Rick. It's nostalgia for older folks and a cult film for younger people – a winning marketing combination.

Using Age to Define Euro-Consumers

After 1968 – or as youth grew up with parents who protested the Vietnam war at Berkeley or in Paris with Danny the Red – nothing is the same on both sides of the North Atlantic.

Today's younger people study as history Watergate, America's defeat in Vietnam, the rise of Japan, and double-digit inflation. Their life experiences are Communism's collapse in Europe, America's victory in Desert Storm, and the universality of western, largely American consumer culture. Younger age-period peer groups of the 1980s and 1990s are tied together by "the same hairstyles, the same jeans, the same short skirts, the same films, the same music, the same fast food,"[18] and their anthem, the hit single "Hope I die before I get old," sung by the Who in the compact disc, "My Generation."

Here are some examples from Europe.

French-Europeans. Joël-Yves le Bigot, the founder of France's Institute de L'Enfant, points out that segmentation by age (not by sex, income, or family background) matters most today in Europe.[19] Youth under age 21 are independent, autonomous decision makers in the purchase of goods for themselves. When they live with their parents, as 50 percent of them do in France until they are 24 or 25, this younger cohort group influences about 43 percent of the family's purchasing decisions for food, clothes, cosmetics, TVs, stereos, computers, cars, and holidays.[20]

From 11 to 25 years old, these young folks in France get their product information from friends, who devalue brand name products and prefer to make specific purchases among many potential choices.[21] So more than 88 percent drink Coca-Cola, 73 percent have a personal Walkman and go shopping by themselves to a hypermarket, 63 percent wear Levi's, and 40 percent eat Snickers.[22]

Italian-Europeans. In Italy, adolescents (11 to 18 years old) purchase goods with the advice of teenage peers to show off their distinct personality. Sandro Paris from Explorer Marketing Research in Italy points out that these young folks negotiate with their mothers about the costs and use of family money, and they seek out their mothers as experts on the quality of goods to be purchased.[23]

If adolescents buy black leather jackets and torn jeans rather than Benetton sweaters and tailored slacks, these younger people are rebelling against or seeking the comfort of their families.[24] Since over 90 percent of young Italians live with their parents well into their mid-twenties, rebellion through clothes purchased plays a more prominent role than rebellion through communal living with peers.

Finnish-Europeans. Martti Puohiniemi from the University of Helsinki in Finland says 40 percent of Finnish youth (under age 24) are inner-directed.[25] This is their means for coping with almost continuous change in European integration, telecommunications, and the MTV hard rock and rap culture. These young adults like novelty and change, and they are willing to take risks (e.g., move to another European country) to gain personal freedom, erotic fulfillment, equality, and meaningful work.[26] They put a low priority on Finnish nationalism because as modern youth they are European.

During the 1970s, marketers first noticed the preference for Europe over individual countries. The choice for Europe is a consistent value among younger age-period cohort groups who became adults during the 1980s and 1990s. It's easy to detect this fact simply by doing walking-around research in shops selling clothes, music, and consumer electronics.

Framing the Research Problem

Naturally, marketers who want to sell to Euro-consumers must do some formal marketing research, too. For example, among committed Europeans 36 percent of both boys and girls in France have an interest in computers; over 38 percent in each group eat chocolate sweets; and over 86 percent of girls and boys like the advertising from McDonald's. Similarity of purchases between the sexes is the same in both Europe and North America.

Also on both sides of the North Atlantic, sex differences matter most in sports practiced, the heroes followed in the newspapers and magazines, and on TV.[27] In Italy, for example, boys prefer strong, famous make, sporting design sports shoes; they affirm their masculinity by talking about the technical side of sports shoes.[28] Girls choose simpler designs and pay a great deal more attention to colors, for example, a colored Superga sports shoe.[29]

However, traditionalism plays an important role in housing. For example, family cohabitation among 15- to 24-year-olds is the highest in Italy (91 percent), Luxembourg (90 percent), Spain (85 percent), Ireland (84 percent), Germany and Belgium (79 percent), Portugal (77 percent), France (75 percent), Denmark (67 percent), The Netherlands (65 percent), UK (63 percent), and Denmark (48 percent).[30]

The southern European countries are more similar to Mexico and Latin America, and the northern European countries are more similar to the United States and Canada in terms of youth living with their parents. Even in France, breadwinners are fleeing the countryside and are setting up separate households in the towns; in Spain, as incomes rise rapidly, breadwinners are expected to do the same.[31] These separate households create the need for additional sets of furniture, TVs, and white-line appliances.

Estimates of Market Potential

Throughout the 1980s and 1990s, the dominant culture in each country (the French culture in France, or the German culture in Germany) has been absorbing two different yet merging subcultures. One is European where the stress is on strengthening a cross-national or pan-European culture. The other is youth in which teenagers growing into young adults in the 1990s build on values created in fashion, film, and music by those who went before, especially the Yeppies who grew up in the 1980s and who have left the homes of their parents to establish families of their own in the 1990s. Occasionally, older age-period cohort groups follow their children, especially when fashions fit stouter figures, films come via cable to the home, and music gets labeled classic rock.

For example, both young and old in the United States prefer relaxed Fridays at business offices when ties and suits are optional, choose sweatsuits for relaxation at home, and want more leisure time, not less. Within the western consumer culture, youth are the "fashion cognoscenti," the style creators, the opinion leaders. When way-out things become the norm, such as earrings on men, the mainstream culture is changed as followers outnumber resistors, and younger age peer groups take control of markets, market segments, and marketing itself.

As more fashions, films, and music cross national boundaries and become European, cross the North Atlantic and become Euro-American, and cross the Pacific and become Amer-Asian, all the media broadcast the universality of the global, largely American consumer culture. Careful marketing research is the accumulated record of an almost endless process of circulation and exchange among Europe, the United States, and Japan. Such research represents the achievement of making products seem less strange in Japan when they are familiar in Europe and a part of ourselves in the United States.

Similar Market Segments Worldwide

Modern European youth culture offers rebellion and conformity, disorder and achievement, and hedonism and meaningful work. It opposes classical, elegant fashion (Chanel, St. Laurent, or Lacroix) and the elitist superiority of the haute couture.[32]

Marketing the Freedom Lifestyle

Youth fashion is a way of life – for example, the Benetton or Nike mold-breaking personalities, or the culture of the street.[33] Youth culture expects the illusion of reality to be maintained down to the smallest details, down to an adventure in colonial French Africa of *Autour du Monde*.[34] According to Pierre Alexandre d'Huy and Olivier Zahm of Semaphore in France, "Youth fashion loads itself with social content, cultural gestures, aesthetic landmarks . . . and carries with it collective feelings, spontaneous, even savage, movements unruled by any elite of taste or rules of elegance."[35]

What do the youth from 11 to 24 want out of fashion? They want to be themselves by showing a trademark (a symbol of intimacy and true emotions) to their friends. They also want to be different within their own tribe and wear those United Colors of Benetton. Since the youth of France believe in the meaning underlying the trademark rather than the trademark itself, they expect fashion to give them a way of life suitable to carry them forward into the future.[36] This is the subculture that is going mainstream in France and Europe.

Selling to Committed Europeans

William Ramsay from Templeton College in the United Kingdom says Europe's single market (or 1992) caused a discontinuity or disconnection in consumer marketing within Europe.[37] Nothing is the same. The spirit or feeling that marks the new European age is lowering mobility barriers among nations, creating cross-national clusters, and forcing managers to shape an EU-wide marketing strategy. All this favors the rapid ascendancy of Europe's youth culture in the EU and in eastern Europe.

However, according to Simon Sylvester, Planning Director of Burkitt Bryant Weinreich Clients & Company, "Young people [in Great Britain] still tend to look to the US before Europe."[38] Mick Williamson of Britain's Yo! Youth Opinion International reports that the United States is seen by youth in England as the best source for smart music (60 percent), soft drinks (68 percent), trendy product design (62 percent), TV serials and soaps (57 percent), and cartoon characters (59 percent).[39] Moreover, British youth similar to American youth and most youth throughout continental Europe, rate Japan as the best source for hi-fi equipment (74 percent), computers (68 percent), and video games (55 percent).

Finding Similar Customers Worldwide

Jeanne Binstock van Rij of the Honeycomb Institute in the United States draws these conclusions about an emerging European-American-Asian identity:

> *The values and expectations of Japanese and Turkish youth, so far apart seemingly in economy and cultural background, appear to be converging, brought together by America's entertainment industry . . . In [both countries], American movies, television programs and music, saturated with the American mentality, have introduced the American way of life, provided American role models and aspirations, and have generally influenced the young at every social class level . . .*

> *The values of American culture which most attract young people include, first, the belief in the respect for the individual and his or her right to freedom of choice; second, the honor bestowed on those who achieve material success through talent and hard work, regardless of family background; and third, the freedom of action and right to non-interference in the pursuit of social mobility . . .*

> *Worldwide TV culture, already shaping younger generations' wants and needs as consumers and workers and their expectations for the future, may yet play a role in shaping the rate of change and direction of their evolving national economies and even the global economy. The socio-political and cultural as well as economic significance of a global village dominated by American values needs to be examined . . .*

American movies, music, and television sit-coms, ubiquitous in worldwide TV culture, spread the themes of US culture around the world, communicating a sub-text of American values – American Expressive Individualism. Absorption of American values via TV culture is a major source of socio-cultural change around the globe.[40]

Preparing for Global Fashion

Notwithstanding the preference for American and Japanese goods among British youth, the trend in fashion is to give up distinctive British clothes and choose European-style jeans, sweatsuits, leather jackets, and sports shoes whose original idea comes from the United States. In fashion, British youth are no different from other European youth, Japanese youth, Mexican youth, and youth in many other countries of the world.

The secret is to find a common cultural bond among youth. Music is their common interest. Pop video is their common popular art form. Here's what youth wants to see in ads for their favorite products: a degree of chaos, a degree of black humor, slightly high-tech, veiling the true identity, and tampering with existing molds.[41]

Some 204 million households, in 41 countries, across six continents watch these ads on MTV.[42] Over 30 million households in Europe tune in MTV-Europe with its separate music and pop video programming for European youth.[43] All signs point to the dominance of the global, largely American consumer culture.

Realizing Trend Is Not Destiny

Now a word of caution about Europe as a single market, American cultural influence over Europe, and youth's acceptance of global products and lifestyles. Most marketers quoted in this section have a blind faith in these marketing propositions. They are doing bungee jumping with their clients' products and money, and they are living dangerously in a world that might not quite come out as the trends suggest.

Let's conclude this section with a few of the weaknesses or flaws in their analysis.[44]

First are the trendsetters a social avant-garde who might come across resistance from followers? The British do prefer the United States over continental Europe.

Second, what unforeseen events might reduce the power of the United States and divert the attention of Europe away from North American culture? The Yeppies as a pan-European market segment constitute a microtrend full of import for the future of European fashion, film, and music.

Third, is it possible that the individualization of consumption might strengthen rather than weaken French or Italian, or Vendée or Mezzogiorno, purchasing behavior? For all the discussion about the single market (1992) or Maastricht, Europe is not a country with a true national character.

Many marketers are guilty of clumsy vetting when they do demographic research on Europe. They have failed to situate the European Community in its historical context – a reaction to two World Wars, the looming threat of the former Soviet Union, and the American view of what Europe should be until the eastern countries are reconnected to western Europe. Most young people can't remember World War II; many think of Communism as the dancing bear in the circus; and only a few really want a federal United States of Europe.

To avoid "humbling" feedback, marketers must pay attention to the real national differences between the French and the Germans, the British and the Italians, the Mexicans and the Americans, and the Japanese and all other Asians. Caution and care in marketing research give us better products and more satisfied clients.

Summary: Scanning Age-Period Cohort Groups

Marketers make European sales by paying close attention to age, income, sex, and other demographic variables. Living as a part of an age-period cohort group affects purchases for clothes, food, and other consumer goods. Within both Europe and North America, younger age groups are different from older age groups. This disconnection persuades the former to choose jeans, fast foods, and other American-style goods. Notwithstanding the current cultural bilingualism, these youth are Euro-consumers (or Yeppies) with their own cross-cultural preferences in music, entertainment, and sports that differ in detail from these of North American youth. That's the impact of EU.

National Marketing Decisions

Marketers manage final demand by signaling detailed national information about France, Germany, and other European nation-states; see Exhibit 4-6.

Exhibit 4-6.
National Marketing Analysis: Europe
The Marketing Scan

Traditional Frame Analysis for Global Marketing
Firm-Specific 4Ps Analysis and Decision Making Under Uncertainty
Gain initial market entry

Create first-mover advantage

Increase rate of product diffusion

Measure coefficient of imitation

Succeed from expansion of national market

Grow through European and global rationalization

Firm-Specific 4Ps Analysis and Marketing Strategy
Imagine a new generation of age-period cohort groups

Pay attention to the availability of sophisticated technology

Build on the deregulation of industries

Appreciate the impact of harmonization policies

Recognize the importance of the time effect on product diffusion

Believe in the word-of-mouth effect for imitation purchases

Acknowledge real cross-country similarities

National Marketing Decisions and Marketing Forecasts
Continuing trend captures European youth for freedom lifestyle

Amplifying trend uses aggressive marketing to increase share

Doubling trend converts older age-period cohort groups

Nontraditional Frame Analysis for Global Marketing
Cultural Context and National Character
Cultural-free typologies
Uncertainty avoidance

Individualism

Power distance

Masculinity

European lifestyle
Young adults, fashion trendsetters, business executives

Monoculturalism, biculturalism, and multiculturalism

Rainbow coalition of western and eastern Europeans

Bazaar of global goods

Freedom lifestyle

Marketing executives also govern final demand by acknowledging hyphenated Europeans (e.g., French-Europeans or German-Europeans) as an important market segment within the EU. Moreover, marketers expand final demand by catering to Euro-youth in all the nation-states of Europe.

Marketing Scan: National Character

Young adult Euro-consumers show a marked disinterest in the institutional framework of EU beyond their ability to travel freely and work anywhere in Europe. They speak enough English to facilitate their communication with one another about fashion, film, and music. Their youth gives content to the expectations about use of goods within the peer group. Moreover, the continued consumption of these products signals to parents the freedom lifestyle of both the peer group and the individual young adults.

Nevertheless, both content and style are shaped by national character, not an ambiguous European character or an amorphous European-American character. To suggest otherwise sows confusion among marketers.

Modeling National Character

Since each country has its own collective mental image of itself, marketers use four cultural-free typologies to ask national cultural questions.[45]

Uncertainty avoidance. Does the expert's role of Italian mothers in the buying behavior of their teenagers and young adults stem from a national character of weak uncertainty avoidance? Do Italians accept and handle uncertainty without much discomfort? Does the preference for shopping with one's peers in France stem from a national character of strong uncertainty avoidance? Do the French feel threatened by ambiguity and uncertainty?

Individualism. Does the preference for the United States over continental Europe among British youth reflect strong individualism, a desire for variety, and a preference for pleasure? Does the willingness among Finnish youth to become European mean weak individualism, a desire for conformity, and a preference for work?

Power distance. Do the wide inequalities in wealth and power in France mean that none of the Scandinavian countries are good role models for France? Do the relative equalities in wealth and power in Denmark and Austria mean they are not good role models for France?

Masculinity. Finally, where demographic data about sex is important, do masculine countries, such as Austria and Italy, get showered by Nike ads showing assertiveness, super-achiever status, the acquisition of money and material possessions? Do feminine countries, such as The Netherlands and Denmark, get sprinkled by sports shoe ads showing nurturing, a concern for the environment, and championing of the underdog?

Here is the bottom line about national character. If cultural distance is small, as it is between the United States and Britain, American products do well in the United Kingdom and vice versa. In this case, a great deal of harmony exists between the four cultural-free typologies and the two national characters.

However, if the cultural distance is wide, as it is between Germany and France, German products do not do as well in France and vice versa. In the latter case, little harmony exists between the four typologies and the two national characters.

Searching for a European National Character

Because the cultural distance between France and Germany is wide, and their cross-cultural distance is even wider with Britain and the southern European countries, let's safely conclude that no European national character exists.

Who are the Europeans? They are French, German, Italians, Dutch, Belgians, Luxembourgers, British, Irish, Danes, Greeks, Spanish, and Portuguese, plus Swiss, Austrians, Norwegians, Swedish, Finnish, Icelanders, and Poles, Czechs, Hungarians, Estonians, Latvians, Lithuanians, Byelorussians, Ukrainians, Russians, Moldovans, Rumanians, Bulgarians, Georgians, Armenians, Azeris, and the Turks. These are ancient peoples.

What are the Europeans? They are a lifestyle, a new form of multicultural- ism, in which the media tries to dilute and sanitize centuries-old national cultures. Ancient and stern demands about Italian mothers as authority fig- ures are watered down into "values" about negotiation between children and parents. In this naive version of culture, the Italians are less identified with the role of mothers in multigenerational families than with Benetton sportswear.

Where to find the Europeans? They are in the fashion ads for living free with *Nike* sports shoes, and with *Pepe* and *Levi's* jeans; and they are on MTV's European service where cross-cultural music plays to a "Rainbow Coalition" audience. The media push the false logic that Europe's cultural differences are merely a colorful bazaar of clothes, film, music, food, and quaint family customs. A European lifestyle slights the power of national memory.

How to deal with the Europeans? They are the people not laden with the past, powerful traditions, and beliefs, and with strict obligations within families, to peer groups, and with outsiders. The European lifestyle is essentially American, but Europe's national character is always French, German, Italian.

In short, US marketers tend make errors about European national character because to be European in their eyes is to live a lifestyle modeled after America's youthful freedom lifestyle. From time to time, marketing executives need to receive "humbling" feedback about their perceptions of Europe so that they are neither over or under confident about selling American-origin products in the EU.[46] Here are some useful ways to turn quick action into results.

Strategies for Increasing Marketing Effectiveness

Start by imagining each new generation as a unique set of political, cultural, economic, technological, and commercial forces as it passes through its life cycle. According to the proponents of age-period cohort analysis,[47] those who became adults in the 1980s and 1990s are going through and learning to live with an unprecedented, ongoing telecommunications revolution. No signals are given to marketing executives about what is really European and what is really Euro-American about telephone products. These products need different marketing strategies from jeans and sportswear because the former are more technologically sophisticated and rely less on knowing all the ins and outs of local national character.

Using a Diffusion Model

Then track the diffusion of telecommunications products within the EU. European deregulation of the telecom industry is incomplete. Within the United Kingdom, convergence exists among telephone and cable so that multimedia can be transmitted through wire and wireless services. Elsewhere in Europe alliances, partnerships, and joint ventures are springing up (e.g, between France Telecom and Deutsche Telekom) to counter the effort of both BT and AT&T to dominate the global outsourcing telephone business between Europe and North America. Moreover, virtually all European and American telephone companies are competing for the right to set up wire and wireless links throughout eastern Europe. All European-based telecommunications firms must deal with EU directives about harmonization in certification procedures, common patenting, opening up the public procurement market, and deregulation of national monopolies. (See chapters 3, 7–14.)

Even though some European countries lag behind the United States and the United Kingdom in providing a deregulated environment for the telecommunications industry, the time between first innovation and wider distribution is shortening. This means the *time effect* is now more important than the *country effect* in the installation and sale of telecommunications products on both sides of the North Atlantic. This tells marketers that many potential new customers exist in Europe for smart telephones and other communications products, some of which are already available in the United States and Canada.

Applying the Coefficient of Imitation

Follow up with an examination of imitation purchases. European imitators buy American products and emulate American lifestyles. Cultural bilingualism already exists across the North Atlantic and between the EU and eastern Europe. Moreover, successful American ideas that make life easier are usually adapted in Europe, especially when European imitators, who are primarily influenced by the number of previous buyers, start making their initial purchases. Call this the *word-of-mouth effect.*

Apply the concept of imitation to telecommuting within the United States and Europe. For wire and wireless services, cellular phones, and other personal communications services, the European imitators market segment is the most important one for US marketers. Real cross-country similarities exist between the United States and Europe in the telecommunications industry because telecommuting is a part of the freedom lifestyle on both sides of the North Atlantic.

Marketing Implementation

Here are the effects of age-period cohort groups and typologies of national character upon Benetton. (The firm represents all firms who market goods and services to Euro-consumers.) As the jeans generation forms families, becomes middle aged, and sees its children leave the household, the freedom lifestyle extends to more age-period cohort groups within the United States, Europe, and Japan. These Yuppies and Yeppies buy more sportswear to enjoy a more relaxed lifestyle. Benetton increases its sales when those who grew up in the 1970s form families in the 1980s and carry with them the commitment to spread the freedom lifestyle among their teenagers in the 1990s.

Three forecasts. The "continuing trend" forecast is the easiest to make because things go on as before. The freedom lifestyle captures even more people as younger age-period cohort groups grow up and form families. This will happen.

The "amplifying trend" forecast assumes Benetton, Levi's, Pepe, and Nike aggressively market their sportswear and more younger people purchase these goods. This also will happen.

The "doubling trend" forecast assumes the industry converts older people to the freedom lifestyle and the purchase of sportswear. This is the most likely forecast. Remember the following: Product diffusion occurs more rapidly in western Europe and more slowly in eastern Europe. Power distance, the inequality of incomes, and the lack of disposable income are problems throughout eastern Europe, Russia, and the Commonwealth of Independent States (CIS). This information should give marketers pause before they casually think the European sportswear market is the same from the Atlantic Ocean to the Ural Mountains.

Summary: Scanning National Character

US marketers bring an American bias to the use of national character within an age-period cohort analysis. Even though a youth culture exists across Europe, there is no European national character. Clothes personify young adults, peers, and sometimes parents, but they reflect national preferences, too. Telephones personify all persons, and they reflect a global preference for faster communications. For both products, tried and true marketing research concepts, such as diffusion and imitation, need to be applied to ensure an expansion of sales throughout Europe.

Inclusive Contexts for Global Marketing

Exhibit 4-7 shows the inclusive contexts for global marketing in the case of Europe. We examine microeconomic reforms in terms of the EU and show their impact on our demographic analysis for the European nation-states.

Exhibit 4-7.
Inclusive Contexts for Global Marketing
_____

Country Risk (A)
Microeconomic reforms within European Common Market
   Pool economic sovereignty among 15 nation-states
   Reinvent nation-state within Europe
Political reforms within European Union
Political Frame
_____

Country Risk (B)
Demographic analysis
   Age-period cohort analysis and disconnection among groups
   Youth culture and freedom lifestyle
   Cultural bilingualism and national character
Regional, cross-cultural, cross-national lifestyles
Cultural Frame
_____

Firm-Specific 4Ps Analysis
Decision making under EU uncertainty
   Long-term planning horizon: country risk equals the United States
   Diffusion of sophisticated technology and time effect
   Deregulation of industries and country effect
   Harmonization of macro- and microeconomic policies
   Word-of-mouth effect for imitation purchases
   Real cross-country similarities
Industry analysis
Marketing teamwork: segmentation, positioning, tailoring
Foreign direct investment
Relationship marketing
Marketing Management Frame
_____

National Marketing Decisions
Socio-cultural information
   Individualism versus power distance
   Uncertainty perceptions about pace and diffusion of change
   Formal and walking-around research
   CETSCALE: Ethnocentrists and nonethnocentrists
_____

Continued on next page

Exhibit 4-7. *Continued from previous page*

Opportunities, analysis, decisions
  Who uses the product?
  How to increase market share?
  How to provide value?
  What customer signals show changes in local markets?
Clumsy vetting
Decision making under EU uncertainty
Multimarkets across nation-states, technologies, industries
Technological Frame

Copyright © Douglas F. Lamont. All rights reserved.

These give us an altered view of country risk. Also we inspect managerial decision making under EU uncertainty. This, too, shows the importance of free-trade agreements and common markets in creating a long-term planning horizon for firms. Moreover, we carry out both formal and walking-around research of socio-cultural information and the opportunities for sales in the youth culture of western and eastern Europe. These results show global marketers how to avoid humbling feedback because they do clumsy vetting of both qualitative and quantitative data. The case of Europe within the EU offers hints about marketing within eastern Europe and the Slavic nations of the former Soviet Union.

Conclusions

Demographic data are about age, age-period cohort groups, and typologies of national character. Income, sex, race, education, and all the other demographic factors play a smaller role in situating the demographic story within its future freedom lifestyle context in Europe and the United States. Today, the youth culture travels as the crucial cargo of America media.

Let's return to our initial three learning objectives:

1. Discuss the need for predictability in cross-cultural lifestyles to carry out successful country risk analyses.

   You should have a clear understanding of the perceptions of marketers about the uncertainties of cross-cultural lifestyles within Europe, and you should be able to make some good decisions about exports to and sales within some the EU nation-states. As you read chapter 4, you should learn the country risk ideas and those from the cultural frame. We further define the important concept of reinventing nation-states through pooling economic sovereignty. Also we introduce many important concepts from demographic analysis (e.g., age-period cohort analysis, cultural bilingualism, national character, youth culture, and the disconnection among age groups). Moreover, we spell out managerial decision making under uncertainty to broaden our concept of firm-specific 4Ps analysis. Finally, we link formal and walking-around research as an improved means to help us make better national marketing decisions. All of these responsibilities are crucial to being successful in Europe under the EU.

2. Outline the use of age-period cohort analysis in marketing similar products across national boundaries.

   You should be able to apply age-period cohort analysis to gain market share and become profitable in Europe. It's clearly an improved way to carry out decision making under uncertainty. You should be able to apply this marketing analysis to sports clothes and telephones.

3. Explain the importance of national character to cultural bilingualism, product diffusion, and imitation purchases.

   You should be aware that the diffusion of new products is taking place much faster today in the new Europe, but marketers still face many difficulties because of national character. You should be able to combine both walking-around research and formal marketing research to build up market share in Europe.

We thought we knew who are the Europeans. Instead, we should have known that these Europeans are really French, Germans, British, and . . . Making the EU future happen in eastern Europe is the work of global marketing executives.

Notes

1. Gianluigi Guido, "What US Marketers Should Consider in Planning a Pan-European Approach," *The Journal of Consumer Marketing*, 9:2 (Spring 1992): 30-131. The six EU cross-cultural clusters were developed by S. Vandermerwe and M. L'Huillier of the World Bank and of Carta Gen DemoGraphics in Geneva, Switzerland.

2. Ibid, 30.

3. Ibid, 31.

4. Tony Horwitz, "Continental Shift: Europe's Borders Fade, and People and Goods Can Move More Freely," *The Wall Street Journal*, May 18, 1993, A10.

5. Gary Mead, "Hunting the Euro-Consumer," *Financial Times*, June 28, 1993, 4. The data in the paragraph come from Mead's article.

6. Yves Marbeau, "Harmonisation of Demographics in Europe 1991: The state of the art, Part 1: Eurodemographics? Nearly there!" *Marketing and Research Today* 20:1 (March 1992): 33–40. Jean Quatresooz and Dominique Vancraeynest, "Part 2: Using the ESOMAR harmonised demographics: External and Internal Validation of the Results of the EURO-BAROMETER test," *Marketing and Research Today* 20:1 (March 1992): 41–50.

7. Alan Riding, "The French," *The New York Times Magazine*, March 21, 1993, 24.

8. Ibid., 51.

9. John Rockwell, "French Culture Under Socialism: Egotism or a Sense of History?", *The New York Times*, March 24, 1993, B3.

10. Peter Schneider, *The German Comedy: Scenes of Life After the Wall*, trans. by Philip Boehm and Leigh Hafrey, (New York: The Noonday Press, Farrar Straus Giroux, 1991), 49.

11. Schneider, 59, 66, 67, and 108. This is not an exact quote, but a compilation of Schneider's observations. Egon Krenz, the former secretary general of the Socialist Unity Party, East Germany's ruling Communist Party, introduced "from the present perspective" to explain how he landed on his feet after the DDR regime collapsed, and the East German landers were incorporated within a reunified Germany. Silesia, which was once Austrian, Prussian, and German, is now Polish; Silesia is a metaphor for all Germans who live outside Germany, claim Germany as their national allegiance, and give Germany its national character within Europe.

12. William E. Schmidt, "In Europe, America's Grip on Pop Culture Is Fading," *The New York Times*, March 28, 1993, 3.

13. Ibid.

14. Yves Boutonnat, Ana Bauer, and Marshall Ottenfeld, "North American and European Markets . . . Is Each Homogeneous or Heterogeneous?", *Applied Marketing Research* 31:1 (Spring-Summer 1991): 9–12.

15. Schmidt, 3.

16. Alan Zakon and Richard W. Winger, "Consumer Draw: From Mass Markets to Variety," *Management Review* (April 1987): 20. The preliminary research for the Benetton case comes from a research paper prepared by William R. Brooks, Jr., Kevin Cadden, Laurence Rosenberg, and Melissa George, all graduate students at the Kellogg Graduate School of Management of Northwestern University.

17. Vincent Canby, "Melanie Griffith Plays a Classic Dumb Blonde," *The New York Times*, March 26, 1993, B3.

18. "Britain and France: So near, and yet so far," *The Economist*, April 30, 1994, 21.

19. Joël-Yves le Bigot, "Marketing to Young Consumers: Segmentation plus Life-Style: A Terrific Cocktail," Seminar on *Children and Young People: Are They the New Consumers?* (Amsterdam, The Netherlands: Esomar, 1992), 69.

20. Ibid., 71.

21. Ibid., 72.

22. Ibid., 74.

23. Sandro Paris, "The Significance and Value of Fashion on the Transition from Childhood to Adolescence," Seminar on *Children and Young People: Are They the New Consumers?* (Amsterdam, The Netherlands: Esomar, 1992), 55.

24. Ibid.

25. Martti Puohiniemi, "Value-Based Segmentation, Social Change and Consuming Orientations," Seminar on the *Growing Individualisation of Consumer Lifestyles and Demand: How Is Marketing Coping with It?* (Amsterdam, The Netherlands: Esomar, 1991), 55–56.

26. Ibid., 56.

27. le Bigot, 74.

28. Paris, 60.

29. Ibid.

30. Ibid., 76.

31. *Europe in the Year 2000* (London: Euromonitor Publications Limited, 1990), 84.

32. Pierre Alexandre d'Huy and Olivier Zahm, "Semiology of Youth Fashion Communication (France Market 1992) "Teenagers of 1992: From Fashion Victims to Fashion Masters," Seminar on *Children and Young People: Are They the New Consumers?* (Amsterdam, The Netherlands: Esomar, 1992), 221.

33. Ibid.

34. Ibid., 224.

35. Ibid.

36. Ibid., 225–26.

37. William Ramsay, "International Marketing Strategy – Mainstream or Niche," The 44th ESOMAR Marketing Research Congress: *Marketing in the New Europe* (Amsterdam, The Netherlands: Esomar, 1991), 145–147, 159.

38. Roger Tredre, "Style Conscious Teenagers Adopt a Euro-identity," *The Independent*, January 13. Cited by Mick Williamson, "To Find Opportunities in the Youth Market – Take the Global View," Seminar on *Children and Young People: Are They the New Consumers?* (Amsterdam, The Netherlands: Esomar, 1992), 123, 125.

39. Ibid., 126.

40. Jeanne Binstock van Rij, "Global Growth of US Values Among Youth: American Influence Thru [sic] the Media," Seminar on Children and Young People: Are They the New Consumers? (Amsterdam, The Netherlands: Esomar, 1992), 103–104.

41. Ibid., 128.

42. Vox, October 1991. Cited by Williamson, 128.

43. Tredre, cited by Williamson, 128.

44. "Trend is not destiny" comes from Lewis Mumford. Cited in S. Nora and A. Minc, *L'informatisation de la Société* (Paris: Seuil, 1978). Cited by Vanal Codeluppi and Daniel Weber, "The Ten C's: How to Use Socio-Trends Analysis in Marketing Strategy," Seminar on *Is Marketing Keeping Up with the Consumer: Lessons from Changing Product Attitudes and Behavior* (Amsterdam, The Netherlands: Esomar, 1989), 294.

45. Sudhit H. Kale and John W. Barnes, "Understanding the Domain of Cross-National Buyer-Seller Interactions," *Journal of International Business Studies* 23:1 (First Quarter 1992): 105–106. The four etic typologies were suggested by Geert Hofstede, *Culture's Consequences: International Differences in Work-related Values* (Beverly Hills, CA: Sage Publications, 1980).

46. Jayashree Mahajan, "The Overconfidence Effect in Marketing Management Predictions," *Journal of Marketing Research* 29:3 (August 1992): 329–42.

47. Joseph O. Rentz and Fred D. Reynolds, "Forecasting the Effects of an Aging Population on Product Consumption: An Age-Period-Cohort Framework," *Journal of Marketing Research* 28:3 (August 1991): 355–60.

Chapter Format

Learning Objectives

After reading this chapter, you should be able to:

- Discuss the need for predictability in national character to carry out successful country risk analyses

- Outline the use of culturally based consumer information in marketing similar products across national boundaries

- Explain the importance of routine purchasing behavior to sales of foreign goods within culturally different countries

Cultural Insights

chapter 5

Introduction

Marketers direct final demand by researching international markets. In this chapter, we look at Japan. Although we stress its traditional political and cultural differences with the West, we look at its youth culture for signs of change in the use of imported goods from the West. Does product assimilation mean faster cultural adaptation of western concepts (such as individualism versus power distance, or the disconnection between older and younger age groups)? No. Japan maintains a unique set of socio-cultural values that are different from those found in the United States or Europe. These cultural differences will help us better understand the difficulties in generalizing about East, Southeast, and South Asia (see chapters 6 and 15). Let's stretch our analysis of global marketing.

Scanning Global Markets

Environmental scan: Japanese market segments. Japan's ability to maintain its unique national character even in the face of the global, largely American entertainment culture stands as a model of success. The former's cultural insights include collectivism, material success, and *nihonjin*. They establish market segments (e.g., young working males, working women) for *manga*, Japanese comic books. These unique market segments translate into large markets for Japanese products and smaller markets for foreign products. Notwithstanding the current level of cultural bilingualism within Japan, marketing executives foresee slightly higher levels of imitation and somewhat more accelerated rates of product diffusion as Japan accepts more American products into its lifestyle.

Competitive scan: consumer information. Marketers make Japanese sales by paying close attention to humor, fantasy, harmony, *nihonjin*, and other cultural insights. Marketing executives also make sales to Japanese juniors and other younger age-period peer groups by building assertiveness, green chic, value, and casual fashion into their products. Moreover, marketers make sales to Japanese younger and older age-period cohort groups by promoting collectivism and material success. This Japan is more different from than similar to Europe and America.

Marketing scan: routine purchasing behavior. Higher levels of consumption among Japanese consumers involve an extremely slow move away from collectivism toward an almost imperceptible amount of individualism. This change in cultural attitudes is most noticeable among Japanese juniors but much less conspicuous among adult working males, working women, and baby boomers. For juniors to express their individualism, new (foreign) products must compare favorably in terms of quality with existing, competing products. Moreover, for juniors to purchase imported products these goods must go through a slow adaptation to Japanese humor, fantasy, harmony, and *nihonjin*. These four cultural insights are crucial to success in Japan.

Traditional Contexts for Global Marketing

Exhibit 5-1 outlines the traditional contexts for global marketing in the case of Japan. We examine government-business relationships, product diffusion, and socio-cultural values. The first delineate the active role government agencies play in helping business firms make their exporting and foreign investment decisions. The second recounts what marketers can measure about product diffusion within Japan – that is, the time effect depends on the country effect. The third underscores Japan's unique traditions, national character, and cultural values. The cases of Japan as seen through *manga* and the assimilation of foreign foods into Japanese culture are specific to Japan.

Exhibit 5-1.
Traditional Contexts for Global Marketing

Country Risk
Microeconomic investment suggestions
Demographic and cultural information
Political (government-business) relationships

Firm-Specific 4Ps Analysis
Decision making under uncertainty
   Teamwork and collectivism
   Segmentation, positioning, tailoring decisions
Product diffusion: time effect dependent on country effect
Market segments

National Marketing Decisions: Cultural Context (A)
Socio-cultural values
   Honne (internalized truth) versus *tatemae* (public truth)
   Dominant homogeneity, or *nihonjin* boosts pop culture
   Collectivism strengthens material success
   Humor shows assertiveness
   Fantasy demonstrates value
   Harmony promotes a lifestyle
Individualism versus power distance: not useful in Japan

National Marketing Decisions: Research Tasks (B)
Formal marketing research
   Self-referencing criteria of language, religion, history
   Focal option (focus of comparison)
   National character (collectivism, material success)
   Coefficient of imitation (stress cultural bilingualism)
   Time effect of product diffusion, first-mover advantage
   Country effect of product diffusion, market share estimates
Walking-around research: compare imports to Japanese products
Who uses the product?
   Self-referencing criteria: collectivism over individualism
   Youth subculture
How to increase market share?
   Work with slow product assimilation
   Compare imports to Japanese products

Continued on next page

Exhibit 5-1. *Continued from previous page*

How to provide value?

    Time effect dependent on country effect

    Quality required: design, packaging, customer service

What customer signals show changes in the local market?

Clumsy vetting

    Trend is not destiny because of national character

    Situate country within historical context

    Humbling feedback

Copyright © Douglas F. Lamont. All rights reserved.

Nontraditional Contexts for Global Marketing

Exhibit 5-2 spells out the nontraditional contexts for global marketing in Japan. We examine reinventing Japan as a capitalist development state, government agencies targeting technologies to gain market share abroad, traditional national character and the emerging youth culture, and decision making under uncertainty. All four stop us with a red light. They warn us that country risk is more than the summation of political and economic risk; that firm-specific 4Ps analysis must include real cross-national differences; and that national marketing decisions must come from a clear understanding of socio-cultural values, customs, and traditions. When the light turns green, one must use a new road map of political, technological, cultural, and marketing management frames to do global marketing within Japan. We are going down a new road in global marketing.

Governing the market. First, let's look at the political frame. Japan's economic success takes place within an environment of active government encouragement for business firms. Japanese culture encourages collectivism, and this carries over into government-business relationships and cooperation among families of firms (or *keiretsu*).

Marketing decisions under uncertainty. Second, let's study the technological frame. Some Americans believe Japan's Ministry of International Trade and Industry has exceptional foresight about the future of multimarkets, technologies, and industries. In their view, MITI assists Japanese firms to capture market share abroad, and it restricts foreign access to Japanese markets. Others go further. They call this cooperation the capitalist development state and label it as culturally different from the Anglo-American approach to free enterprise capitalism.

Exhibit 5-2.
Nontraditional Contexts for Global Marketing

Political Frame: International Rules (A)

Pool economic sovereignty within Asia and the Pacific

Reinvent nation-state within international economy

   General Agreement on Tariffs and Trade (GATT)

   Organization for Economic Cooperation and Development (OCED)

Political Frame: Domestic Rules (B)

Reinvent country as capitalist development state

   Positive government appraisal of business plans

   Government agencies encourage exports

   Cooperation among families of firms (*keiretsu*)

Long-term planning horizon for business firms

Technological Frame

Decision making under uncertainty

Multimarkets across nation-states, technologies, industries

Government agencies target technologies to gain market share

Information technologies

Cultural Frame: Who Are the Customers? (A)

Demographic analysis

   Distribution of ages

   Family background

Age-period cohort analysis, national character, and family status

   Strong traditionalists:

   Older age groups (became adults before 1970s)

   Middle-age parents (became adults in 1970s)

   Weaker traditionalists, experiment with western goods:

   Younger marrieds (became adults in 1980s)

   Unmarried males (became adults in 1980s)

   OL or office ladies (became adults in 1980s)

   Weakest traditionalists, stronger experiment with imports:

   Teenagers (became adults in 1990s)

   Pre-teenagers

Disconnection among age groups: not as strong as in the West

Continued on next page

Exhibit 5-2. *Continued from previous page*

Youth culture
  Assertiveness
  Green chic
  Value
  Casual fashion
  Ease of use
  Weak preference for western goods
Freedom lifestyle: not as strong as in the West
Cultural bilingualism
  Traditionalism, national character, collectivism:
  Chinese ideograms
  Four systems of writing
  Imitate English words
  Skim information
  Totality of Japanese culture
  Cross-cultural lifestyles, material success
National character
  Devoted nationalists
  Modern, trans-Pacific lifestyle of business executives

Cultural Frame: Where Are the Customers? (B)
Regional analysis: similar consumption patterns within Japan
Cross-national clusters: none today

Marketing Management Frame
Industry analysis
Decision making under uncertainty
  Long-term planning horizon: country risk equals US and EU
  Diffusion of sophisticated technology and time effect
  Government-business relationships and country effect
  Harmonization of macro - and microeconomic policies
  Word-of-mouth effect for imitation purchases
  Real cross-country differences
Foreign direct investment
Pool manufacturing, build distribution capacity
Segmentation, positioning, and tailoring decisions

MITI has a mixed record in choosing technologies for future marketing success at home and abroad. We discuss only two – namely, automobiles and computer-based telecommunications (see chapters 7–9 and 13–14). We place MITI's successes and failures within the context of Japan's unique political and cultural frames of reference. Japan's approach to marketing its new technology overseas is a product of how the Japanese government-business relationship works on behalf of this capitalist development nation-state.

The Japanese approach toward governing the market is an appropriate model for subsequent market developments in Korea, Taiwan, Singapore, and elsewhere in East Asia. Thus, marketers who sell products within Japan and elsewhere in Asia must adjust to the economic, cultural, and political realities of Japanese and East Asian society.

Hunting for Japanese consumers. Third, let's examine the cultural frame. Japanese consumers present marketers with real cultural differences. Unfortunately, many marketers are guilty of clumsy vetting when they do cultural research on Japan. They fail to situate Japan in its historical context – a closed society, a rapid race for industrialization ending in war and defeat, and a quick study of American material success (see Exhibit 5-2). Through all the ups and downs Japanese consumers focus on Japanese ideas, products, magazines, humor, and comic books.[1] The Japanese share a closeness, an emotional degree of intimacy attached to goods made by other Japanese.

What is the impact of the global, largely American entertainment culture on Japanese youth? Are the latter's social values converging with those of American and European youth? Unlike the situation of American products in Europe, Japanese consumers view imports from the United States and Europe with coolness. Theirs is an emotional separation from foreign goods. These alien products must prove themselves by going through a slow cultural adaptation within Japan. Once accepted within Japanese society, these products become copy-cat versions of the American youth-oriented culture with potential sales also in China and elsewhere in East Asia.

In chapters 3 and 4, we made six suggestions about increasing marketing effectiveness within Mexico and Europe. Do they apply to Japan?

1. Grow the market through cross-cultural clusters without regard to national boundaries. Japan has a strong set of socio-cultural values, traditions, and customs. Most are unique to Japan. No other countries

within East Asia are similar to Japan. Thus, this concept of cross-national clusters does not apply to marketing in Japan.

2. Pay attention to the self-referencing criteria (SRC) of language, religion, history, and geography and their impact on social groups. Add the focal option (or focus of comparison). Japanese prefer their own products and ideas because these values reflect their own SRC. These concepts are important to marketing in Japan and are effectively translated as *Ware Ware Nihonjin* ("We Japanese").

3. Accept differences in national character. Although Japanese seek out material success, this is done collectively (or through social groups, such as families and firms) rather than as a product of individualism or power distance. Some marketing concepts require cultural adaptation before they can be used effectively in Japan.

4. Apply the coefficient of imitation with an emphasis on cultural bilingualism. Japanese cultural truths dominate consumer choices while global, largely American preferences find their way into fashion, luxury goods, and technologically sophisticated products. Moreover, some age-period cohort groups, such as the youth, are more prone to try western goods once their peers adopt these products into the freedom lifestyle. However, older age-period cohort groups, such as middle-aged parents, are not as likely as American and European parents to follow the consumption habits of their children. This marketing concept does not translate one-for-one in Japan among all age-period cohort groups, but it is useful in discussing inroads of the global youth culture in Japan.

5. Use the time effect of product diffusion (or the time between innovation and wider distribution) to capture first-mover advantage during the growth phase of the product-development life cycle. Foreign-origin products (i.e., manufactured in Japan, technologically superior to locally made goods, and adapted to Japan's unique cultural identity) are able to use the time effect of product diffusion to capture market share in Japan. Nevertheless, the time effect depends on the country effect (or Japan's unique national character) of product diffusion. These relationships are crucial to marketing success in Japan.

6. Exploit the country effect of product diffusion (or the role of nonethnocentrists versus ethnocentrists) to estimate market share among Japanese who are adopting the global, largely American freedom lifestyle. Although Japanese youth do imitate their counterparts in the United States, virtually everyone in Japan believes in *nihonjin*. Thus, the discriminating role of nonethnocentrists versus ethnocentrists in the application of the country effect of product diffusion does not apply in Japan.

Segmentation, positioning, and tailoring decisions. Finally, let's look closely at the marketing management frame. Foreign marketers have difficulty predicting Japanese consumer tastes because many of them are unobservable to those from the West. Even though marketing executives offer standardized Japanese products, Japanese consumers impose differentiation of their own based on high-quality attributes only dimly perceived by foreign marketers. Value creation takes place within a regulatory framework created by the Japanese nation-state, through *keiretsu* and other close bonding relationships among Japanese firms, and the marketing needs of Japanese consumers.

Organizing global marketing experience. The simultaneous existence of these four different contexts forces marketers to research Japanese markets carefully, to position some global brands in Japan, and to watch for different national signals from Japan. Let's do two things in this chapter. First, we will discuss the impact of Japanese cultural insights on the creation of new market segments among the young and old, men and women, and other age-period cohort groups. Then we will apply this country analysis to how marketing teams make decisions about selling comic books, chocolates, and fast food to the Japanese; see Exhibit 5-3.

Country Risk Questions

Marketers manage final demand by researching international markets, such as Japan; see Exhibit 5-4. Today, marketing executives rate Japan (i.e., its country risk) as equal to the United States and Europe, and less speculative than Mexico and China.

Marketing audit. Even as Japan goes from strength to strength, it offers marketers a long-term planning horizon for the sale of consumer goods, industrial products, and services. There's money to be made in Japan–that is, if one knows how to go about studying the Japanese market.

Exhibit 5-3.
Country Risk Analysis: Japan
The Environmental Scan

Traditional Frame Analysis for Global Marketing

Firm-Specific 4Ps Analysis and Market Segmentation

Young working males

OL or office ladies become working women

Young girls and boys

Firm-Specific 4Ps Analysis and Marketing Research

Ask questions

Know rate of product diffusion

Compare traditionalists with emerging youth culture

National Marketing Decisions and Research Tasks

Pick up cultural truths from walking-around research

Flesh out details of national differences with formal research

National Marketing Decisions and Marketing Opportunities

Accept slow adaptation of foreign products into Japanese culture

Appreciate the importance of quality in design and packaging

Recognize the importance of American entertainment culture

Nontraditional Frame Analysis for Global Marketing

Political Context and Domestic Rules

Govern the market

Government-business relationships

Keiretsu

Capitalist development state

Cultural Context and National Character

Self-referencing criteria

Nihonjin

Collectivism of families and firms

Material success

Manga

Time and country effect of product diffusion

Cultural Context and Cultural Bilingualism

Recognize impact of Chinese ideograms

Pay attention to four systems for writing Japanese

Accept desire to imitate English words

Learn to skim information

Appreciate the integrated totality of Japanese culture

Exhibit 5-4.
Japan Buys US Beef

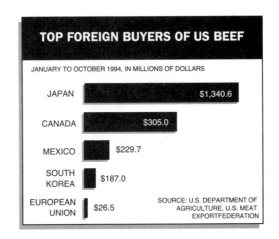

TOP FOREIGN BUYERS OF US BEEF

JANUARY TO OCTOBER 1994, IN MILLIONS OF DOLLARS

JAPAN	$1,340.6
CANADA	$305.0
MEXICO	$229.7
SOUTH KOREA	$187.0
EUROPEAN UNION	$26.5

SOURCE: U.S. DEPARTMENT OF AGRICULTURE, U.S. MEAT EXPORTFEDERATION

Courtesy of Journal of Commerce

Environmental Scan: Japanese Market Segments

Successful marketing executives spend a great deal of time reading Japanese comic books. These *manga* are designed for Japanese readers who share attitudes, values, and customs, many of which are unknown outside of Japan. Marketers gain insights into Japan's popular culture because the comic books provide readers with a common memory about Japanese heroes.

More than one-third of all books and magazines published in Japan are *manga*.[2] The most popular of all comic magazines, *Shukan Shōnen Jampu* (or *Jump*), has a weekly circulation of five million copies, 50 percent greater than *Time* and twice as many copies as *People* magazine.[3] Let's work our way through the formal research on *manga* to see how we come up with market segments. The data translate into market segments that are different from those marketers would anticipate from research work completed in the United States or Europe.

Segment #1: Young Working Males

For example, young Japanese males in their twenties tend not to be married, and they live in dormitories or other all-male shared quarters sponsored by their firms. Unmarried Japanese males in their thirties are forced into marriage advisory services by their bosses and families. Japanese males in their forties are usually married with households separate from those of their parents and their firms.

All three groups of males together buy six million comic books weekly. They form two marketing categories:

- *Shōnen "monster" manga*: These are comic books for both teenage boys and adult males. Thus, the ads in *Shōnen Jump* are for CD players, video games, motorcycles, body-building equipment, electric guitars, tanning lotion, language tape courses, movies, beer, cigarettes, canned coffee, banks, and men's fashion.[4]

- *Seinen "adventure and sex" manga*:[5] These comic books are for young working men, newly married males, and recent fathers with young children. Here, too, the ads in *Big Comic* (a biweekly with circulation of more than one million) and *Giga* (a more recent entry with weekly sales of more than 300,000, whose Chinese ideogram means "playful pictures") appear in the inside front and back covers, and in between stories, promoting male-oriented goods and services.

Segment #2: OL or Office Ladies

Starting in 1980, young female office workers and housewives gave up perusing the *manga* of their boyfriends and husbands. Instead, they began reading *Big Comic for Lady, Be Love*, and 16 other comic books. These give them love stories about how "Boy has to meet girl somehow, someday, somewhere, or our species and its odd mating rituals would soon be history."[6] The ads in the OL *manga* are for clothes, jewelry, pearls, chocolates, tennis, skiing, travel, and marriage services.

Redefining Segment #2: Working Women

Thirteen years later, in 1993, "the princess boom" gave the *manga* for office ladies the chance to become competitive equals with those for men. This category is redefining itself around the concept of feminine elegance, a far cry from what is found in the comic books of the 1980s.

The public event. On June 9, 1993, Masako (Feminine Elegance) Owada, eldest daughter of Hisashi Owada, the Director-General of the Treaty Division of the Foreign Ministry, married Hiro no Miya (Shrine of Broad Vision) Naruhito, the eldest son of the Japanese Emperor.[7] Sometimes, very public spectacles shake up marketing categories, introduce marketing niches, and redefine market segments. The royal wedding in Japan is such an event.

A working woman. Until her marriage, the crown princess lived at home with her parents and the family terrier called (in French) Chocolat, and did the housework along with her mother and sisters.[8] Her lifestyle living arrangements were similar to those of other working women who live at home, want more important work, and travel abroad with girlfriends.

Before the royal wedding, the crown princess worked as a fast-track civil servant in the Foreign Ministry.[9] Her employment was the hope of the future for Japanese women who wanted to break into formerly all-male careers. She was a *sogoshoku* who, similar to men, pledged 9-to-midnight loyalty and a willingness to be assigned anywhere, anytime.[10]

A royal princess. In short, the new crown princess carries both memories of the past and hopes of the future for Japanese working women. She has "crooked teeth (Japanese call them 'eight-tiered teeth,' radiating a smile in eight directions, and find them fetching like Western dimples)." Yet girl met boy, and she is loved and protected. This is one of the oldest story lines in *manga*.

This marketing segment has in the crown princess a model, an image builder, and a spiritual descendant of the samurai scholars who test their skills today as highly motivated middle managers. She gives inspiration to the female millions Japanese call OL, office ladies, who want careers as working women *and* marriage, not just marriage.

Segment #3: Crossover Comic Books

Manga exist for young girls (ages 6–15) and for young boys (ages 8–18), and many of these are read by adults, too. "The general consensus among readers in Japan seems to be that comics have as much to say about life as novels or films . . . As the Japanese describe them, their comics are 'wet,' as opposed to 'dry'; that is, they are unashamedly human and sentimental . . . All are an integral part of Japan's popular culture and as such reveal legacies from the past, ideals of love, attitudes to work and perfection, and a basic love of fantasy."[11] The most popular comics are compiled into paperback books, then into hardback books for collectors.

Assessing the Totality of Japanese Culture

The Japanese are predisposed to visual forms of communication because Chinese ideograms are pictures that represent ideas. Historically, *manga* comes from two ideograms for "involuntary" or "morally corrupt" and "in spite of oneself"; it could be translated as "whimsical sketches." Today, *manga* carries the connotation of "playful pictures," "crazy pictures," "Punch pictures," "drama pictures," and *komikkusu* (or the English word "comics" adopted into the Japanese language).[12]

In fact, the Japanese language employs four writing systems: the ideograms imported from China; two different syllabic scripts, *hiragana*, which is cursive, and *katakana*, which is more angular; and the Roman alphabet. Most Japanese write a blend of all four systems, and Japanese artists use all writing systems to create different moods.[13]

For example, foreign words from western languages are written in *katakana*. To make a point about the exotic nature of ideas, products, or services, artists will use actual American English words in the Roman alphabet (BANG! POW!). Sometimes the Japanese employ a slaphappy use of decorative English that makes no sense to native English-speaking people.[14] Nevertheless, when American-origin products are no longer exotic (e.g., Coke, McDonald's, Kentucky Fried Chicken, and 7-11), artists change advertising copy and brand names from the Roman alphabet into *katakana*.[15]

Reading Japanese comic books also teaches marketers how to skim over the page, absorb the information from the drawings, and look at the printed word only for support of the ideas of artists. Skimming the page, scanning all the pages, and taking the comic book in as a whole: these are acquired skills. However, this is what foreigner marketing executives must do to master their craft in Japan. They must skim category information, scan markets, and take Japanese culture as an integrated totality.

Initial Analysis of Market Opportunities

If the cowboy symbolizes America and the Gascon rooster represents France, the samurai warrior illustrates Japan. Throughout Japan's long feudal period, which ended only in the 1860s, samurai were the elite. Today, modern samurai give their loyalty to Japan, where they work hard in factories and offices. The comic books show today's samurai as good men, strong men, and men of modern Japan. These *manga* superheroes help Japanese men get through long days at the office.

Some are even baseball heroes who go through rigorous training and hazing in their total devotion to their team. Actual Japanese and American baseball players appear in the comics to show their total devotion to the sport. Even American professional football with its emphasis on teams fits into what Japanese men like to read in *manga*. They, too, are affected by "the princess boom" with light love stories first appearing in girls' comic books now finding their way into boys' *manga*.

The Japanese learn their craft as apprentices who give their loyalty to their teachers and who, in turn, become masters. The Japanese take pride in their work as the best photographer, best salesperson, and best carpenter. They are craftsmen who excel in bringing new, better products to the market. Some are Japan's salary-men, hard-working, blue-suited, briefcase-toting organization men who get along in harmony with everyone else in the office. Others are working women who dream of doing what the crown princess did: career and marriage, to be respected for competence, and to be loved for lithe beauty.

Asking Research Questions

Let's assume significant differences in national character continue to exist between Japan, the United States, and Europe – that is, Japan's country risk is both low and predictable. Now let's shift the focus of our risk analysis to the uncertainty perceptions of marketers over the combined strength of collectivism and material success among age-period cohort groups in Japan. Here are several appropriate firm-specific marketing questions:

Who uses the product? Which Japanese consumers use collectivism and material success as their crucial self-referencing criteria? How do the Japanese incorporate non-Japanese products into their modern lifestyles?

How to increase market share? Which American products pour into Japan because some Japanese prefer new and different goods? Are there local Japanese producers? Are American and European firms producing locally, and are they able to capture the Japanese desire for slow cultural adaptation of all things strange, alien, and foreign?

How to provide value? How does Japan define value? Is value based on standardized marketing strategies on price, customer service, quality, and timeliness, and on a willingness to accept experimentation from marketers? Or does Japan define value in terms of quality – namely, good ingredients, design, packaging, and customer service? Are Japanese brand names preferred? Does the stronger impact of collectivism and material success in Japan speed up the rate of product diffusion? Does Japan's different national character force the time effect to be dependent on the country effect of product diffusion?

What customer signals show changes in the local market? Are American products seeping into the cultural values of Japan? Are they viewed positively when they affect Japanese preferences for food, clothes, and entertainment? To what extent will these non-Japanese products be accepted in Japan? Will the combined weight of collectivism and material success speed up the rate of change in the product-development life cycle?

Knowing the Rate of Product Diffusion

The impact of American marketing practices, business experiences, and cross-cultural products is a bit more intrusive today than previously in Japan. Some standardized advertising campaigns push global, largely American products (e.g., Coke, McDonald's, Bud). These marketing efforts target Japanese consumers.

Nevertheless, national character plays the crucial role in determining whether local or foreign products are accepted within Japan. To speed up the rate of product diffusion within Japan, marketers search for useful fragments of cultural information – such as the superheroes from *manga*. Then they dress the samurai in baseball uniforms and give the local culture an appeal found alluring by Japanese youth. Finally, marketers might add a very limited number of ruffles and flourishes of the global, largely American culture now found in North America, Europe, and elsewhere in East Asia.

Clues to Capturing Customers

Marketing within Japan builds on national character, collectivism, material success, *nihonjin* self-referencing criteria, and many other cultural insights. Japan is different and will remain different. Nevertheless, social change is slowly seeping into Japan as a byproduct of the global, largely American entertainment culture. Marketers call this cultural bilingualism – that is, a largely American gloss with Japanese thinking about marketing practices.

Marketers are most at home with known market segments of Japan (e.g., young working males, working women). Because young adults in Japan have a bit more in common with other young people in the United States than they do with their own parents, marketing executives anticipate that young people from Japan and elsewhere in East Asia will become accomplished trans-Pacific consumers, too. Because similar market segments exist all across the Pacific basin, marketing executives can use their knowledge of marketing in the United States to make sales to trans-Pacific business executives and their families who live part of their lives in Japan. This is a significant clue to capturing customers throughout Japan.

Summary: Scanning Japanese Market Segments

Japan's ability to maintain its unique national character even in the face of the global, largely American entertainment culture stands as a model of success for other East Asian countries. The former's cultural insights include collectivism, material success, and *nihonjin*. They establish market segments (e.g., young working males, working women) for *manga*, or Japanese comic books. These unique market segments translate into large markets for Japanese products and smaller markets for foreign products. Notwithstanding the current level of cultural bilingualism within Japan, marketing executives foresee only slightly higher levels of imitation and somewhat more accelerated rates of product diffusion as Japan accepts more American products into its lifestyle.

The Firm-Specific Assignment

Marketers manage final demand by positioning global products within Japan; see Exhibit 5-5. Japanese government agencies (such as the Ministry of International Trade and Industry or MITI) offer marketing executives a long-term planning horizon for exports to and sales within Japan. The former change the perceptions of marketers about firm-specific uncertainties on cultural bilingualism, national character, and local market segments. Today, marketing executives rate Japan (i.e., its firm-specific risk) as equal to North America and Europe, and more predictable than China and East Asia.

Understanding Cultural Context

Right now, Japanese consumers present two lifestyles to marketers:

- Devoted nationalists

- Accomplished trans-Pacific peoples

Younger age-period cohort groups tend to be accomplished trans-Pacific peoples. Young working male adults purchase *Levi's* jeans, sweat suits, *Nike* sports shoes, and leather jackets for their weekend, leisure time. Working women travel throughout the Pacific to buy luxury goods more cheaply than at home. These routine purchasing activities fit the perception of peer groups about the global, largely American consumer culture – that is, the freedom lifestyle culturally adapted to Japanese pursuits of recreation, leisure, and play. As we approach the new century, the Japanese youth culture

Exhibit 5-5.
Firm-Specific Analysis: Japan
The Competitive Scan

Traditional Frame Analysis for Global Marketing

National Marketing Decisions and Formal Research

Pay attention to uniformity of national tastes

Recognize preference for collectivism

Appreciate importance of focal option (or focus of comparison)

Accept desire to imitate trendsetters among youth groups

Build market segments through slow diffusion of products

Establish market share during product-development life cycle

Acknowledge the impact of youthful Japanese consumers

National Marketing Decisions and Walking-Around Research

Noodles and green tea from China

Pork chops from Portugal

Black tea from England

Curry from India

Designer packaged chocolate candy from Europe and US

Hamburgers, pizza, ice cream, and cola drinks from US

KFC flavored chicken from US

Disneyland, Aunt Stella cookies, American coffee from US

Nontraditional Frame Analysis for Global Marketing

Cultural Context and Traditional, Nationalist Lifestyle

Humor shows assertiveness

Fantasy demonstrates value

Harmony promotes a lifestyle

Nihonjin boots pop culture

Cultural Context and Modern, Trans-Pacific Lifestyle

Save time for recreation, leisure, and play

Buy copy-cat goods hot in Tokyo, New York, Paris

Look like everyone else in Japan

Purchase reputation of domestic and foreign goods

Consume luxury goods and services

Search for highest quality

remains a collective work of the imagination, just beginning because older age-period cohort groups, such as parents, prefer more traditional lifestyles.

Competitive Scan: Consumer Information

The interaction of age-period cohort groups and lifestyles within a nation's population affects the consumption of products. That is the received information. More useful are cultural insights about humor, fantasy, harmony, and *nihonjin*. Such prior knowledge systematizes the vision marketers have about a nation's values and their effect on consumption. Let's look at these four cultural insights and see how marketers use them to sell products in Japan.

Using Humor to Show Assertiveness

"Humor . . . enhance[s] recall . . . when the humorous message coincides with [the ad] . . . and is viewed as appropriate for the product category."[16] For example, Japanese juniors, aged 18 to 21, who are children of the twenty-somethings of the 1980s (called *shinjinrui*, new breed, or baby boomers), are a market segment that likes ads mocking rivals in a frank and funny way. So "PepsiCo Inc. rocked Japan with a spot in which rap star Hammer depicted market leader Coke as the beverage that turns you into a nerd. Pepsi's cola sales in Japan jumped 19%" in 1991.[17]

Humor allows juniors to see contrasts between expected and unexpected situations. Humor also works well when consumers have a low involvement with the product. Moreover, humor must suggest a possible or plausible situation in a playful or nonthreatening mode, and must trigger an implied response from both Americans and Japanese:[18] Buy Pepsi's cola.

Employing Fantasy to Demonstrate Value

Japanese have "a deep feeling for fantasy," says Toshio Kagami, the senior managing director of Oriental Land, the Japanese company that manages Tokyo Disneyland.[19] They want an undiluted Disneyland with all its rules, roles, and symbols; they know when they come to Tokyo Disneyland they are coming to the United States, the world of America, but located within Japan. The Japanese prefer to take on new roles – the cowboy, Mickey Mouse, the Scottish bagpiper. Role playing is part of Japan's fantasy world because it's how the Japanese escape from their daily work.

Then we have the fantasies about Aunt Stella's sweet-smelling cookies. "The cookies themselves are somewhat American, although smaller and harder, like sweetened traditional Japanese rice crackers. But the flavors ('American coffee,' for instance) seem to sustain the foreign image."[20] They are sold in souvenir boxes and cans with drawings of wide-open American farms within one of the 56 stores in the chain.[21] Japanese women can sit in early American furniture while they choose cookies packaged in Aunt Stella dolls. Although Japanese women think these are American products, they are made in Japan by Joseph Dunkle, an American resident of Japan. This is called "warm heart communication" among Japanese marketers.

Exploiting Harmony to Promote Lifestyle

Both women and men (whether they are juniors or baby boomers) agree that chocolate must be given on Valentine's Day, February 14, and one month later on White Day, March 14. Even though chocolate first came to Japan from Mexico in the 1600s, it did not become an integral part of Japanese culture until the American occupation after World War II. Today, all Japanese adore chocolate as an adult liquor-spiked candy.

On Valentine's Day, women give dark whiskey-laced, apple-shaped chocolate (called *Eve's Seduction*) to men as a sign of romantic interest.[22] If these women are OL, they give the same dark chocolate (called *Obligation* or *Giri de gomen neko*) in the shapes of pipes, neckties, or golf clubs to their bosses and other executives at work.[23]

On White Day, men give white chocolate to those women who gave them dark chocolate one month before. They are either showing romantic interest or reciprocating an obligation through the gift giving of chocolate.[24] Although White Day gift giving became absolutely required of men only during the rise of the baby boomers to middle-aged prosperity, it is now so much a part of Japanese culture that this chocolate has become an indispensable part of the Japanese lifestyle. Everybody gives chocolates as gifts of romance and as gifts of obligation. Not even the juniors are immune from this aspect of collectivism.

Maximizing *Nihonjin* to Boost Pop Culture

"We Japanese" have flavored chicken in Japan, so who needs Kentucky Fried Chicken?[25] Twenty years ago, Japanese focus group research came up with this negative answer. Today, KFC is the most successful franchise in Japan, even more successful than Mister Donut, Pizza Hut, Baskin Robbins, McDonald's, and 7-11.

Kentucky Fried Chicken used to serve biscuits in its dinner sets to preserve "warm heart communication" for the Japanese who hear the strains of "My Old Kentucky Home" at the food stores. Now KFC serves *yaki-musubi* (or grilled riceballs) in its dinner sets, and the ad promoting this change reads: *Kentakkii ni au na, kore* (This goes with KFC, doesn't it).[26]

"We Japanese" want authentic foreign chicken presented with Japanese quality.[27] For example, dark meat chicken is thought to be tastier than white meat. Drumsticks and wings are preferred over breasts. Chicken, french fries, and *yaki-musubi* must come in dinner sets. And all must be presented visually so that one look at the whole package gives the Japanese the sense of good value, top quality, and an affordable price.

At the beginning, KFC's American roots were stylish and appealing to the Japanese. Over the years, "We Japanese" want foreign food to become Japanese food. Mister Donut introduced *an* (sweet bean paste) to replace jelly in its donuts, and a new line of muffins with a fried sweet potato flavor and black sesame (*daigaku imo* or University Potato).[28] Baskin Robbins offers *matcha* (green tea) and *ogura* (sweet red bean) ice cream. McDonald's does not offer ketchup with its french fries because Japanese think it is too messy for finger food; instead, it offers four types of seasoned salts: *nori* (seaweed), curry, barbecue, and Mexican.[29] And KFC sells rice balls.

"We Japanese" want foreign-origin Japanese food to find a cultural niche within the rituals of Japanese life. KFC introduced roast chicken during the Christmas holidays (*Kurisumasu*) with the chicken legs tied decoratively at the "ankle" with silver foil and red ribbon, and with *dekorēshon kēki* (cake with gobs of decoratively piped buttercream).[30] Since Christmas is a foreign secular holiday in Japan, the Japanese celebrate it with foreign foods.

"We Japanese" want acculturation. Through separate subsidiaries, KFC sells *yakitori* (chicken grilled on skewers) and *wa-fū bentō ten* (Japanese-style boxed lunches). McDonald's (*Makudonarudo*) offers *kare raisu* (curry rice) that bears no resemblance to the curries originally imported from India in the 1800s, and *omiotsuke* (miso soup).[31] These examples show creative adaptation at work in Japan.[32])

Estimates of Market Potential

Japanese juniors (ages 18–21), similar to other Japanese seek out humor, fantasy, harmony, and *nihonjin* in their products. These consumers subordinate their individual goals to those of their peer groups, families, friends, and firms. Yet collectively Japanese juniors as a new market segment want the following from their products:[33]

- Assertiveness (Pepsi Cola, General Motors, Compaq)

- Green chic (Body Shop)

- Value (L.L. Bean, Dell Computer, Tokyo Disneyland)

- Casual fashion (J. Crew, Levi's, Gap knockoffs)

- Ease of use (Macintosh computers)

All these cultural insights give value to products because they have both Japanese and universal appeal to the 18–21 age-period peer groups throughout the world.

Framing the Research Problem

Today, a great deal of marketing research done in Japan concerns the following questions:

1. Is the self-expression found in juniors the birth of a youth culture? According to Terue Ohashi, the marketing director at Daiko Advertising Inc. in Tokyo, four new cultural characteristics are now embedded in the 18–21 age-period cohort group.[34] First, strengthened by the influence of the "princess boom," women are leaving household work and expressing themselves through outside employment. Second, with more income, consumption rather than savings defines individualism for both women and men. Third, men are marrying later and families are getting smaller. And fourth, families want more Western-style living space and leisure activities.

2. Are these juniors more collectivist than their counterparts in Europe or the United States? Although Japanese juniors are too young to be nostalgic for the 1950s, they like to buy products from that era because they find a sense of comfort in the past.[35] For example, Coca-Cola has revived its old red-seal Coke-bottle logo as the youth culture reaches for permanence.[36] Japanese juniors have their own distinctive herding instincts that are reinforced by Japan's collectivist society, and these herding instincts remain intact when juniors marry and form families.

3. Do juniors (similar to their parents) harmonize their individual, independent self-expression within the whole of Japanese society? Is the "We Japanese" syndrome still alive in Japan?

Yes, says Australian George Fields, a Japanese insider (*nakama*). He was born in Japan, lived there for his first 16 years, and came back in 1965 to found ASI Survey Research Group Japan. Fields does focus group research and now is Japan's leading consumer marketing guru.

Fields concludes that the concept of Japanese homogeneity exists among those born during the Great Depression and immediately after World War II, baby boomers who are now middle-aged parents, and even among the juniors. He believes this homogeneity comes from the uniformity of the Japanese educational system.[37]

But times are changing, says Fields. Women are marrying later, having fewer children, putting their kids into kindergarten, seeking out leisure-time travel, and going back to work.[38] Women are no longer *okusan* (traditional Japanese wives) even though their husbands, the salaried office executives, prefer the older ways of thinking about "We Japanese."

Similar Market Segments Worldwide

Japan is an eclectic culture in which indigenous Japanese values are intermixed with those from China, Europe, the United States, and other foreign nations. The latter are acculturated and made Japanese through use, ritual, and time. Yet these imported concepts also change lifestyles, culture, and values within Japan. Today, a new consumer exists in Japan.[39]

Is the new Japanese consumer queer, fantastic, unfathomed, secretive, odd, enigmatic, where nobody is quite as he or she seems? Is this new consumer Different with a capital D? Or is this new Japanese consumer different with a small d similar to the difference one finds in Mexico, Canada, the United States, France, Germany, Italy, or Britain? Yes, Japan is different, but not so different.[40]

Foreign marketers must remember that two truths exist in Japan. The first is *honne*, or the truth you feel in your heart, and the second is *tatemae*, or the truth you utter in public. When George Fields asked his Japanese focus group whether fried chicken from KFC would sell in Japan, he received public truth; "We Japanese" like our traditional chicken. The private truth was that "We Japanese" would try something new, something foreign. *Honne* was the real reality for Kentucky Fried Chicken in Japan.

Understanding the Modern Japanese Consumer

Here are seven important points to remember about the new Japanese consumer.

First, the new Japanese consumer wants ways to save time. The capsule hotel, in which guests sleep in cubicles stacked one on top of the other, exists as an inexpensive alternative for those who don't want to take the long two- to three-hour train ride home. Moreover, 24-hour golf ranges, tennis courts, and convenience stores exist to expand the use of time when offices have closed for the day.

Second, the new Japanese consumer wants to purchase only those goods considered hot in Tokyo. All consumption trends, such as the slight shift toward a liberal (modern, western) lifestyle[41] have started in this city. This is most apparent in consumption, fashion, and pop culture among Japanese under 35 years old.

Third, the new Japanese consumer wants to be similar to all other Japanese consumers. Virtually all Japanese think of themselves as middle class. They pay careful attention to dressing alike, but look for small differences in products to express individuality. The Japanese are amused by youthful indiscretions (e.g., wearing jeans instead of business suits), but they know juniors eventually marry, form families, and become middle class.

Fourth, the new Japanese consumer wants products that have "established reputation." Sometimes this means famous brands. More often this means famous brands bought at an honored store. Most often this means famous brands bought at an honored store that come with a reputation of success from Europe or the United States. Image instead of content is the most important criterion that determines whether the famous brand gift bought at an honored store meets the obligation required on White Day.

Fifth, the new Japanese consumer cannot afford to own houses. So the treat is to buy luxury overseas travel, richly appointed watches and jewelry, expensive cars, highly prized opera tickets, and a sumptuous night on the Queen Elizabeth II. Liquid assets rather than fixed assets make the affluent consumer in Japan.

Sixth, the new Japanese consumer wants the highest quality possible in goods and services. And the packaging of these products must reflect the care one takes in selling these goods and services to the consumer in Japan. Every detail is dwelt upon as essential. The task of wrapping individual items, packaging all items in a box, wrapping the box, and putting ribbons around the total package supercedes all other tasks. The Japanese practice the art form of concentrated quality in which the wrapped package succeeds or fails entirely insofar as it achieves concentration.[42] Beauty is not so much in the product itself, but in the concentration of preparing the package for the customer.

Seventh, the new Japanese consumer receives so much more information from *manga*, magazines, books, newspapers, radio, TV, and online computer services than do European and American consumers. All Japanese get the same information from Tokyo 24 hours each day, seven days per week, 365 days per year. They use this information to determine which goods and services are of the highest quality, and which of these are the trends of emerging new lifestyles appearing from the interaction of western ideas and Japanese values.

To avoid "humbling" feedback, US marketers must pay attention to the real national differences between Americans and Japanese. Also marketers must recognize that Japanese consumers are changing along with other groups in the world, but Japanese consumers are changing at a much slower pace than are the Americans and the Europeans. Caution and care in collecting good consumer information gives us better products, higher sales, and more satisfied customers in one of the toughest markets in the world, Japan.

Summary: Scanning Consumer Information

Marketers make Japanese sales by paying close attention to humor, fantasy, harmony, *nihonjin*, and other cultural insights. Marketing executives also make sales to Japanese juniors and other younger age-period peer groups by building assertiveness, green chic, value, and casual fashion into their products. Moreover, marketers make sales to Japanese younger and older age-period cohort groups by promoting collectivism and material success. This Japan is more different from than similar to Europe and America.

National Marketing Decisions

Marketers manage final demand by signaling detailed national information about Japan; see Exhibit 5-6. Marketing executives also expand final demand by catering to juniors, young working males, working women, married baby boomers, older people, and retired people in Japan. These are important Japanese market segments.

Let's be careful in our analysis. No strong disconnection exists between older and younger age-period cohort groups. Yes, World War II and Vietnam are history; poodle skirts and the twist are retro products again sold in Japan. However, the events of 1968 in Europe and the United States did not invade Japan nor did the ideas of rebellion and freedom come to divide Japanese youth from their elders. This disconnection is a demographic fact only in western Europe and North America.

In Japan, national character (humor, fantasy, harmony, and *nihonjin*) connects all age-period cohort groups to their past, present, and future. In fact, Japanese national character carries more weight today than trans-Pacific values (i.e., leisure, luxury goods, and copy-cat services) among all age groups, even Japanese juniors.

Nevertheless, Japanese juniors are moving ever so slowly along the continuum from collectivism toward a little bit more individualism. In other words, juniors are adapting some trans-Pacific, mostly American values about material success to fit within their national culture. This process of slow cultural adaptation is seen in rising imports of western goods and American fast food services by both juniors and their parents, the baby boomers. When Japanese consumers compare imported products with existing domestic goods and find the latter less favorable, then juniors and baby boomers tend to choose imported luxury products or foreign-origin, copy-cat goods manufactured within Japan. Only under these limited conditions can marketers conclude similar market segments exist among European, American, and Japanese youth. To say more is to draw inappropriate conclusions about the relative strengths of trans-Pacific cultural similarities versus Japanese national character.

Marketing Scan: Routine Purchasing Behavior

Because juniors are behaving in ways considered socially appropriate for the 1990s, their peer group takes its place along with their parents social group, the baby boomers, as those to be imitated within Japanese society. Juniors prefer assertiveness, and they want green chic and ease of use in their products. Over time their view of what is right and proper in clothes, food, personal care products, and computers will come to dominate purchase decisions

Exhibit 5-6.
National Marketing Analysis: Japan
The Marketing Scan

Traditional Frame Analysis for Global Marketing
Firm Specific 4Ps Analysis And Decision Making Under Uncertainty
Gain from initial market entry
Succeed from expansion of the national market
Grow through global rationalization
Firm-Specific 4Ps Analysis And Purchasing Behavior
Pay attention to individualism, independence, uniqueness
Recognize up-to-date fashion choices
Appreciate change fits into tradition, ritual, values
Build on a priori preferences
Accept selective influence of foreign ads
Establish import of group membership, conformity, collectivism
National Marketing Decisions and Marketing Forecasts
Continuing trend captures more juniors for freedom lifestyle
Amplifying trend uses aggressive marketing with little success
Doubling trend does not convert other age peer groups

Nontraditional Frame Analysis for Global Marketing
Cultural Context and Traditional Cultural-Based Typologies
Humor, fantasy, harmony, *nihonjin*
Collectivism
Cultural Context and Modern, Trans-Pacific Typologies
Leisure time, luxury goods, foreign travel, copy-cat services
Individualism
Cultural Context and Composite Japanese Lifestyle
Devoted nationalists, traditionalists, and older groups
Successful, trans-Pacific business executives
Prosperous young working males, working women, baby boomers
Accomplished modern, juniors age-period cohort group
Marketing Management Context and Cultural Change
Compare new to existing products (focal option)
Study good, bad, fuzzy, and selective memory
Pay attention to dominant homogeneity

during the years of family formation, child rearing, and middle-aged prosperity. In this way, Japanese juniors are little different from their counterparts in Europe and America.

However, Japanese juniors, young working males, working women, and baby boomers are different in detail from similar market segments elsewhere in the world. For example, Japanese consumers pick goods and services because of the products' value in expressing traditional or trans-Pacific, largely American lifestyle choices. Even juniors give chocolate on Valentine's Day and White Day because nowhere else in the world do products maintain their symbolic importance as gifts of obligation as they do in Japan.

Modeling Purchasing Behavior

Why do juniors go along with this Japanese cultural idea? What's in it for them to maintain the practice even though giving chocolate on Valentine's Day is an American import, and doing it again on White Day is a 1980s cultural adaptation? Here's how marketers model purchasing behavior to explain routine social acts on the part of Japanese juniors.[43]

Individualism. Similar to peer groups throughout the world, juniors want to show their individuality; they do so by purchasing distinctive clothes, jeans, movies, music, and electronic equipment. Moreover, women in Japan are especially concerned about their independence and uniqueness. However, as juniors grow into parents, their preference for individualism declines as they conform to the traditions, rituals, and values of Japanese culture, especially in gift giving.

Desire to be current. Juniors in Japan, Europe, and the United States want to be up to date in their fashion choices. However, juniors in Japan don't want to stray too far from the cultural values thought important by all Japanese. So juniors will purchase only candy copy-cat items that are entirely appropriate for the two chocolate gift-giving days.

Attitude toward change. "We Japanese" like change when it fits into tradition, ritual, and values. So juniors eat roasted chicken from Kentucky Fried Chicken at Christmas, consume donuts with *an* (red bean paste) from Mister Donut, and buy retro products to link themselves to the past.

Strength of a priori preferences. In Japan more so than elsewhere, juniors are conditioned by the gift-giving practices of their parents, office colleagues, and peers. Unless romance is in the air, the giving of dark and white chocolate with the brand name *Eve's Seduction* is inappropriate. Juniors know without being told that the appropriate symbol is *Obligation* chocolate.

Selective influence. Juniors learn about new fashion choices from their peers, *manga,* advertising, and TV. Some juniors are more connected to European and American peer groups through music and sports; the latter provides an overlapping competing and complementary set of influences on juniors. Yet, when push comes to shove, juniors are more influenced by Japanese values than by foreign ideas.

Group membership, conformity, and collectivism. Juniors choose *Levi's* jeans because their Japanese and foreign peer groups prefer this brand, too. However, juniors choose rice balls with their Kentucky Fried Chicken because of the "We Japanese" syndrome. This specific cultural value is by far the most important one in understanding the emerging Japanese consumer society.

Clearly, the influence of Japanese society as a whole plays a crucial role in setting the boundary between appropriate and inappropriate choices for juniors. Because everyone gives chocolate, juniors rush to join the bandwagon and give chocolate, too. To not do so is inappropriate behavior. When juniors have more income they spend their money on more expensive gifts, luxury goods, and, especially for working women, foreign travel. To do this is appropriate routine purchasing behavior for juniors and other Japanese. In this way, product diffusion occurs within Japan for both domestic and foreign goods.

Employing the Focal Option Why do Japanese juniors add new products to their routine purchases? How do they decide to buy new products instead of existing products? Consumers make comparisons about competing products, comparing new (sometimes foreign or imported) goods against existing products. Marketers call this the focus of comparison (or focal option).[44]

For example, personal computers from NEC are in the memory of the juniors. Since these young adult consumers use Chinese ideograms and the other three writing systems available to the Japanese language, they find keyboard-based operating systems awkward. When these PCs are the focal option, juniors compare NEC's awkwardness to the ease of use of Apple's icons (or modern ideograms) in Macintosh PCs.

Context is crucial to choice. Bad memory of a comparative product makes it easier to choose the alternative or new product. However, good memory of a comparative product does not necessarily make it more difficult to choose the new product. We need to know what facts are remembered and how such selective memory fits into a consumer's comparison of preferences. Moreover, in time, memory becomes fuzzy or uncertain, but retains more of the good than the bad about events, products, and ideas. These problems face marketers all over the world when they employ the focal option for modeling routine purchasing behavior.

Using Quality for Niche Marketing

With the introduction of the Mary Engelbreit designer packaged candy from the Sweet Shop in Fort Worth, Texas to the Japanese market, baby boomers remember *Eve's Seduction* and *Obligation* chocolate. Their memory is good because both are high-quality candies and are packaged properly for romance and obligatory gift giving. Mary Engelbreit candy is also of the highest quality, and each piece in the box is individually wrapped for presentation to the Japanese. For imported candy to sell in Japan, the sales pitch must include highest grade chocolate, elegant packaging, luxury status, and acceptance by the high-income groups in America. These four comparisons are credible. By making these comparisons, Mary Engelbreit candy finds a niche market during Valentine's Day and White Day in Japan.

The same marketing pitch is used for the coordinated accessories from Ginnie Johansen Designs of Dallas, Texas, Brown's Velvet Ice Cream from Louisiana, and the decorative wall accessories from American Accents by Ditto in Winnsboro, Texas. In the case of the frozen gourmet dinners of shrimp gumbo, and red beans and rice from Good Tastes, Inc. of Houston, Texas, the sales pitch is altered to convey a sense of foreignness, something Japanese can enjoy without traveling to the Gulf Coast of the United States.

Should these American imports gain a very large following in Japan, they will be altered slowly and carefully to fit into the tradition, ritual, and values of Japanese society. Their marketing success will be confirmed when their original foreignness is lost to memory (such as Chinese noodles, Portuguese pork cutlets, and Indian curry), and they become staples in the diet of the Japanese similar to Kentucky Fried Chicken, McDonald's, Mister Donut, and Baskin Robbins.

Strategies for Increasing Marketing Effectiveness

Japan is different from the United States and Europe. For example, gender differences between Japanese men and women have a stronger pull on individual purchases of *manga*, electronics, chocolates, and many other traditional products. Marketers find weak homogeneity among age-period cohort groups, such as juniors and baby boomers. These peer groups are not as powerful in promoting fashion trends as are their counterparts in Europe and the United States.

On the other hand, marketers detect dominant homogeneity among the market segments derived from younger age-period cohort groups. For example, Japanese working adult males and working women do have separate and distinct spending patterns. However, these two market segments do not have equivalent segments in the United States or Europe. Thus, our ability to compare similar market segments across national boundaries flounders when we seek to match young working adults in Europe or the United States with young working adult males and working women in Japan.

Nevertheless, Japanese juniors, working adult males, and working women share some of the same values as do young working adults in Europe and the United States. Their clothes (casual fashion), music (punk rock and rap), and personal care products (green chic) are similar. However, big differences do exist. Japanese juniors do not wear casual clothes to work, as is done in the United States. Their parents, the past, and Japanese traditions preclude juniors from moving too far away from tried and true Japanese cultural norms.

Since most Japanese juniors, working women, and working adult males live with their parents or in inexpensive housing provided by their employers, they have more disposable income to spend on gifts, chocolates, clothes, music, poodle skirts, foreign travel, and luxury goods. Marketers should look for goods to sell to these important Japanese market segments.

Marketing Implementation

Here are the effects of routine purchasing behavior on American exports to Japan. As juniors become a separate market segment within Japan, they become a part of the freedom lifestyle that includes 18- to 21-year-olds throughout the world. These young adults buy more jeans, sportswear, music, and luxury goods as part of the emerging global, largely American lifestyle.

As these young adults become parents, they may extend the freedom lifestyle to more age-period cohort groups within Japan. Marketers don't know whether this will happen because traditional lifestyles are still strongly evident throughout Japan.

Three forecasts. The "continuing trend" forecast is the easiest to make because things do go on as before. The freedom lifestyle captures the same number of people in the juniors' age-period cohort group. This is the most likely trend.

The "amplifying trend" forecast assumes that Japanese firms aggressively market their copy-cat and luxury goods and that more juniors, adult working males, and working women purchase these goods. This could happen, but centuries of tradition are ready to do battle against the global, largely American culture.

The "doubling trend" forecast assumes Japanese firms convert older people to the freedom lifestyle. This is the least likely forecast. Product diffusion occurs slowly in Japan and only when goods are vetted through many years of cultural adaptation by juniors, young adults, baby boomers, and older Japanese. This information should give marketers pause before they casually think Japanese market segments are similar to those found in the United States and Europe.

Summary: Scanning Routine Purchasing Behavior

Higher levels of consumption among Japanese consumers involve an extremely slow move away from collectivism toward an almost imperceptible amount of individualism. This change in cultural attitudes is most noticeable among Japanese juniors but much less conspicuous among adult working males, working women, and baby boomers. For juniors to express their individualism new (foreign) products must compare favorably in terms of quality with existing, competing products. Moreover, for juniors to purchase imported products these goods must go through a slow adaptation to Japanese humor, fantasy, harmony, and *nihonjin*. These four cultural insights are crucial to success in Japan.

Inclusive Contexts for Global Marketing

Exhibit 5-7 presents the inclusive contexts for global marketing in the case of Japan. We examine reinventing Japan as a capitalist development state and show its impact on our country risk analysis. We also study decision making under uncertainty. This, too, shows the importance of cross-country differences. Moreover, we apply traditional socio-cultural values to both formal and walking-around research, and we discuss the opportunities for international sales within Japan. These results tell global marketers to be careful with data and information about Japan. Generally, they don't add up to what marketers expect in the United States and Europe. Japan is a unique country for which the old adage "Think global, act local" is most appropriate for global marketers.

Exhibit 5-7.
Inclusive Contexts for Global Marketing

Country Risk (A)
Pool economic sovereignty within Asia and the Pacific
Reinvent nation-state within international economy
    Microeconomic investment suggestions
    Demographic and cultural information
    Political (government-business) relationships
    Reinvent country as capitalist development state
Long-term planning horizon for business firms
Political Frame

Country Risk (B)
Demographic analysis
    Age-period cohort analysis and national character
    Traditionalism, collectivism, and youth culture
Regional analysis: similar consumption patterns within Japan
Cultural Frame

Firm-Specific 4Ps Analysis
Decision making under uncertainty
    Real cross-country differences
    Industry analysis
    Teamwork and collectivism
Segmentation, positioning, tailoring decisions
Market segments

Marketing Management Frame
Continued on next page

Exhibit 5-7. *Continued from previous page*

___

National Marketing Decisions

Socio-cultural values

  Honne (internalized truth) versus *tatemae* (public truth)

  Slow rate of product assimilation into traditional lifestyle

  Formal and walking-around marketing research

Opportunities, analysis, decisions

  Who uses the product?

  How to increase market share?

  How to provide value?

  What customer signals show changes in local markets?

Clumsy vetting

Decision making under uncertainty

Multimarkets across nation-states, technologies, industries

Government agencies target technologies to gain market share

Technological Frame

___

Conclusions

Scanning for cultural insights is about looking at religion, language, writing systems, gift giving, the role of women, music, luxury goods, and social relationships. Humor, fantasy, harmony, quality, and *nihonjin* play a crucial role in helping market researchers understand "We Japanese."

Let's return to our initial three learning objectives:

1. Discuss the need for predictability in national character to carry out successful country risk analyses.

    You should have a clear understanding of the perceptions of marketers about interpreting national character within different cultures abroad, and you should be able to make some good decisions about exports to and sales within key Japanese market segments. As you read this chapter, you should learn the ideas from the political and cultural frames; they enhance your understanding of country risk within an East Asian country. Many of the ideas we discussed in chapters 3 and 4 about North America and Europe do not apply to Japan. We also show the need to do more walking-around research rather than less, even in a well-developed, information-based society such as Japan. All of these efforts are crucial to being a success in Japan.

2. Outline the use of culturally based consumer information in marketing similar products across national boundaries.

    You should be able to apply consumer information to gain market share and become profitable in Japan. You should be able to apply this marketing analysis to *manga*, chocolates, and KFC.

3. Explain the importance of routine purchasing behavior to sales of foreign goods within culturally different countries.

    You should be aware that the diffusion of new (foreign-origin) products takes place in Japan only as these goods go about the process of being adapted to the norms of Japanese culture. You should be able to make comparisons of existing and new goods as a part of your marketing research effort in Japan.

We thought we knew the Japanese were different from the Americans and Europeans. But we did not know that Japanese history, tradition, and culture preclude even young adult Japanese from making significant changes in their routine purchasing behavior. Fitting foreign products into Japanese culture is the work of global marketing executives.

Notes

1. Donald Richie, "Gaijin: A Foreigner, an Alien," *Discover Japan: Words, Customs and Concepts* (Tokyo: Kodansha International Ltd., 1982), Vol. I, 158–159.

2. This figure is calculated by number of copies shipped, or 5.73 billion copies in 1989. Shuppan Kagaku Kenkyujo. Cited in "The Manga Market," *Mangajin* 9 (April 1991): 14–17.

3. Ibid., p. 14. Frederik L. Schodt, *The World of Japanese Comics* (Tokyo: Kodansha International Ltd., 1986), 13.

4. "The Manga Market," 17. Schodt, 13.

5. "The Manga Market," 17.

6. Murray Sayle, "How to Marry a Mikado," *The New Yorker*, May 10, 1993, 43.

7. Ibid., 44.

8. Ibid.

9. Ibid.

10. David E. Sanger, "The Career and the Kimono," *The New York Times Magazine*, May 30, 1993, 29.

11. Schodt, 16.

12. Ibid., 18.

13. Ibid., 23.

14. Jonathan Rauch, *The Outnation: A Search for the Soul of Japan* (Boston: Little, Brown and Company, 1992), 10-11.

15. Schodt, 23.

16. Dana L. Alden, Wayne D. Hoyer, and Chol Lee, "Identifying Global and Culture-Specific Dimensions of Humor in Advertising: A Multinational Analysis," *Journal of Marketing* 57:2 (April 1993): 65. They cite Cliff Scott, David M. Klein, and Jennings Bryant, "Consumer Response to Humor in Advertising: A Series of Field Studies Using Behavioral Observation," *Journal of Consumer Research* 16 (March 1990): 498.

17. Karen Lowry, "You Just Can't Talk to These Kids," *Business Week*, April 19, 1993, 106.

18. Alden, Hoyer, and Lee, 65-66.

19. Robert Thomson, "Japan Enters the World of Fantasy," *Financial Times*, May 6, 1993, 8.

20. Yumiko Ono, "Japan Eats Up 'U.S.' Food Never Tasted in America," *Wall Street Journal*, April 4, 1990, B4.

21. Ibid., B1.

22. Elizabeth Andoh, "A Taste of Culture: Chocolate," *Mangajin* 24 (March 1993): 18.

23. Ibid.

24. Ibid., 19.

25. "An Interview with George Fields," *Mangajin* 22 (December 1992): 10.

26. Elizabeth Andoh, "A Taste of Culture: The Japanification of American Fast Food," *Mangajin* 25 (April 1993): 16.

27. Ibid.

28. Ibid., 16-17.

29. Ibid., 17-18.

30. Ibid., 18.

31. Ibid., 27.

32. Richard Wood, "Makudonarudo (McDonald's restaurant-chain)," in *Discover Japan: Words, Customs and Concepts* (Tokyo: Kodansha International Ltd., 1983), Vol. II, 4-55.

33. Lowry, 104.

34. Terue Ohashi, "Marketing in Japan in the 1990s: Homing in on the Holonic Consumer," *Marketing and Research Today*, November 1989, 221.

35. Dave Barrager, "Retro Power," *Brandweek*, March 15, 1993, 16.

36. Ibid., 15.

37. "An Interview . . . ," 10.

38. "An Interview . . . ," 11.

39. These seven points are excerpted from the article by Masaru Ariga, "Seven Crucial Viewpoints to Understand the Japanese Consumer," *Japan 1991: Marketing and Advertising Yearbook* (Tokyo: Dentsu Inc., 1990), 85-91.

40. Rauch, 10-11.

41. "Changing Lifestyle," *Japan 1991: Marketing and Advertising Yearbook* (Tokyo: Dentsu Inc., 1990), 115.

42. Rauch, 37-39.

43. Christopher M. Miller, Shelby H. McIntyre, and Murali K. Mantrala, "Toward Formalizing Fashion Theory," *Journal of Marketing Research* 30:2 (May 1993): 142-57.

44. Ravi Dhar and Itamar Simonson, "The Effect of the Focus of Comparison on Consumer Preferences," *Journal of Marketing Research* 29:4 (November 1992): 430-40.

Chapter Format

Introduction

Country Risk Questions

Environmental Scan: Political Reforms

Initial Analysis of Marketing Opportunities

Clues to Capturing Customers

The Firm-Specific Assignment

Competitive Scan: Sales of Foreign Goods

Estimates of Market Potential

Similar Market Segments Worldwide

National Marketing Decisions

Marketing Scan: Overseas Chinese Cultural Values

Strategies for Increasing Marketing Effectiveness

Marketing Implementation

Conclusions

Cases: Star-TV, Avon, P&G, Coke, Motorola

Learning Objectives

After reading this chapter, you should be able to:

- Discuss the need for predictability in political reforms to carry out successful country risk analyses

- Outline the use of information about market size and sales targets in marketing similar products across national boundaries

- Explain the impact of East Asian, trans-Pacific overseas Chinese cultural values on sales within mainland China

Political Realities

chapter 6

Introduction

Marketers create final demand by researching international markets. In this chapter, we look at China. Here, too, we stress its political, economic, and cultural differences with the West and with Japan. China is a limited market economy – that is, a ruling Communist Party, socialist theory, and state-owned firms restrain managerial decision making about technology, product, distribution, promotion, price, selling, and value marketing.

We use regional analysis to explain what is going on in southern and coastal China. In their own ways, Guangzhou is tied to Hong Kong, Malaysia, Indonesia, and the United States; Xiamen to Taiwan; Shanghai to Japan and Singapore; and Jilin to North and South Korea, and to the Russian Far East.

We also use cross-cultural analysis to underscore the impact of the overseas Chinese on mainland China. This expanded view of country risk fits in with our notion that successful global marketing requires a deeper understanding of the socio-cultural forces at work in promoting economic growth through markets in the world economy.

The case of China offers other countries in East and South Asia and sub-Saharan Africa lists of things to do (and not to do). All of them seek a place in a global economy dominated by the GATT/WTO, OECD, EU, and NAFTA and by free-market-oriented global business firms. Once more, let's extend our analysis of global marketing.

Scanning Global Markets

Environmental scan: political reforms. China's ability to deliver an increasing number of middle-class customers to American and Japanese marketers stands as a model of choice for poorer Asian, African, and Latin American nations. China's realities include political direction, governing the market, market-oriented reforms, economic risks, competition among regions, and cultural insights from overseas Chinese. Notwithstanding the current higher level of country risk, marketing executives foresee higher levels of imitation and more rapid accelerated rates of product diffusion as China accepts more America, Japanese, and global products into its lifestyle.

Competitive scan: sales of foreign goods. Marketers make Chinese sales by paying close attention to the political realities of market-oriented reforms. All foreign firms need local partners from the state sector, private interests, or both. Foreign firms in China also must produce goods for both domestic use and for export. Moreover, foreign firms need the help of overseas and Hong Kong Chinese to be sure American or Japanese marketing practices don't get in the way of selling products in mainland China. The potential consumer market is very large, but the sales reality is smaller, profitable, and open to more growth in the future.

Marketing scan: overseas Chinese socio-economic values. Higher levels of consumption among Chinese consumers involves a gathering union with overseas Chinese, or the East Asian, trans-Pacific overseas Chinese culture. This meshing of all Chinese forces the Chinese government to make China another economic "tiger" in East Asia. This is the goal of the government's market-oriented reforms. The risks are high for the government because of an over-heated economy and a deepening unrest among the peasants and factory workers. China's reality is a metaphor for most countries in the world today.

Traditional Contexts for Global Marketing

Exhibit 6-1 lists the traditional contexts for global marketing in the case of China. We examine party-government-market relationships, producing for

Exhibit 6-1.
Traditional Contexts for Global Marketing

Country Risk

Political direction from Communist Party

Market-oriented macroeconomic reforms

Regain control over money supply

Reduce double-digit inflation

Market-oriented microeconomic reforms

Construct legal system for business transactions

Deregulate some industries

Privatize some state-owned firms

Encourage foreign investments

Rebuild infrastructure

Cultural insights from overseas Chinese

Firm-Specific 4Ps Analysis

Decision making under uncertainty

Product diffusion: time effect dependent on country effect

Produce for domestic and export markets to earn foreign exchange

National Marketing Decisions: Cultural Context (A)

Socio-cultural values: dominant homogeneity

Uncertainty perceptions about size of market

National Marketing Decisions: Research Tasks (B)

Formal marketing research

Cross-cultural clusters across national boundaries

Self-referencing criteria of language, religion, history

Focal option (focus of comparison)

National character (collectivism, material success)

Coefficient of imitation (stress cultural bilingualism)

Time effect of product diffusion, first-mover advantage

Country effect of product diffusion, market share estimates

CETSCALE: overseas and traditional Chinese

Walking-around research: watch out for people error

Who uses the product?

Self-referencing criteria: collectivism over individualism

Overseas Chinese subculture

Continued on next page

Exhibit 6-1. *Continued from previous page*

How to increase market share?

Work with product assimilation to build brand loyalty

Compare American imports to Japanese products

How to provide value?

Time effect dependent on country effect

Word-of-mouth promotion

What customer signals show changes in the local market?

Clumsy vetting

Get the numbers right

Situate country within historical context

Humbling feedback

Copyright © Douglas F. Lamont. All rights reserved.

export to earn foreign exchange, and socio-cultural values. The first spells out the guiding force of the Communist Party on the development of global marketing within the country. The second underscores what marketers must do to be successful within the market-oriented regions of China. The third recounts the unique contribution of the overseas Chinese in blending traditional and modern socio-cultural values to reinvent China. The cases of China as seen through the sale of foreign cosmetics and the diffusion of up-to-date satellite TV and wireless telephone communications, are prototypes of how new products might become assimilated within India, South and Central Asia, and the rest of the world.

Nontraditional Contexts for Global Marketing

Exhibit 6-2 enumerates the nontraditional contexts for global marketing in China. We examine reinventing China as a socialist market economy, importing foreign technology, applying regional and cross-cultural analysis, and carrying out managerial decision making under uncertainty. Again we must come to a full stop. The old, dusty, country risk road is closed. In its place is a new highway posted with political and cultural signs that lead us to reinventing nation-states. As we travel down our new superhighway, we now pay close attention to demographic analysis, cultural bilingualism, national character, and regional analysis. When we get to our destination we can go about our business of making better marketing decisions under the uncertainty of a market economy with socialist characteristics. This too is global marketing.

Exhibit 6-2.
Nontraditional Contexts for Global Marketing

Political Frame

Long-term planning horizon for business firms

Reinvent country as a market with socialist characteristics

Technological Frame

Decision making under uncertainty

Multimarkets across nation-states, technologies, industries

Information technologies

Cultural Frame: Who Are the Customers? (A)

Demographic analysis

   Triangle as model for income distribution

   Rich and poor social classes

   Family connections to Communist Party

Age-period cohort analysis, national character, and family status

Cultural bilingualism

   Devoted Communists among government officials

   Committed consumers among younger business executives

   Accomplished trans-Pacific, overseas Chinese

National character

   Confucian tradition

   Family orientation

   Social network of friends

   Question of face

   Paternal hierarchy within family, among friends

   Restraints in dealing with foreign-owned firms

   Little desire for experimentation

Cultural Frame: Where Are the Customers? (B)

Regional analysis

   Guangzhou-Hong Kong (Pearl River)-southern China

   Shanghai-Wuhan (Yangtze River)-middle China

Cross-national clusters

   Xiamen-Taiwan

   Jilin (Yanbian)-Kore–Russian Far East

Continued on next page

Exhibit 6-2. *Continued from previous page*

Marketing Management Frame

Industry analysis

Decision making under uncertainty

Long-term planning horizon: country risk higher than Mexico

Diffusion of technology and time effect

Party relationships and country effect

Word-of-mouth effect for imitation purchases

Real cross-country differences

Foreign direct investment

Pool manufacturing, build distribution capacity

Segmentation, positioning, and tailoring decisions

Governing the market. First, let's look at the political frame. China's sprint toward economic prosperity is taking place within the embedded constraints of one crucial socio-political convention – namely, the drive of a Communist government to retain political control while at the same time speeding up market-oriented reforms (see Exhibit 6–3). The government calls its effort market reforms with socialist characteristics. The government began deregulating some industries, privatizing many business enterprises, and encouraging overseas, Hong Kong, and Taiwan Chinese and their American and Japanese partners to make direct investments in China. Today, many see China as on the way to becoming another economic "tiger" in East Asia.

Marketing decisions under uncertainty. Second, let's study the technological frame. The Chinese who are both Chinese-speaking and English-speaking (or overseas Chinese) and who live throughout East Asia and the Pacific are the biggest benefactors of China's market-opening measures. Their overseas Chinese values of material success are seeping into mainland China and finding converts among the youth, entrepreneurs, and business executives.

Most Chinese are peasants, and factory workers (i.e., the vast majority of the people in mainland China) want the Communist government to do more for them and less for the new rich class of overseas Chinese. As a consequence, the central government continues to reassess the wisdom of its market-oriented reforms. These economic dislocations and political uncertainties increase China's country risk, slow down the introduction of new computer-based information technologies, and delay the development of multimarkets across all industries.

Exhibit 6-3.
China's GDP

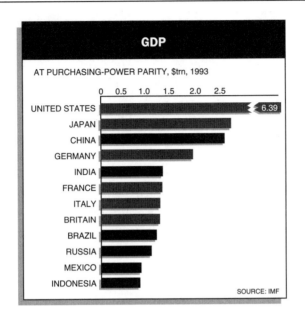

Courtesy of The Economist

Hunting for Chinese consumers. Third, let's examine the cultural frame. What is the impact on Chinese youth of the global, largely American culture and its copy-cat versions from Japan and the overseas Chinese societies of East Asia? Do younger groups within China drive older groups, such as their parents and government officials, to copy the emerging overseas Chinese lifestyle of Chinese youth?

In chapters 3 through 5, we made six suggestions about increasing marketing effectiveness within Mexico, Europe, and Japan. Do they apply to China?

1. Grow the market through cross-cultural clusters without regard to national boundaries (e.g., Hong Kong and southern China). These relationships are crucial to marketing success in China because they transmit overseas Chinese business practices to the youth, entrepreneurs, and business executives within China.

2. Pay attention to the self-referencing criteria (SRC) of language, religion, history, and geography and their impact on social groups. Add

the focal option (or focus of comparison). Chinese prefer overseas Chinese over Japanese products and the latter over American products. Overseas Chinese products reflect their own SRC because these are from Chinese who live overseas. In some cases, Japanese products also reflect Chinese SRC too. American and European products tend to be western, foreign, and exotic; they must be sold on the basis of something completely new and different for Chinese lifestyles.

3. Accept differences in national character. Although Chinese seek out material success, this is done collectively (or through social groups, such as extended families) rather than as a product of individualism. Some marketing concepts require political acceptance before they can be used effectively in China. This is especially true when marketers seek to collect demographic facts and other economic information about the Chinese.

4. Apply the coefficient of imitation with an emphasis on overseas Chinese cultural bilingualism. Chinese political realities and overseas Chinese economic facts dominate consumer choices while global, largely American and Japanese preferences find their way into fashion, luxury goods, and technologically sophisticated products. Moreover, the youth are more prone to try western goods once their peers adopt these products into the overseas Chinese lifestyle. However, older groups, such as parents and party officials, are not as likely as American and European parents to follow the consumption habits of their children. This age-period cohort group concept does not translate one-for-one in China, but it is useful in discussing inroads of the global, mostly overseas Chinese youth culture in China.

5. Use the time effect of product diffusion to capture first-mover advantage during the growth phase of the product-development life cycle. Foreign-origin products (i.e., manufactured in East Asia, the United States, and Japan, technologically superior to locally made goods, and adapted to China's unique cultural identity) are able to use the time effect of product diffusion to capture market share in China. These relationships are crucial to marketing success in China as long as they meet the tests of success suggested by overseas Chinese.

6. Exploit the country effect of product diffusion (or the role of nonethnocentrists versus ethnocentrists) to estimate market share among

Chinese who are adopting the global, largely American overseas Chinese lifestyle. Although Chinese youth do imitate their counterparts in the United States, virtually everyone in China accepts the political realities of China. Thus, the discriminating role of nonethnocentrists versus ethnocentrists in the application of the country effect of product diffusion does not apply in China. Instead, we must divide the population between overseas Chinese and traditional Chinese to study the country effect of product diffusion within mainland China.

Segmentation, positioning, and tailoring decisions. Finally, let's look closely at the marketing management frame. Marketers have difficulty predicting consumer choices as traditional and overseas Chinese tastes become more heterogeneous. Even though marketing executives offer standardized Japanese and western products, Chinese consumers impose differentiation of their own based on culturally based attributes unknown to foreign marketers. Value creation takes place within a Chinese market governed by socialist characteristics, through competitive analysis of both western and Japanese firms, and the marketing needs of mainland and overseas Chinese consumers.

Organizing global marketing experience. The simultaneous existence of these four different contexts forces marketers to research Chinese markets carefully, to position more global brands in mainland China, and to watch for different national signals from southern and coastal China versus more remote, inland China. Let's do two things in this chapter. First, we will discuss the impact of Chinese political realities on the creation of new market segments among the young and old, men and women, and overseas Chinese and other Chinese groups. Then we will apply this country analysis to how marketing teams make decisions about selling to the Chinese.

Country Risk Questions

Marketers manage final demand by researching international markets, such as China; see Exhibit 6-4. Its Communist government supports market-opening measures, and these are leading to explosive economic growth throughout southern and coastal China. All effort is directed toward rapid increases in labor productivity, per capita gross domestic product (GDP) output, and per capita income.[1] For example, in the 1980s, "the average gross national product grew more than twice as fast as it did in Europe and America."[2] That striking gap is widening in the 1990s.

Exhibit 6-4.
Country Risk Analysis: China
The Environmental Scan

Traditional Frame Analysis for Global Marketing
National Marketing Decisions and Marketing Opportunities
Pool manufacturing between Hong Kong and southern China
Build competing center in Shanghai and coastal China
Accept cultural bilingualism among overseas Chinese
Recognize the impact of overseas Chinese
Acknowledge the force of satellite TV on product diffusion
Remember the impact of Chinese culture on East Asia
Recall trend is not destiny

Nontraditional Frame Analysis For Global Marketing
Political Context and Market-Oriented Reforms
Keep control over political process
Institute market-oriented reforms
Privatize state-owned enterprises
Rebuild infrastructure
Regain control over the money supply
Watch out for overheated domestic economy
Pay attention to double-digit inflation in cities
End peasant and labor unrest
Couple industry to international trade
Construct legal system for business transactions
Cultural Context and Cultural Bilingualism
Devoted Communists among older government officials
Committed consumers among younger business executives
Accomplished trans-Pacific, overseas Chinese people

"The World Bank's exchange rate conversion methods give China a per capita GNP of US $370 in 1990 . . . But figures from the United Nations International Comparison Program, based on purchasing power parities, give per capita GDP as US $1,950. This makes China the world's second biggest economy, larger than Japan but well behind the United States. The International Monetary Fund . . . puts China's per capita GDP at about US $1,300, ranking the economy among larger European countries."[3] Other experts put income per head lower, at just over US $1,000. They conclude that China will become a crucial (but relatively poor) economic player in Asia by the end of the century.[4]

Marketing audit. Even as China's income per head grows, China will remain poor for the rest of the decade. China does not offer marketers a long-term planning horizon, only a series of short one- to three-year planning horizons. Therefore, the Chinese consumer market is relatively small and growing each year, but it does not include the total 1.1 billion Chinese who are often quoted in the press as the market for nondurable and durable consumer goods. More on these details later.

Environmental Scan: Political Reforms

The Chinese government seeks market-led prosperity without the capitalism practiced in the United States, Europe, and Japan, and without the disruptions from socialism's demise in Russia and eastern Europe. Chinese leaders are pushing a gradualist approach that experiments with limited changes in the southern and coastal provinces before trying them out throughout the country.

Government first improved agriculture so that peasants no longer feared famine; they soon came to feel wealthy enough to invest in new seeds, fertilizers, and machinery. Then government fostered the development of non-state (aka private) industry rather than trying to reform the loss-ridden state-owned industry. In 1993, only 7 percent of total industrial output was subject to central planning; 83 percent of all sales went through the market.[5] As a consequence, China is one of the world's larger markets for nondurable and durable consumer goods, factory machinery, transportation equipment, and telecommunications goods. It sucked in goods valued at US $104 billion in 1993.[6]

The coastal cities of Guangzhou (up the Pearl River from Hong Kong) and Shanghai (at the mouth of the Yangtze River) are the high value-added centers, providing technology, management, and financial services to the inland cities. Both coastal (Xiamen is across from Taiwan) and inland cities (Wuhan is up the Yangtze River) are establishing their own locally controlled factories without substantial interference from the central government in Beijing. This gives local Communist Party officials a stake in economic reform, change, and long-term market-led prosperity. Such competition among cities (and provinces) gives foreign investors, especially Hong Kong and overseas Chinese, the opportunity to negotiate the best deal possible on wages, fees, and taxes.

The good news: run-away economic growth, a current-accounts surplus, and a cheaper Chinese currency in terms of the US dollar. The results are impressive. Chinese exports are cheaper overseas, China builds up reserves to invest in its megaprojects, and Chinese manufacturers have more goods to supply a wealthier internal consumer market.

The bad news: peasants moving to the cities looking for work, out of control city and provincial leaders bringing in imports without regard to China's foreign exchange reserves, 30-percent annual expansion of the money supply, double-digit inflation (about 23.9 percent annually in China's biggest cities),[7] capital flight to Hong Kong, and the potential for demonstrations and strikes. More than 100 million Chinese (or about 9 percent of the population) live in absolute poverty, and they are coming to the cities as illegal rural migrants looking for work.[8]

Forecasting Country Risk

Clearly, China is not done with change. Have the government's market reforms gone so far as to end a return to the command economy of the Communist past? Will China's GDP continue to grow at 9.0 percent or better? Can Chinese industry be coupled more closely to international trade with the United States, Europe, and Japan? Can the central government reestablish controls over the money supply and cut the rate of price inflation? Will the dispossessed peasants and unemployed factory workers find work in the new market-driven economy? Will the wealthier southern and coastal provinces pay more in taxes to subsidize the poorer northern and interior provinces? Are there more post-command economy hangovers in store for the Chinese government? Will China follow the model set by its prosperous Asian neighbors – South Korea, Taiwan, and Singapore? Or will China remain a relatively poor country throughout the 21st century?[9]

These country risk questions affect all marketing decisions by Chinese, Japanese, and American marketing executives. The answers translate into a continuing trend of higher sales to the youth, entrepreneurs, and business executives who are more comfortable with the overseas Chinese lifestyle. More on this marketing forecast later.

Initial Analysis of Market Opportunities

"Whosoever enters first is master,"[10] is a traditional Chinese saying. Let's see how it applies to marketing. Long before the Communist government, Unilever sold *Lux* soap in China. Today, facial soap is called Lux. The same is true for *Squibb* tablets, *Schindler* elevators, *Sony* consumer electronics products, *Johnson* wax, Coke, Pepsi Cola, and *Singer* sewing machines.[11] These foreign-origin products got in first, are doing well, and have become household names in China.

Asking Research Questions

Let's assume the Communist government continues to sponsor market-oriented reforms for the next one to three years. Also, let's forecast 9-percent GDP economic growth and 24-percent price inflation. Moreover, let's admit peasants and factory workers want jobs, and reporters and business executives want more personal freedom. In addition, let's allow for all Chinese to speak out more frequently about the abuses of Communist government officials and the slowness of managers to push their state factories into privatization. Furthermore, let's conclude that those in control won't give up their economic perks without a fight.[12] That is, China's country risk is higher and less predictable than similar perils in Mexico, Europe, and Japan.

Now let's shift the focus of our risk analysis to the uncertainty perceptions of marketers about the size of the Chinese market, and the combined strength of collectivism and material success among the young, the entrepreneurs, and business executives in China. Here are several appropriate firm-specific marketing questions:

Who uses the product? Which Chinese consumers use collectivism and material success as their crucial self-referencing criteria? How do the mainland Chinese incorporate overseas Chinese, American, and Japanese products into their modern lifestyles?

How to increase market share? Which products pour into China because some overseas Chinese prefer these goods? Are there competing American and Japanese products? Are there local Chinese producers? Are American, Japanese, and East Asian firms producing locally? Are they all equally capable of capturing the Chinese desire for faster adoption of successful overseas Chinese products?

How to provide value? How does China define value? Is value based on standardized marketing strategies on price, customer service, quality, and timeliness, and a willingness to accept experimentation from marketers? Or does China define value in terms of word-of-mouth promotion from overseas Chinese? Are American brand names preferred? Does the stronger impact of collectivism and material success in China speed up the rate of product diffusion? Does China's different national character force the time effect to depend on the country effect of product diffusion?

What customer signals show changes in the local market? Are American, European, and Japanese products seeping into the cultural values of China? Are these products viewed positively when they affect Chinese preferences for food, clothes, and entertainment? To what extent will these non-Chinese products be accepted in China? Or must these products be pretested by overseas Chinese before they are accepted freely by mainland Chinese? Will the combined weight of collectivism and material success speed up the rate of change in the product-development life cycle?

Knowing the Rate of Product Diffusion

The impact of American and Japanese marketing practices, business experiences, and cross-cultural products is a lot more intrusive today than previously in China. Some standardized advertising campaigns push global, largely American products (e.g., Coke, McDonald's, Avon). Other goods and services are coming from Hong-Kong–based Star Television. Everyone from Japan to Jordan with satellite dishes, which cost as little as a few hundred dollars or the price of a VCR, can receive "Lifestyles of the Rich and Famous," "Dallas," "The Bold and the Beautiful," or any of the upscale, luxury-oriented soap operas from the United States. Or they can watch the news from the British Broadcasting Corporation's World Service or Cable News Network, cricket or tennis matches on Prime Sports, and MTV. In June 1992, Asian viewers amounted to about 45 million, with perhaps as many as 25 million in China, and at least 2 million in Taiwan.[13]

The results:

- Teenage girls wear miniskirts to the discos, and they buy Whitney Houston's "Bodyguard" album.

- Dressmakers and tailors copy the outfits and clothes of the famous TV stars for the new Chinese rich.

- Unified advertising pitches for upscale products are made with modern MTV-type graphics for all Asians.

How did the world reach China? Michael Johnson, an American entrepreneur, took an option to buy AsiaSat I, then persuaded Hutchison Whampoa Ltd. and its cautious billionaire chairman, Li Ka-shing, to back the venture.[14] Today, AsiaSat is owned by Li's Hutchison, Britain's Cable and Wireless, and China's international investment company, Citic.[15] Also Li's Star TV went into joint venture partnerships with BBC, Prime Sports, MTV, and a Mandarin Chinese station to guarantee programming for pay TV channels.

When AsiaSat 2 was put in place in late 1994, Star TV began to reach 75 percent of the world's population – from Tokyo to Berlin, and Ulan Bator (in Mongolia) to Hobart (in Australia).[16] This coverage preempts American and European coverage and may break the control the United States has on the world's media. According to George Yeo, Singapore's Minister of Information, East Asia's economic strength translates into cultural power, and China's overseas Chinese civilization will contest Western domination of global media by the turn of century.[17]

Hundreds of thousands of satellite dishes exist in China, and many millions of Chinese live connected to and sometimes within the global village. Here's their routine. They watch Star TV and listen to the Voice of America and the BBC on short-wave radios. The Chinese direct-dial their international telephone calls and send faxes worldwide. Moreover, many Chinese communicate with all parts of the world through electronic bulletin boards and electronic mail.[18]

As marketers add the ruffles and flourishes of the global, largely American culture and its copy-cat versions from Japan and the overseas Chinese, and as these are transmitted through electronic media to mainland Chinese, the trend for the next three years is for more rapid diffusion of American, overseas Chinese, and Japanese products within China. Do remember the admonition in chapter 3: Trend is not destiny. China's higher country risk could still get in the way of marketers making money from the opportunities open to them in mainland China.

Clues to Capturing Consumers

Marketing within China builds on cross-cultural clusters. For example, the Cantonese (or the Chinese from Guangdong province, the Pearl River valley, and many Hong Kong Chinese) are leading China through market-oriented reforms. Although Hong Kong has been a leading financial center during the last 20 years, the role of market-opening leader is new for the people of southern China.

Throughout all the ups and downs of Chinese history – that is, until the boom in the 1990s – the Shanghainese (or the Chinese from Shanghai and the Yangtze River valley) led in producing China's industrial output and manufacturing goods for China's consumers. Until the beginning of World War II, Shanghai's Bund was China's financial center and the regional seat for many European and American banks in East Asia. Today, the Shanghainese want to take back this leadership role in finance and manufacturing from the Cantonese. The Shanghainese want to dominate steel, autos, petrochemicals, energy, telecommunications, computers, the stock market, the commodities exchanges, and the foreign exchange center.[19] Both the Shanghainese and the Cantonese are competing for dominance in China's race to modernize industry, build financial centers, and grow consumer markets.

According to an old Chinese saying: For the Cantonese, life revolves around food. For the Shanghainese, life revolves around clothes, wearing them to show off on Nanking Road, always China's best shopping street. And for the Chinese in Beijing, life revolves around politics.

Don't jump to conclusions. The Chinese in Beijing also buy *Gucci* shoes, *Dunhill* cigarette lighters, and *Johnnie Walker* scotch at the Yaohan department store, part of a Japanese chain with outlets throughout Asia and in North America and Europe.[20] Imported brand-named goods are a status symbol throughout all of China.

Today, 60 million Chinese have an annual income greater than US $1,000; with the continuing economic boom, the number could grow to more than 200 million Chinese by the year 2000.[21] Because housing, transport, education, and health costs are heavily subsidized, the Chinese tend to have a relatively high percentage of disposable income. This is a significant clue to capturing Chinese consumers.

Summary: Scanning Political Reforms

China's ability to deliver an increasing number of middle-class customers to American and Japanese marketers stands as a model of success for poorer

Asian, African, and Latin American nations. China's realities include political direction, governing the market, market-oriented reforms, economic risks, competition among regions, and cultural insights from overseas Chinese. Notwithstanding the current higher level of country risk, marketing executives foresee higher levels of imitation and more rapid accelerated rates of product diffusion as China accepts more America, Japanese, East Asian, and global products into its lifestyle.

The Firm-Specific Assignment

Marketers manage final demand by positioning global products within China; see Exhibit 6–5. Given the political realities surrounding market-oriented reforms (i.e., higher country risk), the Chinese government is unable to offer marketing executives the same long-term planning horizon found in Japan. Instead, we must plan for the short run, between one and three years.

To make matters worse, the Chinese government cannot immediately change the perceptions of marketers about firm-specific uncertainties. For example, exporters are never sure Chinese factory output meets the quality, packaging, and most-favored-nations (or MFN) requirements of overseas importers, distributors, and retailers. Also, importers are never confident they will be paid in full by the Chinese because China lacks foreign exchange. Moreover, investors believe they have weak legal protection of intellectual property rights (or copyrights, trademarks, and patents) within China.

Today, marketing executives rate China (i.e., its firm-specific risk) as more speculative than Mexico, Europe, Japan, and many countries in East Asia.

Understanding Cultural Context

Right now Chinese consumers present three lifestyles to marketers:

- Devoted Communists among older government officials

- Committed consumers among younger business executives

- Accomplished trans-Pacific, overseas Chinese

Younger persons speak both Chinese and English (or overseas Chinese), act as trend setters, and make their living as business executives in the private

Exhibit 6-5.
Firm-Specific Analysis: China
The Competeive Scan

Traditional Frame Analysis for Global Marketing
National Marketing Decisions and Probability Sampling
Lack of demographic data

Nonresponses and costs of responses

Unfamiliarity with marketing research techniques

Difficulty in interpreting results

Get the numbers right

National Marketing Decisions and Formal Research
Cluster (convergent and divergent) purchasing power

Measure coefficient of imitation

Track the diffusion of products and services

Measure country and time effects

National Marketing Decisions and Walking-Around Research
Create brand loyalty

Employ direct selling

Team up with savvy partners

Carve luxury niche

Find opinion leaders

Nontraditional Frame Analysis for Global Marketing
Cultural Context and Demographic Analysis
Use the triangle as model for income distribution

Divide social classes into rich and poor

Separate consumers into mainland Chinese and overseas Chinese

Vet market size from Hong Kong point of view

Cultural Context and National Character
Confucian tradition, family orientation, paternal hierarchy

Social network of friends

Question of face

Little desire for experimentation

Cultural Context and Regional Analysis
Guangzhou-Hong Kong-southern China

Shanghai-Wuhan-middle China

Xiamen-Taiwan

Jilin-Korea-Russian Far East

sector. Their routine purchasing activities fit the perceptions of other groups about the global, largely American consumer culture and their copy-cat Japanese and overseas Chinese material cultures. Their lifestyle is culturally adapted to Chinese pursuits of politically stable, market-oriented reforms under the rule of the Communist Party. As we approach the new century, the overseas Chinese, East Asian trans-Pacific culture goes from strength to strength as the composite work of overseas and mainland Chinese.

Competitive Scan: Sales of Foreign Goods

China's huge internal market is a mirage. China's 1.1 billion people constitute the world's largest consumer market. Both contradictory statements are the received information.

Carrying Out Formal Research

Let's start our formal research with what we can observe from a Hong Kong vantage point. (See chapters 3 through 5 for United States, European, and Japanese points of view.)

Cross-cultural clusters. Construct a cluster of purchasing behavior for the Hong Kong-Guangzhou region to show convergence (e.g., in the consumption of food and cola drinks) and to show divergence (e.g., in the consumption of newspapers and magazines) between consumers who live in Hong Kong and Guangzhou. If disposable income is similar, both Hong Kong residents and Cantonese Chinese tend to make similar purchases. If power distance exists between wealthier overseas Chinese and poorer mainland Chinese, then routine purchasing behavior will be different between the two groups of Chinese.

Coefficient of imitation. Follow up with an examination of imitation purchases. Cantonese imitators buy foreign products consumed by Hong Kong overseas Chinese. Since a more homogeneous culture exists within southern China based on the Cantonese dialect of Chinese, the transfer of ideas comes quickly between Hong Kong and other Chinese in southern China.

Investment funds, new technologies, export connections, and new lifestyle ideas come from Hong Kong. Mobile phones, apartments, satellite dishes, and Japanese-style *karaoke* bars are as commonplace in Shenzhen,

Guangzhou, Dongguan, Shunde, Zhongshan, and Zhuhai as they are in Hong Kong, Kowloon, and the New Territories.

Per capita income in Guangzhou province is about US $600, or double that of China as a whole. This is where Avon, P&G, Pabst Brewing Co., Lockheed, and 16,000 other factories are located, with 85 percent of their investment funds from sources in Hong Kong.[22] Hong Kong's choices about lifestyle, consumption habits, and work ethic are fast becoming the standard for Guangzhou province.

Product diffusion. Then track the diffusion of goods and services. Chinese culture (or the country effect) binds devoted ethnocentrist Communist officials to the past, but connects accomplished East Asian trans-Pacific overseas Chinese to the future. The latter adopt improved products faster (or the time effect) and fit them into the reality of modern China.

All Chinese share common cultural traits about Confucian tradition, family orientation, the social network of friends, the question of face, paternal hierarchy within family firms, restraints in dealing with foreign-owned firms, and little desire for experimentation. Theirs is a collectivist society.

The political economy of Singapore offers an example for China. The government of the island nation seeks to create a virtuous business cycle based on the blend of Confucian tradition, government strategic targeting, ordered foreign direct investment, and broad-based economic prosperity. This system has more appeal to mainland Chinese than the free market approach of Hong Kong and Taiwan.

Right now, both Hong Kong and Taiwan are the workhorses in spreading the western market economy into China. The process of diffusion of western goods and western marketing ideas is accelerating because of Hong Kong-based Star TV. If the diffusion model works in China too, we know two important marketing facts. First, additional innovations are introduced even faster than before, and each new innovation reaches its peak sales in a shorter period of time. Right now the marketing pace is quickening in China as more overseas Chinese have higher levels of disposable income to spend on luxury goods.

CETSCALE. Finally, prepare research questionnaires using the CETSCALE. Do Chinese ethnocentrists believe the purchase of foreign products is wrong and unpatriotic? Do overseas Chinese nonethnocentrists evaluate products more objectively, regardless of the country of origin? In China, the time effect is a function of the country effect, and this one piece of information helps shape sales and marketing decisions for American, Japanese, and East Asian firms.

Let's carry out cross-national validation of the CETSCALE for China, Singapore, Taiwan, and Hong Kong. Both mainland Chinese and East Asian overseas Chinese are, for the most part, ethnocentrists who prefer Confucian values and Chinese traditionalism. Even though Japan is also a collectivist culture, none of these Chinese nation-states choose a lifestyle imported from Japan. Moreover, even though many Chinese live in North America and Europe, none of the Chinese nation-states want to import a western lifestyle. In short, all marketing effort within China must recognize that mainland Chinese are mostly ethnocentrists who favor traditional consumption habits.

Using Probability Sampling

Nevertheless, extreme care must be taken in doing marketing research because of the higher chance for human error within China. Here's how Hong-Kong–based marketing research firms resolve this problem.[23] (See chapter 3 and compare the research situations in Mexico and China.)

Sampling. Since all Chinese are registered, it is not too difficult to find households from which to draw samples.[24] Individual members of these households are used in focus group comparisons and to determine what "the average Chinese" thinks about new products. On the other hand, probability sampling and the weighting of information based on demographic data and cultural information are a great deal harder to do because the statistics aren't collected or available from government sources.

Nonresponse. If individuals are given permission to be interviewed by the appropriate city resident committee, then local Chinese representatives can get the comparative information required by marketers. Without permission, the nonresponse rate is high.

Quality of response, timing, and costs. Good responses take time. Researchers must establish a rapport with the appropriate persons in the city resident committees. The former must convince the latter that the information requested is not classified, privileged, or state secrets, but simply marketing intelligence. With permission, time must be spent getting to and obtaining the information from individuals. All of these items make research more costly in China.

Limited understanding of western marketing techniques. Until recently, advertising branded goods was a novelty to most Chinese outside the reach of television from Hong Kong. However, as Star TV adds more Chinese households to its satellite system, this problem will diminish, but not go away. Knowledge about the world's products among the Chinese is limited.

Difficulty in interpreting results.[25] Even with a guarantee of 500 million gross impressions per week, a 60-second radio spot is very cheap on China radio (a penny per thousand impressions). But what does the advertiser get? No outside media groups provide count numbers from paper diaries or metered TV sets. Direct-response promotions rather than traditional advertising offer more information about what sells within China. (See chapter 11.)

Carrying Out Walking-Around Research

On a regular basis, China fever sweeps through foreign business executives. They see 1.1 billion potential customers. That's too high. Instead, marketers must concentrate on the frequency of product usage internally, producing large numbers of goods for export, promoting the use of more sophisticated products in the future, and increasing demand for the core global goods of the product line. Marketing executives will find customer markets in China, but they will have to work at translating these into sales.

Estimates of Market Potential

Are foreign firms doing well in China? Yes. They are selling their products and repatriating their profits because they follow these few simple competitive rules.

Building Brand Loyalty

According to Donald Altfeld, the president of ChinAmerica (an advertising agency that places ads on China's radio and TV channels), the Japanese approach to China is one that US advertisers would be wise to follow. "The Japanese advertise two to three years ahead of a product introduction, which is effective since the Chinese are very brand loyal."[26] Here are several American examples.

Employing Direct Selling Avon's commercials appeared on Hong Kong television long before *Avon* products were introduced into Guangzhou.[27]

Avon has its sales force (all women) call on customers in their factories and at their work sites to sell them facial toner, cleansing lotion, day cream, night cream, and eye cream. It does not have to push its products into the distribution system by cultivating wholesalers, nor does it have to coax retailers to pull its products onto their shelves. Avon carries the image of high quality for Chinese women, and they get the added advantage of shopping where they work or where they go to school.

Avon's China partner is Guangzhou Cosmetics Factory, and its Hong Kong partner is David Li, the chief executive of Hong Kong's Bank of East Asia.[28] Li convinced the Cantonese government to try direct selling, which in 1989 was a novel concept in China. Today, Avon is a US $60 million business in China.

Teaming Up with Savvy Partners Procter & Gamble sells four shampoos – two versions of Head & Shoulders, Rejoice, and a reformulated local brand called Jiejua.[29] P&G also sells two types of Oil of Ulan skin cream (Oil of Olay elsewhere), nine types of Whisper sanitary napkins, and Pampers disposable diapers. All are sold through TV advertising at pennies per thousand impressions where P&G gets to saturate the market. P&G's partners are Li Ka-Shing, his Hutchison China Trade Co., and Guangzhou government's Construction Import & Export Corp.

Carving a Tiny Luxury Niche in a Huge Market The cola wars are alive and well in China. Both Coca-Cola and Pepsi send delivery trucks and motorcycles with their international logos in Chinese characters to every nook and cranny retail outlet in coastal and inland China. These American cola drinks are simple luxury items, where as the orange drink and an herbal cola drink (Tianfu Cola) are the cheap alternatives.[30] Nevertheless, Coke sold 73 million cases in 1992 and its unit sales are 10 times higher in China than in the rest of Asia.[31] Clearly, the luxury international cola niche is growing within China where well-paid factory and office workers buy Coke along with their Avon cosmetics and P&G personal care products.

Overcoming the Lure of the Billion-Buyer Market

China's income distribution looks like a triangle. The wealthy are few, but they are powerfully connected in Beijing. The middle class is small. Virtually everyone is poor.

Ge ti hu. Very few Chinese are the entrepreneurial elite. Here are some examples:[32]

- Wang Junjin. He and his brother own Sky Dragon Charter Airline Company with reported revenue of US $2 million. Wang wears a US $420 double-breasted suit and a US $600 24-karat gold bracelet.

- Zhou Jiangning. He owns a jade carvings factory in Wenzhou. Zhou wears a US $16,000 diamond-studded gold Rolex watch.

- Mr. Zhao, "the hair lotion king," or the Red Fat Cat. He produces Formula 101, an herbal hair-growth tonic, and is a member of the Chinese parliament. Mr. Zhao has a driver to drive his Mercedes 280 SEL, owns a penthouse flat in Beijing, and a 1,000-square-meter mansion in his home town, Wenzhou.

All these new "fat cats" have only one interest: Make money while the current boom lasts in China and hope that chaos won't return to China.

Mang liu. Almost all Chinese are peasants. Some in southern China, in the village of Pan Shi of Guangzhou province, in which the Taishan dialect is the preferred Chinese language among its 440 peasants, "now live in brick homes, lit with electric light bulbs, and they enjoy such fruits of economic liberalization as refrigerators, two-story homes, and foreign romance novels . . . In 1987, for instance, the entire village had only a dozen black-and-white televisions. Now, about 80 percent of the homes have televisions, about half of them color."[33]

The villagers earn about US $185 a year, more than the national average for peasants.[34] Even though they see Hong Kong television and can go to Shenzhen to work, they must compete with other *mang liu* (or peasant immigrants into the cities), some who speak Cantonese and others who come from inland Sichuan and Hunan to better their lives in Guangzhou province and will work for less than local people.[35] With the end of internal travel documents, over 80 million peasants are searching for jobs far from home, driving wages down in coastal China and, eventually, looking for ways to be smuggled to North America.

Looking for Opinion Leaders

Business executives must target their products to the small but growing middle class. These Chinese used to work in the factories or offices, saved up their wages, and finally set up their small retail businesses; or they are the sons and daughters of the business elite driven from their companies during the turbulent 1950s, 1960s, and 1970s who are starting out again. These middle-class Chinese are neither "fat cats" nor peasants.

Here is the important piece of economic data. The personal income of the new Chinese middle class is about 21 percent greater in Guangzhou than of average factory workers.[36] What do they buy with their greater disposable income? They are heavy consumers of media, Hong Kong TV, national radio in the local dialects, four or more newspapers a day, and at least four magazines per month.[37] These government office workers and private business people are well informed about changing consumer tastes.

The new middle class is the universe from which to draw samples for polls of focus groups. The China Market Research Institute contacts between 500 and 3,000 families for each of its product surveys.[38] Yuan Yue, the Institute's assistant president, says the response rate is about 60 percent, very high by western standards. Another marketing research firm, Connections Consulting Company, interviews Chinese distributors to find out how foreign firms can improve their business connections. Li Kan is one of the founders of Connections, and he says, "In five years' time the demand for marketing will be big. We are ahead of domestic demand."[39]

Getting the Numbers Right

Motorola produces 10,000 pagers weekly in its plant in the northern port city of Tianjin.[40] All are sold within China for about US $200 (which includes a one-year service contract). The projected annual demand for pagers is four million units for the mid-1990s. So Motorola has no production left over for export. There's the problem and the lesson to be relearned once again in China. The Chinese government needs foreign exchange, frowns on foreign investments that don't earn dollars or yen, and won't let foreign business firms repatriate their profits without earning equivalent foreign exchange.

"The profit that really matters is repatriated profit."[41] Here are the choices. Sell products for cash as do the Japanese. If Guangzhou or Shanghai must be a low-cost production site for Asia, enter into counter-trade and sell Chinese goods for hard currencies. If one production site is all right for both North America and Asia, set up Mexican border plants (maquiladoras) where government permits foreign firms to repatriate profits.

Motorola is putting hard currency into China. However, it must export pagers, simple integrated circuits, cellular phones, or something else to earn the foreign exchange to pay off its US $120 million investment *and* repatriate its profits from its sales within China. Estimates of market potential must be tempered with a realistic plan for paying back foreign investors. Otherwise, the Chinese market is indeed a mirage for foreign firms.

Similar Market Segments Worldwide

Although consumer markets are alive and well in southern China and in the coastal cities to the north, it is premature to think of China as having similar market segments with the global economy. Star TV brings MTV, the Sports Channel, and the BBC to many middle-class Chinese. Over time, their expectations about brand-named goods change and they slowly add new products to their lists of "luxuries" and necessities. Moreover, anticipation of the good life in the future depends on the willingness of the overseas Chinese to invest in China's future. And that future counts on continued political stability. Perhaps, by the year 2000, China will have the younger market segments similar to those in Mexico, Europe, and Japan.

Summary: Scanning Sales of Foreign Goods

Marketers make Chinese sales by paying close attention to the political realities of market-oriented reforms. All foreign firms need local partners from the state sector, private interests, or both. Foreign firms in China also must produce goods for both domestic use and export. Moreover, foreign firms need the help of overseas and Hong Kong Chinese to be sure American or Japanese marketing practices don't interfere with selling products in mainland China. The potential consumer market is very large, but the sales reality is smaller, profitable, and open to more growth in the future.

National Marketing Decisions

Marketers manage final demand by signaling detailed national information about China; see Exhibit 6-6. Marketing executives also expand final demand by catering to newly rich business executives and the growing middle-class opinion leaders. These are important developments in consumer marketing within China.

Exhibit 6-6.
National Marketing Analysis: China
The Marketing Scan

Traditional Frame Analysis for Global Marketing

Firm-Specific 4Ps Analysis and Decision Making Under Uncertainty

Gain from initial market entry

Succeed from expansion of the national market

Grow through global rationalization

Firm-Specific 4Ps Analysis and Purchasing Behavior

Use fashion to position market offerings among younger groups

Compare overseas goods to existing products (focal option)

Pay attention to dominant homogeneity

National Marketing Decisions and Marketing Forecasts

Continuing trend captures youth for overseas Chinese lifestyle

Amplifying trend uses aggressive marketing with some success

Doubling trend does not convert other age-peer groups

Nontraditional Frame Analysis for Global Marketing

National Character

Cultural Context and Cultural-Free Typologies

Invest with family, avoid market ambiguities

Uncertainty avoidance

Wide inequalities in wealth and power

Power distance

Cultural Context and Cultural-Based Typologies

Language, family orientation, social networks

Food-loving Cantonese

Style-conscious Shanghainese

Politically adept folk from Beijing

Collectivism

Cultural Context and Overseas Chinese, Trans-Pacific Lifestyle

Younger age-period cohort groups

Entrepreneurial spirit

Material success

Collectivism

Cultural Context and Traditional Chinese Lifestyle

Devoted Communists, government officials, and older groups

Successful state-sector business executives

Let's be careful in our analysis. No strong disconnection exists between older and younger age-period age groups. Yes, World War II, Chairman Mao's cultural revolution, and the Communist command economy are history. However, the events of 1968 in Europe and the United States did not invade China, nor did the ideas of freedom divide Chinese youth from their elders. This disconnection is a demographic fact only in western Europe and North America.

In China, national character connects all age-period cohort groups and all mainland Chinese and overseas Chinese to their past, present, and future. In fact, Chinese national character carries equal weight today with overseas Chinese values about material success. Moreover, overseas Chinese values or the extension of Chinese values about collectivism throughout Chinese-speaking East Asia are fast becoming the strongest challenger to American values about individualism throughout the same English-speaking Pacific Basin countries.

Marketing Scan: Overseas Chinese Cultural Values

Clearly, country risk is higher in China than in other countries of the Pacific and East Asia. Most of the reasons for this assessment come from the unknown about China's political future and the long-term direction of its market-oriented reforms. Today, China has an overheated national economy with all the risks of rapid price inflation, peasant and labor unrest, and shortages of raw materials. Most marketers predict these difficulties will continue into the indefinite future. Nevertheless, similar to Mexico, marketing executives believe they must do business in China or place themselves at a competitive disadvantage in the long run.

Demographic facts are hard to come by for China. The Chinese don't know the details about age-period cohort groups, income distribution, and gender divisions. Access to information is still closely guarded by the Chinese government. Hong-Kong–based research firms, together with local associates, can provide some facts about cross-cultural clusters, the coefficient of imitation, and country and time effect of product diffusion so long as they employ the CETSCALE in developing their questionnaires. Given the similarities between overseas Chinese cultural values and Chinese national character, many marketing research techniques developed for use among ethnic Chinese in the west and in East Asia are good substitutes for use in China.

Marketers also can fall back on anecdotes, simplistic associations, and fragmented studies about the cultural habits of overseas Chinese. For example,

Hong Kong is a financial microcosm for Guangzhou in southern China, and Taiwan is a marketing prototype for Fujian province in southeastern China. Moreover, southern China shares some cultural habits (e.g., power distance) with the northern coastal provinces of China. But the food-loving Cantonese are different from the style-conscious Shanghainese, and both are different from the politically adept Chinese living in Beijing. Even with the introduction of satellite TV, these regional differences among the Chinese remain strong because Star TV broadcasts in Cantonese, Mandarin, and the other major language groups within China.

Furthermore, China shares a few cultural insights with Japan (e.g., Japanese words are written with Chinese ideograms). But the two East Asian countries differ over power distance. Japan does not have wide inequalities in wealth and power. China does. Some Chinese are very wealthy, but almost all of the 1.1 billion Chinese are poor peasants. This is China's fundamental economic problem and the one that drives all discussions about China's political realities. The overseas Chinese who live throughout East Asia and the Pacific are good examples for the mainland Chinese in their quest for economic growth coupled with political stability.

Applying National Character

As we learned in chapters 3 through 5, marketers generally ask national cultural questions when they search for the answer to "What is national character?" We discovered in this chapter that power distance is crucial to understanding Chinese national character. Very wide inequalities in wealth and power exist within China. This is true in part within Hong Kong, valid to some extent in Taiwan, but not generally the case in Singapore.

Nevertheless, all Chinese within and outside mainland China share many similar cultural traits (e.g., language, family orientation, and social networks of friends) even though they live in different nation-states. If we look at the overseas Chinese in Malaysia, Indonesia, the Philippines, Australia, on the Pacific Coast of South and Central America, in the United States, in Canada, in England, and in Portugal – all places in which overseas Chinese are large minorities within a Malay, Javanese, and Anglo-American culture – they too share these same similar cultural traits.

Today, mainland China is opening up once again. Even after decades or a century of separation, overseas Chinese, together with the Hong Kong Chinese and Taiwanese, are reconnecting with their families and social networks within China. All want China to become another economic "tiger" within East Asia.

Is there a Chinese national character? Yes. We can find power distance and uncertainty avoidance. The Chinese prefer to shop and invest with their families, friends, and coworkers so that they can avoid the market ambiguities sought by most Anglo-Americans and many Europeans. These attributes of national character are common among mainland Chinese and between them and Chinese outside of China. This overseas Chinese marketing fact is often overlooked by western marketers.

Matching Cultural Typologies with Lifestyles

Hong Kong, Taiwan, Singapore, and many overseas Chinese communities provide us with cross-sectional age differences to forecast patterns of consumption as cohort groups age through the decades. *Older age cohort groups* witnessed World War II, the Japanese occupation, the end of British, Dutch, and French colonialism, and the emergence of independent Malay- and Japanese-dominated nation-states in southeast Asia. *Younger age cohort groups* observed the American defeat in Vietnam, rampant Japanese capitalism throughout East Asia, and the rise of wealthy Chinese communities on both sides of the Pacific Ocean.

Some of these young adults and teenagers wear jeans, comfortable clothes, and sportswear. They want to enjoy the freedom lifestyle, but they also want to live this life within the Chinese cultural context of close family and social relationships. This Confucian marketing fact is often overlooked by western marketing executives.

Reducing Overconfidence or "Humbling" Feedback

Clearly, when marketers study China they must consider additional information. Here are some crucial questions. How quickly will China's economy develop? Will overseas Chinese, western, and Japanese investments come in at an increasing rate? Will the internal Chinese market develop its own ability to generate capital for new investments? Will the Chinese become savers in the Japanese tradition or continue to be consumers in the Cantonese and Shanghainese tradition? To what extent will China's political economy follow in the footsteps of Singapore or those of Hong Kong and Taiwan? Will instability reoccur in China when Deng Xiaoping passes from his role as leader of the Peoples' Republic of China?

No doubt China is on the move. Several roads are open for China to travel down (see Exhibit 6-7). Intuition tells us that Hong Kong and Taiwan will

Exhibit 6-7.
China's Foreign Trade with the US

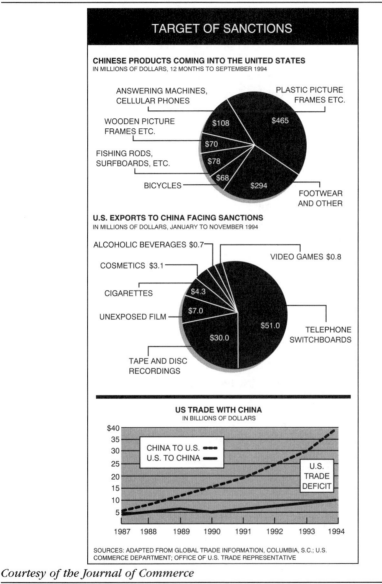

TARGET OF SANCTIONS

CHINESE PRODUCTS COMING INTO THE UNITED STATES
IN MILLIONS OF DOLLARS, 12 MONTHS TO SEPTEMBER 1994

- ANSWERING MACHINES, CELLULAR PHONES — $108
- PLASTIC PICTURE FRAMES ETC. — $465
- WOODEN PICTURE FRAMES ETC. — $70
- FISHING RODS, SURFBOARDS, ETC. — $78
- BICYCLES — $68
- $294 — FOOTWEAR AND OTHER

U.S. EXPORTS TO CHINA FACING SANCTIONS
IN MILLIONS OF DOLLARS, JANUARY TO NOVEMBER 1994

- ALCOHOLIC BEVERAGES $0.7
- VIDEO GAMES $0.8
- COSMETICS $3.1
- CIGARETTES $4.3
- UNEXPOSED FILM $7.0
- $51.0 — TELEPHONE SWITCHBOARDS
- $30.0 — TAPE AND DISC RECORDINGS

US TRADE WITH CHINA
IN BILLIONS OF DOLLARS

CHINA TO U.S. ●●●
U.S. TO CHINA ━━━

U.S. TRADE DEFICIT

$40, 35, 30, 25, 20, 15, 10, 5 — 1987 1988 1989 1990 1991 1992 1993 1994

SOURCES: ADAPTED FROM GLOBAL TRADE INFORMATION, COLUMBIA, S.C.; U.S. COMMERCE DEPARTMENT; OFFICE OF U.S. TRADE REPRESENTATIVE

Courtesy of the Journal of Commerce

have a strong impact on China during the mid-1990s. However, the transition to a post-Deng China at some point in the decade will force China to shift its course toward Singapore. This political news is a marketing fact often overlooked by western marketers.

Strategies for Increasing Marketing Effectiveness

Cultural information is key to understanding the Chinese market. Fashion in particular plays an important role in positioning market offerings within China. The use of the focal option is appropriate when comparing new products from overseas Chinese (so-called overseas Chinese goods and services) with existing products in mainland China. Paired comparisons are less useful when equating new American and Japanese products to enduring products in China.

Modeling Purchasing Behavior

The mainland Chinese with disposable personal income are consuming Western cosmetics, personal care products, consumer electronics, TV productions, cellular phones, credit cards, and many other goods and services. These Chinese are following in the footsteps of their conationals in Hong Kong and Taiwan in the desire to be current with the rest of the world. Both choose change when it fits into tradition, conformity, collectivism, and family values.

Right now, the diffusion model of fashion is occurring throughout coastal China. For example, "in Shanghai, in the peacock parade in front of the Garden Hotel, in the old French quarter of the city, 22-year-old Li Chiu is wearing a passable imitation of a Chanel blouse in cream silk, black pants and gold jewelry that is a hot seller in the stores. Her companion [wears] a double-breasted pearl-gray suit, custom-made shirt and flashy gilded watch."[42] If the diffusion model continues to deepen its hold in Guangzhou and Shanghai, it will gather speed and create a bandwagon effect in other parts of China.

Marketing Implementation

China is in transition from its past to its future. Chinese products (such as herbal medicines and hair-growing lotions) have served local consumers for decades, centuries, and even millennia. Their performance is known among Chinese.

On the other hand, Japanese and western products are new for local Chinese consumers. Their performance is unknown. If competing Chinese products rate a good past performance, then they are the focus of comparison (or focal option) for foreign, imported products from the West.

When no competing Chinese products exist, the success of imported goods depends on their integration within the cultural habits of the Chinese. Today, a vast number of foreign-origin products are entering the Chinese market. Most of these have no Chinese products for comparison. Hence, the focal option technique is not universally useful to market researchers in mainland China.

Three forecasts. The "continuing trend" forecast is the easiest to make because things do go on as before. The overseas Chinese lifestyle captures the same number of people in the younger age-period cohort groups. This is the most likely trend.

The "amplifying trend" forecast assumes Chinese and foreign firms aggressively market their copy-cat and luxury goods and more younger people purchase these goods. This could happen, but centuries of tradition are ready to do battle against the global, largely American culture and its recent copy-cat versions from Japan and the overseas Chinese societies of East Asia.

The "doubling trend" forecast assumes Chinese and foreign firms convert older people to the overseas Chinese lifestyle. This is the least likely forecast. Product diffusion occurs slowly in China because power distance, inequality in incomes, and the lack of disposable income all exist in mainland China. This information should give marketers pause before they casually think the Chinese market is divided into market segments similar to those found in the United States, Europe, and Japan.

Summary: Scanning Overseas Chinese Values

Higher levels of consumption among Chinese consumers involve a gathering union with overseas Chinese or the East Asian, trans-Pacific culture. This meshing of all Chinese forces the Chinese government toward making China another economic "tiger" in East Asia. This is the goal of the government's market-oriented reforms. The risks are high for the government because of an overheated economy and a deepening unrest among the peasants and factory workers. China's reality is a metaphor for most countries in the world today.

Inclusive Contexts for Global Marketing

Exhibit 6–8 sums up the inclusive contexts for global marketing in the case of China. We examine reinventing China as a market economy with socialist characteristics and show its impact on our country risk analysis. We also

Exhibit 6–8.
Inclusive Contexts for Global Marketing

Country Risk (A)
Political direction from Communist Party
  Market-oriented macro-* and microeconomic reforms
  Reinvent country as a market with socialist characteristics
Cultural insights from overseas Chinese
Long-term planning horizon for business firms
Political Frame

Country Risk (B)
Demographic analysis
  Age-period cohort analysis and national character
  Traditionalism, collectivism, family status within party
Regional analysis and cross-national clusters
Cultural Frame

Firm-Specific 4Ps Analysis
Decision making under uncertainty
  Teamwork and collectivism
  Segmentation, positioning, tailoring decisions
Product diffusion: time effect dependent on country effect
Produce for domestic and export markets to earn foreign exchange
Marketing Management Frame

National Marketing Decisions
Socio-cultural values: dominant homogeneity
Uncertainty perceptions about size of market
Opportunities, analysis, decisions
  Who uses the product?
  How to increase market share?
  How to provide value?
  What customer signals show changes in local markets?
Walking-around research: watch out for people error
Clumsy vetting
Decision making under uncertainty
Multimarkets across nation-states, technologies, industries
Technological Frame

study decision making under uncertainty. This too shows the importance of regional analysis in deciding where to invest and with what set of partners. It also reminds foreign investors to pay particular attention to exporting products to earn badly needed foreign exchange. Moreover, we apply traditional socio-cultural values to both formal and walking-around research, and we discuss the realities for sales within mainland China. These results tell marketers to discount many of the stories about the very big mainland Chinese market. Generally, success in China is measured in smaller numbers, local markets, regional connections, and family relationships. Success in mainland China comes from following the path opened by overseas Chinese.

Conclusions

Scanning for political realities is about looking at government policies toward market-oriented reforms or governing the market. Within China, these changes are taking place under the auspices of a Communist government and with the skills and money of overseas Chinese, Japanese, and Americans.

Let's return to our initial three learning objectives:

1. Discuss the need for predictability in political reforms to carry out successful country risk analyses.

    You should have a clear understanding of the perceptions of marketers about interpreting political change, and you should be able to make some good decisions about exports to, imports from, and sales within mainland China. As you read chapter 6, you should learn the ideas from the political and cultural frames; they enhance your understanding of country risk within all East Asian countries whose citizens and commercial residents are overseas Chinese. Many of the ideas discussed in chapters 3 through 5 about North America, Europe, and Japan do not apply to China. We also show the need to do more walking-around research because of the problems inherent in doing probability sampling within emerging markets, such as both Mexico and China. All of these tasks are crucial to being a success in China.

2. Outline the use of information about market size and sales targets in marketing similar products across national boundaries.

    You should be able to apply sales information to gain insights into the use of nondurable consumer products in mainland China, and you should be able to put together information from sources available within mainland China.

3. Explain the impact of East Asian, trans-Pacific overseas Chinese cultural values on sales within mainland China.

    You should be aware that the diffusion of new (foreign-origin) products takes place in mainland China only as these goods are introduced by overseas Chinese. You should be able to weigh country risks, demographic facts, cultural insights, and political realities as a part of your marketing effort in mainland China.

We thought we knew the Chinese were different from the American, Europeans, and Japanese. But we did not know that Chinese history, tradition, and culture strongly influence overseas Chinese as well as those who live in China itself. Finding acceptable foreign products among the overseas Chinese, who will transmit them to mainland Chinese, is the work of global marketing executives.

Notes

1. Michael Prowse, "Miracles Beyond the Free Market," *Financial Times,* April 26, 1993, 15. Urban C. Lehner, "Belief in an Imminent Asian Century is Gaining Sway," *The Wall Street Journal,* May 17, 1993, A12.

2. Leslie H. Gelb, "Wealth Crosses the Pacific," *The New York Times,* March 25, 1993, A15. Marcus W. Brauchli, "The Outlook," *The Wall Street Journal,* February 24, 1994, A1.

3. Alexander Nicoll, "China's Unique Path Towards the Free Market," *Financial Times,* May 24, 1993, 15.

4. Nicholas Lardy, *International Economic Insights.* Cited by Nicoll and by "Big," *The Economist,* April 30, 1994, 78.

5. Cyril Lin of St Antony's College, Oxford. Cited by Nicoll.

6. Brauchli, A1.

7. "Inflation has China Running Scared," *Business Week,* June 14, 1993, 48-49. Brauchli, A1.

8. Edward Balls, "Unstable Foundations of the Chinese Economic Miracle," *The Financial Times,* January 17, 1994, 19.

9. Both Nicholas Lardy and *The Economist* believe China will remain poor for a very long time. See "Big," 78. This is my opinion, too.

10. Xu Bai Yi, *Marketing to China: One Billion New Customers* (Lincolnwood, IL: NTC Business Books, 1990), xxvi.

11. Ibid.

12. Julia Leung and Craig S. Smith, "Some Chinese Factory Bosses Live It Up," *The Wall Street Journal*, March 15, 1994, A16.

13. Simon Holberton, "Shooting Star Aims for Domination," *Financial Times*, June 8, 1993, 21. Marcus W. Brauchli, "Star-Struck: A Satellite TV System Is Quickly Moving Asia into the Global Village," *The Wall Street Journal*, January 14, 1993, A1 and A8.

14. Ibid.

15. Holberton, 21.

16. Ibid.

17. Lehner, A12.

18. Nicholas D. Kristof, "Via Satellite, Information Revolution Stirs China," *The New York Times*, April 11, 1993, 1, 6.

19. Joseph Kahn and Urban C. Lehner, "Shanghai Thrives on Beijing's Favoritism," *The Wall Street Journal*, May 10, 1994, A15.

20. Tony Walker, "Consuming Passion of Chinese Shoppers," *Financial Times*, April 24/25, 1993, 7.

21. Survey by McKinsey Hong Kong. Cited by Walker, 7.

22. Ford S. Worthy, "Where Capitalism Thrives in China," *Fortune*, March 9, 1992, 71-75.

23. Henry C. Steele, "Marketing research in China: The Hong Kong Connection", *Marketing and Research Today*, August 1990, 155-65.

24. Steele reports that Yau H. M. Oliver finds it very difficult to obtain a sample in China. Sin Y. M. and Yau H. M. Oliver, "Marketing Research in China," *Ming Pao Monthly*, May 1986 (published in Chinese). Cited by Steele, 160, 164.

25. Betsy Sharkey, "Getting to Know You," *Adweek*, June 6, 1988, G34.

26. Ibid., G38.

27. James McGregor, "US Companies in China Find Patience, Persistence and Salesmanship Pay Off," *The Wall Street Journal,* April 3, 1992, B1.

28. Andrew Tanzer, "Ding-Dong, Capitalism Calling," *Forbes*, October 14, 1991, 186.

29. McGregor, B1.

30. "Coke and Pepsi Carve Tiny Niche in Huge Market," *Advertising Age,* June 9, 1986, 56, 60.

31. "Coke v Pepsi (cont): Chinese Fizz," *The Economist,* January 29, 1994, 67-68.

32. Nicholas D. Kristof, "Entrepreneurial Energy Sets Off a Chinese Boom," *The New York Times,* February 14, 1993, 1, 6. Tony Walker, "The Tale of the Red Fat Cat," *Financial Times*, June 12/13, 1993, I.

33. Sheryl WuDunn, "China Village Prospers But Retains Old Ways," *The New York Times,* January 17, 1993, 8.

34. Ibid.

35. George Melloan, "All Is Bustle on China's Capitalist Road," *The Wall Street Journal,* March 15, 1993, A13.

36. Louis Tong, "A Close Look at China's Opinion Leaders," *Media International,* June 1988, 37.

37. Ibid.

38. Lynne Curry, "Charting the Tastes of China's Consumers," *Financial Times,* April 8, 1993, 12.

39. Ibid.

40. "Motorola in China: A Great Leap Forward," *Business Week,* May 17, 1993, 58-59.

41. Paul Beamish and Lorraine Spiess, "Post Tiananmen China: Should You Invest," *Business Quarterly,* Spring 1991, 72.

42. Suzy Menkes, "Chinese Go Shopping for Western Fashion," *The New York Times,* June 21, 1993, B1.

Part Three

Positioning
Global Brands

Chapter Format

Introduction

Marketing Questions

Environmental Scan: Future Watch

Initial Analysis of Marketing Opportunities

Clues to Capturing Customers

The Firm-Specific Research Assignment

Competitive Scan: Interactive Connectivity

Estimates of Market Potential

Similar Market Segments Worldwide

National Marketing Decisions

Marketing Scan: Nonroutine Partnerships

Strategies for Increasing Marketing Effectiveness

Marketing Implementation

Conclusions

Cases: AT&T, BT, MCI, Baby Bells, Nextel, Iusacell, Mobilcom

Learning Objectives

After reading this chapter, you should be able to:

- Discuss the need for predicting the future of telecommunications to carry out successful marketing analysis

- Outline how interactive connectivity conveys information about spanning technological, cultural, and managerial boundaries

- Explain the impact of nonroutine partnerships on growing share in the wireless cellular and mobile radio market

Marketing Teamwork

chapter 7

Introduction

Marketers manage final demand by research-ing international markets (chapters 3–6), posi-tioning global brands (chapters 7–10), and signaling detailed national information (chap-ters 11–14). In this chapter, we look at the telecommunications industry. Here we stress market (rather than country) risk analysis within a regulated industry that is going through denationalization, deregulation, pri-vatization, and liberalization throughout the world. We also spell out the process by which companies do their firm-specific 4Ps analysis, and we detail several positioning strategies now in vogue within the industry. Moreover, we show what formal and walking-around research must be done for us to develop the habit of teamwork within telecom firms.

Let's break some new ground. In chapters 3–6, country risk and the political frame gave us the idea of reinventing nation-states. In this chapter, let's reinvent an industry (telecommunications) and several telecom firms (AT&T, BT/MCI, and the Baby Bells). Let's call this market risk analysis.

Scanning Global Markets

Environmental scan: future watch. Marketers know that government policies of deregulation, privatization, and liberalization mean the end of the existing wired (or landlines) telephone business. In some markets, wired networks could even be replaced by wireless networks. Moreover, *teams of marketing executives* are asking questions about the future. Are cellular, mobile radio, or satellite transmissions going to dominate the wireless market? What role will computer communications firms play in the conversion of wireless data systems to hand-held personal communications systems? What's the future role of wired telephones? This is the decision-making environment that telecommunications firms face.

Competitive scan: interactive connectivity. Marketers are pushing technological and service changes into global markets with an *imperfect understanding of the preferences* of business customers. The latter want to be interactive with their voice and data transmissions connected worldwide. Successful marketing executives position AT&T to dominate the global outsourcing business through wired and wireless connections within the United States and Canada, and through World Source in East Asia. Teams of marketers at MCI, the Baby Bells, and at other telcos look for ways to position services in mature markets, by product-line extensions, and to become global outsourcers.

Marketing scan: nonroutine partnerships. Even though many customers don't have a clear idea of what they want from the telecommunications industry, marketers believe the wireless telephone, data service, and multimedia businesses are ready to roam the world's stage. Successful marketing executives are finding partners from within and outside the telecommunications industry to develop new products and services for household customers who have high incomes and will be the first to adopt new telecom technologies. Teams of marketers work to *span boundaries* among telephones, cable TVs, and computers. Even with soft information, many telecommunications firms fail to pass the *marketing vision* test. The most successful teams have the very best partners, that is, those who can develop a marketing strategy for matching technology to customer preferences.

Traditional Contexts for Global Marketing

Exhibit 7-1 records the traditional contexts for global marketing in the case of the telecommunications industry. We examine a reinvented business

Exhibit 7-1.
Traditional Contexts for Global Marketing

Market Risk

Govern the market through reinvented business environment

Deregulation of industry

Privatization of state-owned firms

Planning horizons and range of market risk

Foreign investment

Imperfect information about decisions of competitors

Unknown competitive possibilities among emerging technologies

Firm-Specific 4Ps Analysis

Demand analysis

Who uses the product?

How to increase market share?

How to provide value?

What signals show changes in market?

Cultural analysis and age-period cohort analysis

Positioning strategies

Mature markets: through promotion and price

New markets: through value-added product extensions

Emerging markets: competing as a global outsourcer

Product positioning

Competitive destruction of cellular technologies

Product-development life cycle

Time effect of product diffusion

Status symbols

Business tools

Price segmentation and bundled prices

National Marketing Decisions

Supply analysis

Technological choices

Ambiguities about nonroutine partnerships

Span managerial boundaries

Scanning potential markets, offerings, segments

Continued on next page

Exhibit 7-1. *Continued from previous page*

Formal and walking-around research

    Changing versus stable industry

    Usefulness of soft information

    Market is immature

    Humbling feedback

    Focal option

Vision test

Remember trend is not destiny

environment, positioning strategies, and research variables. The first alerts us to the monumental changes sweeping the telecommunications industry from decisions made by national governments. The second reminds us that telcos decide how to position themselves in terms of their individual market risk. The third shows us the research still to be done before we can predict the future of the telecommunications industry. The wired versus wireless case, the competing cellular claims, and the other emerging telecom technologies are symbols of how new industries are being created for a future global economy.

Nontraditional Contexts for Global Marketing

Exhibit 7-2 names the nontraditional contexts for global marketing in the telecommunications industry. We survey reinventing an industry and its firms, the creative destruction of alternative telecommunications technologies, cross-cultural analysis, and carrying out managerial teamwork under uncertainty. Again we break new ground because reinventing nation-states goes hand-in-hand with reinventing industries (e.g., telecommunications) and competing telecom firms (or telcos). We also begin again by focusing on the creative destruction of analog wired (or landlines) technology at the hands of wireless technologies, and the end of some or all at the hands of computer-based interactive telecommunications. (The economics of the creative destruction of technologies will be a theme throughout chapters 7–12.)

As we venture forth onto the new information highway, we do not know who our customers will be and what they will choose as their long-term technologies. However, from our past work on cross-cultural analysis, we do know three facts: disconnection occurs between older and younger age groups; available disposable income helps the more affluent adopt newer

Exhibit 7-2.
Nontraditional Contexts for Global Marketing

Political Frame

Govern the market through reinvented business environment

Modified Final Judgment (US)

Technological Frame

Interactive connectivity

Convergence between telephone and cable TV

Computer modems and video servers transmit multimedia

Interactive broadband information highway

Creative destruction to winnow out winners and losers

Analog versus digital wired (or landlines) systems

Wired versus wireless (or cellular, GSM, satellite) systems

Computer-telecommunications

Information highway as unknown competitive future

Cultural Frame

Disconnection among older and younger age-cohort peer groups

Cross-cultural analysis

Similar self-referencing criteria

Imitate affluent lifestyles of peer groups

Sustainable higher levels of disposable income

Preference for products with new technology

Value creation and multiplying bits of information

Marketing Management Frame

Industry analysis

Stable industries and past experience

Changing industries and new information

Managerial decision making under uncertainty

Teamwork

Role ambiguities, boundary spanners, collective work products

"Juice" teams

Change corporate culture

Nonroutine partnerships

Open new markets, gain new skills, share fixed costs

Commit to a long-term economic relationship with suppliers

Stress the quality of the relationship as the crucial asset

Continued on next page

Exhibit 7-2. *Continued from previous page*

Learning organization

    Unstructured marketing decisions

    Trust and cooperation

    "Soft" information

    Walking-around research

things faster; and within all countries some people (with similar self-referencing criteria) adopt the newest technologies faster than others.

Finally, we are beginning to recognize that only learning organizations survive during periods of reinventing nation-states, industries, and firms. These firms must participate in long-term nonroutine partnerships and insist their managers work as a team to resolve ambiguities, span boundaries, and change the corporate culture. Teléfonos de Mexico, Bell Atlantic, AT&T, BT/MCI, and other telcos are all reinventing themselves through the creative destruction of technologies and the establishment of learning organizations. It's not clear which will survive, but that is the essence of a global industry reinventing itself in the last half of the 1990s.

Governing the market. First, let's look at the political frame. Government sets the pace for economic reforms by making choices about deregulating industries, privatizing domestic firms, permitting foreign competition, and encouraging alliances. The tempo of reinventing industries speeds up as nation-states pool their economic sovereignty through free-trade agreements, and the weaker learn to deal with stronger competition from abroad. Success in governing the market leads to decreased market risk.

Making decisions under uncertainty. Second, let's study the technological frame. Today, government forces on the telephone industry are changing. Some governments (such as those of the United States and Canada) deregulate existing services; others (those of Mexico and Britain) privatize state-owned firms; still others (those of France and Germany) encourage government-owned telephone companies to form alliances; and many governments (China's included) build telecom networks from scratch. The process of telecom reforms varies widely throughout the world.

The world's very knowledgeable customers want interactive connectivity or the ability to communicate ideas, politics, and interests through computer modems, telephone or cable TV lines, and radio paging or satellite transmissions. Theirs is the information highway. Somewhat belatedly, governments are trying to set rules about access to, use of, and protection of cultural values.

Many informed customers want voice and fax services from wired and wireless systems today, not tomorrow. Theirs is a copper and fiber-optic digital telephone (or cable TV) line. Governments administer rate-of-return pricing in return for local monopolies. The process of matching government preferences with technological change and customer experience varies even more widely throughout the world.

Most of the competitive argument among telephone and cable firms is about the business context of telecommunications. It's very similar to the question "How do we add the picture to a radio?" It's the wrong question because radio and television are two different technologies. Telephone and cable TV firms have created a convergence circus without paying attention to the real needs of their customers.

Consumers don't care who makes the equipment, who administers the switches, and what the government does or does not do to make the information revolution happen. The smartest consumers want to receive and react to TV programs, Internet messages, and word processing results on their computer screens – interactive computer communications. This means broadband networks to carry multimedia from telephone and cable TV lines through video servers within personal computers to customers.

Success in working together among government, business, and consumer experts leads to decreased country risk, improved interactive connectivity, and increased telecom sales. Although the information revolution is truly upon us, governments still can't decide how to govern the market, and business firms resist going through the creative destruction necessary to winnow out winners from losers.

Hunting for consumers. Third, let's examine the cultural frame. The best marketers search for ways to network information, improve connectivity and communications, and increase marketing effectiveness. Interactivity is their future, and the future is malleable. Future-oriented marketing executives experience, move, and convey information. They also look at information in new ways, change it, and probe information for new facts. Since their point of view is considered relevant, future-oriented marketers move swiftly, conveniently, and interactively to provide new ideas to executive teams. All marketing executives add value by multiplying the availability of information among all participants, both at home and abroad.

Segmentation, positioning, and tailoring decisions. Finally, let's look closely at the marketing management frame. In chapters 3 through 6, you experienced new information about country risk:

- Mexico is the prototype emerging country that stakes its future on free trade with the developed countries to the north.

- The EU is a set of age-period cohort groups who bet their European loyalty is more important than national fealty.

- Japan is the unique culture in the world, but it finds ways to accommodate both the United States and China.

- China is the prototype East Asian challenger to the dominant orthodoxy of Anglo-American capitalism.

By probing together for new demographic, cultural, and political facts, we found three characteristics that define global telecom consumers. First, spenders display similar SRCs (e.g., nonethnocentrist Mexicans, North American, and Euro-consumers; trans-Pacific Japanese business executives; and overseas Chinese) about the need for new interactive communication devices. Second, shoppers imitate the affluent lifestyles of peer groups elsewhere in the world and demand the latest telephone equipment and service. Third, customers prefer products that use new technology and provide better service to gain first-mover advantage at home and abroad. For example, these accomplished consumers show their "street smarts" in communicating with friends and clients around the world by using the Internet or pocket cellular phones. Both are status symbols for Americans and crucial business tools for the overseas Chinese. Success in positioning computer communications products leads to increased telecom sales.

Organizing global marketing experience. The simultaneous existence of these four different contexts forces marketers to research traditional telephone markets, to position wired and wireless telephone services, and to watch for different national signals about personal communications systems (PCS), smart radio, direct satellite, and other telecom technologies. Let's do two things in this chapter. First, we will discuss the impact of interactive connectivity on decision making by marketing teams within the telecommunications industry. Then we will apply this marketing analysis to the sale of equipment, lines, and services among all competitors, some of whom think they know the future.

Market Risk Questions

Marketers manage final demand by researching international telecommunications markets; see Exhibit 7-3. Country risk and the political frame are merging into a new view of market risk. Decision making under uncertainty occurs through the new international trading rules of the GATT/WTO, NAFTA, and the EU. The institutional framework for market decisions within nation-states includes new domestic edicts about deregulation, privatization, and liberalization. Both sets of rules offer marketing executives a long-term planning horizon for investments, joint ventures, and licensing locally and throughout the world.

Paying Attention to Deregulation

In the telecommunications industry, global marketers encounter familiar market risks (e.g., deregulation, privatization, foreign competitors, and limited foreign exchange). Their task is to make deals with national governments even though the latter are not sure which telecom service should be sold, how much market share should be given to foreigners, and whether competition is good for the national industry. Everyone is uneasy because of the rapid diffusion of new, competing wireless technology. All players (including governments) are making technological choices and marketing management decisions under conditions of imperfect information and market uncertainty.

Researching Demand

Throughout virtually all parts of the world, the overall demand for new telecom connections, equipment, and services is strong, growing, and limitless. No part of the world is untouched by this relentless pursuit of personal and business communications. In this sense, the telecom industry is a global industry.

Nontraditional frames. However, "the devil is the details." Everywhere, local, regional, and national demand for wired versus wireless service depends on the impact of the four nontraditional frames for global marketing:

- *Political context:* the speed at which governments open up national markets to new competitors, technologies, and services

Exhibit 7-3.
Market Risk Analysis: Telecommunications
The Environmental Scan

Traditional Frame Analysis for Global Marketing

Market Risk Analysis, and Deregulation and Privatization
Govern the market through reinvented business environment
Permit foreign investment in former state-owned PTOs
Deal with imperfect information
Accept unknown competitive possibilities

Firm-Specific 4Ps Analysis and Demand and Price Segmentation
Who uses the product: Age-period cohort analysis
How to increase market share: Creative end of technologies
How to provide value: Time effect of product diffusion
What signals show changes in market: Bundled prices

Firm-Specific 4Ps Analysis and Product Positioning
Forget US cellular technology
Accept GSM (European) cellular technology
Speed up the product-development life cycle

National Marketing Decisions and Technological Choices
Scan future of wired versus wireless service
Exploit ambiguities about nonroutine multimedia business
Span boundaries across technology, marketing, finance

National Marketing Decisions and Marketing Opportunities
Position communications products as status symbols
Position telephone products as business tools
Offer e-mail, collaboration, information, direct marketing
Remember trend is not destiny

Nontraditional Frame Analysis for Global Marketing

Technological Frame and Interactive Connectivity
Forget convergence circus between telephones and cable TV
Use computer modems and video servers to transmit multimedia
Build interactive broadband information highway
Employ creative destruction to winnow out winners and losers

Marketing Management Frame and Value Creation
Multiply available bits of information
Spenders display similar SRCs for interactive communications

Continued on next page

Exhibit 7-3. Continued from previous page

Shoppers imitate the demand of peers for latest services

Customers prefer new technology

Marketing Management Frame and Teamwork

Establish "juice" teams

Create collective work-products

Focus on real needs of customers

Build global outsourcing network

- *Cultural context:* the willingness of older, middle-aged, and younger age-period cohort groups of customers to change their telecommunications lifestyle

- *Technology context:* the extent to which existing wired analog service is installed and how fast countries can be rewired for digital and satellite service

- *Marketing management context:* the perceptions about the cost-quality-price of new technology and the time it will take for privately owned firms to recoup their investments

Given the impact of these four circumstances on demand analysis in the telecommunications industry, global marketers must "think global, but act local." Here are some examples:

Who prefers wired service? American, European, and Japanese customers prefer wired over wireless service; see Exhibits 7–4 and 7–5. Their installed base of home and office telephones already is wired to central and PBX exchanges. They will examine wireless telecommunications as an add-on to their basic service rather than as a way to carry out all their telephone connections. Thus, prices must come down quickly for these new technologies to gain significant market share.

Who prefers wireless service? Mexican, Chinese, and other customers want wireless services. They cannot wait for landlines to be installed across their countries. Their pent-up demand for worldwide telephone connections makes them willing to try these new technologies even when they come at premium prices.

Competitive analysis. Competition exists between alternative forms of telecom services. Right now, telecom firms have no set of correct answers about matching customer preferences with future market segments. Their marketing executives are scanning the future before they commit capital, time, and talent.

Understanding Technological Choices

Real differences do exist among technologies chosen by telecom firms. For example, AT&T promotes its expanding public switch network; it creates value by selling equipment, connections, and the use of its global outsourcing network by global firms. In Asia, AT&T sets up World Source with local, mostly government-owned telcos, and business firms use the AT&T network for global voice and data transmissions. In the United States, AT&T views the convergence of wireless communications with computer technologies as a means to keep the Regional Bell Operating Companies (Baby Bells) from dominating crucial cordless telephone markets. This is why AT&T acquired McCaw's Cellular One.

Exhibit 7-4.
Landline Telephones in East Asia

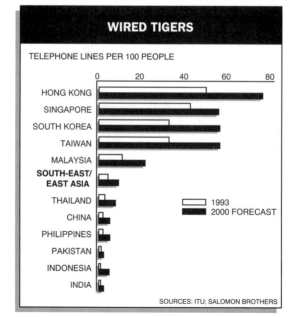

WIRED TIGERS

TELEPHONE LINES PER 100 PEOPLE

HONG KONG
SINGAPORE
SOUTH KOREA
TAIWAN
MALAYSIA
SOUTH-EAST/
EAST ASIA
THAILAND
CHINA
PHILIPPINES
PAKISTAN
INDONESIA
INDIA

□ 1993
■ 2000 FORECAST

SOURCES: ITU; SALOMON BROTHERS

Courtesy of The Economist

Exhibit 7-5.
Landline Telephones in the World

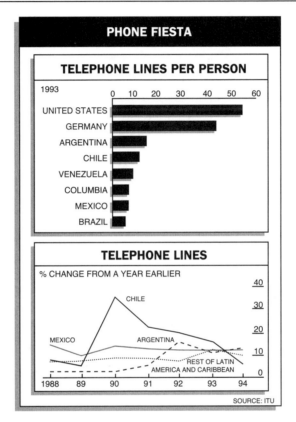

PHONE FIESTA

TELEPHONE LINES PER PERSON

1993

TELEPHONE LINES

% CHANGE FROM A YEAR EARLIER

SOURCE: ITU

Courtesy of The Economist

On the other hand, Nextel (once known as Fleet Call) offers local connections through specialized mobile radio (SMR) carriers. These are the old two-way taxi, trucker, and oil rig radio transmissions updated with Motorola's SMR digital technology. Nextel, with the help of Motorola, Comcast (a cable TV firm), Masushita, and Nippon Telephone and Telegraph, seeks to compete directly against AT&T's McCaw Cellular One with a seamless national digital wireless telecommunications network based on mobile radio transmissions. Who will win the conversion to wireless service is anyone's guess, but we pay marketers to predict the future.

Creating Value

This is just the beginning of the information revolution. Business customers want portable telephones that roam the world, give them fax, e-mail, and other connections with their computers, and offer to store, retrieve, and recalculate data. Most choose answering machine or voice mail capability, and many seek fax service for their home offices. Although some customers know they need online computer services, most don't buy these enhanced telephone services even though more than 30 percent of US homes now have PCs. These consumers fall victim to the "fatal disconnection" discussed in chapters 3–5.

Who uses the product and age-period cohort analysis? Let's remind ourselves once again what age-period disconnection means to global marketers. Older age-cohort groups who became adults before the 1980s have difficulty integrating new technology into their businesses and lifestyles. Tradition strengthens this resistance among ethnocentric Mexicans, rural French and Germans, and middle-aged Japanese. Younger age groups who became adults in the 1980s and afterward do not share these same fears, phobias, and dislikes. Their desire to participate fully in a global telecom lifestyle spurs them on to try new technologies to find those that suit them the best. Thus, the future telecommunications revolution waits for younger age-period cohort groups to become decision makers with substantial disposable income to buy one or more of the new services just coming onto the market.

Environmental Scan: Future Watch

Many competitive possibilities are simply unknown, some present imperfect information, and only a few offer assurance about the future. Governments alone (or together with telco executives) find it difficult to predict the future. Moreover, to get from telephones to telecommunications, then to telecomputers, and now to multimedia, requires major revisions in the way marketers conduct their future watch. Here's how firms predict the future.

Employing Teamwork

Modern management employs teams to gather data, compare alternatives, and make decisions. These teams of engineers, technicians, factory supervisors, marketers, and finance personnel (sometimes together with outside suppliers and customers) assemble the details and turn them into alternative action plans about the future direction of an industry. This is a crucial process in understanding what is going on in telecommunications.

Exploiting ambiguities. At first, multimedia (as either an extension of or a new business separate from telecommunications) forces negotiation between marketing and other executives about the former's ambiguous, sometimes conflicting roles within teams. "Role ambiguity is . . . the discrepancy between the information available to the persons and that which is required for adequate performance of the role."[1] These marketing executives want to be boundary spanners, or team members who cross from telecommunications to computers, and to provide innovative solutions to the nonroutine problems of the multimedia business.[2]

Spanning boundaries. Role ambiguity is not necessarily dysfunctional. Boundaries are crossed between technology, marketing, and finance, or between boss and subordinate, and marketers play different, multidimensional roles within teams.[3] For example, even though the chief executive officer or boss makes the final decision, Robert Allen's role within the telecommunications, data management, and multimedia teams at AT&T is to collaborate with and take responsibility for the performance of the firm's teams.[4] If something goes wrong, as it did when European state-owned telcos refused to join World Source, Allen must step in and force the teams to rethink AT&T's strategy in Europe.

Creating "juice" teams. Teams at AT&T are known as "juice" teams. Executives pump themselves up with heavier commitments to share marketing intelligence.[5] They use "soft" information to implement strategies, redefine market segments, and plan for the future. These are "collective work-products," that is, the joint contributions of all members of the team.[6] Here are examples.

Carrying Out 4Ps Analysis

With a better understanding of market risk, AT&T teams promote the worldwide web of wired landlines, computers, optical fiber, and software as the firm's basic core business. Governments want installed capacity or what is known in the United States as universal access, but governments want the telcos to pay for laying digital wires without subsidy from the ministry of post, telephone, and telegraph. These competing goals bedevil the process of decision making under uncertainty. Nevertheless, global marketers must make marketing decisions regarding the following issues.

Product positioning. Provide universal global outsourcing for voice, data, and graphics transmissions. Transform the public switch network into a private system, with lower costs passed on to the largest business customers. These are the goals of AT&T.

Price segmentation. Price each service separately to determine whether a competing telecom firm is offering a better deal. Offer bundled pricing (see chapter 12) for interactive connectivity–that is, one telephone line to bring the world to homes and offices and to respond to the world's questions through the Internet. These too are the goals of AT&T.

Industry analysis. Can AT&T (or BT/MCI or Sprint) put the largest business firms on specialized urban loops while retaining the public network for smaller and medium-sized firms and for individual consumers? Can AT&T enhance its tailored private corporate networks through strategic alliances with Asian telcos? Can AT&T (or other telcos) put in place "virtual" networks based on wireless cellular and mobile radio transmissions as the cheapest way of linking offices together in Third World countries?

Initial Analysis of Marketing Opportunities

Here are several crucial marketing decisions facing landline telephone firms and their wireless competitors. These choices are made regarding the long-term planning horizon provided by national governments worldwide. They are as follows:

- *Learning curve:* get out in front of business customers, and create first-mover advantage

- *Positioning:* position all new telecom products and services in terms of values important to customers

- *Market segmentation:* offer expanded use of wireless, mobile radio, and computer services to all potential market segments

- *Tailoring:* feed all products and services at different rates into the global telecom outsourcing network

- *4Ps:* choose carefully from a wide range of product, place, promotion, and price strategies to gain scale economies quickly, because several new technologies will come and go before both business and consumers make their long-term choice

- *Marketing strategy:* grow the business worldwide under deregulation, privatization, and state-owned telecommunications

If the current group of wired and wireless telecom companies cannot compete effectively in the changing telecommunications industry, then more competitors from the direct satellite and computer industries are waiting in the wings. We will discuss this topic in more detail in chapter 8.

Comparing Technological Choices

Let's look at the current technological choices available to marketers when they do their *positioning* analysis. First, Cellular One from McCaw Cellular Communications, together with its parent, AT&T, packages cellular and long-distance services together for ease of use by business and household customers in North America. Second, the pan-European GSM (Global System for Mobile communications) digital standard has rolled out in more than 18 European countries; the GSM service is built around the Smart Card, which means customers don't have to own a cellular or wireless telephone. All the billing instructions are in the Smart Card; this feature makes it very different from Cellular One.

Both cellular wireless services are different from two-way digital-based specialized mobile radio technology. The latter could make an end run around existing American cellular services and give the United States a seamless national digital SMR cellular network that bypasses the Baby Bells.

Positioning Within the EU and in Mexico

The problem of setting up mobile radio communications is more complicated in Europe. In 1994, four different digital radio systems were in place. AT&T/NCR uses one part of the radio spectrum for its cordless telephones, and Olivetti uses another part, the ISM portion of the radio spectrum. The EU still needs to develop a single frequency and a single standard for radio-based local area networks (LANs). Until then, European mobile radio communications will be a Cinderella story rather than a mainstream competitor for GSM digital cellular service.

Within Mexico, Grupo Iusacell has formed an alliance with Bell Atlantic, an American Baby Bell, to gain market share in the local wireless telephone markets of Mexico City and central Mexico. The partners will get themselves ready to compete in the long-distance market against Telmex when the latter's monopoly ends in 1996. Grupo Pulsar also took a 15-percent stake in Ionica, a British fixed wireless telco that uses a digital-radio frequency to ship video and other types of electronic information.[7] The competition between cellular and radio wireless service is now in Mexico.

Moreover, MCI put together a nonroutine partnership with Grupo Financiero Banamex Accival (or Banacci) to build a long-distance network within Mexico.[8] It will be operational in 1996 when Telmex's monopoly ends. And Nextel forged another nonroutine partnership with Corporación Mobilcom to build a network of cellular telephones, message paging, and two-way radio services.[9] Mobilcom already owns radio frequency licenses for about 75 percent of the Mexican population.

Put all of these deals together. It looks as if SMR services are going to be a major competitor of analog and digital cellular services throughout North America. Establishing partnerships is one way that newer telcos are getting ahead of their business customers and their telephone competitors.

Asking Research Questions

It seems American telcos are failing to answer several basic marketing questions.

Who uses the product? Right now, younger age-period cohort groups who became adults in the last two decades and who are accomplished business executives use analog cellular phones. Americans put up with roaming problems because the alternative GSM system is not available in North America. Americans might buy the cheaper mobile radio system when it becomes widely available in the mid-1990s. Older age-period cohort groups will not join the rush to analog cellular service because the technology is not as easy to use as is GSM and seems to be more expensive than the forthcoming SMR system.

How to increase market share? Cellular One doesn't have sales opportunities in Europe and East Asia. Moreover, most emerging countries will leapfrog over the vintage cellular technologies; they will either invest in GSM or go directly into interactive radio paging and direct satellite services. Most US cellular investments in both North America and overseas will go through many years of creative destruction before a few telecom or radio paging firms become winners.

How to provide value? Cellular customers throughout the world want interference-free telephone communications. This is how they define quality, and business customers will pay higher prices for quality. For cellular telephones and many other computer communications devices, the time effect of product diffusion is the single most important criterion in deciding what to buy and when to put it in use. Future-oriented marketers already see analog cellular fading, GSM gaining, and radio and satellite transmissions exploding. This is their marketing forecast.

What customer signals show changes in local markets? Cellular customers in the emerging countries want these services even sooner than do their counterparts in the developed countries. Customers in emerging countries lack installed capacity; this fact alone pushes cellular customers in Asia, Latin America, and elsewhere in the world to purchase cellular telephones at very high prices. This should spur telecom providers to speed up the product-development life cycle for less expensive, better performing alternative telecom products.

Knowing the Rate of Product Diffusion

The impact of optical fiber cables, digital telephone and cable TV lines, radio paging and satellite transmissions, interactive computers with video servers, and wireless-based software on cellular telephone service is simply unknown. Business customers want the delivery of electronic (or e-) mail, team collaboration, information gathering, direct marketing, and advertising on two-way communications systems. Consumers with PCs in the home will want their computers to be telephone and TV switches, too. On this, consumers in Mexico, the United States, the EU, Japan, China, and East Asia all agree – the future for cellular telephone service is unknown, but the existing technology within the United States is a few years away from extinction. Trend is definitely not destiny.

Clues to Capturing Consumers

Let's repeat what we know. Governments everywhere are deregulating and privatizing telecommunications, and they are pushing national PTOs (or post telephone organizations) into networks of global alliances. Telecommunications, computers, and video are converging to create a single multimedia industry. AT&T wants to provide the equipment, the know-how to link it up, and the communications network through which to transmit the traffic. This is probably not enough because customers want networked information, communications connectivity, and worldwide interactivity. Either AT&T, BT/MCI, the Baby Bells, McCaw Cellular, the cable-TV companies, Nextel, and the computer firms will provide transparent solutions to the difficult communications problems of their customers, or pieces of these companies will be picked off by a collection of smaller, smarter, more nimble niche firms. Consumers want solutions to their interactive communications problems.

Summary: Scanning the Future

Marketers know that government policies of deregulation, privatization, and liberalization mean the end of the existing wired (or landlines) telephone business. In some markets, wired networks could be replaced by wireless networks. Moreover, teams of marketing executives are asking questions about the future. Will digital cellular transmissions, specialized mobile radio, or satellite transmissions dominate the wireless market? What role will computer communications firms play in the conversion of wireless data systems to hand-held personal communications systems? What's the future role of wired telephones? This is the decision-making environment that telecommunications firms face.

The Firm-Specific Assignment

Marketers manage final demand by positioning global products within government-sponsored, market-oriented reforms of the telecommunications industry; see Exhibit 7-6. Marketing executives succeed when they are finely attuned to how governments oversee the market. Global marketers prosper when they bring together political strategies for reinventing industries, estimates of market risk, and decisions about planning horizons.

Paying Attention to Planning Horizons

Given the political, technological, and cultural realities surrounding the information revolution, marketing executives equate lowest market risk with the longest planning horizon and higher market risk with shorter times to recoup investments. Here are three scenarios that all global marketers face in the telecommunications industry.

Deregulation Delivers Lowest Market Risk The deregulation of privately owned firms delivers the lowest market risk. The political arguments are over who can provide local and long-distance service, how much it will cost the public to merge wired and wireless firms, and whether foreign

Exhibit 7-6.
Firm-Specific Analysis: Telecommunications
The Competitive Scan

Traditional Frame Analysis for Global Marketing

Market Risk Analysis and Planning Horizons
Deregulation delivers lowest market risk
Privatization without competition dispenses higher market risk
State-owned PTOs dole out the highest market risk

Firm-Specific 4Ps Analysis and Positioning Strategies
Positioning in a mature market through promotion and price
Positioning through value-added product extensions
Positioning by competing as a global outsourcer

National Marketing Decisions and Marketing Research
Exploit changing industry
Employ unstructured marketing decisions
Accept incomplete information
Realize experience helps weigh relevant information
Accept usefulness of "soft" information
Remember market is immature

Nontraditional Frame Analysis for Global Marketing

Marketing Management Frame and Industry Analysis
Stable Industries
Experience helps managers make routine decisions
Managers avoid role ambiguity
Managers refuse to span boundaries

Changing Industries
New information forces managers to use nonroutine processes
Managers practice role ambiguity
Managers accept boundary spanning as part of teamwork

Marketing Management Frame and Teamwork
Create "juice" teams
Accept foreign partners as members
Focus on real skills for foreign investments
Change corporate culture
Promote connectivity

firms with different cellular, radio paging, and satellite transmission technologies may compete in the national market. The task for government (especially the US government) is to create a "level playing field" so that returns from managerial wisdom are market driven.

Privatization Dispenses Higher Market Risk Privatization of state-owned firms dispenses higher market risk at first because governments set conditions on the sale (e.g., maintain jobs) and grant privatized firms monopoly powers for a few years. Once partnerships between local and foreign telecom firms compete against former monopolies, governments dictate less and regulate more through licensing, taxation, and other ways of governing the market. These activities lower market risk, increase sales, and raise returns on equity.

State-Owned PTOs Dole out Highest Market Risk State-owned post telephone organizations dole out the highest market risk. These government ministries want to control the existing cash flow from telecommunications services by charging the highest prices per transmission rather than make their money by lowering prices and widening the total market for telecom services. Both customers (who buy secret satellite receivers) and foreign firms (who transmit through wireless devices) learn how to bypass PTOs. Authoritarian governments jail citizens, seize equipment, and dismiss foreigners while democratic governments cut deals to limit programming from the global, largely American entertainment culture. Over time, government PTOs become wasting assets as politics, technology, and culture stress freer trade with the world.

Employing Industry Analysis

"What is the real interplay between managers' experience and their decision making?"[10] Is experience within the telephone industry appropriate for making decisions about the telephone, telecommunications, computer telecommunications, and multimedia industries?

Here's what we know. Within *stable industries* experience helps managers use routine decision-making procedures to buy and sell, enter into joint ventures, and plan for the future.[11] No role ambiguity exists here.

Within *changing industries* all kinds of new information helps experienced managers use nonroutine decision-making processes to make *conservative* (more orthodox, moderate, or restrained) judgments about the future.[12] All managers face role ambiguity, and experienced managers know how to span boundaries within the firm.

Deregulation, privatization, technological change, and customer demand tell us that the telecommunications industry is changing rapidly. Within the industry unstructured marketing decisions include recommending a cellular and wireless strategy, novel product decisions about linking computers to microelectronics and both to global telecommunications networks, and choices about multimedia's future. All of them involve incomplete information. Thus, experience is crucial to weighing relevant information and making nonroutine (unprogrammed) decisions as regulated monopolies give way to global competition.

Deepening Teamwork

AT&T's "juice" teams train associates to value more sources of practical, real-world marketing intelligence and to include "soft" information in the environmental, competitive, and marketing scans.[13] Do the AT&T teams make good decisions? Are these judgments optimal within AT&T's market segments? Can we learn from AT&T's choices about product positioning? Is it possible to capture AT&T's marketing expertise and use it to turn novices into experienced managers? Let's look to the competitive scan for answers.

Competitive Scan: Interactive Connectivity

Today, AT&T is an aggressive and innovative competitor with aggressive marketing and cut-rate prices for loyal customers. It continues to build on its collective team approach to managerial decision making. This change in corporate culture is reinforced continually by hiring executives from outside the telephone industry who bring new ideas for increasing AT&T's profit. AT&T's goal is to improve interactive connectivity for all.

Positioning in a Mature Market

For example, in the long-distance market, every market share point means about a half-billion dollars gained or lost.[14] In 1991, AT&T had a 62-percent share, MCI a 15-percent share, and Sprint a 14-percent share. By 1993, the long-distance market in the United States again was mature. Once more, the product was a commodity that forced all long-distance operations to cut prices. Notwithstanding Sprint's third-place showing, both AT&T and MCI spent millions on advertising to win the battle for market share. Moreover, outside executives new to AT&T repositioned long distance in an enhanced core network for business firms.

Positioning Through Product Extension

As the forces of competition changed, global alliances became crucial to success in long-distance (and international) lines. AT&T entered into high-profile long-distance (and international) partnerships. Through its alliance, World Source, AT&T linked up with Kokusai Denshin Denwa (Japan's international carrier), Singapore Telecom, Canada's Unitel Communications Inc., and carriers in Australia and South Korea. AT&T launched its World Source service first in the Asia-Pacific region because the region has the world's fastest growing telecom sector.

Positioning to Become Global Outsourcers

MCI was not far behind. In 1993 MCI sold 20 percent of its shares to British Telecommunications (BT), a recently privatized national telephone company from the United Kingdom.15 BT asked the FCC for permission to link US customers on the public fixed network with the UK–something only US carriers are permitted to do. AT&T asked British regulators for the same rights.

This was just the beginning of an immature market growing, prospering, seeking new ways to become mature. Moreover, the market was not simply long-distance lines within the United States. The market was international long distance. AT&T and its World Source competed against the BT/MCI joint venture. MCI marketed phone service to multinationals in North and South America and the Caribbean, and BT did the same throughout the rest of the world.

Making Decisions Under Uncertainty

The race was on to become the "global outsourcer" for the telecommunication needs of the world's multinational firms. Here are the strategies of the telecom competitors.

AT&T did not want to do these telecommunications deals alone; it prefers foreign nonequity partners for its global alliances. If the latter want to buy into AT&T's collective team approach for decision making, that's okay. However, foreign partners are not required to participate in "juice" teams, role ambiguity, and boundary spanning.

On the other hand, BT planned to go down the road with its one American equity partner, MCI. The managerial problem was their two different corporate cultures. "MCI is scrappy and entrepreneurial, while stodgy BT still has some characteristics of the British postal system from which it is descended."[16] Neither partner seemed willing to create a set of collective teams to make better unstructured marketing decisions; without these joint corporate teams, little bonding occurred among top, middle, and lower management.

And Sprint . . . probably is an also-ran, that is, unless Sprint makes its deal with Deutsche Telekom, France Telecom, and other European PTOs work.

Estimates of Market Potential

During the last 10 years, the Baby Bells did what they do best. They ran deregulated and privatized wired telephone companies for foreign governments (e.g., New Zealand's) interested in getting out of the telecommunications business. However, "they have had mixed results where they are least experienced: operating cable TV franchises . . . [and] the votes are still being counted on a third type of venture, the risky business of building cellular phone systems in developing countries that for years have neglected their basic phone networks."[17] Today, these overseas investments continue to consume cash rather than put dividends in the hands of American shareholders.

Unfortunately, the Baby Bells are "old companies in a new age . . . [These] ponderous monopolies don't work in an era of new technology, high-speed management, and adroitness."[18] They are looking for a vision, a new corporate culture, a new approach to managerial decision making.

Will the seven Baby Bells (Ameritech, Bell Atlantic, Bell South, Nynex, Pacific Telesis, Southwestern Bell, and US West) find ways to offer value-added services similar to AT&T's? All the Baby Bells need "juice" teams, executives who play ambiguous roles, associates who span boundaries, groups that make unstructured marketing decisions, and a corporate culture for collective managerial decision making. All the Baby Bells need better managerial decision making in an era of governing the market through privatization and subsequent deregulation.

Similar Market Segments Worldwide

Although the telecom markets are alive and well wherever accomplished consumers live, it is premature to think of a global telecommunications industry. The deregulation concerns of the United States are different from the privatization efforts of Mexico. The preference for private-sector decision making is frowned on in many countries throughout Asia, Africa, and Latin America. Time has not changed the way some governments oversee the market. Instead, they seek to have the best of both worlds—modern forms of connectivity for their citizens without giving up control over cash flow and culture to outside, foreign interests. All the telecom firms will cooperate with government because traditional managers prefer known risks over uncertainty, ambiguity, and watching the future. Nevertheless, the future belongs to those who span boundaries of technology and marketing to compete in the new (and not yet formed) telecommunications industry of the 21st century.

Summary: Scanning Interactive Connectivity

Marketers are pushing technological and service changes into global markets with an imperfect understanding of the preferences of business customers, who want interactive links with their voice and data transmissions connected worldwide. Successful marketing executives position AT&T to dominate the global outsourcing business through wired and wireless connections within the United States and Canada, and through World Source in East Asia. Teams of marketers at MCI, the Baby Bells, and other telcos look for ways to position services in mature markets, by product-line extensions, and to become global outsourcers.

National Marketing Decisions

Marketers manage final demand by signaling detailed national information about telecommunications connectivity (i.e., telephone or cable TV lines and equipment, local and outsourcing services, and business and multimedia applications); see Exhibit 7–7. Marketing executives also expand final demand by convincing younger, newly affluent business executives and then other age-period cohort groups to expand their use of interactive telecom connections. Many telecom marketers go into partnerships with other firms to improve interactive connectivity. These are important developments in marketing telecommunications throughout the world.[19]

Exhibit 7-7.
National Marketing Decisions: Telecommunications
The Marketing Scan

Traditional Frame Analysis for Global Marketing

Firm-Specific 4Ps Analysis and Decision Making Under Uncertainty

Signal national wired landlines information

Gain from initial wireless cellular market entry

Succeed from expansion of wireless GSM technology

Grow through radio frequencies rationalization

Pay attention to alternative telecommunications lifestyles

National Marketing Decisions and Marketing Research

Scanning Potential Markets

Target markets

Product offerings

Market segments

Marketing Changes

Avoid "humbling" feedback

Compare existing and new products with focal option

Disaggregate the product-development life cycle

Forget trends

Pass the vision test

National Marketing Decisions and Marketing Forecasts

Continuing trend is unrealistic in emerging markets

Amplifying trend requires role ambiguity and boundary spanners

Doubling trend is unrealistic in mature markets

Nontraditional Frame Analysis for Global Marketing

Marketing Management Frame and Relationship Marketing

Teamwork Through Nonroutine Partnerships

Open new markets

Gain new skills

Share fixed costs

Commit to a long-term economic relationship

Stress the quality of the relationship as the crucial asset

Teamwork Through a Learning Organization

Employ role ambiguity

Span boundaries

Make unstructured marketing decisions

Promote trust and cooperation

Act on good "soft" information

Understanding Relationship Marketing

Clearly, cross-border alliances, joint ventures, and partnerships are the up-and-coming way business leaders in the telecommunications industry choose to participate in the global marketplace. Partners go into alliances to *open new markets, gain new skills,* and *share fixed costs.*[20] Their bargaining over rights and responsibilities (in research and development, wired and wireless service, analog or digital equipment, long-distance and local connections) commits the participating telecoms to a long-term economic relationship in which all partners deal with the competitive changes in the industry world-wide.[21] The crucial asset is the *quality of the partner relationship.*

Employees take their cue from the *corporate culture* of the firm, and from the commitment of the CEO and top management to the vision of the firm's future.[22] If the CEO fails to convey that *role ambiguity is not detrimental* to their careers, then executives fail to identify the role ambiguities they face within the team.[23] If the CEO provides strong leadership for *organizational learning,* then employees use the positive aspects of role ambiguity to *span boundaries* within the firm and in its many alliances.[24]

To *embed inter-firm cooperation* within firms requires collective leadership from teams at the top – and role ambiguity for all levels of management. A positive attitude about spanning boundaries within firms and through alliances is crucial to winning the technological battle over the convergence of computers and telephones into multimedia business. When "juice" teams make *unstructured marketing decisions* their alliances end up differently from how they began. Marketing teamwork energizes the dynamic properties of alliances and partnerships within the telecommunications industry.

Marketing Scan: Nonroutine Partnerships

Teamwork among partners requires trust and cooperation because telecommunications firms share technology, manufacturing process, sales and marketing information, and other proprietary knowledge.[25] AT&T believes McCaw Cellular provides the competitive means to bypass the Baby Bells in connecting long-distance service to local customers. The seven Regional Bell Operating Companies (RBOCs) know they must work together or they will lose market share to AT&T, other telcos, and foreign-based, mostly European telecoms. BT recognizes its global network only can compete with AT&T

only when MCI's long-distance service is directly connected to international service based in the United Kingdom.

Moreover, by the mid-1990s, telecom marketers can make more informed judgments about partners before entering alliances. Some Baby Bells (such as Southwestern Bell, Bell South, and Bell Atlantic) do indeed use teamwork to fashion themselves into new AT&Ts. These deals include customer focus, trust, cooperation, and a common quest for market share, cash flow, and profits.

Now that telecom executives know which Baby Bells are highly successful performers and which are not good achievers in global markets, experienced managers from AT&T and BT/MCI collect information about potential partnerships only from the successful group.[26] These decision makers have a high probability of acting on good information from highly successful telcos, and a low probability of using good information from less successful Baby Bells. This is how top-flight executives in the telecom industry make decisions.

Scanning for Target Markets

Telecommunications firms need vision about their common futures. Those that remain tied to wired (or landline) connections, such as the regulated RBOCs and the state-owned telecoms in Europe, are not subject to market disciplines within the traditional telephone business. Their target market must be the wireless and cellular business unregulated by government rules on rate-of-return pricing. Most important: The Baby Bells must develop their expertise quickly so they can transfer it from North America to Europe before local competitors (such as Vodafone in the United Kingdom) acquire unassailable scale economies.

Scanning for Product Offerings

Telecommunications firms need to carry out expeditionary marketing.[27] Those cellular services that don't provide the Smart Card for international roaming and customer billing, such as McCaw in the United States, will find their technology obsolete long before it wears out. Their product offerings must match new digital GSM technology with the expectations of potential customers about product characteristics and a planned selling price. Most important: AT&T and the Baby Bells must tie wireless and cellular into a full range of global network services before European telecoms transfer their expertise to the United States and Canada. Mobile radio or SMR technology is, perhaps, the way to compete in both North America and Europe.

Scanning for Market Segments

Telecom firms must turn their informal business associations into formal working groups, and these into networks of strategic alliances. Those outsourcers (Deutsche Telekom, France Telecom, and other European telecoms) that don't link up with AT&T's World Source, the BT/MCI joint venture, and opportunities presented by the Regional Bell Operating Companies will find themselves outside looking in. Most important: Global outsourcing for multinational firms is the crucial value-added service for which a premium price can be charged by telecommunications firms.

Reducing "Humbling" Feedback

Clearly, when marketers study telecommunications they must consider new information provided by nonroutine partnerships. All these nonequity joint ventures cross the cooperative membrane of participating firms. The alliances bind partners together across continents. Even though the details of the partnerships change, the totality of the alliance relationship is stable. The quality of the teamwork also becomes an asset of great value to all partners. Successful partners from among the seven Baby Bells are jewels of incalculable worth. Moreover, through role ambiguity, boundary spanning, and unstructured marketing decisions the partners promote a cooperative (not an adversarial) competitive strategy for the industry. Thus, the focus of the marketing scan must be on how nonroutine partnerships help us search for all possible target markets, product offerings, and market segments. This is what interactive connectivity means to marketers.

Strategies for Increasing Marketing Effectiveness

Partnership information about country risk, technology, and cultural change helps managers better understand the telecom market. The task of top management is to embed its marketing teamwork skills into alliances. AT&T does this very well. Some of the Baby Bells and now BT/MCI are showing their competitive strength by learning how to be effective team players, too. Organizational learning is a shared responsibility within firms, among alliance partners, and by governments.

Employing the Focal Option

The focal option, in particular, plays an important role in positioning telecom offerings throughout the world. Our accomplished customers in

Europe and East Asia compare new telecom products and multimedia applications from American-owned telcos with existing products in the European Union, eastern Europe, Japan, China, and southeast Asia. Paired comparisons show that new cellular offerings from the United States are less useful than the existing Smart Card-based GSM technology within Europe. Most East Asians are choosing wireless technology based on GSM because it mirrors their collective quest for change within conformity. Right now, the diffusion model for the product-development life cycle of wireless telecom equipment favors GSM.

Forgetting Trends

Although Americans with disposable personal income are purchasing more cellular telephones, many of the better informed are aware of other ways to go wireless in the future. These choices are also a part of the worldwide information revolution.

Technological Choices 1995 begins the fierce technological competition in which new wireless telephone and data services plan to serve people on the go. Traditional cellular services – today's fashion – have about 16 million customers. If the diffusion model for traditional cellular services continues to deepen its hold on business executives, these competing cellular partnerships will gather speed and create a bandwagon effect throughout the United States, Canada, and Mexico.

An alternative technology exists – specialized mobile radio carriers. Nextel Communications (with Motorola) uses new digital technology to transform radio frequencies reserved for taxi and truck dispatching services into wireless telephone and data networks. Nextel has licenses that cover 180 million Americans, about two-thirds of the United States.

Firm-Specific 4Ps Analysis Moreover, new radio frequencies are being opened by the US Federal Communications Commission. They offer twice as much capacity as do traditional cellular services. The bidders for these radio frequencies are AT&T (and McCaw), the regional Baby Bells, Nextel (and Motorola), and others. Their long-term goal is to use interactive wireless radio connections as the low-cost alternative to traditional, high-cost wireless cellular connections. In this way, two-budget conscious groups in the United States – the younger age-period cohort groups who are just beginning to form families and the much older-period peer groups who are retired – plus Mexicans, Chinese, and others whose disposable income is lower can participate in the wireless information revolution.

Governing the Market The United States is deregulating wireless communications by creating a "level playing field" in licensing radio frequencies. Other countries may choose to follow this approach to governing the telecom market. Or, their state-owned PTOs may seek to keep control of cash flow from traditional wired and cellular services. It's too soon to know how China will decide the issue, but Mexico has decided to follow the United States and open up its radio frequencies.

Teamwork Through Nonroutine Partnerships The connectivity decisions made by AT&T, the Baby Bells, BT/MCI, Nextel, and others show the ability of marketers to enter into nonroutine partnerships and go forward spanning the boundaries of technological diffusion, cultural change, and the information revolution. The past is not helpful; the trends are misleading. This is the time and place in which marketers earn their reputation as brilliant, far-sighted executives.

Passing the Marketing Vision Test

With the coming convergence of computers and telephones to make digital wireless service a universal reality, any bias against computer-based communications is an unwise structured marketing decision. Such decisions fly in the face of the public's demand for interactive connectivity. Teams must be set up so that boundary spanners can play the key role in discussing the use of new technology within an unplanned future. If the talent is not available in-house, then telcos must go outside and form alliances to help both partners make better decisions about the future of the telecommunications industry.

Marketing Implementation

Telecommunications is in transition from its present to its future. For many decades, wired landline telephones have served local consumers as their primary form of interactive connections with the outside world. The performance of these traditional telephones is known.

On the other hand, wireless cellular telephones, computer-based interactivity, and multimedia applications are new for most consumers. Although time-pressured business executives use wireless telephones and younger computer-literate experts link themselves around the world electronically, the performance of these new telephones is unknown to most people.

If competing wired telephones rate a good past performance, then they are the focus of comparison (or focal option) for wireless telephones. Right now, the price of wireless service is too high compared to traditional wired telephone service. Thus providers of wired and wireless telecom services are looking at radio frequencies as a way to offer a lower-priced alternative in the telecom market. Their success means wireless telecommunications moves closer to universal service.

Three forecasts. The "continuing trend" forecast is the easiest to make because things go on as before. The wired telephone conforms to traditional lifestyles in Europe, the United States, and Japan. All three have high levels of installed capacity. More people will be added to the telecom networks as population grows. Where installed capacity is low (e.g., Mexico and China), the wired telephone does not conform to the global, largely American lifestyle of the future. Most people are looking for alternatives to the wired telephone connection; this is especially true for the younger, upper-income business executives. The "continuing trend" forecast is unrealistic in Mexico and China.

The "amplifying trend" forecast assumes that telco firms aggressively market their wireless equipment, services, and applications (i.e., they push interactive connectivity) and that more younger people purchase these goods with their available disposable income. In the United States, Europe, and Japan, these routine purchases are status symbols, but in Mexico and China these acquisitions are business necessities. This trend will develop because we are at the beginning of a major information revolution, with no end in sight. Only marketers who favor role ambiguity and spanning boundaries will be successful in the changing industry known as telecommunications.

The "doubling trend" forecast assumes that telco firms convert older people to the wireless telecom lifestyle. This is the least likely forecast in the United States, Europe, and Japan. Product diffusion occurs slowly because these three markets have installed capacity. Given the inequality in incomes and the lack of disposable income within Mexico, mainland China, and throughout much of East Asia and Latin America, product diffusion will probably occur slowly among their older age-period cohort groups. This one piece of information should give marketers pause before they casually think the telecommunications market is similar across the world.

Summary: Scanning Nonroutine Partnerships

Even though many customers don't have a clear idea of what they want from the telecommunications industry, marketers believe the wireless telephone, data service, and multimedia businesses are ready to roam the world's stage. Successful marketing executives are finding partners from within and outside the telecommunications industry to develop new products and services for household customers who have high incomes and will be the first to adopt new telecom technologies. Teams of marketers work on spanning boundaries among telephones, cable TVs, and computers. Even with soft information, many telecommunications firms fail to pass the marketing vision test. The most successful teams have the very best partners, that is, those who can develop a marketing strategy for matching technology to customer preferences.

Inclusive Contexts for Global Marketing

Exhibit 7-8 summarizes the inclusive contexts for global marketing in the telecommunications industry. We examine reinventing the industry and its competing firms. We also study two types of decision making under uncertainty: culturally based demand analysis and organizationally based supply analysis. These two focuses help us direct our research to answering important questions, such as who will be our customers and what will they want in the future. Moreover, we deal with technology as a driving force in managerial decision making under uncertainty. We are uncertain about the success of alternative technologies, the price-cost-quality relationships, and what new forms of telecommunications can do for us as customers. Our choices will determine whether we will succeed at global marketing.

Conclusions

Global telecommunications is more than telephones, wired and cellular services, mobile radio, cable TV, telecomputers, and interactive multimedia. It is all of these combined in new ways in which innovative technologies and changing market demand are reshaping firms and reinventing an industry. Global telecommunications is interactive connectivity for all.

Exhibit 7-8.
Inclusive Contexts for Global Marketing

Market Risk

Govern the market through reinvented business environment

Deregulation of industry

Privatization of state-owned firms

Planning horizons and range of market risk

Imperfect information about decisions of competitors

Unknown competitive possibilities among emerging technologies

Political Frame

Firm-Specific 4Ps Analysis (A)

Culturally based decision making under uncertainty

Demand analysis

Who uses the product

How to increase market share

How to provide value

What signals show changes in market

Cultural analysis and age-period cohort analysis

Disconnection among older and younger age-cohort peer groups

Cross-cultural analysis

Value creation and multiplying bits of information

Cultural Frame

Firm-Specific 4Ps Analysis (B)

Organizationally based decision making under uncertainty

Industry analysis

Change corporate culture

Teamwork

Nonroutine partnerships

Learning organization

Product positioning

Competitive destruction of cellular technologies

Product-development life cycle

Time effect of product diffusion

Price segmentation and bundled prices

Marketing Management Frame

Continued on next page

Exhibit 7-8. *Continued from previous page*

National Marketing Decisions
Supply analysis
Scanning potential markets, offerings, segments
Formal and walking-around research
  Interactive connectivity
  Creative destruction to winnow out winners and losers
Information highway as unknown competitive future
Vision test
Remember trend is not destiny
Technological Frame

Let's return to our initial three learning objectives:

1. Discuss the need for predicting the future of telecommunications to carry out successful marketing analysis.

    You should have a clear understanding of how teamwork helps firms prepare for the future and carry out competitive marketing strategies in the telecom industry. You need to develop the habits of role ambiguity and spanning boundaries to be successful in global marketing.

2. Outline how interactive connectivity conveys information about spanning technological, cultural, managerial boundaries.

    You should be able to discuss how deregulation led to the use of "juice" teams at AT&T and what they are deciding about interactive connectivity. You should prepare a list of their successes and failures in telephones, telecommunications, online computers, and multimedia. This list will help you understand the competitive force behind the creative destruction of technologies worldwide. It will help you decide which firms are doing both culturally based and organizationally based decision making under uncertainty. Those that do both are sure examples of higher sales, dominance in all major markets, and continued profitabilty.

3. Explain the impact of nonroutine partnerships on growing share in the wireless cellular and mobile radio market.

    You should be able to offer a partnership rationale for focusing on potential wireless customers. Make some decisions and decide which customers are most likely consumers of wired or cellular connections and of global outsourcing services.

All of these nontraditional and nonroutine managerial assignments are the work of global telecommunications executives.

Notes

1. R. L. Kahn, D. M. Wolfe, R. P. Quinn, and J. D. Snoek, *Organizational Stress: Studies in Role Conflict and Ambiguity*, (New York: John Wiley & Sons, Inc. 1964), 73. Cited in Jagdip Singh and Gary K. Rhoads, "Boundary Role Ambiguity in Marketing-Oriented Positions: A Multidimensional, Multifaceted Operation-alization," *Journal of Marketing Research* 28:3 (August 1991): 329.

2. Kahn et al. Cited in Singh and Rhoads, 329.

3. Singh and Rhoads, 325.

4. Singh and Rhoads, 327.

5. Jon R. Katzenbach and Douglas K. Smith, "The Discipline of Teams," *Harvard Business Review* 71:2 (March–April 1993): 112.

6. Katzenbach and Smith, 113.

7. Craig Torres, "Telex Monopoly to Face Fight from Wealthy Mexican Investor," *The Wall Street Journal*, May 3, 1994, A10.

8. Edmund L. Andrews, "MCI Joins Mexican Phone Venture," *The New York Times*, January 26, 1994, C3.

9. Anthony DePalma, "Nextel in $175 Million Deal with Mobilcom of Mexico," *The New York Times*, June 7, 1994, C4.

10. W. Steven Perkins and Ram C. Rao, "The Role of Experience in Information Use and Decision Making by Marketing Managers," *Journal of Marketing Research* 27:1 (February 1990): 1.

11. Dipankar Chakravarti, Andrew A. Mitchell, and Richard S. Staelin, "Judgment Based Decision Models: An Experimental Investigation of the Decision Calculus Approach," *Management Science* 25:3 (1979): 251–63. Cited by Perkins and Rao, 1.

12. Perkins and Rao, 2.

13. Perkins and Rao, 9.

14. Dan Cray, "Hold the Line," *Mediaweek* March 25, 1991, 18.

15. "Who's Afraid of AT&T?" *Business Week*, June 14, 1993, 33.

16 Ibid.

17. Andrew Kupfer, "Ma Bell and Seven Babies Go Global," *Fortune*, November 4, 1991, 118-19.

18. "The Baby Bells' Painful Adolescence," *Business Week*, October 5, 1992, 125.

19. The ideas in this section are drawn from Douglas Lamont, "Strategies for Managing U. S.-Japanese Cross Border Alliances and Joint Ventures" (St. Louis, Missouri: Center for the Study of American Business, Working Paper 148, August 1992) 1-2.

20. Joel Bleeke and David Ernest, "The Way to Win in Cross-Border Alliances," *Harvard Business Review* 69:6 (November-December 1991): 127.

21. Bruce Kogut, "The Stability of Joint Ventures: Reciprocity and Competitive Rivalry," *The Journal of Industrial Economics* 38:2 (December 1989): 183-98.

22. Singh and Rhoads, 331.

23. Ibid., 332-33.

24. Ibid., 334-35.

25. Ideas in this section come from Lamont, 3-10.

26. Perkins and Rao, 9.

27. Gary Hamel and C. K. Prahalad, "Corporate Imagination and Expeditionary Marketing," *Harvard Business Review* 69:4 (July-August 1991): 81-92.

Chapter Format

Learning Objectives

After reading this chapter, you should be able to:

- Discuss the importance of industrial organization to competitive marketing strategy

- Outline the marketing mix, four product market segments, and positioning strategies in the telecom services industry

- Explain the usefulness of telecom alliances to build up market share in the interactive wireless services industry

Marketing Strategy

chapter 8

Introduction

Marketers manage final demand by positioning global products, services, and brands. In this chapter, we look at the telecom services industry. Here we stress changing market risk and its impact on reinventing industries and competing firms. We also describe the process by which companies do their firm-specific 4Ps analysis, and we detail several segmentation strategies now in vogue within the industry. Moreover, we show how joining industrial organization and marketing helps us develop a comprehensive marketing strategy.

Let's reinforce the new ground we broke in chapter 7. In this chapter, let's reinvent another industry (telecom services) and several telecom firms (BT/MCI and Time Warner). Let's work through our firm-specific 4Ps analysis to be sure we understand all the nuances of decision making under uncertainty.

Scanning Global Markets

Environmental scan: future business. Marketers find four market segments among consumers of telecommunications products and services within the United States, Europe, and Japan. Successful marketing

259

executives use data about household income, consumer demand, technological sophistication, and industry analysis to make good decisions under
uncertainty. Teams of successful technology-oriented managers compare
alternative ways to position new telecom services to a wide range of cross-
border buyers and sellers. With economic uncertainty and limited information, many choose alliances and joint ventures to gain access to markets
undergoing government-directed liberalization, deregulation, and privatization. This is the environment facing the telecom services industry.

Competitive scan: interactive wireless services. Marketers learn what consumers want before providing them with wired or wireless telecom services.
Successful marketing executives from three Baby Bells (Ameritech,
Southwestern Bell, US West) position cable TV (with concurrent telephone
service) in the United Kingdom to compete against British Telecommunications. Effective marketers from Star TV position direct broadcasting satellite TV throughout Asia to compete against local television services.
Teams of successful technology-oriented managers compare alternative ways
to position new wireless telephone, television, and computer telecom services to a wide range of English-, Spanish-, and Chinese-speaking buyers and
sellers. With "soft" information about future consumer demand, many suppliers of telecom services choose *nonroutine partnerships* to gain access to
technology and markets. The most successful teams choose the very best
partners, those who can match technology to business change.

Marketing scan: telecom alliances. Marketers select partners with skills in
cellular, cable TV, direct satellite, and personal communications services.
Successful marketing executives bridge the connections between technology and business change through cross-border comarketing alliances. Teams
of successful technology-oriented managers compare alternative ways to
position new wireless telephone, television, and computer telecom services
to the high-income, first-adopters market segment. With "weak" information
about future consumer use, many suppliers of telecom services choose
comarketing alliances to gain control over new products markets. The most
successful partnerships develop a marketing strategy for matching technology to business change.

Traditional Contexts for Global Marketing

Exhibit 8–1 lists the traditional contexts for global marketing in the case of
the telecom services industry. We will study a reinvented business

Exhibit 8-1.
Traditional Contexts for Global Marketing

Market Risk

Govern the market through reinvented business environment

> Deregulation or reinventing telecommunications industry

> Privatization or reinventing telecom firms (telcos)

Foreign investment, joint ventures, nonroutine partnerships

Unknown competitive possibilities and imperfect information

Firm-Specific 4Ps Analysis

Decision making under uncertainty

> Reinvented industries and competing firms

> Unstructured marketing decisions

> Incomplete "soft" information

Demand analysis, cultural analysis, age-period cohort analysis

Positioning strategies Product: preference for different technologies

> Place: support for logistics EDI systems

> Promotion: who are key decision makers

> Price: value of final goods to users

Value creation

> Multiply uses of information

> Permit freedom of entry through substitute products

> Change industry structure and increase power of competitors

> Expose revenues to competition

National Marketing Decisions

Supply analysis

Scanning potential markets, offerings, segments

Formal and walking-around research

Segmentation strategies

> Older, traditional, price-conscious users

> Middle-aged, recent converts to data services

> Younger, online computer jockeys

> Upscale, high-income multimedia sophisticates

Continued on next page

Exhibit 8-1. *Continued from previous page*

Marketing strategy

Which activities, and where?

Which products, and for whom?

Who are our customers, and do they exist across borders?

What is our added value?

Can we do better than our competitors?

Do we have a competitive marketing strategy for ourselves?

Do we have a competitive marketing strategy for our partners?

Should we find better competitors?

What is the makeup of our industry?

Are the competitive forces changing in our favor?

Is the overseas environment conducive to our products?

Vision test

Remember trend is not destiny

environment, value creation, and marketing strategy. The first reinforces our observation about the changes occurring in the telecom services industry. The second reminds us that telecom service firms must create value through use of the information on their networks. The third readies us for the hard task of preparing and implementing a marketing strategy. The wireless television case is another symbol of how new industries are being created for a future global economy.

Nontraditional Contexts for Global Marketing

Exhibit 8-2 names the nontraditional contexts for global marketing in the telecommunications industry. We survey reinventing an industry and its firms, alternative entry models for new technology, adoption of new market offerings, and improving the effectiveness of nonroutine partnerships. Again, we break new ground because reinventing industries goes hand-in-hand with reinventing telecom service firms. We also focus on alternative entry models that can be used in the creative destruction of older technology at the hands of wireless television and computer-based interactive telecommunications.

Again, as we venture forth onto the new information highway, we do not know who our customers will be or what they will choose as their long-term technologies. However, from our past work on value creation, we do know about unanswered questions and how these must be included in our marketing analysis.

Exhibit 8-2.
Nontraditional Contexts for Global Marketing

Political Frame
Govern the market through reinvented business environment
> Modified Final Judgment (US)
> Telecommunications directive (EU)

Technological Frame
Alternative entry models
> Interactive connectivity
> Information highway as unknown competitive future
Creative destruction to winnow out winners and losers

Cultural Frame
Disconnection among age groups and adoption of new offerings
> Late adopters: ethnocentrists, older persons
> Early adopters: nonethnocentrists, younger people
> Price-quality relationship deemed acceptable to customers
Cross-cultural analysis, similar self-referencing criteria
Value creation and multiplying bits of information

Marketing Management Frame
Managerial decision making under uncertainty
Industry analysis
> New entrants
> Opportunity cost of substitute products
> Micro factors and exposure to world competition
> Macro forces and unexposed revenues of state-owned PTOs
> Bargaining power of buyers and sellers
Segmentation
> Define industry around two product market segments:
> High incomes or market segment #4
> Young adults or market segment #3
Teamwork, nonroutine partnerships, relationship marketing
> Develop clear view of managerial goal line
> Prepare for uncertainty as industry realigns itself
> Embed inter-firm cooperation among partners
> Commit equal resources and management time
> Provide for projects with high payouts
Value creation and learning organization
> Which unanswered questions remain unresolved?
> What will people use?
> What will people pay for?

Finally, we are beginning to realize that only learning organizations survive during periods of reinventing industries and firms. These firms must participate in long-term nonroutine partnerships and insist that their managers work as a team to resolve ambiguities, span boundaries, and change the corporate culture. BT/MCI, Time Warner, and other telecom service firms are all reinventing themselves through the creative destruction of technologies and the establishment of learning organizations. It's not clear which will survive, but that is the meaning of a global industry reinventing itself in the last half of the 1990s; see Exhibit 8-3.

Governing the market. First, let's look at the political frame. Government quickens the pace for economic reforms by making choices about the availability of substitute products, the bargaining power of buyers and sellers, and the costs of doing business. The tempo speeds up as nation-states open

Exhibit 8-3.
Interactive TV Connections

DOWN THE TUBE			
SELECTED INTERACTIVE TV TRIALS			**PROJECTED USERS, 1995**
MAIN COMPANY	**LOCATION**	**START DATE**	
UNITED STATES			
BELL ATLANTIC	NEW JERSEY	1994	7,000
	VIRGINIA	1994	2,000
US WEST	OMAHA	1994	40,000
NYNEX	NEW YORK	1994	800
TIME WARNER	FLORIDA	DEC-94	4,000
TCI	WASHINGTON	1995	2,000
VIACOM	CALIFORNIA	1995	NA
BRITAIN			
BT	COLCHESTER/ IPSWICH	MID 95	2,500
ON LINE MEDIA	CAMBRIDGE	SEP-94	250
GERMANY			
DEUTSCHE TELEKOM	SIX CITIES	1995	6,000
JAPAN			
JAPANESE GOVERNMENT	KYOTO	JUL-94	300
TOKYO CABLE NETWORK	TOKYO	DEC-93	400
HONG KONG			
HONG KONG TELECOM	HONG KONG	LATE 95	NA
AUSTRALIA			
INTERACTIVE TV AUSTRALIA	ADELAIDE	NOV-94	1,500
SOURCES: JUPITER COMMUNICATIONS; FORRESTER RESEARCH; THE ECONOMIST			

Courtesy of The Economist

up domestic markets to global firms. By increasing the number of competitors, government enhances freedom of entry, alters industry structure, and offers marketers new opportunities.

Making decisions under uncertainty. Second, let's study the technological frame. When government sanctions deregulation, privatization, and foreign direct investment, future-oriented marketers identify a range of competitive problems, examine a set of feasible alternatives, and evaluate the effectiveness of marketing decisions. This is *marketing strategy.*

For example, with the breakup of America's national telephone monopoly in the mid-1980s, the seven Regional Bell Operating Companies (or the Baby Bells) were left with local narrowband (or voice) telephone monopolies in their service regions. Within the United States, the rules governing the market were set down by the courts and the Federal Communications Commission. The Baby Bells could not offer local service outside their home region, could not compete in long-distance service, and could not provide cable TV service. For the first 10 years after the breakup, freedom of entry within local and cable TV markets of the United States was restricted by government policy.

Teams of future-oriented marketers began examining several *feasible marketing alternatives* outside the United States. They found competitive opportunities in broadband (or voice, data, pictures, and other multimedia) cable television markets in the United Kingdom. Three Baby Bells (US West, Nynex, and Southwestern Bell) built the largest cable TV networks in the United Kingdom. More importantly, these cable TV systems also carried interactive voice and data telephone transmissions. British Telecommunications (BT) protested competition from American-owned Baby Bells, but Britain's Office of Telecommunications (Oftel) continued to approve new telephone-cable TV competitors for the United Kingdom.

Governing the market in the United States led to a *change in strategy* by telecom marketing executives; both affected how markets are governed in the United Kingdom. If the governments of the United Kingdom and the United States were paying attention, they should have drawn three important conclusions about the future of interactive connectivity:

1.   The convergence of telephone and cable TV brings about *substitute products* in the global telecommunications industry.

2.   Telephone companies as cable TV operators and the latter as telcos change their *bargaining power* within the United Kingdom and the United States.

3.   The *costs of doing business* change as the freedom to enter all market segments of the telecom services industry is confirmed by government, the new industry competitors, and successful marketing executives.

Based on business experience in the United Kingdom, Southwestern Bell, a Texas firm, bought and sold cable TV systems in the Washington, DC area; US West went into a joint venture with Time Warner to manage the latter's cable TV systems outside the Rocky Mountain states. Both strategic initiatives were contested in American courts to determine whether they fit within the telecommunications policy of the United States.

Today, in the United Kingdom and the United States, a new industry is being forged among suppliers of analog and digital, wire and wireless, narrowband and broadband, and voice, data, pictures, and other multimedia connections. It's not the telephone industry of the mid-1980s; it's not the cable TV industry of the late 1980s; and it's not the long-awaited convergence of the two into a new telecommunications industry. Our future watch in chapter 7 suggests wired and wireless interactive connectivity, a computer-based telecommunications industry, in which the United States at least will work on developing a "level playing field" for all competitors.

Success in working together among government and business leads to the following *marketing audit:* decreased country risk, changed industry structure, improved interactive connectivity, and increased telecom sales. When governments decide to open up domestic markets, recently privatized state-owned firms (such as BT) resist these changes at the risk of slowing down their own transformation into market-based firms. This is a lesson for Telmex and other wired telephone companies.

Hunting for consumers.[1] Third, let's examine the cultural frame. Effective marketing strategy leads to creative destruction among winners and losers. Here's how executives go about developing a marketing strategy.

First, marketers ask *what goods and services to produce and in what quantity.* The limited variety of narrowband telephone services to households and the wider variety of broadband telecommunications services to business determine the *scope* of the telecom supplier firm.

All telephone, telecommunications, and telecomputer firms are forming alliances among themselves and with owners of movies, TV situation comedies, educational software, games, bank services, and home shopping. These suppliers of telecom services are trying to determine what quantity of multimedia goods to supply across emerging broadband networks. When these alliances, partnerships, and joint ventures make decisions about the quantity of services to be supplied, we will know the *scale* of the firms within an emerging industry (i.e., the suppliers of telecom services).

Second, marketing executives also ask *what markets to enter, both as seller and buyer*. With good demographic data, telecom suppliers segment customers as follows:

#1. Older, traditional, price-conscious telephone users

#2. Middle-aged, recent converts to voice, fax, and data telecommunications services

#3. Younger, online telecomputer jockeys

#4. Upscale, high-income multimedia sophisticates from the generations who became adults in the 1980s and 1990s

All telecom suppliers want to produce high-value goods and services targeted to segment #4, and products useful at reduced prices to segments #2 and #3. No future exists for high rates of return in producing goods for segment #1. Hence, all telecom suppliers buy technology, equipment, personnel, and alliance partners suitable for segments #2 through #4.

Segmentation, positioning, and tailoring decisions. Finally, let's look closely at the marketing management frame. In chapter 7, you acquired new information about marketing telecommunications products and services:

- AT&T is the prototype customer-driven firm that stakes its future on acquiring wired and wireless telecom services.

- BT/MCI is a nonroutine partnership that bets its teamwork on global outsourcing, long distance, and radio communications.

- GSM is the unique wireless service from Europe; the Baby Bells and others must find ways to accommodate it in the United States.

- Nextel is the prototype specialized mobile radio challenger to the dominant orthodoxy of wired and wireless communications.

By inspecting new marketing facts, we found that AT&T's research, marketing, and alliance strategies are a great success. AT&T enters markets with some information about the product, price, place, and promotion characteristics of its customers. AT&T takes strategic actions based on decisions of customers and other telecom suppliers. Other international competitors view AT&T as a master player in sharing imperfect information among its internal teams and partners. The payoffs to other firms in subsequent decisions depend on AT&T's marketing strategies.

Organizing global marketing experience. The simultaneous existence of these four different contexts forces marketers to research strategies of competitors, to create a firm-specific 4Ps strategy, and to watch for different national signals about help from local governments for locally owned telecom service firms. Let's do two things in this chapter. First, we will discuss the importance of industrial organization to competitive marketing strategy. Then we will apply this analysis to an emerging global industry, the suppliers of worldwide telecom services.

Market Risk Questions

Marketers manage final demand by researching international telecom service markets; see Exhibit 8-4. *Market risk* tells us about how government policies affect the rate at which new technologies reinvent industries and firms. This is our macro business environment.

Understanding the Importance of Culture

The *cultural frame* offers us clues about the resistance to new competitive offerings or the speed with which they will be adopted by customers worldwide. Among ethnocentrists, traditions about socio-cultural conventions get in the way of adopting new products or services. Among older age groups, learned behavior impedes the ability to make changes in lifestyle. Both slow down the creative destruction of existing technologies.

On the other hand, nonethnocentrists and younger age groups are open to change, and they will adopt new technologies as these prove their usefulness within a price-quality relationship that customers deem acceptable. We use *cross-cultural demographic analysis* to find these early adopters, determine their segment size, and sell them products.

Exhibit 8–4.
Market Risk Analysis: Telecom Services
The Environmental Scan

Traditional Frame Analysis for Global Marketing

Market Risk Analysis and Reinvented Business Environment

Reinvent telecom services industry

Reinvent telcom firms (telcos)

Firm-Specific 4Ps Analysis

Product: preference for different technologies

Place: support for logistics EDI systems

Promotion: who are key decision makers?

Price: value of final goods to users

Firm-Specific 4Ps Analysis and Value Added

Multiplying uses of information

Permit freedom of entry

Introduce substitute products through convergence of services

Change bargaining power of competitors

Lower costs of doing business

Alter industry structure

Expose revenues to competition

National Marketing Decisions and Marketing Opportunities

Older, traditional, price-conscious telephone users

Middle-aged, recent converts to data telecom services

Younger, online telecomputer jockeys

Upscale, high-income multimedia sophisticates

Nontraditional Frame Analysis for Global Marketing

Technology Frame and Alternative Entry Models

Telephone switching centers for global outsourcing

Cable TV needs US and UK markets to gain scale economies

Direct broadcast satellite TV

Small satellites for voice, data, paging, and radio services

Rate of product diffusion within affluent young adults segment

Cultural Frame and Rate of Adoption of New Market Offerings

Late adopters: ethnocentrists, older persons

Early adopters: nonethnocentrists, younger people

Price-quality relationship deemed acceptable to customers

Continued on next page

Exhibit 8-4. *Continued from previous page*

Marketing Management Frame and Industrial Organization
Industry analysis
Opportunity cost of substitute products
Micro factors and exposure to world competition
Macro forces and unexposed revenues of state-owned PTOs

Information from the cultural frame is crucial for teams of managers to carry out their *firm-specific 4Ps analysis* successfully. This combination of culturally based information and 4Ps analyses gives us an up-to-date way to focus on demand for new technologies, products, and services, and to make better *managerial decisions under uncertainty*.

Carrying Out Firm-Specific 4Ps Analysis

In chapter 7, we used our cross-cultural analysis to assist firms in doing their *demand analysis* and to help them carry out their *positioning and pricing strategies*. Both lead to *value creation*, first by multiplying bits of information, then by multiplying uses of information. These are the products of the computer-based telecommunications revolution now sweeping the world. All of these topics form a major part of our *firm-specific 4Ps analysis*.

Here is the 4Ps scheme widely used by marketing educators:

- *Product:* What technologies do customers want from telecom products? Will interactive computer-driven communications replace older cellular services among all age-period cohort groups?

- *Place:* Why do customers prefer wired or wireless, cellular, GSM, and SMR mobile radio? Can these technologies be used to support modern EDI systems within national and global industries?

- *Promotion:* Who are the decision makers? Are they the same in each country? Why do they decide to switch to interactive connectivity based on computer communications?

- *Price:* How do customers value telecom services in terms of price and after-market support services? Will they pay for these services through bundled pricing schemes, or must marketers continue charging them for individual transactions?

The 4Ps scheme has utility when it helps marketing executives identify a set of customer-oriented marketing actions with future payoffs. Can marketers identify market segments among consumers of telecommunications products and services within the United States, Europe, and Japan? The environmental scan yields some answers.

Environmental Scan: Future Business

Let's use the tools of *demographic analysis* discussed in chapters 4 and 7 to show how *models of consumer demand* are really models of a firm's product markets. This is the crucial insight from *industrial organization*, industry analysis, and competitive analysis. Industries and firms reinvent themselves when new technologies come to market and are put into use by suppliers, customers, and consumers. It is this second part of the equation that we are waiting for in the rush toward computer-based communications via wired, wireless, or satellite technology.

Pursuing Segmentation

Now let's take this competitive information and turn it into *market segments*. This is the key wisdom from *marketing management*. By combining intelligence from industrial organization and marketing, let's assemble a rich array of possible marketing strategies for the suppliers of telecom services.

Product Market Segment #1: Basic Telephones for Older Persons Some customers who came of age before 1968 still prefer rotary phones, but most people who became adults during the 1940s, 1950s, and 1960s want push-button, digital phones. They can pay their bills and call 1-800 emergency services from home. These older consumers may try some of the new telephone services, such as call waiting and call forwarding, but they often get confused and discontinue using these "time-saving" services. As they approach retirement, these customers become more sensitive to price increases for local and long-distance communications.

Product Market Segment #2: Enhanced Telephones for Middle-Agers Virtually all customers who became adults in the 1950s, 1960s, and 1970s want push-button, digital phones with enhanced voice, fax, and data services. They learn about these enhanced services at work and try them out at home. If they set up a small business at home, they are good prospects for most enhanced "time-saving" telephone services. These customers may shop for price differences initially, but once connected to local and long-distance systems, they remain loyal to their local and long-distance carriers.

Product Market Segment #3: Online Telecomputers for Young Adults Customers who became adults in the 1980s and 1990s are products of the computer generation, and they see immediately the advantage of linking telephones and computers. They have been experimenting with telecomputer-based data systems in high school and college. As their parents retire within the next 10 years, these younger age-cohort groups will dominate the work force. When they purchase their own PCs and online services, these customers shop for price differences among telemarketing and mail-order services. These young, newly married adults know what's inside the telecomputers, and they have the skills to repair their own equipment.

Product Market Segment #4: Telecom Services for Rich Persons Customers with high incomes, whose motto is "time is our most precious asset," and who can bridge the gap between rapid changes in technology and slower rates of personal adoption of new high value-added goods, are willing to pay any price for new telecom products. They are the first to adopt products for use in their offices, cars, homes, and corporate jets. As prices drop for new multimedia products, the choices made by these rich "players" will trickle down to younger, online telecomputer jockeys.

Forecasting Marketing Opportunities

Once the trickling-down effect begins (e.g., for PCs, fax machines, online telecomputers, and multimedia telecom products) we get a much richer description of the characteristics of mass consumer demand. This model of consumer behavior represents the product markets of suppliers of telecom services. Between now and the end of the decade, the focus of all telecom firms must switch to product market segments #3 and #4, to the young computer experts and to the rich business executives.

Those telephone, telecommunications, and telecomputer firms that develop successful marketing mix strategies for the purpose of becoming suppliers of telecom services will increase market share and maximize profits. They get out in front of their business customers, and they position their new telecom services properly. We will discuss this global marketing forecast in more detail later.

Initial Analysis of Marketing Opportunities

Let's look at how the suppliers of telecom services are trying to position their new telecom services. Throughout the world, wireless or cellular, online computer, mobile radio, and satellite services are *substitutes* for traditional wired telephone connections. These new telecom services, which are priced for customers with higher incomes and who wish to be the first to adopt new technologies, are capturing an increasing share of the European market.

Here are the data that confirm this *industry analysis*. For example, in 1991 the European market for telecommunications services was Ecu 110 billion (US $137.5 billion).[2] About 85 percent of these revenues came from basic landlines or wired telephone connections; the rest came from data services and mobile wireless connections. By the year 2001, the EC and Scandinavian market for telecom services will be Ecu 250 billion (US $312.5 billion). Moreover, only 65 percent of these revenues will come from basic telephone connections, and some 35 percent will come from online computer services and mobile wireless connections. That's a fivefold increase in revenues from new, substitute, nontraditional telecom services!

Exposing Revenues to Competition

What marketing intelligence is available for scanning the European environment? How should marketers interpret the changing policies of national governments? What are the economic costs facing the telecom services industry?

Micro factors. Throughout Europe, governments are deregulating, liberalizing, and privatizing local and long-distance services. Today, all long-distance revenues of AT&T (US), BT (UK), and KDD (Japan) are exposed to competition; 80 percent in Sweden; and 6 to 8 percent in Germany, France, Belgium, and other EC countries. Moreover, under pressure from the telecom directorate of the European Commission, by 1998 a minimum of 30 percent of long-distance service in all EC countries must be exposed to competition.[3]

Macro forces. After a decade of pressure from Oftel (Britain's telecom watchdog), Mercury, a subsidiary of Cable and Wireless, controls 10 percent of Britain's residential and business wired telephone markets, and BT controls the rest. Moreover, 30 cable TV companies supply voice and data services to

British customers. Everyone wants to reduce BT's control over unexposed revenue to about 80 percent in 1997.

Opportunity cost. The longer BT resists new entrants in traditional UK telecom markets the faster alternative substitute technologies will come into the UK market from foreign-owned telecom suppliers. The cost to BT is high. By failing to speed up the process by which "juice" teams match technology to business change, BT falls further behind AT&T in the worldwide race for supremacy in the telecommunications industry.

Implementing Alternative Entry Models

Nevertheless, BT is learning important lessons abroad. In *Europe* BT is going after the existing business of Deutsche Telekom, France Telecom, and other European telecoms. For example, at BT's Eurocentre in Paris, its multilingual staff provides hassle-free telecom services to European multinationals, such as the Axa financial group of Paris. Since London is the electronic switching center for the overseas communications of 39 percent of US multinationals, BT provides the same service in English to American, Canadian, Swedish, and Japanese multinationals.[4] In the *United States* BT/MCI is battling AT&T for direct access to the American public telephone networks. BT wants to compete against AT&T in planning, installing, and managing internal corporate communications (or outsourcing) systems.

Alternative Cable Networks Cable TV networks are alternative digital, wire and wireless broadband networks. In Britain, the cable TV rivals of BT are American-owned. In the United Kingdom, suppliers of British cable service provide both voice telephone communication and entertainment services, and they gain scope economies unavailable in the United States

Alternative Satellite Networks Hughes Electronics, a subsidiary of General Motors, is launching satellites to beam movies, cable TV programs, and sporting events to anyone in the United States and Canada. Its DirecTv markets satellite services straight to the consumer in competition with cable TV companies. This is called *direct broadcast satellite TV* (or DBS).

Of course, since the early 1990s, DBS has been used by Hong-Kong-based *Star TV*, a supplier of telecom and entertainment services owned by Rupert Murdoch's News Corp., in China and Asia. Its Asian customers are middle class, and they are in product market segments #2 (middle-aged converts) and #3 (younger computer jockeys). These Asian customers prefer to watch

TV or listen to TV reports, music, and sports than dabble in the politics of change facing most East Asian countries.

Star TV makes big money in India with English- and Hindi-language programming. For example, presenters from its MTV channel receive rock star receptions. Over 3.3 million Indian households receive Star's five channels, and they get a heavy dose of cricket plus high-action music videos.[5] With a Mandarin movie channel, and English- and Chinese-language programming, Star TV expects to make long-term profits in Taiwan, China, and Hong Kong by signing up about 30 million households in this part of East Asia.

Knowing the Rate of Product Diffusion

By the year 2000, super carriers (such as AT&T, BT/MCI, KDD/NTT, and Star TV) will provide global network management for multinational business firms. Product market segment #4 will be their primary target market. The upscale demands of the entertainment and financial industries will become the business market demands for such industries as purchasing, transportation, home shopping, and government services.

Then product market segment #3 (younger telecomputer jockeys) will be the second target market. Youthful, mass consumer demands for all telecom services will become the norm throughout the world. Both product market segments will want low-priced, high-quality local telephone fixed-wired and mobile services with broadband multimedia products either from telephone or cable TV companies or through DBS services.

Clues to Capturing Customers

With BT setting up its Eurocentre in Paris, "competition will decrease our market share in France . . . we expect new revenues from foreign operations to compensate," says Jacques Cuachy, head of international business development for France Telecom. His goal for the year 2000: "To get 10 percent of France Telecom's revenue from other European countries."[6] Today, France ranks second as the electronic switching center for the overseas communications of 17 percent of US multinational firms.

France Telecom and Deutsche Telekom are joining forces to build up a rival outsourcing venture, Eunetcom, to BT's Syncordia. Although France Telecom remains a state-controlled enterprise, it's the first among the European telecommunications firms to recognize the importance of audiotex telecom services – that is, combining computer processing power with traditional telephone services.[7] Now France Telecom is trying to extend audiotex services within the EC and across the continent. These are potent marketing tools for developing a firm's computer-based communications markets.

Summary: Scanning Future Business

Marketers find four market segments among consumers of telecommunications products and services within the United States, Europe, and Japan. Successful marketing executives use data about household income, consumer demand, technological sophistication, and industry analysis to make good decisions under uncertainty. Teams of successful technology-oriented managers compare alternative ways to position new telecom services to a wide range of cross-border buyers and sellers. With economic uncertainty and limited information, many choose alliances and joint ventures to gain access to markets undergoing government-directed liberalization, deregulation, and privatization. This is the environment that the telecom services industry faces.

The Firm-Specific Assignment

Marketers manage final demand by positioning global products within a reinvented telecom services industry; see Exhibit 8–5. Competing telecom firms make *unstructured marketing decisions*, such as allowing information and entertainment programming to be delivered directly to the home through *nonroutine partnerships* of telephone and cable TV firms. Marketers have *incomplete "soft" information*, and their success depends on intuition, hunches, good guesses, and experience.

Understanding Decision Making Under Uncertainty

Since the mid-1980s, Britain has promoted competition in telecommunications by encouraging joint telephone-cable operations. Three Baby Bells from the United States are major forces in British cable, and they deliver telephone services over the same lines that deliver cable television. Their telephone rates are about 15 percent below those of BT because cable TV does what long-distance service used to do. Cable TV *cross-subsidizes* local telephone service.

Exhibit 8–5.
Firm-Specific Analysis: Telecom Services
The Competitive Scan

Traditional Frame Analysis for Global Marketing

Firm-Specific 4Ps Analysis and Decision Making Under Uncertainty

Reinvented industries and competing firms

Unstructured marketing decisions

Incomplete "soft" information

Firm-Specific 4Ps Analysis and Demand for Wireless Television

Who uses the product: consumers near microwave networks

How to increase market share: keep costs under wired service

How to provide value: fewer rather than more channels

What signals show changes in market: segments #3 and #4

National Marketing Decisions and Marketing Research
Positioning

Interactive data and multimedia services

Wireless telephone and television transmissions

Mobile radio and personal communications systems

Satellite down links to direct broadcasting

Share Building

English-speaking countries

Spanish-speaking nations

East and South Asian lands

Nontraditional Frame Analysis for Global Marketing

Marketing Management Frame and Nonroutine Partnerships

Prepare for marketing uncertainties

Define the industry carefully

Understand the dynamics of the industry

Develop the habits of role ambiguity and boundary spanning

Get out ahead of customers

Marketing Management Frame and Industry Analysis

Define industry around two product market segments:

High incomes or market segment #4

Young adults or market segment #3

Marketing Management Frame, Value Creation, Marketing Strategy

How to put together routine partnerships?

Which unanswered questions remain unresolved?

What will people use?

What will people pay for?

Things are different in the United States. Although the US Cable Television Act of 1984 limits the intermingling of telephone and cable service in the United States, it does not prohibit the Baby Bells from buying cable TV firms as long as the latter are outside the multistate territory of the regional telephone companies. Early in 1993, Southwestern Bell, the Baby Bell from Missouri to Texas, bought two cable systems in the Washington, DC area from Hauser Communications, then sold them in 1994. Nynex, the Baby Bell for New York state and New England, started carrying the cable TV service of Manhattan's Liberty Cable because of the difficulty in laying more broadband fiber-optic cable underground in densely populated New York City.

Forging Nonroutine Partnerships

In May 1993, Gerald Levin was only five months into his role as chairman of *Time Warner*, itself a merger of the publishing interests of *Time Magazine* and the entertainment business of Warner Communications. His publishing executives from *Time* thought they worked in a stable industry in which routine decisions protected their fiefs. His entertainment executives from Warner thought they worked in a changing industry in which nonroutine decisions kept them ahead of their cable TV rivals. Both couldn't be correct.

To bring order out of chaos, Levin created technology alliances to market Time Warner entertainment products:[8]

- Silicon graphics from 3DO to make interactive video games

- Advanced cable converter boxes from Toshiba

- Interactive video games from Sega of America

- High-speed digital switches from AT&T to route programming to individual subscribers

- A telephone network that operates on cable from US West

Levin's deal with US West forces both sets of Time Warner executives to join forces and recognize technology's impact on consumer demand for information and entertainment. The partners are upgrading Time Warner's cable systems and its movie programming (such as Home Box Office). The films are being put into digital form and sent to homes through the telephone and cable lines of the new partnership. US West could have invested its US $2.5 billion overseas, but it chose to put its money into the domestic cable TV business. This is another way for a Baby Bell to become a key player in the emerging telecom services industry.

Competitive Scan: Interactive Wireless Services

Interactive wireless television from CellularVision of New York (a Bell Atlantic partner) "doesn't pose any important competitive threats," says Richard Aurelio, president of Time Warner's New York City Cable Group. "It has severe limitations, including limited channel capacity and problems with signal quality and reliability."[9] Aurelio believes CellularVision won't do the job expected in New York City.

Market Segments

Video servers built into home-based networked PCs do make interactive wireless television a reality in New York and elsewhere in the world. In fact, Oracle produces them. More importantly, customers with high incomes (market segment #4) are already buying them as they replace two-year-old, out-of-date PCs. Can young adult customers who are the vidkids of the recent computer revolution (market segment #3) be far behind?

Decision Making Under Uncertainty

Where has Aurelio gone wrong in his marketing analysis? Aurelio defines the industry incorrectly; he believes he works in the cable TV industry rather than in the interactive telecom services industry. Then he misunderstands the dynamics of both cable TV and interactive telecommunications; he believes stability reigns within the technology and marketing characteristics of his industry. In fact, Aurelio is competing within a fast-changing industry.

Teamwork

Aurelio needs to develop the habits of role ambiguity, boundary spanning, and getting out ahead of his customers. He needs a dose of marketing vision before he does the even harder work of trying to position Time Warner cable products in New York City.

Employing Demand Analysis

Who uses wireless television? This means no more digging up the streets, putting holes into basements, running wires up through floors and walls, and keeping the TV against the wall near the cable connection wire. The wireless service will use a microwave network, that is, radio frequencies approved by the US Federal Communications Commission. This network is already in place from the early days of television, and it is not used a great deal because telephone and cable TV firms switched to transmitting voice and video over fiber-optic networks.

How to increase market share of wireless television? The wireless service delivers TV programs through a flat, four-square-inch antenna that's mounted on the window and pointed in the direction of the signal. In fact, the wireless service is another form of direct broadcasting – without the cost of sending satellites into space. This means wireless service costs half as much as a wired cable TV service.

How to provide value in wireless television? The consumer might want wireless television with fewer channels than the 500 or more proposed by futurists in the telephone-cable TV-entertainment-multimedia industry It's hard to determine what demand will be 5 to 10 years in the future. Right now, consumers are confused with the 50 or so channels they currently receive through cable TV. We do know consumers don't want to pay more for cable TV, and local American municipalities again have the legal right to put price ceilings on cable TV services.

What signals show changes in the market? No one knows whether consumers really want interactive, multimedia television. Consumers in product market segment #4 (the rich, the sophisticated, the leaders) will buy the new antenna and try the service out. If the new wireless television service doesn't work out, they will throw away CellularVision's antenna and buy whatever is the current technological rage. Consumers in product market segment #3 (the younger telecomputer jockeys) will wait until the price comes down or will find a way to try the new wireless television service without paying for it.

Technological Changes

We do know this about wireless services: Cellular telephone services took off before most telephone firms knew what was happening within the telephone industry. Interactive computer communications became very popular before most Internet users really knew how to drive down all the lanes of the information superhighway. Wireless television services could do the same before most cable TV firms know what will happen within the telecom services industry. To wait too long is to forgo future business.

Positioning in the Wireless Category

The race is on to become a voice and video wireless telecom supplier. These players are asking consumer-based marketing questions.

Bell Atlantic, the Baby Bell serving the middle of the eastern US seaboard, took a minority stake in CellularVision to provide a variety of interactive data and multimedia services, such as basic and enhanced bill-paying telephone connections, financial and reservations transactions, information retrieval, and entertainment. These wireless telephone services could be transformed into wireless television services just as the latter now carries the former in the Bell Atlantic–CellularVision alliance within New York.

By acquiring McCaw Cellular, AT&T alters its cost functions and the payoffs of its competitors. Right now 45 cents of each US dollar spent on a long-distance cellular phone call goes to the Baby Bells and other local telephone companies. By getting away from wires, AT&T provides long-distance cellular telecommunications service without using the local telcos.

Creating Value

In the United Kingdom it is the American-owned telecom suppliers (i.e., *nonroutine partnerships* between three Baby Bells and several US cable TV companies) against the entrenched local, long-distance, and global outsourcer, British Telecommunications.

In the United States it is the Baby Bells and their cable TV entertainment partners versus a newly reinvented wireless, computer-based, and global outsourcer, AT&T.

Across the globe it is broadband technology, connected through wires and wall-mounted telephone and cable jacks, versus wireless cellular services and hand-held phones, microwave towers, fixed antennas, and rotating satellites. The telecommunications industry is moving down the road toward an information superhighway. Along the way, a few firms have taken detours into international privatizations. Others have chosen the slower cellular voice and cable TV video lanes. Still other companies decided to travel down the express lanes of wireless voice, data, video, and other interactive multimedia. Again, we have a few *unanswered questions* for marketers.

In summary, the competitive scan really depends on what customers want from their telecom suppliers. Here's what Robert E. Allen, chairman and chief executive officer of AT&T, says about the crucial question of how to conduct a competitive scan. "In the final analysis, customers will have a lot of choices, not only in telephones, but in access to information services and entertainment. . . The great unanswered question is what do people want? What will people use? That's the fuzziest part of it for me."[10]

Preparing a Marketing Strategy

Marketers ask what goods and services to produce and in what quantity. One set of competitors (Mercury, BT, and some Baby Bells) answers wired services. The other set of competitors (three Baby Bells in the UK cellular and cable telephone business, AT&T, and most Baby Bells in the United States) answer wireless service. Until Bell Atlantic went into wireless television and AT&T went into wireless telephone services, laying new fiber-optic wire was the smart move. Now all bets are off.

Marketing executives also ask what markets to enter, both as seller and buyer. For example, local telephone companies will have to lower their access charges to AT&T, or AT&T will push more of its business onto McCaw's cellular network. Each 1-percent cut in access charges translates into a US $400 million cost reduction for AT&T.[11] That's $400 million more to invest in new wireless products and services. Both broadband and wireless telecommunications services to households and businesses make up the scope of the telecom supplier firm called AT&T, and the potential scope for Bell Atlantic, Bell South, Southwestern Bell, and BT/MCI.

Estimates of Market Potential

In the free-for-all to create wireless interactive voice, data, and video telecom services, AT&T wants to shift the pricing of telecommunications services from a commodity basis to a foundation based on value-added services. AT&T seeks to dominate product market segment #4 by providing all types of communication services to rich, sophisticated business executives, anywhere and any time. Allen insists that AT&T grow its long-distance service business at the industry rate of 8 percent to 10 percent a year, or higher.[12] Through the integration of McCaw Cellular, AT&T expects to provide one telephone number to all subscribers for use in telephone, interactive multimedia, and portable computing services.

Will AT&T be able to provide these services, do all these tasks well, and capture significant market share across the full range of telecom services? Will BT/MCI, the Baby Bells, and other telecom suppliers be able to mount an effective challenge to AT&T? The answer lies not in technology, but in how the firms put together their nonroutine partnerships for marketing telecom services to business and household customers throughout the world.

Similar Market Segments Worldwide

Across the English-speaking world, American, Canadian, British, Australian, Indian, and Hong Kong telecommunications are shedding their parochial image. It's possible to travel from New York to London and then to Sydney and watch the same English-language news from Cable News Network (CNN), Canadian Broadcasting Corporation (CBC), British Broadcasting Corporation (BBC), and Australian Broadcasting Service (AUBS). Moreover, the same North American situation comedies, talk shows, and sporting events travel regularly to Britain, India, Australia, and Hong Kong, and vice versa. Some do well, and others are culturally unsuitable for their new environments.

Positioning in Mexico and Latin America

Across the Spanish-speaking world, American, Mexican, Venezuelan, and Argentine telecommunications are shedding their parochial image, too.[13] It's possible to travel from Chicago to Mexico City and on to Caracas and Buenos Aires and watch the same Spanish-language programs from CNN, Univision, Time Warner, MTV-*Olé*, Mexico's Televisa and Telemundo, and translated programs from Brazil's TV Globo. Virtually all use PanAm Sat, the satellite company in the Americas, have agreements with Tele-Communications, Inc. to provide cable and satellite TV service, and provide CineCanal movies on wireless cable television through Televisa's Multivision.

Positioning in China and East Asia

Moreover, across the Chinese-speaking world, from Hong Kong to Guangzhou, Shanghai, Beijing, and to the overseas Chinese communities throughout East Asia, Star TV provides Mandarin- and Cantonese-language programs through satellites feeding into fixed antennas in homes and offices. The list of satellite-based wireless television services without the use of copper wires, fiber-optic wires, and cable TV connections grows every day; all of these services handle telephone voice and data transmissions as well. These non-US voice, data, and video wireless connections are forcing American, Canadian, and British policy makers and telecommunications firms to reconsider their commitment to maintaining the traditional wired services of the Baby Bells, Bell Canada, and BT.

Positioning Around the World

Wherever one goes in the Spanish-, Portuguese-, Chinese-, Russian-, German-, and French-speaking worlds, English-language programs are available from

CNN, BBC, and Star TV. One similar market segment worldwide is business travellers from the United States and the United Kingdom; their ranks are joined by English-speaking tourists; the numbers are swelled by local people who want to learn English as a second language. All are the richest consumers, most likely to buy new cars, consumer durables, wireless telecommunications services, and satellite television programs. As the cost of wireless and satellite technology falls, the market expands rapidly from product market segment #4 to product market segment #3. This is the future of the telecom services industry; see Exhibit 8–6.

Summary: Scanning Wireless Services

Marketers learn what consumers want before providing them with wired or wireless telecom services. Successful marketing executives from three Baby Bells position cable TV (with concurrent telephone service) in the United Kingdom to compete against British Telecommunications. Effective executives from Star TV position direct broadcasting satellite TV throughout Asia to compete against local television services. Teams of successful technology-oriented managers compare alternative ways to position new wireless telephone, television, and computer telecom services to a wide range of English-, Spanish-, and Chinese-speaking buyers and sellers. With "soft" information about future consumer demand, many suppliers of telecom services choose

Exhibit 8-6.
Cable TV Connections

HOLD THE LINE

TOP TEN OPERATORS, JUNE 1994

	HOMES CONNECTED, '000	AS % OF TOTAL FRANCHISE
TELEWEST	133	6.0
COMCAST	120	8.5
SOUTHWESTERN BELL	93	8.4
VIDEOTRON	81	7.4
NYNEX	78	3.1
TELECENTIAL	46	7.3
BELL CABLEMEDIA	37	2.2
GENERAL CABLE	33	3.0
DEVANHA	26	12.5
BT	12	10.5
TOTAL	**660**	**5.5**

SOURCES: ITC; MORGAN STANLEY RESEARCH

Courtesy of The Economist

nonroutine partnerships to gain access to technology and markets. The most successful teams choose the very best partners, those who can match technology to business change.

National Marketing Decisions

Marketers manage final demand by signaling detailed national information about interactive telephone and television wireless services; see Exhibit 8–7. Marketing executives expand final demand by convincing affluent business executives and then younger telecommuters to expand their use of interactive telecom connections. Many telecom marketers go into nonroutine partnerships with other firms to improve interactive wireless connectivity. These are important developments in marketing telecommunications throughout the world.

Understanding Marketing Strategy

The crucial marketing question is as follows: Do alliance partners *stretch themselves and leverage their combined assets* to form a more competitive marketing relationship?[14] Does top management at Bell Atlantic, US West, Time Warner, AT&T, MCI, and BT have a clear view of the *managerial goal line?* Compare their aspirations and partnerships to those of Pacific Telesis, Sprint, and Deutsche Telekom. The former are leveraging the scope of their existing telecommunications businesses into newer, customer driven telecom opportunities. The latter are content with the scale of their existing telephone business. This strategy is a portent for disaster among some Baby Bells and the also-ran, state-owned European telephone monopolies.

The first approach, a stretch-and-leveraging competitive marketing strategy, is worthy of the best companies worldwide. This strategy "stress[es] the importance of *information* and *uncertainty* as explanations for the organization of activities within the firm."[15] Nonroutine partnerships and acquisitions are designed to reduce uncertainty, get more information about technology and demand, and obtain more realistic production costs. If *interfirm cooperation* is embedded within the managerial teams of both partners, then the alliance prospers, transforms itself into an equity joint venture, and winds up with one partner acquiring the whole business (e.g., AT&T takes over McCaw Cellular). What of the other telecom alliances?

Exhibit 8-7.
National Marketing Decisions: Telecom Services
The Marketing Scan

Traditional Frame Analysis for Global Marketing
Firm-Specific 4Ps Analysis and Decision Making Under Uncertainty
Signal national interactive wireless information
Succeed from expansion of interactive wireless TV technology
Grow through radio frequencies rationalization
Pay attention to alternative telecom services lifestyles

Firm-Specific 4Ps Analysis and Marketing Strategy
Stretch and leveraging
Managerial goal line
Information and uncertainty
Inter-firm cooperation

National Marketing Decisions, and Alliances and Strategy
Which activities, and where?
Which products, and for whom?
Who are our customers, and do they exist across borders?
What is our added value; can we do better than our competitors?
Do we have a competitive marketing strategy for ourselves?
Do we have a competitive marketing strategy for our partners?
Should we find better competitors?
What is the makeup of our industry?
Are the competitive forces changing in our favor?
Is the overseas environment conducive to our products?

National Marketing Decisions and Marketing Forecasts
Continuing trend is unrealistic in the US and the UK
Amplifying trend requires role ambiguity and boundary spanners
Doubling trend is realistic in observable market segments

Nontraditional Frame Analysis for Global Marketing
Marketing Management Frame and Relationship Marketing
Develop clear view of managerial goal line
Prepare for uncertainty as industry realigns itself
Embed inter-firm cooperation among partners
Commit equal resources and management time
Provide for projects with high payouts

Continued on next page

Exhibit 8-7. *Continued from previous page*

Marketing Management Frame and Industry Analysis

New entrants

Substitute products

Micro forces

Macro forces

Bargaining power of buyers and sellers

Marketing Scan: Telecom Alliances

BT and MCI recognize the need to improve linkages across telecommunications systems and decide to *share proprietary technologies* across the globe. Theirs is a complementary product or *comarketing alliance*. Both partners practice "mutual recognition and understanding [because] the success of each firm depends in part on the other . . ."[16] Coordination extends to marketing, research and development, and manufacturing production. These *horizontal cross-border ties* help the BT/MCI partners leverage their long-distance and global outsourcing businesses, and they will be used again as this partnership tries to become the preeminent group in personal communications systems (PCS). Will BT gain at the expense of MCI, or will both gain at a high cost to still unnamed partners for PCS?

Making Partnerships Work

Both partners must commit equal resources and management time to make the alliance work well.[17] Also, "well-planned projects with high payouts in relation to cost are most likely to be successful."[18] Moreover, alliances tend to be more successful in turbulent environments. These partnerships are "a superior vehicle to gain access to new complementary products or technologies without all the risks of internal development."[19]

An analysis of the telecom services industry suggests that some alliances provide their partners with superior results. (For example, overseas privatization deals between two Baby Bells, cellular service in Latin America and Europe between one or more Baby Bells and other telecom suppliers, telephone and cable TV joint ventures in the United Kingdom, and some of the deals put together by AT&T.)

Joining Marketing and Industrial Organization

These partnerships underscore the importance of marketing's relationship to industrial organization. Know what customers want before committing to the production of goods and services, and before entering markets as buyers or sellers. With market objectives clearly in mind, then form a nonroutine alliance to add value through the complementarity of products from both partners. If both partners agree on what customers want in the future, then the partnership has a good chance of success.

Strategies for Increasing Marketing Effectiveness

The task of top management is to embed its partnerships and alliances within its targeted product market segments. In chapter 7, we discussed how BT became a *new* entrant in the global outsourcing segment and how AT&T stunned cellular firms by setting up an alliance with McCaw Cellular. In this chapter, we explained how US West teamed up with Time Warner and how this joint venture became a new entrant in the cable TV business.

Telecom Services Industry

Our analysis of the telecom services industry shows it to be *unstable* because of the threat of *many new entrants*, some of whom are unknown at this time. We have a hunch that AT&T (and its wholly owned subsidiary, McCaw Cellular) might just go after the Baby Bells in the wireless cellular service segment of the market. We also think that BT/MCI might just go after AT&T in the mobile radio PCS segment of the telecom market.

Industry Analysis All these new telecom technologies are *substitutes* for one another: wireless easily replaces wired landlines; interactive wireless television cuts into fiber-optic cable TV; and smart messaging repeals the need for fixed phone connections. They are chosen because of *micro factors*, such as emerging new needs of buyers, stronger bargaining power of suppliers, and changing policy directions from government. These new technologies are successful because of *macro forces*, such as economic costs, cultural adaptation, and political impact, or forces governing the market. Such *industry analysis* is the necessary first step in understanding how to position competitive products within the emerging telecom services industry.

Product Market Segments In chapters 7 and 8, we have done a great deal more. We did several competitor analyses. We looked at their past records, identified their strategies, evaluated their resources, and chose those competitors we thought would be the most successful for product market segment #1 (the lackluster regulated telephone monopolies, or Baby Bells), #2 (Southwestern Bell, Nynex, and Pacific Telesis), #3 (Bell Atlantic, Bell South, and BT/MCI), and #4 (US West and Time Warner, AT&T and McCaw Cellular).

Reinvented Telcos Clearly, those telecom suppliers that compete for market share in product market segment #4 are the best competitors in the industry. This is the segment with the greatest potential demand for the highest value-added products and with money to pay for these new technologies. If successful, the rates of return for these competitors in product market segment #4 will be high compared to all other telecom suppliers. This additional cash flow will be invested in speeding up the product-development life cycle for newer interactive multimedia products. And these telecom competitors will go from strength to strength in positioning new competitive product offerings in the fast-changing telecom services industry.

Preparing a Marketing Strategy

Here is a sample list of questions for executives to use in developing a marketing strategy:

1.   Which activities, and where?

2.   Which products, and for whom?

3.   Who are our customers, and do they exist across borders?

4.   What is our added value, and can we do it better than our competitors?

5.   Do we have a competitive marketing strategy for ourselves and for our partners?

6.   Are our competitors worthy of our interest, or should we find better competitors?

7.   What is the makeup of our industry, and are the competitive forces changing in our favor?

8.   Is the overseas environment conducive to our products, technologies, and marketing efforts?

Marketing Implementation

To be successful, all telecom suppliers must have an organizational mechanism to integrate technological and strategic thinking at a time of industry upheaval.[20] Have Pacific Telesis, other Baby Bells, and the state-owned European telecoms missed crucial plays in cellular wireless service that are now obvious in hindsight? Yes. Has AT&T found executives within NCR who grasp the connections between technology and business change? No. Does AT&T have these bridging people in McCaw Cellular, and does BT have these crucial executives in MCI? Yes.

Managers who are able to grasp the tie between technological progress and business change apply return-on-investment and product life-cycle models to the management of research, marketing, and partnership investments. Let's return to our key example of successful teamwork: "AT&T has high-level teams of technologists and business executives devoted to mastering business evolution. Some of these teams function within existing business units, and others focus on the 'white space' between. But the primary long-term benefit of these approaches is that some of the best technical minds in places like Bell Labs and across the AT&T businesses are creating new approaches for business strategy in the alliance-driven world of computers, communications, and consumer electronics."[21]

Three forecasts. The "continuing trend" forecast is the easiest to make because things do go on as before. Wireless telephone and cable TV services don't conform to traditional lifestyles in Europe, the United States, and Japan. Interactive wireless services are so new that the "continuing trend" is unrealistic in the United States and the United Kingdom.

The "amplifying trend" forecast assumes computer-driven telecommunications firms aggressively market their wireless services; more younger people purchase these interactive services with their available disposable income. In the United States and the United Kingdom, these routine purchases are crucial parts of their lifestyle. This trend will develop because we are at the beginning of a major information revolution with no end in sight. Only marketers who favor role ambiguity, are boundary spanners, and conduct industry analysis will be successful in the changing telecom services industry.

The "doubling trend" forecast assumes telecom service firms convert older people to interactive wireless services. If we define this older age-period cohort group as highly successful business executives, then this is the most likely forecast in the United Kingdom and the United States. Product diffusion occurs rapidly because high-income business executives want these new interactive wireless services. This one piece of information helps marketers in putting together an effective marketing strategy for the UK and the US interactive wireless telecom services industry.

Summary: Scanning Telecom Alliances

Marketers select partners with skills in cellular, cable TV, direct satellite, and personal communication services. Successful marketing executives bridge the connections between technology and business change through cross-border comarketing alliances. Teams of successful technology-oriented managers compare alternative ways to position new wireless telephone, television, and computer telecom services to the high-income, first-adopter market segment. With "soft" information about future consumer demand, many suppliers of telecom services choose comarketing alliances to gain access to proprietary technology and new markets. The most successful teams have the very best partners, those who can develop a marketing strategy for matching technology to business change.

Inclusive Contexts for Global Marketing

Exhibit 8-8 sums up the inclusive contexts for global marketing in the telecom services industry. We examine reinventing the industry and its competing firms. We also study two types of decision making under uncertainty: culturally based demand analysis and organizationally based industry analysis. These two focuses help us direct our research to answering important questions: what will our customers do with our products, and how will they use our products in the future? Again, we deal with technology as a driving force in managerial decision making under uncertainty. Our choices determine whether we will be a success at global marketing.

Conclusions

Suppliers of global telecom services come in many different packages: telephone companies, cable TV firms, direct broadcasting satellites, mobile radio communications, and entertainment multimedia programmers. All of these combined (and with many more new entrants on the way) make up the telecom services industry.

Exhibit 8–8.
Inclusive Contexts for Global Marketing

Market Risk
Govern the market through reinvented business environment
Foreign investment, joint ventures, and nonroutine partnerships
Unknown competitive possibilities and imperfect information
Political Frame

Firm-Specific 4Ps Analysis (A)
Culturally based decision making under uncertainty
Demand analysis, cultural analysis, age-period cohort analysis
Value creation and multiplying uses of information
Cultural Frame

Firm-Specific 4Ps Analysis (B)
Organizationally based decision making under uncertainty
Industry analysis
  New entrants
  Opportunity cost of substitute products
  Micro factors and exposure to world competition
  Macro forces and unexposed revenues of state-owned PTOs
  Bargaining power of buyers and sellers
Change corporate culture and relationships marketing
Segmentation, positioning strategies
Value creation and learning organization
  Which unanswered questions remain unresolved?
  What will people use?
  What will people pay for?
Marketing Management Frame

National Marketing Decisions
Supply analysis
Scanning potential markets, offerings, segments
Formal and walking-around research
Marketing strategy
  Which activities, and where?
  Which products, and for whom?

Continued on next page

Exhibit 8-8. *Continued from previous page*

Who are our customers, and do they exist across borders?

What is our added value?

Do we have a competitive marketing strategy for ourselves?

Should we find better competitors?

What is the makeup of our industry?

Are the competitive forces changing in our favor?

Is the overseas environment conducive to our products?

Alternative entry models and information highway

Vision test: remember trend is not destiny

Technological Frame

Let's return to our initial three learning objectives:

1. Discuss the importance of industrial organization to competitive marketing strategy.

   You should have a clear understanding of how global marketing strategy fits into models of industrial organization, consumer behavior, and industry analysis. You need the wisdom from both schools of thought to be successful in global industries.

2. Outline the marketing mix, four product market segments, and positioning strategies in the telecom services industry.

   You should be able to discuss the 4Ps scheme and the segmentation and positioning strategies of buyers and sellers within the telecom-services industry. You should draft an international marketing plan for the major markets of the world, then choose which markets to enter as the main source of competitive revenues for the future.

3. Explain the usefulness of telecom alliances to build up market share in the interactive wireless services industry.

   You should be able to offer the pros for going into or the cons for staying out of technology and comarketing telecom alliances. Make some decisions and decide which telecom firms are the best partners.

All of this is the work of global marketing executives.

Notes

1. This section draws extensively from Daniel F. Spulber, "Economic Analysis and Management Strategy: A Survey," *Journal of Economics & Management Strategy*, 1:3 (Fall 1992): 538-51.

2. All the data in the paragraph come from Daiwa Institute of Research. Cited by Andrew Adonis and Andrew Hill, "Lifting the Lid on Liberalisation," *Financial Times*, May 10, 1993, 13. The US dollar figure comes from Richard W. Stevenson, "Telephone Upheaval in Europe," *The New York Times*, May 31, 1993, 21.

3. Daiwa, cited by Adonis and Hill, 13.

4. Richard L. Hudson, "France Telecom and BT Rivalry Grows," *The Wall Street Journal*, August 3, 1992, A9.

5. Simon Davies, "Murdoch Bets on Channels' Star Potential," *Financial Times*, August 3, 1993, 16. Pete Engardio, "Murdoch in Asia: Think Globally, Broadcast Locally," *Business Week*, June 6, 1944, 29.

6. Hudson, A9.

7. Della Bradshaw, "On the Line to a Wider Service," *Financial Times*, July 29, 1993, 21.

8. "Time Warner's Techie at the Top," *Business Week*, May 10, 1993, 60-61.

9. Mary Lu Carnevale, "Bell Atlantic Takes on Cable in Wireless Pact," *The Wall Street Journal*, August 5, 1993, B7.

10. Edmund L. Andrews, "AT&T Reaches Out (And Grabs Everyone)," *The New York Times*, August 8, 1993, F6.

11. Robert B. Morris III of Goldman Sachs & Co. Cited by John J. Keller, "AT&T Agrees to Buy McCaw Cellular," *The Wall Street Journal*, August 17, 1993, A3.

12. John J. Keller, "AT&T Sees McCaw Deal as Way to Spur Growth, Offer New Consumer Services," *The Wall Street Journal*, August 18, 1993, A3.

13. Damian Fraser, "Latin American TV Sheds Parochial Image," *Financial Times*, July 27, 1993, 23.

14. Gary Hamel and C.K. Prahalad, "Strategy as Stretch and Leverage," *Harvard Business Review* 71:2 (March-April 1993): 75-84.

15. Spulber, p. 553.

16. James C. Anderson and James A. Narus, "A Model of Distributor Firm and Manufacturer Firm Working Partnerships," *Journal of Marketing* 54 (January 1990): 42–58.

17. Louis P. Bucklin and Sanjit Sengupta, "Organizing Successful Co-Marketing Alliances," *Journal of Marketing* 57:2 (April 1993): 43.

18. Ibid.

19. Ibid.

20. James F. Moore, "The Tough Interface Between Execs and Techs," *The Wall Street Journal*, August 16, 1993, A14.

21. Ibid.

Chapter Format

Learning Objectives

After reading this chapter, you should be able to:

- Discuss the importance of standardization and adaptation to product positioning strategy

- Outline the impact of consumer heterogeneity, category purchase, and market response segmentation on product positioning

- Explain the usefulness of brands in building up market share in the interactive multimedia industry

Product Positioning

chapter 9

Introduction

Marketers manage final demand by positioning global products, services, and brands. In this chapter, we look at the multimedia industry. Here we stress changing market risk, unknown competitive possibilities, and imperfect information. We also spell out the process by which companies do their firm-specific 4Ps analysis, and we detail value creation during the product-development life cycle. Moreover, we show how joining together competitive analysis and marketing helps us develop a comprehensive marketing strategy.

Let's reinforce the new ground we broke in chapters 7 and 8. In this chapter, let's reinvent another industry (multimedia) and two games firms (Nintendo and Sega). Let's work through our firm-specific 4Ps analysis to be sure we understand all the nuances of decision making under uncertainty.

Scanning Global Markets

Environmental scan: modernization. Marketers find preteen and teenage boys are the one key market segment among consumers of interactive fantasies, *manga*, sports, wars, and other video games.

297

Successful marketing executives grow the interactive multimedia market by converting heterogeneous tastes into predictable preferences, then turning games into family entertainment. Moreover, to capture the market segments for young women and newly married families, interactive multimedia stops using personal computers and transforms itself into a new form of TV entertainment. Even under conditions of uncertainty about market structure and limited information about consumer attributes, marketers pursue a product positioning strategy of minimum differentiation or standardization of interactive entertainment.

Competitive scan: interactive multimedia. Marketers know teenage boys are key to family decisions about home interactive multimedia. Right now, they are wedded to Nintendo because the games have more substance than competing products from Sega. Successful marketing executives from AT&T, the cable TV companies, and Hollywood entertainment firms know they must offer the same amount of exciting substance to boys and slant the other multimedia products toward values for girls, women, and young families. The competitive battle is Nintendo's to lose.

Marketing scan: joint ventures. Successful marketing executives realize they don't know everything about consumer habits. During market entry and other phases of the product's life cycle, many cultural choices are unobservable by global marketers and unclear to domestic marketers. With "hard" market response data and with "soft" information about consumer preferences, marketing executives prefer telephone-cable TV-Hollywood joint ventures as the best way to minimize substantial market risks. Through alliances, partnerships, and joint ventures, marketers reduce the possibility of making a category mistake as they position new interactive multimedia products.

Traditional Contexts for Global Marketing

Exhibit 9-1 lists the traditional contexts for global marketing in the case of the telecom services industry. We study a reinvented business environment, value creation, and marketing strategy. The first reinforces our observation about the changes occurring in the multimedia industry and how these are driving innovations in the telecommunications and telecom services industries. The second reminds us that multimedia, telecom services, and telephone firms must create and add value by multiplying the use of information. The third prepares us for the hard task of implementing a marketing strategy with continuous future payoffs. The multimedia case is another symbol of how new industries are being created for a future global economy.

Exhibit 9-1.
Traditional Contexts for Global Marketing

Market Risk

Govern the market through reinvented business environment

Foreign investment, joint ventures, nonroutine partnerships

Long-term planning horizon

Unknown competitive possibilities and imperfect information

Firm-Specific 4Ps Analysis

Decision making under uncertainty

Demand analysis, cultural analysis, age-period cohort analysis

Product life cycle

Entry: simultaneous introduction

Growth: sequential introduction

Maturity: routine purchasing behavior

Saturation: all groups shop for lowest price

Decline: all groups check out new technology

Positioning strategies

Value creation

Multiply uses of information

Restructure category

Formal market research

Product positioning strategy

Product-development life cycle

National Marketing Decisions

Supply analysis

Competitive analysis

Global, largely American popular culture

Generational changes breed uncoupling of age-period groups

Speeding up product life cycle for value-added products

Core meaning of interactive multimedia entertainment

Scanning potential markets, offerings, segments

Formal and walking-around research

Segmentation strategies

Continued on next page

Exhibit 9-1. *Continued from previous page*

Marketing strategy

    Identify customer-oriented actions with future payoffs

    Create a new product market category

    Identify market segments among multimedia consumers

    Classify interactive multimedia into value-added products

    Use information about culture, tastes, behavior

    Make marketing decisions under uncertainty

    Apply contingency perspective to 4Ps marketing mix

    Find better competitors

Vision test

Remember trend is not destiny

Nontraditional Contexts for Global Marketing

Exhibit 9-2 names the nontraditional contexts for global marketing in the multimedia industry. We survey reinventing a product category, multiplying uses of information, matching self-referencing criteria, and making marketing investments. Again, we break new ground because reinventing a product category goes hand-in-hand with reinventing the industry and the competing firms. We also focus on the creative destruction of existing technology at the hands of computer-based multimedia communications.

Again, as we venture forth onto the new information highway, we do not know who our customers will be and how they will use these new products. However, from our past work on value creation, we do know about unanswered questions, unknown competitive possibilities, and imperfect information.

Finally, we are beginning to realize that only learning organizations survive during periods of reinventing product categories, industries, and firms. These firms must make good marketing investments, leverage their assets, and seek customers from all income groups and social lifestyles. Nintendo, Sega, and other multimedia firms are all reinventing themselves through the creative destruction of current games and other multimedia products. It's not clear which will survive, but that is the meaning of a global industry reinventing itself in the last half of the 1990s.

Governing the market. First, let's look at the political frame. Government steps up the pace of modernization by allowing global and domestic marketers the freedom to compete. Privatization leads to open, more liberal

Exhibit 9-2.
Nontraditional Contexts for Global Marketing

Political Frame

Govern the market through reinvented business environment

Reinvent product category

Technological Frame

Alternative entry models

Creative destruction to winnow out winners and losers

Value added

Multiplying bits of information

Multiplying uses of information

Cultural Frame

Disconnection among age groups and adoption of new offerings

Cross-cultural analysis of similar self-referencing criteria

Value creation and multiplying bits of information

Marketing Management Frame

Managerial decision making under uncertainty

Industry analysis

Segmentation

Teamwork, nonroutine partnerships, relationship marketing

Value creation and learning organization

Which unanswered questions remain unresolved?

What will people use?

What will people pay for?

Marketing investments

Look for unobservable habits

Carry out unconventional thinking

Establish long-term goals in emerging multimedia industry

Seek quality, high-profit consumers

Attack switchable customers

Gain significant market share

Leverage investments in products and services

Return on investment

Convert installed capacity to interactive multimedia

Quality of market share keeps home-based customers with us

Seek customers from all lifestyles

markets, especially in telecom services and interactive multimedia. The tempo accelerates as marketing executives sell brand-named products, supply logistics information systems, provide advertising copy, and offer bundled pricing (see chapters 8-11). Success in governing the market leads to new alliances among competitors.

Marketing decisions under uncertainty. Second, let's study the technological frame. Marketers position products by identifying potential consumer choices, matching them to a set of product attributes, and offering a range of innovative goods (and services) during the product's life cycle. Many national markets are growing together into similar, virtually *homogeneous* market segments worldwide; see Exhibits 9-3 and 9-4. The preference for convenience, informality, instant feedback, and popular culture are all observable attributes that influence consumer choice in fast foods, clothes, telecommunications, and multimedia. Marketing professors call this a *standardization strategy*.

Sometimes, national (regional and local) markets display significant and continuing consumer *heterogeneity*. Marketing executives don't know precisely what influences consumer choice because unobservable attributes affect purchase decisions.[1] Then marketers tailor products and services to fit cultural differences and use both price and nonprice competition (e.g., distribution channels and promotional advertising) to position products to meet the needs of religion, language, social class, and nationality. Marketing professors call this an *adaptation strategy*.

Exhibit 9-3.
Future Consumers of North Atlantic Products

BOTTOM OF CLASS			
1988-89 FROM:	ASIAN STUDENTS IN: EUROPE	AMERICA	AMERICA AS MULTIPLE OF EUROPE
CHINA	6,110	58,016	9.5
ASEAN	13,721	35,274	2.6
TAIWAN	NA	28,680	NA
JAPAN	3,081	26,900	8.7
SOUTH KOREA	5,613	19,567	3.5
HONG KONG	6,397	10,126	1.6
TOTAL*	34,922	149,883	4.3

*EXCLUDING TAIWAN
SOURCES: CORRADO LETTA, LUIGI BOCCONI UNIVERSITY, MILAN

Courtesy of The Economist

Exhibit 9-4.
Global, Largely American Sports Culture

UNAMERICAN			
FOREIGN STUDENT-ATHLETES IN NCAA INTERCOLLEGIATE SPORTS	SEX	NO. OF PARTICIPANTS	% OF TOTAL*
SOCCER	MALE	820	15.7
TENNIS	MALE	731	14.0
ICE HOCKEY	MALE	546	10.5
TRACK	MALE	483	9.3
TENNIS	FEMALE	389	7.5
SWIMMING	MALE	252	4.8
GOLF	MALE	219	4.2
TRACK	FEMALE	217	4.2
BASKETBALL	MALE	206	3.9
FOOTBALL	MALE	179	3.4
VOLLEYBALL	FEMALE	126	2.4
SWIMMING	FEMALE	118	2.3
BASKETBALL	FEMALE	94	1.8
CROSS COUNTRY	MALE	90	1.7
BASEBALL	MALE	82	1.6

SOURCE: NCAA 1993 STUDY   *THERE ARE ALSO 20 OTHER SPORTING CATEGORIES, WHICH TOTAL 12.7%

Courtesy of The Economist

Finally, add the complexity inherent in industry analysis (see chapter 8). Marketers select positioning strategies based on a "firm's international experience, the technology orientation of the industry, and the competitiveness of the export market."[2] Sometimes standardization is feasible and desirable. At other times, new markets require significant adaptation at first, but fewer changes later.[3] Marketing executives carry out a different mix of marketing activities during and after market entry, and these multiple efforts improve overall global marketing performance. Marketing professors call this approach to product positioning a *contingency perspective*.

Hunting for consumers. Third, let's examine the cultural frame. In global marketing, economic and demographic changes, the impact of western popular culture on religion and social identity, and the rush of new technology affect consumer choices. Sometimes, we are unable to predict initial purchase decisions, the diffusion of products and services, and the constant quest for variety among the world's consumers. These are the unobservable attributes of consumer choice.

Are consumer choices homogeneous (the same) when matched in terms of unobservable attributes? An affirmative answer persuades marketing executives to export duplicate products overseas without thought to the differences in culture. Most horror stories are written about marketers who fail to use marketing intelligence about real cultural differences. A negative answer misses the success of *global brands* (i.e., products with common features, names, and advertising) even though they are a special case and inappropriate for some international marketing situations.

Are consumer choices heterogeneous (different) when matched in terms of observable attributes? An affirmative answer persuades marketing executives to recreate product lines overseas without thought to life-cycle preferences for variety and industry characteristics. A negative answer relegates product positioning to a second-best marketing strategy.

Within the multimedia industry, consumer choices are heterogeneous. Most attributes about consumer choice are unobservable by marketers. This is a new market whose structure is not yet formed. The industry lacks clear boundaries and the competitors come from a wide variety of industrial backgrounds. These firms don't know whether consumers want online information, financial services, and entertainment (commonly referred to as the 500-plus TV channels), or the point-to-point switched services so familiar in the telephone and telecommunications industry. Thus, marketing executives cannot predict with confidence consumer choices about multimedia products.

Segmentation, positioning, and tailoring decisions. Finally, let's look closely at the marketing management frame. Marketers have difficulty predicting consumer choices as tastes (or the unobservable attributes) become more heterogeneous. Even though marketing executives offer standardized products (i.e., goods similar to the competition on the observable attributes), consumers impose differentiation of their own based on attributes unknown to marketers. This happens after market entry, especially during the growth and maturity phases of the product life cycle.

Global marketing is different because so many consumer choices depend on local cultural characteristics unknown to marketers. The safest product positioning decision is for global marketers to flood overseas markets with standardized product offerings, then let consumers make their own implicit differentiation, unknown to marketing executives. This decision leads to lower levels of consumer satisfaction because the difference between what consumers desire and what they get is large and grows larger with additional advertising and other marketing communications from new competitors.

The most aggressive product positioning decision is for marketers to provide differentiated products for overseas markets even when they don't know all the reasons why consumers choose one set of products over another. This decision leads to higher levels of consumer satisfaction in terms of not only prepurchase expectations but also postpurchase perceived performance. The costs of this positioning decision are high. However, if future competitors are kept out of an important overseas market, then maximum differentiation is well worth the expense.

Organizing global marketing experience. The simultaneous existence of these four different contexts forces marketers to research multimedia markets, to position alternative one-way and interactive delivery systems, and to watch the choices made by customers in different nations. Let's do two things in this chapter. First, we will discuss the importance of standardization versus adaptation (or minimum differentiation versus maximum differentiation) to product positioning. Then we will apply this analysis to the contingencies of an emerging global industry, the suppliers of interactive multimedia products worldwide.

Market Risk Questions

Marketers manage final demand by researching international multimedia markets; see Exhibit 9-5. *Market risk* offers advice on dealing with unknown competitive possibilities and imperfect information, and their effect on the product positioning, segmentation, and tailoring strategies of multimedia competitors. This, too, is a part of our macro business environment.

Understanding the Importance of Information

In chapters 7 and 8, we discussed the transport of bits of information by telephone and cable TV firms and how some of these firms also own the bits of voice, data, and video information. That is yesterday's story.

Long-Term Planning Horizon In the future, money will be made by *adding value to bits of information.*[4] Here are examples:

- AT&T sells "fat minutes" (or multimedia dial-tone traffic) and charges two times the price of regular phone calls.[5]

Exhibit 9-5.
Market Risk Analysis: Multimedia
The Environmental Scan

Traditional Frame Analysis for Global Marketing

Market Risk Analysis and Reinvented Business Environment

Unknown competitive possibilities and incomplete information

Long-term planning horizon

Firm-Specific 4Ps Analysis and Observable Attributes

Recognize homogeneous and heterogeneous markets worldwide

Apply standardization, adaptation, and contingency strategies

Acknowledge the importance of global brands

Provide nondifferentiated and differentiated products

Gain higher levels of consumer satisfaction

Firm-Specific 4Ps Analysis and Unobservable Attributes

Avoid category mistakes

Create new product market category

Convert heterogeneous tastes into predictable preferences

Identify market segments

Render durable goods obsolete through cost-reducing innovations

Gain commitment from buyers

Promote TV paradigm

National Marketing Decisions and Marketing Opportunities

Segmentation

Parents who became adults in the 1970s, in the 1980s

Teenage boys, early adopters, adult men, technophiles

Adult women

Positioning

Minimum differentiation or standardization

Contingency choices

Maximum differentiation or adaptation

Tailoring

American teenage and adult males: more violence

Japanese teenage and adult males: less violence and more story

German teenage and adult males: even less violence

Teenage and adult women: stories about love and travel

Continued on next page

Exhibit 9-5. *Continued from previous page*

National Marketing Decisions and Marketing Strategy
Identify customer-oriented actions with future payoffs
Classify interactive multimedia into value-added products
Apply contingency perspective to 4Ps marketing mix
Find better competitors

Nontraditional Frames for Global Marketing
Technology Frame and Value Added
Multiplying bits of information
Multiplying uses of information

- Oracle, a software giant, provides media servers that use copper telephone and cable TV wires to transport entertainment and business products to homes and offices.[6]

- Electronic Arts Inc. produces computer disks, called CD-ROMs, with video clips, animation, sound, and text for transport over AT&T wires and through Oracle set-top boxes.[7]

This is the *long-term planning* horizon of interactive multimedia.

4Ps Scheme The first P is *Product*: Are interactive multimedia products digital services from telephone or cable TV firms? Are interactive multimedia products movies or games from entertainment companies? Are interactive multimedia products data networks from online computer services? These are three ways to define the product in the minds of manufacturers, suppliers, and retail sellers.

Category Mistake All these marketers make a category mistake.[8] They don't know answers to the following consumer-based product questions.

What bits of information do *customers want* in terms of multimedia products from the telephone, cable TV, and entertainment industries? How will customers use these bits of information to enhance or change their lifestyle? To what extent are these bits of information and their uses *observable* or *unobservable?* How do these influences affect *consumer choice?*

Does digital technology drive multimedia toward *standardization* (or *minimum differentiation*)? Do cultural differences force product *adaptation (maximum differentiation)?* Do industry and *market contingencies* push adaptation first and standardization later?

Category mistakes are easy to make.[9] We patched them over in chapters 7 and 8 by adopting the distinction between telephones and telecom services. Wire and wireless digital telephones are hardware that offer customers speedy point-to-point interactive voice and data communications. Cable TV is hardware that offers consumers "500" choices of video and entertainment services. Multimedia blurs this distinction and makes these two sets of hardware functionally identical.

Marketing Strategy Here are crucial questions for global marketers:

1.   Which activities? Can we identify a set of customer-oriented actions with future payoffs?

2.   Which products, and for whom? Can we create a new product market category?

3.   Who are our customers? Can we identify market segments among consumers of multimedia products and services?

4.   What is our added value? Can we classify interactive multimedia into value-added products?

5.   Can we do better than our competitors? Can we use information about culture, tastes, and behavior to make good marketing decisions under uncertainty and with incomplete information?

6.   Do we have a competitive marketing strategy for ourselves? Do we have a competitive marketing strategy for our partners? Can we gain significant market share by applying a contingency perspective to the 4Ps marketing mix?

7.   Should we find better competitors? What is the makeup of our industry? Are the competitive forces changing in our favor? Is the overseas environment conducive to our products?

Environmental Scan: Modernization

A new product category is emerging from the romance of Hollywood with the graphic capability of Silicon Valley, and their digital convergence with the telephone and cable TV industries. It is called interactive amusements, motion pictures, and multimedia and involves or interacting with the TV, the computer, or both. This new category is changing market structure. For example, in the helter-skelter race to place multimedia products in the hands of consumers, telephone and cable TV monopolies are becoming more similar to entertainment oligopolies. All firms are increasing their R&D expenditures; this rush of innovation is shaping the market structure of the multimedia industry.[10]

Market Structure

Under the assumption of imperfect foresight and within concentrated industries, cost-reducing innovation renders durable goods obsolete. The least competitive firms cut their R&D expenditures, sell themselves to others, and eventually drop out of the industry. Therefore, marketers do their utmost to add value through innovation, sell rather than rent their newest products, and charge a high fee for service for all multimedia entertainment products.

Commitment from Buyers

Commitment from potential customers is crucial to the success of firms within the multimedia industry. However, to get a pledge from buyers requires sellers to make a crucial product decision. Do multimedia marketers increase R&D expenditures and future costs, and thus presume their products are durable in the minds of consumers? Or do they reduce innovation levels and future costs, and thus assume their products are nondurable in the minds of their customers? Because marketing executives cannot uncover consumers' *unobservable attributes*, they don't know whether to offer differentiated or standardized differentiated products, or one at time of market entry and the other afterward. This is the *contingency environment* in which they must develop a product positioning strategy.

Modeling Consumer Behavior

What do we know about consumer demand for multimedia products? Buyer *tastes are heterogeneous*. The supply consists of traditional standardized products from the telephone, cable TV, and entertainment industries. Because firms lack knowledge about consumer preferences, they prefer to sell existing movies, TV programs, and computer games through expanded multimedia delivery systems. Notwithstanding all these "bells and whistles" from the 4Ps scheme (deals on monthly and pay-per-view *prices*, pre-existing *place* or cable delivery systems, and aggressive advertising *promotion*), consumer satisfaction is low.

Product Positioning Strategy of Maximum Differentiation

Without marketing research, consumer preferences are unknown and buyer decisions are unpredictable. Marketers continue to offer products adopted from the telephone, cable TV, and entertainment industries as imperfect substitutes for innovative multimedia products. This *product positioning strategy of maximum differentiation* does not lead to higher levels of consumer satisfaction for multimedia products.

Product Positioning Strategy of Minimum Differentiation

However, if marketing research finds heterogeneous tastes and if these translate into predictable results, marketers end category mistakes and introduce standardized multimedia products across local, regional, national, and international markets. This *product positioning strategy of minimum differentiation* leads to higher levels of consumer satisfaction for multimedia products.

Because the multimedia industry is relatively new, most marketing questions remain unanswered, and marketing executives must prepare themselves for a wide array of industry, market, and cultural possibilities. We will show how marketers uncover facts about customers, get commitments from buyers, and create a new product category, industry, and market structure.

Initial Analysis of Marketing Opportunities

Throughout the world, preteen and teenage boys call interactive multimedia by its popular brand names, Sega Genesis or Super Nintendo. Super Mario Brothers, Sonic the Hedgehog, Street Fighter II, and Mortal Kombat are interactive video game movies that rival passive prime-time television and standard Hollywood fare. Here are the *market facts*. In the United States, sales of video games equal $5.3 billion and sales of movie tickets equal $4.9 billion.

British sales from video games are US $1.5 billion, and sales in Italy, France, and Germany total US $250 million. Worldwide revenues from video games now exceed US $10 billion.[11]

Forecasting Market Segments

How did this all come about? First, remember the sweeping technological revolution that moved successive groups of adults to become users of computers in their businesses and VCRs in their homes. Second, recognize the growing passion of governments to privatize the telephone and telecom services industries that we discussed in chapters 7 and 8. Third, recall the discussion in chapters 3 through 6 about the disconnection between those who came of age before and after 1968. All three are "soft" information for our environmental scan.

Parents who became adults in the 1970s. They are home-bound, middle-aged customers whose routine purchasing patterns include owning personal computers. However, few prefer video games over cable TV movies for home entertainment. These parents don't understand how their sons can spend hours playing video games.

Parents who became adults in the 1980s. These younger adults have more facility with personal computers. They tend to prefer cable TV movies and video games over reading for home entertainment. These parents are more visual than previous generations and some join online computer networks simply to play cards, chess, and action games. Some are grown-up video kids.

Product Market Segment #1: Teenage Boys Become Men In the 1990s, these teenage vidkids are becoming men. They are under 25, possibly married, and with one or two children of their own, but these young adult men spend their money extending childhood game-playing habits well into their adult years. Now they play Joe Montana II Sportstalk Football (Sega) and Jordon vs. Bird basketball (Electronic Arts). When they buy the book *Sega Genesis Secrets*,[12] these men learn crucial passwords to improve their performance. For them games are life.

Product Market Segment #2: Adult Women Most young girls can take or leave video games. When they become adult women they prefer books, movies, and television soaps to video games and sports. If young adult women are going to be a part of the multimedia market, Hollywood must tell them stories, Silicon Valley must turn these into interactive games, and the telephone and cable industries must deliver interactive digital products to the home.

For example, Robyn Davidson reads from her own best seller, *Tracks,* as the photographer Rick Smolan creates a multimedia version of his coffee-table book, *From Alice to Ocean,* with short video clips on Australian culture, geography, and animal life.[13] With a CD-ROM player, the video is viewed on a personal computer, and a mouse lets the viewer (male or female) select the side trips each takes within the "virtual reality" of Australia. Clearly, women users are broadening the market for interactive multimedia to include other forms of entertainment, such as travel stories and soap operas.

Asking Questions About Future Business

Today's TV programs and motion pictures can be spun off into tomorrow's interactive multimedia. The task is to predict all the different paths home viewers might want to take within CD-ROM programs. Then the users (father, mother, young adult woman, and teenage boy) are in control. These "early adopters" are technophiles who are eager to try out the latest personal computers, modems, CD-ROM players, and other digital equipment. By the year 2000, the two product market segments (teenage boys become men, adult women) will divide and subdivide several times over. The possibilities are almost endless.

Clues to Capturing Customers

Between 1991 and 1993, AT&T tested interacting with your TV. Here's what the firm learned. Their future customers won't play multimedia products on souped-up personal computers; instead, multimedia players have to be mindlessly simple to operate, and interactive multimedia must be billed as an advanced form of television entertainment.[14] According to Vincent Grosso, a former public relations executive for AT&T, "Nobody got up to get closer to the set. They sat back to be entertained. It's a TV paradigm."[15] Besides providing entertainment, interactive TV has to offer transactions (to buy merchandise or compete for prizes), communications (among family and friends), and information (about superstars and sports figures).[16]

Although potential multimedia customers have heterogeneous tastes, AT&T found that *these preferences are predictable.* Thus, we are able to avoid a category mistake, pursue a product positioning strategy of minimum differentiation, deal with industry and market likelihoods, and raise levels of consumer satisfaction. We do so at the very *beginning of the product life cycle* where growing the interactive multimedia market is the primary concern of all telephone, cable TV, and entertainment firms.

Summary: Scanning Modernization

Marketers find that preteen and teenage boys are the one key market segment among consumers of interactive fantasies, *manga*, sports, wars, and other video games. Successful marketing executives grow the interactive multimedia market by converting heterogeneous tastes into predictable preferences, then turning games into family entertainment. Moreover, to capture young women and newly married families, interactive multimedia stops using personal computers and transforms itself into a new form of TV entertainment. Even under conditions of uncertainty about market structure and limited information about consumer attributes, marketers pursue a product positioning strategy of minimum differentiation or standardization of interactive entertainment.

The Firm-Specific Assignment

Marketers manage final demand by positioning global products within markets committed to modernization; see Exhibit 9–6. Given the cultural realities surrounding the multimedia information revolution, positioning decisions include creating a product category out of product usage, segmenting by market response, and allowing for brand switching. These managerial decisions are based on incomplete "soft" information, and their success depends on avoiding too many category mistakes.

Understanding Decision Making Under Uncertainty

All competitors in the interactive multimedia industry agree that their products are being debugged, refined, improved, and changed. The existing market is small, but the potential market is large. Demand is limited to preteen and teenage boys, but with a few significant changes in the product, demand could grow to include young adult men, young women, and families.

Exhibit 9–6.
Firm-Specific Analysis: Multimedia
The Competitive Scan

Traditional Frame Analysis for Global Marketing
Firm-Specific 4Ps Analysis and Product Life Cycle
Entry: simultaneous introduction among teenage boys
Growth: sequential introduction among young adult families
Maturity: routine purchasing behavior among parents
Saturation: all groups shop for best or lowest price
Decline: all groups check out advent of new technology
Firm-Specific 4Ps Analysis and Value Creation
Multiply uses of information
Restructure category
Formal market research
Product positioning strategy
Product-development life cycle
National Marketing Decisions and Competitive Analysis
Global, largely American popular culture
Generational changes breed uncoupling of age-period groups
Speeding up product life cycle for value-added products
Core meaning of postlinear interactive multimedia entertainment

Nontraditional Frame Analysis for Global Marketing
Marketing Management Frame and Teamwork
Prepare for marketing uncertainties
Acknowledge substitution in use
Promote bundles of benefits
Use care in delineating product categories
Adapt product to match future unanticipated needs
Carry out market response segmentation
Prepare for switching among global brands

Copyright © Douglas F. Lamont. All rights reserved.

Teenage Boys Shape the Multimedia Market Many teenage markets around the world are commercially exploitable simultaneously because buyers are precommitted to Japanese *manga* video games. Yet marketers are spending large sums on R&D to keep their competitors' products off the shelves of retail rental shops and out of the homes of buyers. We are in the *introductory phase of the product life cycle* in the United States, Europe, Japan, and most countries of the world. In the minds of teenage boys, interactive multimedia games are a durable part of their lifestyle.

Yet differences do exist among customers throughout the world. American boys and men prefer more bloodthirsty games. Japanese young adult men prefer games with less violence and role-playing games with some subtlety and complexity. According to Takashi Yamamori, a general manager of the publishing firm Tokuma Shoten Intermedia, American-style action games "are too simple for Japanese."[17] Excessive violence is not popular in Germany, where the public generally prefers nonmilitarism.

Young Adults Grow the Interactive Market In the minds of young women and upscale families, interactive amusements still are a nondurable part of their routine purchasing behavior. Many of these potential markets around the world are commercially exploitable sequentially because buyers are precommitted to Hollywood motion pictures and television situation comedies. Here, too, marketers are spending large sums on R&D to keep their competitors' products off the shelves of retail rental shops and out of the homes of buyers.

When these products become similar to TV entertainment, many middle-aged customers will give their precommitment to firms offering interactive videos on games, foreign travel, home shopping, sports statistics, and new fashion. Then we will be in the *growth phase of the product life cycle*.

Creating a Category Out of Product Usage

Here is the information now available to global marketers in the telephone, cable TV, and entertainment businesses. They "know" interactive amusements, motion pictures, and multimedia are the wave of the future. Thus, they are shipping products with the expectation of sales in final markets.

Value Added However, we don't know how customers are using these products and how they will use these goods in the future. More importantly, we have no idea about how customers will multiply the uses of multimedia products in their personal lives and within their businesses. We can only guess about how added value will be created.

Restructuring a Category No doubt customers will change their perceptions of what is the proper use of these products. Then marketers will have to restructure the product category to fit the opinions of customers. This is one of the most difficult tasks confronting global marketers. Let's look at how one telecommunications firm sought to get better information about the product category.

Formal Market Research Through an online central server system, with microwave radio relays, and fixed directional antennas in the home, AT&T provided families in Chicago with sample multimedia products.[18] Similar to a record of telephone calls, each multimedia choice is recorded. Then marketing research personnel followed a *substitution in use* approach to analyzing the data about simultaneous clustering of usage and revelations about product-market structure.[19] Crucial facts come from the consumers' perceptions of the core meanings of interactive products. They help families choose those categories of interactive multimedia products that can be surrogates for "bundles" of benefits. Using interactive products is a way for consumers to achieve their ends – that is, to be entertained.

New Category The category is postlinear interactive multimedia entertainment or PIME. For membership in the category, products must be similar and typical. They must share common features, and consumers must presuppose the presence of such features. Moreover, these products must serve as props for some culturally defined purpose – that is, for families to be entertained together. Thus, the boundary of the PIME category is based on usage for entertainment, transactions, communications, and information.

Product Positioning Strategy Our product positioning strategy of minimum differentiation (or standardization) offers us the opportunity to communicate the product's suitability for several end uses. This, in turn, facilitates recall and routine purchasing behavior, especially when consumers have fuzzy goals about how to spend their entertainment dollars.

Product-Development Life Cycle However, we don't know two crucial pieces of information: After initial market entry, how will consumers adapt interactive multimedia products for their own unanticipated needs?

What will be the long-term uses of interactive multimedia? Until we know the answers to these contingency questions we cannot discuss the *maturity, saturation,* and *decline phases of the product life cycle* as these pertain to the use and sale of interactive multimedia products within the United States, Europe, or Japan.

Competitive Scan: Interactive Multimedia

Let's segment the PIME category based on choice, response, and usage, so-called *market response segmentation*.[20] This gives us the opportunity to apply the marketing mix, the 4Ps scheme, and the product positioning strategy outlined above to market segmentation.

Minimum differentiation requires video game manufacturers to use *brand choice* as the means to segment multimedia markets. Clearly, Nintendo, Sega, and Electronic Arts are well-known brands. Their usage tells us when and how interactive products move through the product life cycle.

Can we increase usage? If Nintendo updates its games, more new games will be bought and more older games will be rented. New games expand the market. However, if Sega simply lowers price, more games will be rented, but the market will not expand. Teenage boys and young men tend to be price-insensitive when it comes to video games.

Positioning in the Category

Customers increase their use of video games based on new technology and through interaction with the TV. Large numbers of customers switch brands (from Nintendo to Sega, or from both to AT&T) based on digital telephone and cable TV access in homes, in schools, and in video arcades. We call this a *category purchase*.

By examining the impact of changing one or more aspects of the marketing mix on demographic data, cultural information, political news, and other marketing intelligence, we find out about market response segmentation through the actual use of brands among consumers. This is an important way to gain information in global markets when demographic and cultural information is imperfect, scarce, or unavailable.

Teenage boys are loyal Nintendo customers. They don't switch brands on the basis of price and promotion. Moreover, we can preassign new customers based on previous information about market response segmentation; for example, young adult men share many routine purchase patterns with teenage boys. Both insist on new technology and updated video games, and both will buy more interactive multimedia videos when they become available through telephone and cable TV.

Preparing a Positioning Strategy

Our major findings are as follows: High response to technological change in brand choice translates into high response in category purchase. Update video games and more will be bought; the overall market expands. However, high response to price and promotion in brand choice does not translate into high response in category purchase. Lower the price of video games and more will be bought or rented, but the overall market does not expand. In short, product development, technological change, and improved delivery systems are the marketing mix keys to success in the product-development life cycle for interactive multimedia products. This is our positioning strategy.

Estimates of Market Potential

Revenues from Super Mario Bros. 3, Nintendo Entertainment System's hot video game, top $500 million in the United States; only the movie *ET* grossed more money.[21] SMB3 sold 7 million copies in the United States and 4 million in Japan. If it were a record, it would have gone platinum 11 times, a feat accomplished by Michael Jackson.

Today, Nintendo is more successful than Toyota and all other Japanese companies. Nintendo also made more money than all the American movie studios combined, and more than the three television networks combined. Between 1985 and 1990, in just five short years, Nintendo machines and video games made it into more than one-third of all US and Japanese households. Nintendo dominates the product category with an 85-percent market share.

Predicting Potential Sales

AT&T, Time Warner, Viacom, Turner, some Baby Bells, and all Hollywood studios want a piece of the future – combine computer power with home entertainment systems, and integrate television, video recorders, CD sound systems, and the telephone. In Japan, Nintendo already has a Family Computer Communications Network System that provides video game entertainment, does home shopping, asks friends about a sushi order, and obtains movie information. When introduced in the United States, it will dwarf the Prodigy network (a joint venture of IBM and Sears) with 1.3 million subscribers. The *Los Angeles Times* estimates the world interactive (Internet) market to be worth US $3.5 billion annually by the year 2000.

Setting Up New Cultural Standards

Clearly, television defined the culture of parents, and interactive electronic multimedia are defining the culture of their children. As early as 1990, Nielsen Media Research reported that boys spend more time playing Nintendo video games than watching children's television.

Now Nintendo is entering the collective culture of Japan, the United States, Europe, and other parts of the world. Recall our discussion of Japanese culture in chapter 5. We found humor, fantasy, harmony, quality, and *nihonjin* as significant cultural attributes of Japanese society. Super Mario helps children laugh, offers them a way to get out of worlds in which they are stuck, makes them one with nature, shows boys how to do the best job possible, and melds Japanese heroes into universal champions. Is Super Mario more widely recognized than Mickey Mouse? Many advertising people think so. Has Super Mario changed the cultural values of American children? Some students of culture believe it is happening right before our eyes.

Similar Market Segments Worldwide

Nintendo, Sega, NEC, AT&T, IBM, and Sony are *global brands*. Even though Sega and NEC spent a great deal of money trying to switch teenage boys away from Nintendo, little movement occurred within the category purchase. Nintendo kept 85 percent or more of the market. Sega's products, such as Genesis, are flashier, but boys don't find them as exciting as Nintendo's Super Mario products. With very little effort, we have our market response segmentation based on brand choice among our primary customers.

Examining Brand Switching

Because substance is more important than show in the interactive video game business, we can divide customers into two groups. The first group is preteen and teenage boys who are more adept at manipulating the wizardry of the video games and who carry their eye-hand dexterity into manhood. They form the first and primary market segment for Nintendo games, and they give us clues about why cutting price or doing more promotion doesn't work for Sega and others in the video game business.

The second group is preteen and teenage girls who prefer more story and more color and who carry these interests and values into womanhood. This market segment is small and growing year after year. It should be the primary focus of attention for other firms in the video game business, but it is not clear that Sega and others recognize their role within the market structure of interactive video games. However, from this second segment comes video games and other multimedia products for the family.

Positioning a Brand

Let's summarize our *brand positioning strategy*. Within a short period of time, Nintendo customers will have to make a decision. Do they continue with 16-bit or 32-bit Nintendo hardware and software, that is, older technology? Do they go over to a 64-bit system? Do they give up special hardware and switch to multimedia products offered via telephone wireless lines by AT&T or via wired cable TV lines by Time Warner, Viacom, and Turner?

Income Effect Boys from upper-income families will be asked which telephone or cable home entertainment system they would like in addition to the Nintendo system. However, boys from middle-class families will be forced to switch when parents decide they can afford only one system of home interactive multimedia entertainment. Since Nintendo gets the bulk of its sales revenue from this latter group of boys, its products must be so different that they are unique in the minds of these young boys. Or, Nintendo must change its focus and become a complete home entertainment company with ownership in wire or wireless lines, cable TV lines, central server systems, home receivers, and software.

Organizational Learning Such change in organizational focus is very difficult for a successful firm to do in the short period of time required for Nintendo to become competitive with AT&T and the other firms that seek market share in the home entertainment industry. Moreover, it leads to a dilution in brand belief among its primary customers, preteen and teenage boys. Nintendo might lose everything in the coming industry shake-out.

Summary: Scanning Interactive Multimedia

Marketers know preteen and teenage boys are the key to family decisions about home interactive multimedia entertainment systems. Right now they are wedded to Nintendo hardware and software because the games have more substance than competing products from Sega and NEC. Successful marketing executives from AT&T, the cable TV companies, and Hollywood entertainment firms know they must offer the same amount of exciting substance to boys and slant the other multimedia products toward values for girls, women, and young families. The competitive battle is Nintendo's to lose.

National Marketing Decisions

Marketers manage final demand by signaling detailed national information about interactive multimedia services; see Exhibit 9-7. Marketing executives also expand final demand by convincing affluent teenage vidkids and their parents to augment use of interactive video games with newer forms of multimedia. Many multimedia marketers use product usage, market response segmentation, and category information to prepare a product positioning strategy. These are important developments in marketing multimedia throughout the world.

Here are the crucial product marketing decisions: Does Nintendo stay with its standardized proprietary entertainment system and video games? Does Nintendo adapt to changes in the home multimedia market by manufacturing a machine to play games, movies, and TV programs? Does Nintendo take its existing products off the market when they reach the maturity phase of the product life cycle?

Moreover, does Nintendo strike a deal with a telecom services firm to transmit its games over wire and wireless, telephone and cable TV lines? Does Nintendo go into an alliance with an entertainment firm to gain access to new movie and TV characters? What does Nintendo gain and lose by forming partnerships, alliances, and joint ventures similar to AT&T's?

Facing Up to Market Contingencies

Most Japanese consumer electronics firms (e.g., Matsushita, Sony, and NEC) slipped aimlessly through the years 1991–1993.[22] Their family markets for televisions, VCRs, and camcorders and their teenage boys' market for video

Exhibit 9-7.
National Marketing Decisions: Multimedia
The Marketing Scan

Traditional Frame Analysis for Global Marketing
Firm-Specific 4Ps Analysis and Decision Making Under Uncertainty
Signal national interactive multimedia information
Succeed from expansion of interactive multimedia entertainment
Grow through rationalization of computer communications
Pay attention to alternative multimedia lifestyles

National Marketing Decisions and Marketing Strategy
Company Characteristics
International experience
Research and development costs
Marketing expenses

Product/Industry Characteristics
Technology orientation of industry
Core meaning of products
More differentiation

Market Characteristics
Cultural attitudes
Socio-economic preferences
Customization of products
Similar clusters of consumers worldwide

National Marketing Decisions and Marketing Forecasts
Continuing trend is unrealistic in all major markets of the world
Amplifying trend builds on routine durable purchases by vidkids
Doubling trend is realistic for young married, adult males

Nontraditional Frame Analysis for Global Marketing
Marketing Management Frame and Marketing Investments
Look for unobservable habits
Carry out unconventional thinking
Establish long-term goals in emerging multimedia industry
Seek quality, high-profit consumers
Attack switchable customers
Gain significant market share
Leverage investments in products and services

Continued on next page

Exhibit 9-7. *Continued from previous page*

Marketing Management Frame and Return on Investment
   Convert installed telephone capacity to interactive multimedia
   Quality of market share keeps home-based customers with us
   Seek customers from all groups, social classes, and lifestyles
   Leverage investments in connections, servers, and program content

games are saturated; their products are based on research done 10 years ago; their vision about consumer preferences is out of date. Without a change of focus, these Japanese firms may find themselves at the mercy of AT&T, BT, or other telecommunications firms, or in bed with Time Warner, Viacom-Paramount, Star TV, or other entertainment companies. The Japanese consumer electronics companies are in danger of becoming low-cost hardware producers while AT&T and Viacom-Paramount dominate the more profitable interactive multimedia software fields. These are the contingencies facing Nintendo.

The contingency framework of marketing standardization is divided into several categories:[23]

Company Characteristics Nintendo has many years of *international experience* as the firm that dominates the interactive video game category. It operates in most national markets through its own subsidiaries, and it has adapted its games to suit Japanese and American cultural tastes. Given Nintendo's seasoning, the firm should be able to change its products to meet new market situations. However, substantial *research and development costs and marketing expenses* are involved in changing hardware, producing new compatible software, and going after new customer markets. Moreover, Nintendo management is good at selling interactive video games, but it may not be very successful at jointly marketing interactive multimedia that are transmitted via telephone, cable TV, wireless, radio microwaves, and satellites.

Product/Industry Characteristics Although Nintendo games have a *technological orientation*, future competing products within the emerging industry called interactive multimedia are even more technologically oriented.

Nintendo video games are old line. They appeal to the tastes, habits, and customs of preteen and teenage boys. Nintendo products don't cater to the specific cultural needs of families who want home interactive entertainment. In short, Nintendo games are no longer *unique* in the minds of customers.

Market Characteristics Today, consumers around the world are familiar with video games from Nintendo, and Hollywood films from Time Warner, Viacom-Paramount, and Disney. Video games, movies, and TV situation comedies are standardized products with some minimum differentiation to conform to distinct *cultural attitudes* in the United States, Europe, and Japan. *Customization* occurs by translating into local languages and by reducing the use of sexual and violent material in more conservative societies. Further cultural adaptation depends on the ability of firms to build into their multimedia the means by which consumers change their home entertainment to suit their own *preferences*.

Understanding Marketing Strategy

Within the United States, Europe, Japan, and many countries of the world, similar clusters of consumers exist. These telecom customers have the same demand characteristics as they relate to similar wired and wireless products, made anywhere in the world. For example, Nintendo users want standardized video games in which change is built into the category purchase of Super Mario Bros. 3.

At first, some product differentiation is going to be the hallmark of the home interactive multimedia systems chosen by the world's consumers. After initial market entry, consumers in each country will change the first interactive multimedia product to suit their own use. Those multimedia firms that gain worldwide coverage have a chance of doing well commercially at home and abroad. However, global standardization of products and adaptation of other aspects of the marketing mix are no guarantees of financial success.

Standardization might not be the optimal approach in all markets.[24] This has important implications for our cases. Those firms that pursue product standardization coordinate their marketing mix efforts centrally (e.g., Nintendo). Those firms that pursue marketing mix adaptation permit national subsidiaries to carry out their own activities (e.g., AT&T, Time Warner, and others). Given Nintendo's corporate history, the firm may not be able to change the way it does business or to pursue a positioning strategy of product standardization and marketing mix adaptation. Nintendo may fail in its quest to dominate the home interactive multimedia entertainment market.

Marketing Scan: Joint Ventures

"Most research on product positioning supports the idea of differentiation. Product standardization (minimum differentiation) occurs only under very limited assumptions. Yet, similar products are often observed in the market-place."[25] These are worldwide brands bought by similar middle-income consumers in the national telephone market segments of the global market. Unfortunately, marketers always don't know all the reasons why some brands (e.g., Nintendo, McDonald's, and Coke) find favor among consumers throughout the world, and others (e.g., Sega, Burger King, and Royal Crown) fall into disfavor in one or more countries.

Carrying Out Marketing Investments

Marketers must invest in customers and reduce the *uncertainty over unobservable attributes*.[26] Here's an action plan. First, determine which customers to target, then segment them by lifestyles, and finally place them into groups with observable traits. Moreover, use unconventional thinking to uncover those demographic reference groups that help us find our long-term customers. In the quest for first-mover advantage, all multimedia competitors must decide to what extent they will pursue alliances and joint ventures, and a combination of hardware standardization, software adaptation, and marketing mix differentiation in price, promotion, and place strategies. This is their *contingency perspective*.

There are five basic marketing investment questions:[27]

1. What are our long-term marketing goals?

2. What returns are we earning from our marketing investment?

3. What is the quality of our market share – do we have customers who will stay with the product for many years?

4. Which customers should we seek, and which should we avoid?

5. How can we leverage our investments so that we can reduce customer acquisition costs and maximize our returns?

Pursuing Competitiveness

In chapter 8, we noted that successful marketing executives accelerate the product life cycle and form joint ventures with better-informed customers. This *stretch and leveraging competitive marketing strategy* creates a new marketing mindset. Even so, most new products fail. Their intended customers don't buy them, or if customers make initial purchases, they don't make repeat purchases after market entry. Most products never get out of the entry phase of the product life cycle.

Strategies for Increasing Marketing Effectiveness

Also in chapter 8, we noted that successful marketing executives form alliances, partnerships, and joint ventures with better-informed customers. Let's try to match the four phases of the product life cycle to our likely customers.[28]

Entry Phase – High Profit

During the market entry phase of the product life cycle, marketers pay special attention to high-profit customers. Initially, the product is available in limited quantities to those "gadget freaks" who want to be first with the newest in multimedia technology.[29] Will these early adopters pave the way to large sales later?

Growth Phase – Share Determining

The firm gambles the new interactive product will be "adopted by cable networks, satellite television stations, telephone companies, schools, and games arcades."[30] The facts:

Installed base. The video game giants have an installed base of 55 million players in the United States.[31] However, only Nintendo is a runaway marketing success. Worse yet for other firms is that Nintendo's video players are incompatible with those from Sega and with the multimedia formats from Panasonic, IBM, and Apple. More bad news: A VCR player delivers entertainment at a fraction of the cost. So 3DO, the newest noncompatible technology, is battling against stiff odds.

Educational software. What to do? We must go after those customers who will give multimedia players above-average growth. These will determine our market share. According to Bruce Ryon, who directs multimedia research at

Dataquest, parents see the coming merger of arts and technology[32] and want it at home for their children. For example, Knowledge Adventure Inc., a California-based computer company, markets interactive multimedia programming for CD-ROMs. Some of their products include Space Adventure, Dinosaur Adventure, and a children's zoo program.

Unconventional thinking. Since a good chance exists for a new technology to be an orphan, the firm must do something very different. It must engage those with higher levels of disposable income (e.g., grandparents and parents) to engage in storytelling, fantasy, simulation, and role playing with their grandchildren and children through interactive multiplayers.[33] These older demographic groups are important opinion leaders. If older people decide to carry out their cultural role with the help of multimedia, then software for PCs and CD-ROMs will make one of these hardware businesses a great success.

Maturity Phase – Switchable

Money is made in producing software. This includes video games that *are* Hollywood movies.[34] Since Americans now spend more on cartoon-based video games than on movie tickets, they might spend a lot more money on interacting with real persons. Hollywood is "re-purposing" *Aladdin, Jurassic Park, Cliffhanger, The Last Action Hero*, and other films for games, or shooting new films especially for games. Sega sees this as a window of opportunity to switch loyal Nintendo customers to Sega players. That's an expensive marketing investment.

CD-ROM technology. Everyone is jumping on the multimedia bandwagon. Magazines (e.g., *Time* and *US News & World Report*) want to be available through online electronic bulletin boards.[35] David Bowie's single, "Jump They Say," is released on an interactive CD-ROM and bundled with a new Apple PowerCD player.[36] This is a reasonable marketing investment.

Program content marketing. Money is also made in owning programming content and controlling its flow through cable lines. Nynex, the Baby Bell for New York and New England, bought access to programming from MTV, Showtime, and other Viacom-owned networks.[37] As noted in chapter 8, US West, the Baby Bell for the Rocky Mountain states, made a deal on programming content with Time Warner, and Bell Atlantic provides video programming in New York, New Jersey, and Virginia. Nynex-Viacom, US West–Time Warner, and Bell Atlantic see opportunities in switching Nintendo customers to television-based home multimedia. This, too, is a reasonable marketing investment.

Postlinear multimedia marketing. These postlinear, random-access applications from video servers are opportunities to switch customers to new interactive, computer-based technologies. They come to us through a video dial tone; this, too, is a reasonable marketing investment.

Switchability window. Many years ago, Nintendo acquired its customers by default because no one else saw the opportunities to sell video arcade games to preteen and teenage boys. They stayed with Nintendo as they grew into manhood. Now these men are asking for a change. They want something different for themselves. The switchability window is open.

Decline Phase – Loyal High Profit

Will Nintendo customers switch to competing products? Many will stay loyal to Nintendo and continue to buy Nintendo software for Nintendo machines. These customers provide Nintendo with the quality of its existing market share. However, Nintendo cannot leverage its marketing investment in teenage boys and turn it into returns from new customers (e.g., parents who want the newest technology for their children, and grandparents who want to continue to be storytellers for their grandchildren).

Nintendo's earlier marketing investments paid off in later years. It built the category of arcade and home-based video games, and it beat back Sega, NEC, and other competitors. Nintendo created brand loyalty among customers who were willing to pay a premium for its hardware and Super Mario Bros. 3. That era of market share dominance is over.

Marketing Implementation

Let's see where our unconventional thinking takes us. If we make a marketing investment, will we get long-term returns – that is, create a category, grow the total market, increase our market share, and turn quality consumers into loyal, high-profit customers? To put it another way, can we make marketing investments in the entry and growth phases of the product life cycle so that we are the dominant market leader in the maturity phase of the life cycle? Here are our choices.

Invest in existing video game technology. This is the Sega strategy. Produce movies for video games, and make them available on incompatible Sega players. Can Sega spend enough money to switch a majority of Nintendo customers? Probably not. Moreover, will Sega create a new market category, grow the total market, increase its share, and turn consumers into loyal Sega customers? This product positioning strategy is a nonstarter because the returns are not worth the marketing investment.

Invest in newer CD-ROM technology. This is the strategy of Apple, IBM, and Matsushita (Panasonic). Produce CD-ROMs for computer and TV screens, and make them available on many different incompatible systems. Can any one firm spend enough money to convince a majority of customers to buy its product over all others? Does any single firm know all there is to know about customer attitudes toward CD-ROMs? Most attributes are still unobservable. Will these firms create a new product category and grow the total market? Will individual firms increase market share and create loyal, high-profit customers? We simply don't know how customers will apply CD-ROM technology to their own lifestyles during and after market entry. This product positioning strategy is a second-best choice.

Planning the International Product Campaign

Our unconventional thinking takes us to video servers, fiber-optic wire and radio microwave wireless connections, program content, and "thumb surfing" by our home-based consumers. We need to create a new market category. Then we must grow the total market, increase our market share, and turn television customers into loyal consumers. This is a marketing investment worthy of large financial returns, and it must take place continuously during all phases of the product life cycle.

The answers to basic marketing investment questions are as follows:

1. Our long-term marketing goal is to convert installed telephone and cable capacity to interactive multimedia.

2. Our potential return from this product marketing investment is greater than the returns from other marketing investments.

3. The quality of our market share is such that our home-based customers will stay with us.

4. We must seek customers from almost all income groups, social classes, and lifestyles because we want to mass market interactive multimedia.

5. We can leverage our investments in telephone and cable connections, global video server networks, and Hollywood program content so that consumers pay low monthly rental costs and we maximize our financial returns for many years in the future.

Three forecasts. The "continuing trend" forecast is the easiest to make because things do go on as before. Interactive multimedia doesn't conform to traditional lifestyles in Europe, the United States, and Japan. Interactive multimedia is so new that the "continuing trend" is unrealistic in all major markets.

The "amplifying trend" forecast assumes computer-driven multimedia firms aggressively market their interactive entertainment services; more vidkids then purchase these multimedia products. In the United States and Japan, these routine durable purchases are crucial parts of their lifestyle. This trend will develop because we are at the beginning of a major entertainment revolution with no end in sight. Only marketers who create a product category out of product usage and practice segmentation by market response will be successful in the changing interactive multimedia industry.

The "doubling trend" forecast assumes multimedia firms convert parents to postlinear interactive multimedia entertainment. If we define this older age-period cohort group as highly successful young adult, married males, then this is the most likely forecast in the United States. Product diffusion occurs rapidly because high-income married males want these new interactive multimedia services. This one piece of information should help marketers put together an effective marketing strategy for the US interactive multimedia industry.

Summary: Scanning Joint Ventures

Successful marketing executives realize they don't know everything about consumer habits. During market entry and other phases of the product's life cycle, many cultural choices are unobservable by global marketers and unclear to domestic marketers. With "hard" market response data and with "soft" information about consumer preferences, marketing executives prefer telephone-cable TV-Hollywood joint ventures as the best way to minimize substantial market risks. Through alliances, partnerships, and joint ventures, marketers reduce the possibility of making a category mistake as they position new interactive multimedia products.

Inclusive Contexts for Global Marketing

Exhibit 9-8 sums up the inclusive contexts for global marketing in the multimedia industry. We examine reinventing a product category, the industry, and competing firms. We also study two types of decision making under uncertainty: culturally based demand analysis and organizationally based industry analysis. These two focuses help us direct our research to answering

Exhibit 9-8.
Inclusive Contexts For Global Marketing

Market Risk
Govern the market through reinvented business environment
  Reinvent product category
Foreign investment, joint ventures, nonroutine partnerships
Long-term planning horizon
Unknown competitive possibilities and imperfect information
Political Frame

Firm-Specific 4Ps Analysis (A)
Culturally based decision making under uncertainty
Demand analysis, cultural analysis, age-period cohort analysis
Disconnection among age groups and adoption of new offerings
Cross-cultural analysis and similar self-referencing criteria
Value creation and multiplying bits of information
Cultural Frame

Firm-Specific 4Ps Analysis (B)
Organizationally based decision making under uncertainty
Product life cycle and positioning strategies
Value creation
  Multiply uses of information
  Restructure category
Marketing investments
Return on investment
Marketing Management Frame

National Marketing Decisions
Supply analysis
Competitive analysis
Scanning potential markets, offerings, segments
Formal and walking-around research
Segmentation strategies

Continued on next page

Exhibit 9-7. *Continued from previous page*

Marketing strategy

Identify customer-oriented actions with future payoffs

Apply contingency perspective to 4Ps marketing mix

Find better competitors

Value Added

Multiplying bits of information

Multiplying uses of information

Technological Frame

---

important questions: How will our customers multiply the use of our products, and how will we make money on our marketing investments? Again, we deal with technology as a driving force in managerial decision making under uncertainty. Our choices determine whether we will be a success at global marketing.

Conclusions

Providers of interactive multimedia products bring hardware players, program content software, and telecom connections into the global market. Rapid technological change is occurring, and marketers are groping for the most appropriate product strategy.

Let's return to our initial three learning objectives:

1. Discuss the importance of standardization and adaptation to product positioning strategy.

    You should have a clear understanding of differences between standardization (minimum differentiation) and adaptation (maximum differentiation) and of how many situations in the emerging multimedia industry require a contingency perspective.

2. Outline the impact of consumer heterogeneity, category purchase, and market response segmentation on product positioning.

    You should be able to discuss the observable and unobservable habits of customers and the impact of socio-cultural factors on the creation of a new product category. You should draft an international product positioning plan, then invest in crucial market segments to build up market share and revenue.

3. Explain the usefulness of brands in building up market share in the interactive multimedia industry.

You should be aware that the Sega brand has little loyalty among consumers and that the Nintendo and Panasonic brands may not carry these Japanese companies into an interactive multimedia future. You should also recognize that "thumb surfing" is the entertainment preference for most future users of multimedia. Thus, brand names, such as AT&T, US West, Bell Atlantic, and others, may not have any real core meaning to consumers of postlinear interactive multimedia entertainment.

Sorting these facts from fiction is the work of global marketing executives.

Notes

1. Byong-Duk Rhee, Andre de Palma, Claes Fornell, and Jacques-Francois Thisse, "Restoring the Principle of Minimum Differentiation in Product Positioning," *Journal of Economics & Management Strategy* 1:3 (Fall 1992): 475–505. The authors discuss the relationship between unobservable attributes and consumer choice, and their collective impact on product standardization and product adaptation. The next two parts of the Introduction draw heavily from this article.

2. S. Tamer Cavusgil, Shaoming Zou, and G. M. Naidu, "Product and Promotion Adaptation in Export Ventures: An Empirical Investigation," *Journal of International Business Studies* 24:3 (Third Quarter 1993): 497.

3. Cavusgil, Zou, and Naidu, 485–86.

4. Nicholas Negroponte, "Bit by Bit on Wall Street: Lucky Strikes Again," *Wired* (May 1994): 144. He cites Bob Lucky, "Looking Ahead at Telecommunications," *Bellcore Exchange* (November 1993) for the idea.

5. John J. Keller, "AT&T Unveils Video Calling Between PCs," *The Wall Street Journal*, June 16, 1994, A3.

6. "Multimedia: The Oracle speaks," *The Economist*, February 19, 1994, 72–73.

7. Steve Lohr, "The Silver Disk May Soon Eclipse the Silver Screen," *The New York Times*, March 1, 1994, A1, D6.

8. Benjamin Woolley, *Virtual Worlds* (Oxford, UK: Blackwell Publishers, 1992): 68, 101-02. He cites Gilbert Ryle, *The Concept of Mind* (London, UK: Penguin, 1963) for the original idea.

9. Ibid.

10. Gregory E. Goering, "Innovation, Product Durability, and Market Structure," *Journal of Economics & Management Strategy* 1:4 (Winter 1992): 699-702, 720-21.

11. Philip Elmer-Dewitt, "The Amazing Video Game Boom," *Time*, September 27, 1993, 38.

12. Rusel DeMaria and Zach Meston, *Sega Genesis® Secrets* (Rocklin, CA: Prima Publishing, 1992).

13. Lawrence M. Fisher, "The Tools of a New Art Form," *The New York Times*, September 19, 1993, F7.

14. John J. Keller, "AT&T's Secret Multimedia Trials Offer Clues to Capturing Interactive Audiences," *The Wall Street Journal*, July 28, 1993, B1.

15. Ibid., B6.

16. Ibid., B1.

17. James O. Jackson, "Vidkids Everywhere," *Time*, September 27, 1993, 43.

18. Keller, 14.

19. S. Ratneshwar and Allan D. Shocker, "Substitution in Use and the Role of Usage Context in Product Category Structures," *Journal of Marketing Research,* 28:3 (August 1991): 281-95. The rest of the section applies the approach of these authors to interactive multimedia products.

20. Randolph E. Bucklin and Sunil Gupta, "Brand Choice, Purchase Incidence, and Segmentation: An Integrated Modeling Approach," *Journal of Marketing Research*, 29:2 (May 1992): 201-15. Throughout this section, we apply their approach to market segmentation research idea to video games.

21. This section draws heavily from David Sheff, *Game Over: How Nintendo Zapped an American Industry, Captured Your Dollars, and Enslaved your Children* (New York: Random House, 1993): 1-11.

22. David P. Hamilton, "Sharp Gets Set to Ride Hottest Trends in Electronics," *The Wall Street Journal*, October 4, 1993, B3. David P. Hamilton, "Japan Electronics Show

Offers Glimpse of Sleeping Giants Starting to Awaken," *The Wall Street Journal*, October 8, 1991, A11.

23. Cavusgil, Zou, and Naidu, 485–90. Subhash C. Jain, "Standardization of International Marketing: Some Research Hypotheses," *Journal of Marketing* 53:1 (January 1989): 70–79.

24. Saeed Samiee and Kendall Roth, "The Influence of Global Marketing Standardization on Performance," *Journal of Marketing* 56:2 (April 1992): 1–17.

25. Byong-Duk Rhee, Andre de Palma, Class Fornell, and Jacques-Francois Thisse, "Restoring the Principle of Minimum Differentiation in Product Positioning," *Journal of Economics & Management Strategy* 1:3 (Fall 1992): 475.

26. Adrian J. Slywotzky and Benson P. Shapiro, "Leveraging to Beat the Odds: The New Marketing Mind-Set," *Harvard Business Review* 71:5 (September–October 1993): 97–107.

27. Ibid., 98.

28. Ibid., 98.

29. Jim Carlton, "'Multiplayers' Developed by 3DO Enjoy Brisk Sales," *The Wall Street Journal*, October 8, 1993, B3.

30. Julie Pitta, "Hyperinteractive," *Forbes*, September 13, 1993, 228.

31. Ibid., p. 230.

32. Frederick Rose, "At Knowledge Adventure, Tiny Chirps Have Quickly Turned into Mighty Roars," *The Wall Street Journal*, October 8, 1993, B1.

33. Andrew J. Kessler, "In Your Face," *Forbes*, September 27, 1993, 140.

34. John Tierney, "Movies That Push Buttons," *The New York Times*, October 3, 1993, H1.

35. Deirdre Carmody, "For Magazines, a Multimedia Wonderland," *The New York Times*, October 11, 1993, C1.

36. Paul McEnery, "Jamming Good with Weird," *Mondo 2000*, 10 (1993): 17.

37. Dennis Kneale and Gautam Naik, "Hollywood Doesn't Guarantee Stardom for Baby Bells," *The Wall Street Journal*, October 8, 1993, B4.

Chapter Format

Introduction

Marketing Questions

Environmental Scan: Rapid Technological Change

Initial Analysis of Marketing Opportunities

Clues to Capturing Customers

The Firm-Specific Research Assignment

Competitive Scan: Interactive Logistics EDI

Estimates of Market Potential

Similar Market Segments Worldwide

National Marketing Decisions

Marketing Scan: Relationship Marketing

Strategies for Increasing Marketing Effectiveness

Marketing Implementation

Conclusions

Cases: Anchor Abrasives, Intral and Gillette, EDS, TMM

Learning Objectives

After reading this chapter, you should be able to:

- Discuss the importance of the contingency perspective to a logistics positioning strategy

- Outline organizational incentive models to help make better decisions about in-house logistics (or vertical integration) and contracting out logistics (or market-based transaction costs)

- Explain the management decisions taken to exploit virtual logistics EDI (electronic data interchange) networks

Channel Management

chapter 10

Introduction

Marketers manage final demand by positioning global products, services, and brands. In this chapter, we look at the logistics EDI industry, or the combination of physical distribution with information services. Here we stress unknown competitive possibilities, imperfect information, and reinventing a services marketing category. We also spell out the process by which companies do their firm-specific 4Ps analysis, and we detail value creation by multiplying the uses of information. Moreover, we show how joining industry analysis and marketing helps us develop better answers to the six-sigma question: What do I get?

Let's reinforce the new ground we broke in chapters 7–9. In this chapter, let's reinvent another industry and introduce a new services marketing category, logistics EDI. Let's work through our firm-specific 4Ps analysis to be sure we understand all the nuances of decision making under uncertainty.

Scanning Global Markets

Environmental scan: rapid technological change. As governments sell off state-owned

337

firms, marketers create new ways of doing business. The privatization of telecommunications and transportation helps them shape positioning strategies for logistics EDI. Such uncertainty requires suppliers to be open to different marketing strategies and to pay the multiple transaction costs for specialized logistics EDI services. Successful marketers learn how to segment channels of distribution as easily as they now segment consumer markets.

Competitive scan: interactive logistics EDI. Marketers know standardized information protocols are the key to better channel decisions. The near universal use of standardized protocols within the automotive industry keeps transactions costs down for Anchor Abrasives, OEM suppliers, and the large auto firms. Marketing executives also contract out logistics EDI services to acquire expert knowledge on a fee-for-service basis, and the distribution costs are then shared by Gillette and Intral. Moreover, transportation marketers guide shippers to use ocean container services, such as TMM, as the means through which goods move from place to place. These external market transactions compete with internal vertical integration for the soul of channel management.

Marketing scan: relationship marketing. Marketers position logistics EDI services based on services demanded by customers. Successful marketing executives realize they must learn a great deal more about virtual logistics EDI networks before they can offer a total package of services to shippers. Positioning decisions about computer-based logistics EDI systems, wireless technologies to transmit data, and simulators to show users alternative distribution systems are an exciting new business for the future. All service providers who want to manage channels for others must remember their customers' most important question: What do I get?

Traditional Contexts for Global Marketing

Exhibit 10-1 lists the traditional contexts for global marketing in the case of the logistics EDI industry. We study a reinvented business environment, transaction costs, and marketing strategy. The first reinforces our observation about the changes occurring in the logistics EDI industry and how these are driving innovations in the ocean shipping, air freight, and freight-forwarding industries. The second reminds us that distribution-shipping-warehousing firms must pay attention to costs as they seek to add value by multiplying the use of information. The third prepares us for the hard task of implementing a marketing strategy with continuous future payoffs. The logistics EDI case is another symbol of how new industries are being created for a future global economy.

Exhibit 10-1.
Traditional Contexts For Global Marketing

Market Risk
Govern the market through reinvented business environment
    Deregulation of air, rail, trucks
    Privatization of telephone, ocean shipping, ports
    Liberalization of computer-based information
Nonroutine partnerships and relationship networks
Long-term planning horizon
Unknown competitive possibilities and imperfect information

Firm-Specific 4Ps Analysis
Decision making under uncertainty
Demand analysis, cultural analysis, age-period cohort analysis
Value creation
    Multiply uses of information
    Restructure services marketing category
    Reengineer user-based information
Transaction costs
    Marketing bits of information
    Asset specificity and channel volume
    External uncertainty – volatility and diversity
    Fixed costs and scale economies
    Just-in-time and advance ship notices
Teamwork and nonroutine partnerships
    Organizational incentives
    Acknowledge unobservable information or adverse selection
Networks

National Marketing Decisions
Supply analysis
Competitive analysis

Continued on next page

Exhibit 10-1. *Continued from previous page*

Segmentation strategies

OEMs receive direct shipments of high value-added items

OEMs receive shipments through customs brokers

Local partner oversees transport and EDI systems

Positioning strategies

Accept paradigm shift

Classify contract logistics into value-added services

Merge external EDI with existing data management system

Apply contingency perspective

Marketing strategy

Identify customer actions with future logistics payoffs

Create a new services marketing category

Classify contract logistics into value-added services

Reduce transaction costs

Apply contingency perspective to 4Ps marketing mix

Vision test

Remember trend is not destiny

Nontraditional Contexts for Global Marketing

Exhibit 10-2 names the nontraditional contexts for global marketing in the logistics EDI industry. We survey reinventing a services marketing category, multiplying uses of information, matching self-referencing criteria, and making marketing investments. Again, we break new ground because reinventing a services marketing category goes hand-in-hand with reinventing a product category, as well as the industry and competing firms. We also focus on the creative destruction of existing technology at the hands of computer-based logistics EDI.

Finally, we are beginning to realize that only learning organizations survive during periods of reinventing categories, industries, and firms. These firms must make good marketing investments, leverage their assets, and seek customers from all industries. It's not clear which will survive, but that is the meaning of a global industry reinventing itself in the last half of the 1990s.

Governing the market. First, let's look at the political frame. Government steps up the pace of modernization by allowing global and domestic marketers the freedom to compete. Privatization leads to open, more liberal markets, especially in interactive logistics EDI. The tempo accelerates as marketing executives sell transportation services, provide fleet and cargo data, and offer online supplier information. Success in governing the market leads to new relationships among competitors.

Marketing decisions under uncertainty. Second, let's study the technological frame. Marketers manage channels of distribution by building databases to own market niches, delivering targeted information to big companies and small companies alike, forecasting future inventory needs of suppliers, and determining what customers want. These are specific investments in logistics EDI networks.

Marketing educators call this *asset specificity*. Here's a summary of our argument so far.

- Chapter 7: In-house, cross-functional teams evaluate the costs of switching from older, nonredeployable narrowband copper wire technology to newer, broadband fiber-optic and wireless technologies.

- Chapter 8: These investments are the means for restructuring the telephone industry into a telecom services industry. They lead to a marketing strategy favoring the integration of telephone and cable TV technologies.

- Chapter 9: New multimedia product offerings require additional investments in servers, modems, switches, and antennas. Marketers must decide whether these computer-based products should be standardized or adapted to meet the needs of local markets.

Moreover, marketing executives must decide whether to push television- or computer-based interactive connectivity, wired and wireless services, multimedia, and interactive logistics EDI. That's the story of the future.

In this chapter, we add another complexity to our discussion of asset specificity in global marketing. Teamwork, strategy development, and product positioning tend to be activities internal to the firm. However, product positioning strategies are of no use without the surrounding envelope of distribution services. These latter activities are either internal or external to the firm. Asset specificity takes on a new meaning when we choose between internal vertical integration and external channels of distribution, for which we will pay transaction costs.[1]

Exhibit 10-2.
Nontraditional Contexts for Global Marketing

Political Frame

Govern the market through reinvented business environment

    Reinvent services marketing category

Technological Frame

Alternative entry models

Creative destruction to winnow out winners and losers

Value added

    Multiplying bits of information

    Multiplying uses of information

Cultural Frame

Disconnection among age groups and adoption of new offerings

Cross-cultural analysis, similar self-referencing criteria

Marketing Management Frame

Managerial decision making under uncertainty

Industry analysis

    Scale economies: spread fixed costs over multibrand output

    Scope economies: offer a variety of goods in global markets

    Sequence economies: link upstream and downstream activities

Organizational incentives

    Share risks and contract out

    Leverage core competencies

    Fill in white spaces

    Create virtual reality network

Six-sigma question: What do I get?

Virtual reality and paradigm shift

Segmentation

Teamwork, nonroutine partnerships, relationship marketing

Marketing investments

    Look for unobservable habits

    Carry out unconventional thinking

    Establish long-term goals in emerging multimedia industry

    Seek quality, high-profit consumers

    Attack switchable customers

Continued on next page

Exhibit 10-2. *Continued from previous page*

Gain significant market share

Leverage investments in products and services

Return on investment

Convert installed capacity to interactive multimedia

Quality of market share keeps home-based customers with us

Seek customers from all lifestyles

Hunting for consumers.[2] Third, let's examine the cultural frame. In the simplest formulation of a marketing strategy, AT&T lost *channel volume* when the firm gave up the Baby Bells in the mid-1980s. Throughout the last 10 years, AT&T sought to increase channel volume by multiplying the use of its global network (e.g., global outsourcing through World Source Services, wireless voice and fax transmissions with McCaw Cellular, and multimedia and computer connections through WorldWorx). So far, AT&T's strategy of increasing asset specificity through both captive distribution and independent transactions is increasing channel volume.

Faced with such *external uncertainty* from AT&T, British Telecom went into a joint venture with MCI, and partnerships were formed among French and German telecoms, the American Baby Bells, and cable TV and computer companies. Although opportunities abound for absorbing uncertainty through internalizing channels within the firm, such increases in asset specificity through foreign direct investments raise transaction costs; hence, the relative high cost of foreign investments by the Baby Bells in overseas privatizations, cable connections, and cellular services. Moreover, highly integrated captive vertical channels of distribution do not insulate firms from the overseas political and business environment.

Since external uncertainty has many different dimensions, we are forced to fall back on a contingency perspective for positioning logistics services. Marketing executives carry out a different mix of distribution activities based on the volatility and diversity of domestic and foreign markets.

Volatility refers to the rapidity of change, and high volatility means an inability to predict future outcomes. Surely, this is the case in the telephone, telecommunications, multimedia, and EDI industries. Although we are driven to anticipate high transaction costs, we know intuitively that organizational flexibility among all channel members drives us toward sequential decisions about captive versus independent channels in foreign markets.

Diversity refers to the number of sources of uncertainty in the political and business environment. In the industries under discussion, we have many competitors, customers, and final users; in many foreign markets, we have a hard time predicting who these market players are and what information we need to know to do business effectively overseas. Again, we are driven toward organizational flexibility in deciding whether to internalize or incur transactions costs for logistics services.

Segmentation, positioning, and tailoring decisions. Finally, let's look closely at the marketing management frame. Channel management is about bundling logistics services and positioning them along with products to meet the needs of domestic and international customers. Successful marketers gain significant competitive advantages by creating value through tailored logistics. Sometimes marketing executives build up captive distribution systems; at other times they set up independent logistics systems. These systems differ from foreign market to foreign market because levels of channel integration may depend on whether privatization has taken hold in a country's services sector. Ocean shipping lines, air freight services, port facilities, railroads, and telecommunications networks may be owned by governments, domestic private firms, and, occasionally, by foreign multinational firms. Marketing professors call this different mix of logistics activities a *contingency perspective* (chapter 9).

Organizing global marketing experience. The simultaneous existence of these four different contexts forces marketers to research traditional distribution systems, to position logistics EDI services, and to watch for different national signals about selling off state-owned transportation and warehousing facilities. Let's do two things in this chapter. First, we will discuss the importance of transaction cost analysis to positioning tailored logistics services. Then we will apply this analysis to reengineering channels of distribution through up-to-date logistics EDI management.

Market Risk Questions

Marketers manage final demand by researching international markets; see Exhibit 10-3. *Market risk* offers advice on dealing with unknown competitive possibilities and imperfect information and their effect on channel management and the positioning, segmentation, and tailoring strategies of logistics EDI competitors. This, too, is a part of our macro business environment.

Traditional Frame Analysis for Global Marketing

Market Risk Analysis and Reinvented Business Environment

Nonroutine partnerships and relationship networks

Unknown competitive possibilities and incomplete information

Long-term planning horizon

Market Risk Analysis and Privatization

Telephone (PTO), telecom services networks

Ocean shipping and air freight, port facilities

Railroads and trucks

Firm-Specific Analysis and Reengineering User-Based Information

External databases, targeted supplier information

Inventory forecasts

Dial-up modems, virtual logistics EDI networks

Firm-Specific 4Ps Analysis, Transaction Costs, Value Added

Marketing bits of information

Asset specificity and channel volume

External uncertainty – volatility and diversity

Fixed costs and scale economies

Just-in-time and advance ship notices

National Marketing Decisions and Marketing Opportunities
Segmentation

United States: OEMs receive direct shipments of high value-added items

Mexico: OEMs receive shipments through customs brokers

Mexico: Local partner oversees transport and EDI systems

Positioning

Accept paradigm shift

Classify contract logistics into value-added services

Merge external EDI format with existing data management system

Create future logistics payoffs

Apply contingency perspective

National Marketing Decisions and Marketing Strategy

Identify customer-oriented actions with future logistics payoffs

Classify contract logistics into value-added services

Continued on next page

Exhibit 10-3. *Continued from previous page*

Reduce transaction costs
Apply contingency perspective to 4Ps marketing mix
Find better competitors

Nontraditional Frame Analysis for Global Marketing
Technological Frame and Value Added

Multiplying bits of information
Multiplying uses of information

Understanding the Importance of Information

In chapters 8 and 9, we describe the 4Ps scheme used widely by marketing educators. The second P is *Place:* Is logistics EDI the products that move through channels of distribution? Is logistics EDI the digital data that represent goods ordered, containers shipped, titles transferred, and products sold? Or is logistics EDI the convergence of distribution and logistics services with data and information services? This third idea is the *paradigm shift*, a new view of channel management. Here's where firms really add value to bits of information.

Value Added Up-to-date logistics EDI manipulates whatever data are needed to give customers the distribution results they demand – for example, a 24-hour-a-day direct link with the computer systems used by truckers, air cargo carriers, railroads, ship lines, and distribution centers.[3] Customers know at any time the precise location of shipments, and they can display alternative routes to get the right goods to the right places at the right time.

Transaction Costs Because a complete logistics EDI system is expensive, smaller companies need to ask these questions: What data do we need? Can logistics EDI vendors sell us connections to existing data networks? Can we use the information in their EDI format within our existing data management system? After all, any EDI system must be a simulation of the envelope of logistics services surrounding the positioning and sale of products. Also, the *transaction costs* of buying, using, and manipulating this logistics EDI information must be reasonable, competitive, and in line with the costs of products for sale in final markets.

Here is just one example. High value-added products (e.g., computer-based numerical control machines) that require speed in delivery incur the higher costs of air freight. The following documents precede or go with the shipment: irrevocable letter of credit (L/C), shippers' manifest, packing and cartage charges, NVOCC freight and insurance charges, export clearance, landing permits, import documents, through bill of lading, and more. Virtually all documents flow separately, either through courier services or via high-speed computer links.

Banks, nonbank financial institutions (such as factors and forfait houses), exporters, importers, and distributors want to reduce or eliminate the paper documents. More and more foreign trade documents are being transported by modern logistics EDI networks. These are reducing transaction costs.

Marketing Strategy Here are crucial questions for global marketers:

1. Which activities? Can we identify a set of customer-oriented information actions with future logistics payoffs?

2. Which products, and for whom? Can we create a new services marketing category?

3. Who are our customers? Can we identify market segments among customers of Internet, EDI, and other wired technologies?

4. What is our added value? Can we classify contract logistics into value-added services?

5. Can we do better than our competitors? Can we make good support decisions under uncertainty and with very limited hard information? Can we reduce transaction costs?

6. Do we have a competitive marketing strategy for ourselves? Do we have a competitive marketing strategy for our partners? Can we gain significant market share by applying a contingency perspective to the 4Ps marketing mix?

7. Should we find better competitors? What is the makeup of our industry? Are the competitive forces changing in our favor? Is the overseas environment conducive to our products?

Environmental Scan: Rapid Technological Change

A new *services marketing category* is emerging from the underworld of computer hacking, the *demi-monde* of virtual reality, and the universe of logistics EDI, and their digital convergence with wired and wireless telephone, microwave, and satellite technologies. For example, in the rush to reengineer corporations, *contract logistics firms* are using a dial-up modem with existing telephone data networks to manage supplier and distribution channels for manufacturing firms. If the contract logistics firms are more effective than the *captive internal organizations* of the manufacturing companies, these outside logistics companies are paid fees for their expertise in managing transportation and distribution services; hence, our interest in transaction costs.

Privatizing Logistics Services

The political news throughout Europe, the Americas, East Asia, and the rest of the world is the retreat of the state sector and the emergence of *privatization* as a tool to improve the performance of national economies. In chapters 7 and 8, we witnessed the deregulation of telephone networks in the United States and Canada and the sale of government-owned telephone firms (PTOs) in Europe, Mexico and Latin America, and southeast Asia. The same is happening with ocean-going maritime fleets and transcontinental air cargo carriers and, in some cases, with domestic air services, railroads, and trucking lines. As these state-owned enterprises move into the private sector, their new owners must make major investments to bring facilities and data retrieval systems up to world-class standards.

Fixed Costs and Scale Economies Initially, privatization requires greater fixed costs. Multinational firms expect the best service possible from telephone firms providing global outsourcing, transportation companies handling containers, and logistics EDI firms tracking information. Unfortunately, the volume of business does not rise as fast, and per capita transaction costs go up before they go down. These initially higher costs delay internal specialization, the application of specialized marketing management skills, and the benefits from channel integration. Scale economies simply take a longer time to realize when we are dealing with domestic and foreign distribution systems.

Manufacturing firms that have a slow rise in foreign sales volume may decide to use independent foreign distributors – that is, keep fixed costs low, but maintain some illusion of an integrated channel of distribution. Using the market and paying the transaction costs are preferred at reduced volume levels. Nevertheless, even with low asset specificity, volatility (including surprises from customers, competitors, and middlemen) is minimized, and diversity (i.e., many intermediate and final customers) is maintained. Moreover, without any additional fixed costs, we can add products to the foreign channels of distribution and gain some additional scale economies.

Applying the Contingency Perspective to Place

Thus, foreign privatization drives us toward applying the contingency perspective to the second P: *Place*. Here are the choices. Look for market solutions, make deals with the newly privatized transportation companies, and set up logistics EDI to monitor shipments. Second, pay contract logistics firms to manage both the movement of goods and the flow of information required to monitor packages, boxes, and containers. Or, bring some or all of these elements within the firm by internalizing the channel of distribution. How do transaction costs affect these crucial logistics EDI decisions?

Initial Analysis of Marketing Opportunities

Although the automotive industry was not state-owned within most of (western) Europe, Latin America, and East Asia, it has been highly regulated in some countries. For example, France insisted on blocking shares owned by government. Mexico and Brazil required high levels of national content production. And Thailand forced a limit on the number of models assembled and sold within the country. Since the industry was highly regulated up until the current period, those automotive firms that were involved in cross-border assembly and sales spent little time worrying about compatible logistics EDI.

Market Risk and Political Frame

Things are different in the 1990s. Cross-border trading is commonplace within Europe, across North America, and even in East Asia. For example, in Mexico, Ford, Nissan, and GM built three new assembly plants within 300 miles of the border. Ford plants in the United States ship motors, drive trains, and other major components on unitized trains to their Hermosillo, Mexico plant; and fully assembled cars return on these same trains to distribution centers in the western and southern United States. Also, the Mexican and US original equipment manufacturers (OEMs) in the Ford family must be sure that springs, spark plugs, pistons, rods, brakes, glass, computer controls, dashboards, batteries, tires, and everything else for Ford cars are there, too, just in time (JIT). Moreover, suppliers further back in the logistics system (e.g., those who make nut-inserted discs that help OEMs meet the closer tolerance levels of automotive companies in the grinding of engine and transmission parts) must meet JIT requirements as well.

Maximizing Logistics EDI

Why do suppliers, such as Anchor Abrasives, a US $4 million manufacturer of nut-inserted discs for the automotive industry, incur transaction costs from logistics EDI firms? In the automotive industry, Anchor is responsible for providing goods just in time to original equipment manufacturers (OEMs). Anchor's logistics success is measured by on-time Advanced Ship Notices (ASNs).[4] Late ASNs lower overall quality ratings and jeopardize future sales to the OEMs within the automotive supplier systems.

Here's what Anchor and its OEM clients want: standardized software that provides ASN data, including the number of cartons on each pallet, the weight of the shipment, trailer number, receipt acknowledgment, and cumulative total reconciliation. Moreover, here's what both need: standardized software that provides information about fine-tuning logistics EDI as required by OEM plant, sales, and information personnel.

Developing a Global EDI Standard

1994 was a key year for the automotive industry. Before that most US automobile firms still used American National Standards Institute (or ANSI) for the transportation, administration, and control of logistics EDI. In 1994, some began aligning with the new world standard, UN/EDIFACT (United Nations EDI for Administration, Commerce and Transport).[5] If US automotive suppliers were going to pay transaction costs for JIT and ASN success, they preferred to pay these costs once rather than twice with two sets of standards.

External Uncertainty Here is a case in which external uncertainty has multiple dimensions.[6] For Anchor to do nothing, it would have been faced with technological obsolescence in its capacity to be an effective supplier to the OEMs. The logistics EDI environment was changing rapidly, but its volatility precluded Anchor from being able to make good predictions of future outcomes. Also, Anchor faced unforeseen contingencies – for example, when would the automotive industry as a whole begin to use UN/EDIFACT? Anchor had to make several sequential decisions to be sure its plant and administrative personnel kept up with the fast-changing logistics EDI environment – and to keep its internal organizational costs and external transactions costs in line with sales and profits.

Anchor's logistics EDI environment was becoming more diverse, too. Mexico became an important foreign market with many new OEM customers (for springs, valves, and piston rings wipers), similar final users (including US and Japanese automotive firms), and a few new abrasives competitors (such as locally owned Austromex). Also, Anchor had to decide whether to sell directly or indirectly through a Mexican distributor, or to use the latter (Abrasivos Mexicanos Graff) as its manufacturer's representative in Mexico. Moreover, Anchor had to learn how to ship to the border (Laredo) and work with both its Mexican distributor and Mexican OEM customers so that it had on-time ASNs in both North American countries.

Different Marketing Strategies These different contingencies between US domestic distribution and US export logistics to Mexico forced Anchor to develop different marketing strategies. In the United States, Anchor has field sales engineers who are managed directly from headquarters, and it uses Roadway as its independent transportation firm to ship many nut-inserted discs directly to OEM plants. In Mexico, Anchor uses two approaches: (1) direct shipment to some customers through US and Mexican customs brokers, and (2) indirect shipment to other OEM clients through its contractual partner (Graff), who oversees customs clearance, shipping to a central distribution center, and transportation to Mexican customers. In short, Anchor had to develop a more complex dual-channel structure to deal with specialized logistics demands from Mexico.

Transaction Costs Although changes in the competitive conditions of logistics EDI for the automotive industry forced Anchor to implement multiple marketing strategies, Anchor continues to rely on external markets and pay transactions costs for logistics services. None of these changes direct Anchor's management to consider forming captive logistics systems and integrating vertically through the channel of distribution. Its task as a supplier is to follow the lead of its customers, the OEMs, and their customers, the giant auto assembly firms.

Implementing Logistics EDI

Here are the things Anchor learned about logistics EDI:[7]

1. Use computers to do the work of gathering data.

2. Use data models from OEMs and automotive firms.

3. Use EDIFACT standards to improve data flow.

4. Receive purchase orders and send ASNs on compatible EDI files.

5. Logistics EDI makes OEM customers happy and increases sales.

In the transition from ANSI X12 national standards [i.e., the different US industry conventions for the automotive business (AIAG) and for ocean, air, and rail transportation (TDCC)] to UN/EDIFACT, Anchor Abrasives relied on EDS (Electronic Data Systems Corporation) to ensure, that its EDI files are continually compatible with its customers' files. Anchor paid the transaction costs for outside support from specialists in logistics EDI. In this way, Anchor positioned an envelope of logistics EDI services around the manufacture, sale, and distribution of its nut-inserted discs within the US and Mexico.

Clues to Capturing Customers

Tailoring logistics is most important in keeping customers happy. Suppliers who provide an envelope of services around products create value in terms of convenience, reliability, support, and EDI.[8] What products do you want? That's easy because we have a lot of data about segmenting markets and preferences of customers. How often do you want our products delivered? When during the day do you want our products delivered? How often do you want to be billed and on which billing cycle during the month? Shall we set up the products so you can run tests? These are difficult questions. Global marketers are looking for answers because they want to segment customers into cost-effective channels.

Positioning Strategies

Positioning product and distribution strategies together – one standardized or adapted to suit customer needs, the other dependent on the contingencies of the marketplace – is the central task of channel management. EDI offers a way to simplify, enhance, or reinvent the logistics process for participants in the channel. Some examples follow:

- Do just-in-time (JIT) work through Advanced Ship Notices (ASNs), and keep future sales from being trapped in the inventory pipeline.

- Split channels based upon location. Carry out direct shipment to US customers, and provide specialized handling for Mexican OEM clients.

- Split channels based on customers' needs. Get our products to our most demanding customers first, especially those that want unique components delivered on an expedited basis.

- Split channels based on costs. Recover the costs of channel complexity instead of averaging these costs for all customers.

- Reinvent channels based on multiplying uses of information. Restructure all the fixed assets in the channel based on distinct information collected from our logistics EDI system. Suggest new ways to share logistics assets.

The last item on the list is what we have in mind when we label a distribution-shipping-warehousing-recordkeeping process an up-to-date logistics EDI system.

Summary: Scanning for Rapid Technological Change

As governments sell off state-owned firms, marketers create new ways of doing business. The privatization of telecommunications and transportation helps them shape positioning strategies for logistics EDI. Such uncertainty requires suppliers to be open to different marketing strategies and to pay the multiple transaction costs for specialized logistics EDI services. Successful marketers learn how to segment channels of distribution as easily as they now segment consumer markets.

The Firm-Specific Assignment

Marketers manage final demand by positioning logistics EDI within markets committed to rapid technological change; see Exhibit 10–4. Many cooperate, forming networks that are linked to share skills, costs, and services. Common information protocols, such as ASNs, give their collective business the look of vertical integration. Here's how logistics EDI is changing long-standing supplier relationships: Fewer intermediaries are needed; speedier decision making is commonplace; everyone has equal access to data.[9] For example, auto assembly firms tell OEMs, who then notify other suppliers what products are wanted, where, and when, driving them harder than ever on prices. This takes the guesswork out of industrial purchasing, slashing inventory cycles and keeping the most needed parts in stock. We want to explore this new way of adding value to bits of logistics information.

Exhibit 10–4.
Firm-Specific Analysis: Logistics EDI
The Competitive Scan

Traditional Frame Analysis for Global Marketing
Firm-Specific 4Ps Analysis, Teamwork, Nonroutine Partnerships
Organizational Incentives
Practice coordination and central control
Promote bundled pricing
Require on-time deliveries
Prepare for unobservable effort or moral hazard
Acknowledge unobservable information or adverse selection
Logistics EDI Networks
Delegate responsibilities
Distribute more products
Do cross-sourcing among plants
Provide dependable shipping notices
Maintain just-in-time inventory levels
Create flexible response systems

Continued on next page

Exhibit 10-4. *Continued from previous page*

Nontraditional Frame Analysis for Global Marketing
Marketing Management Frame and Industry Analysis
Accept misuse of agency relationships
Scale economies: spread fixed costs over multibrand output
Scope economies: offer a variety of goods in global markets
Sequence economies: link upstream and downstream activities
Reduce total cost through virtual vertical integration
Marketing Management Frame and Organizational Incentives
Add value to bits of information
Share risks and returns within channels of distribution
Contract out shipping or EDI or both
Leverage core competencies
Fill in white spaces
Create virtual reality network for logistics EDI

Organizational Incentives

Organizational incentives create logistics EDI corporations.[10] Advantages are gained from coordination of individual logistics activities and centralized decision making about and control over EDI. Because manufacturers delegate responsibility for on-time deliveries to OEMs, and make a similar delegation to suppliers, prices are less important than no-fault deliveries within the channel. Bargaining and negotiation occur over who does want, how it's done, and when it will be completed. Here is the crucial idea: Each member of the channel is everyone else's agent, and all must pull together to make a successful logistics EDI network.

Transaction Costs

The benefits of EDI are impressive.[11] EDI cuts the costs of sending invoices, processing sales orders, and performing other administrative functions in half, says Dataquest, an information research group in San Jose, California. Also, EDI saves 5 percent in transportation costs and up to 10 percent in consignment values. Moreover, when interruptions occur in intercontinental telecom services, manufacturing firms demand that the value-added networks of AT&T and other global outsourcers fix the problems immediately.

Most importantly, these VANs earn their money by providing ANSI X12 and UN/EDIFACT translations for US and European firms.

Management Strategy

In fact, all the newest logistics EDI information protocols, such as UN/EDI-FACT, seek to minimize the typical problems found in agency relationships. One is unobservable effort (*moral hazard*), in which some agents don't do their share of the work and leave it for others to finish the job. The other is unobservable information (*adverse selection*), in which some agents do not forward or slow down the forwarding of data that contain bad results. When logistics EDI systems are not completely compatible, such as those found in ANSI X12 standards, some agents will succumb to this temptation and limit the effectiveness of the logistics EDI network.

Paying Attention to Relationship Marketing

Let's specify the strategic relationships within logistics EDI networks. First, individual agents calculate their value added in terms of market-based transaction costs. Second, alliances of agents think in terms of customer-dominated vertical integration. Finally, agency networks create logistics EDI networks in which computer-based information technology permits marketers to promote vertical contractual relations, segment channels, and tailor strategies to suit final users.

Cost Economies Here are the costs associated with separate production and distribution by independent firms. For example, Gillette gains *scale economies* when it spreads its fixed production and overhead costs over the output of multiple brand-named goods. Also, Gillette gains *scope economies* when it offers a variety of products and services, individually chosen for specific national markets, to customers throughout the world. These two are commonly understood cost economies.

However, one other type of cost economy is important to our discussion of channels of distribution, and it is less well known. For example, Gillette gains *sequence economies*[12] through vertical integration from upstream suppliers to downstream plants because some common units of production exist in the design, engineering, and manufacturing of its razors, blades, shaving cream, and other products. These organizational advantages (such as technological improvements and an assurance of supplies) give Gillette the ability to reduce total cost through equity-based vertical integration.

In one important area, namely distribution of final branded products to user markets, Gillette realizes sequence economies through logistics outsourcing contracts. Back in 1987, Gillette sold its manually operated logistics system to Intral Corporation (The new entrepreneurs were former employees of Gillette.)[13] Shipment orders were sent by courier because every division had a different configuration of mainframe and midrange computers, and this hodge-podge did not lend itself to logistics EDI.

Downstream Distribution Gillette delegated the responsibility for downstream distribution to Intral. Intral then chose to use existing PCs and modems, purchase off-the-shelf software, and connect all parties through telephone lines and local area networks (LANs). In 1991, Puerto Rico was the first test for the Gillette-Intral logistics EDI alliance. The distribution system included online order checking, real-time responses, and worldwide forecasting. The next year the system was rolled out to Mexico and the UK first, then to all of Latin America, Europe, and East Asia. Gillette contracts for Intral's services on a three-year basis, works with its partner to ensure high performance, and pays the transaction costs of market-based logistics EDI.

Creating a Logistics EDI Network

Intral's work has grown as Gillette has given it responsibility for distributing more products, cross-sourcing among plants, providing dependable shipping notices, keeping inventory promises, and creating a flexible response system. Intral also has the authority to solve some of the headaches of any logistics EDI system (e.g., slow modems, elderly satellites, and failed telephone lines). Moreover, Intral can select (with the consent of Gillette) the most appropriate global outsourcing network among those of AT&T, BT/MCI, and other worldwide providers. All of these are confidence-building measures as both firms negotiate over their respective roles in their logistics EDI network.

Let's close this section by restating the questions asked of suppliers:[14] What added value do you contribute to OEMs and final users? Why should we bind you to us? How will you interpret our joint information? How will you participate in our future success? It is the interrelationships among members in the channel of distribution that counts.

Competitive Scan: Interactive Logistics EDI

Logistics EDI as practiced by Anchor Abrasives and Intral Corporation is an indispensable partner to global production. The rationale is simple: Manufacturers realize that "holding large amounts of inventory was costly and tied up valuable working capital. . . Distribution and logistics . . .lay outside their core activity . . . [So they] began contracting out their distribution to outside specialists and found they could reduce operating costs and improve margins as a result."[15]

European Logistics

The British Institute of Logistics and Distribution Management found that "distribution costs as a percentage of UK companies' turnover fell from 17 percent at the start of the 1980s to 4.7 percent in 1991–1992."[16] Within the European Community, the big companies, such as Unilever, are closing national factories, concentrating production sites, reducing inventory levels, and centralizing distribution to take advantage of pan-European distribution. The intention is to set up regional warehouses and distribution centers to serve different areas of Europe. Unfortunately, the problem for most European companies is that their sales and marketing departments are still organized along national lines, with the director of distribution reporting to the local marketing manager. The local marketing managers have been slow to standardize product lines or bring uniformity to packaging, labels, and EDI. Europe is behind North America in this important activity.

In the United Kingdom, large retailing and manufacturing groups are beginning to reverse themselves about outsourcing logistics to third-party specialists, and they are once again taking direct control over their distribution activities. EDI make this easier to do in today's cost-conscious market. Shocking as it may seem to third-party providers of logistics services, the commercial and distribution committee of the United Kingdom's Freight Transport Association concludes "that the operating cost of an effectively-managed in-house distribution operation was unlikely to differ much from one contracted out. . . The main motivation for a company contracting out its distribution was likely to be the benefit of the contractor's specialised distribution know-how. . . not necessarily [to] save money."[17]

Contracting Out

In the United States, many firms take on the business of contracting out logistics services. For example, KLS, a spin-off of an in-house shipping service at Kaiser Aluminum, puts heavy loads on railroads. Trucking firms (Yellow and TNT), freight forwarders (Harpers), customs brokers (Fritz), banks (Cass Logistics), and telecom EDI service firms (EDS) also provide pieces of the distribution and logistics business. Also, Intral manages the whole distribution system (order processing, packaging, inventory management, warehousing, trucking, ocean shipping, air freight, logistics EDI, and accounts receivable).

According to the US Council on Logistics Management, the industry is in formation. As we see from the partial list above, the logistics industry is highly fragmented; in this section, we have focused on the management of contracting out logistics through EDI. Even with this emphasis, we find many logistics firms are still searching for core competencies. This is another indication that the industry has a long way to go before we can do a traditional industry analysis and determine its market structure.

Estimates of Market Potential

Satellite and radio tracking, the use of bar codes (such as PDS417 checkerboard) and hand-held scanners for data acquisition, and on-board laptop or even dashboard-mounted computers characterize today's logistics EDI industry in Europe. However, different data systems, incompatible systems, and nationally based telephone networks still hinder Europe's distribution system from moving ahead as quickly as its counterpart in the United States.

The goal is the same on both continents: "The fast movement of information . . . to speed goods through the supply chain is what logistics is all about . . . [Also] logistics is all about customer response," says Nick Allen, editor and publisher of *Logistics Europe*.[18] According to David Hobbs, associate director of CMG Consultants, "Clients need . . . client-server systems, wide area networks, and the ability of powerful communications to deliver worldwide logistic information."[19]

Telecomputers Hit the Road

Federal Express pioneered real-time shipment tracking to improve courier productivity. Tracking data are converted to routing labels that can be read by humans or scanned by computers. Now most courier systems use this wireless system to improve their productivity.

In 1993, the American market for wireless data equipment and services was US $2 billion a year, and it is expected to grow to about $15 billion by the year 2000. Arthur D. Little predicts "40 million Americans employed in 130 occupations might use wireless communications for eight hours or more of a typical working week. A similar number . . . in Europe are also potential users."[20] Is the logistics EDI industry ready for a wireless future?

Most firms discussed so far are still trying to sort out information protocols for EDI and to decide whether to support in-house or external logistics services. Few are paying attention to the coming wireless revolution. Those logistics EDI firms that stick with wired telephone connections will surrender their leadership to others, such as the courier and paging firms, that have jumped directly into the wireless future.

Chris Smith, the marketing director for software products at Arthur Andersen Consulting's European Software Center sees this future for logistics EDI:[21]

- Concentrate on business processes, not functional systems.

- Provide client-servers and distributed computing.

- Integrate purchasing, manufacturing, and delivery from all geographic locations.

- Communicate more effectively with outside partners and internally within the firm and network.

Predicting the Future

The continuing battle over in-house versus external logistics EDI services and the coming wireless revolution dominate the self-analysis discussion at EDS.[22] If the firm ignores the return to in-house distribution and transportation services, it is missing a market demand for personal micro-level logistics EDI services. If EDS ignores the demand for wireless communications, it is missing a market demand for faster, personal, all-purpose telecommunications services. Failure here means EDS falls behind the curve, and the firm will find it very hard to catch up in the fast-paced telecomputer R&D environment.

Leverage Core Competencies Today, EDS is discussing revitalization and leveraging core competencies in information technology, systems integration, and network management. Its managers are looking for the "white spaces" or the uncontested, new competitive areas to create radical change in the way EDS serves its clients. One of these "white spaces" is wireless logistics EDI systems.

Here are the questions: Is EDS as a market leader today any different from GM in 1965 or IBM in 1975? Is EDS so large that it is losing its way as the industry changes? Does EDS make the mistake of believing that greater scale and resources will make it a winner in tomorrow's markets? Has EDS failed to pay attention to early warning signs, such as the leveling off of its rate of productivity growth? Is the EDS model out of date in an industry whose boundaries are changing constantly and in unpredictable directions?

Some answers. EDS must reinvent its services products based on five key marketing ideas: Mass customizing of logistics EDI; segmenting channels of distribution for in-house and contracted services; sequencing activities among partners to minimize costs; delivering market-based and vertically integrated support services; and recasting marketing strategies based on customer demands for logistics EDI networks.

Going into Unchartered Markets

As EDS and others cast about for new core competencies in technology-driven markets, their marketing executives must think about the boundaries of the industry, the structure of the market, the future market segments, and the services and products demanded by customers. Marketers must do this future thinking without a large installed base of computer simulators for logistics EDI systems.

The design space for the new logistics EDI industry includes three important components:[23]

- *Environmental reality:* What distribution, transportation, and logistics EDI conditions influence decisions by alliance partners?

- *Personal managerial experience:* Who shares which parts of the channel of distribution? Are all pulling together, or do some shirk their duties?

- *System cost:* Do in-house systems or contracted systems keep costs down and improve productivity?

Here's the assignment for EDS, IBM, Intral, Arthur Andersen Consulting, and others that want to provide state-of-the-art logistics EDI. Develop simulators for small, entrepreneurial clients (such as Anchor Abrasives) to personally experience what is possible within alternative logistics EDI systems. Then answer these questions for clients: Will they get a higher rate of return on their investment? Will their productivity improve through new logistics EDI networks?

The real business of EDS is to create new networks of logistics EDI. According to Hugh W. Ryan, director of new-age systems for Arthur Andersen Consulting, virtual reality (VR) "worlds will be used to simulate business interactions – from sales negotiations . . ."[24] to logistics EDI systems. During the 1990s, VR's big winners in logistics EDI will be suppliers of packaged solutions to specific business problems.[25]

Similar Market Segments Worldwide

One of the most important problems facing shippers is theft of cargo. In the United States, trucking industry losses amount to US $5 billion a year. Losses are much higher in the ports of southern Italy, Argentina, and Mexico, according to Stephen Donati, director of corporate security for Gillette.[26] With five million containers on the move every day aboard planes, ships, trains, and trucks, shippers want to be sure the goods show up in good condition – not wet, overheated, frozen, broken to bits, smashed beyond recognition, or of no use to final customers.

International Cargo Management Systems (ICMS) provides shippers with a new global tracking service. Its electronic sentry is bolted inside the container and pulls in signals from cellular phones, ship-to-shore radios, and communications satellites. The sentry transmits location and other data to computers at a tracking center and permits clients to dial up via modem to check cargo status and view their cargo on computer screens. Intruders are captured on digital film, and their pictures are sent to manufacturers, shipping firms, and insurers.

Examining Container Shipping

Another problem is shipping containers of merchandise between the less well-equipped ports of Mexico and those of the United States, Europe, and Japan. In the North Atlantic trade between North America and Europe, liner shipping is a mature industry with a homogeneous set of services and substantial overcapacity.[27] However, in the United States-Mexico-Latin America trade (and in the trans-Pacific trade between North America and East Asia), the ocean shipping industry has more opportunity to make money; see Exhibits 10–5 and 10–6. The following is a review of just one shipping line that plies the seas between Mexico and the United States.

Industry Analysis

In chapter 8, we explored the ins and outs of industry analysis. Let's apply this approach to Transportación Maritima Mexicana (TMM) and see how this carrier goes about marketing its business within the liner shipping industry.

Threat of competitors. Traditionally, liner shipping conferences have increased the number of sailings as a means to bar entry of non-conference operators. The latter fought back by giving rebates to shippers with a high volume of containers.

Before privatization in Mexico, the Mexican government owned the ports, container terminals, cranes, grain elevators, and oil depots. Mexican flag vessels called at Mexican ports, such as Vera Cruz and Acapulco. Since investments in container ships are both massive and lumpy, carriers, such as Mexican-owned TMM, finance these by equipment-leasing deals and the sale of stock, and through debt. TMM's capitalization costs are high and growing because, with privatization it is acquiring the port facilities of the Mexican government and Pemex, the state-owned oil company.

TMM is procuring specialized ships to carry automobiles between Mexico and Japan. Its return on investment depends on a continuation of a long-term contract with Nissan. The task of TMM's marketers is to provide door-to-door intermodal service to shippers, guarantee delivery of goods, and encourage long-term use of TMM ships over competing lines from the United States.

Threat of substitutes. TMM's ocean shipping business is faced with two sub-stitutes: fast air cargo service between New York, Chicago, and Los Angeles to Mexico City, and intermodal truck and train land service between the United States and Mexico. Marketing executives at TMM are working to counter the latter threat by doing intermodal deals with APL, an American ocean carrier with rail and truck links across the continental United States.

Bargaining power of buyers. High value-added merchandise (such as com-puters, appliances, and luxury goods) and large shippers (Nissan) get pref-erential shipping space at TMM over commodities and small shippers.

Exhibit 10-5.
Cross-Border Trade within the Americas

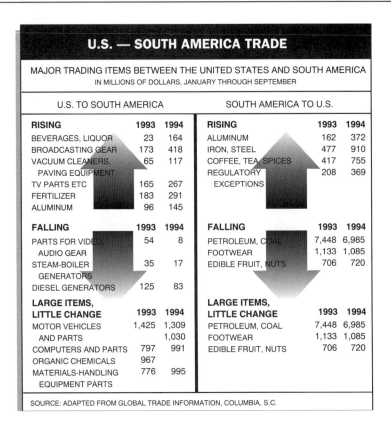

U.S. — SOUTH AMERICA TRADE

MAJOR TRADING ITEMS BETWEEN THE UNITED STATES AND SOUTH AMERICA
IN MILLIONS OF DOLLARS, JANUARY THROUGH SEPTEMBER

U.S. TO SOUTH AMERICA

RISING	1993	1994
BEVERAGES, LIQUOR	23	164
BROADCASTING GEAR	173	418
VACUUM CLEANERS, PAVING EQUIPMENT	65	117
TV PARTS ETC	165	267
FERTILIZER	183	291
ALUMINUM	96	145

FALLING	1993	1994
PARTS FOR VIDEO, AUDIO GEAR	54	8
STEAM-BOILER GENERATORS	35	17
DIESEL GENERATORS	125	83

LARGE ITEMS, LITTLE CHANGE	1993	1994
MOTOR VEHICLES	1,425	1,309
AND PARTS		1,030
COMPUTERS AND PARTS	797	991
ORGANIC CHEMICALS	967	
MATERIALS-HANDLING EQUIPMENT PARTS	776	995

SOUTH AMERICA TO U.S.

RISING	1993	1994
ALUMINUM	162	372
IRON, STEEL	477	910
COFFEE, TEA, SPICES	417	755
REGULATORY EXCEPTIONS	208	369

FALLING	1993	1994
PETROLEUM, COAL	7,448	6,985
FOOTWEAR	1,133	1,085
EDIBLE FRUIT, NUTS	706	720

LARGE ITEMS, LITTLE CHANGE	1993	1994
PETROLEUM, COAL	7,448	6,985
FOOTWEAR	1,133	1,085
EDIBLE FRUIT, NUTS	706	720

SOURCE: ADAPTED FROM GLOBAL TRADE INFORMATION, COLUMBIA, S.C.

Courtesy of the Journal of Commerce

Bargaining power of suppliers. TMM is actively buying from the Mexican government as many land-based facilities as possible or going into alliances with terminal operators, trucking firms, and the national Mexican railroad. In the future, marketing executives at TMM will have to sort out what should be integrated vertically and what should be purchased in the market.

Rivalry among competitors. TMM's marketing strategy is to promote long-term shipping deals with the largest domestic and foreign investors in Mexico, such as Pemex, Nissan, Del Monte, and others. Once shipping (channel) volume, tariff (price), and delivery times are set by contract, logistics EDI takes over to monitor cargo movement. Here's a place in which packaged solutions to real business problems from ICMS and Intral could make a difference to the profitability of TMM.

Exhibit 10-6.
Trade Across the Pacific

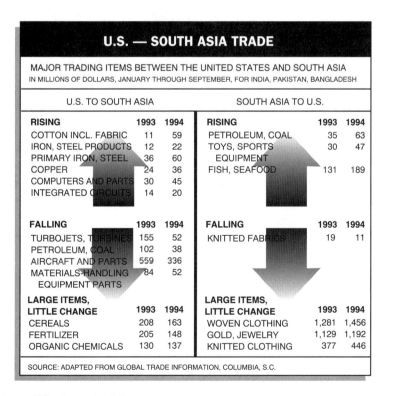

U.S. — SOUTH ASIA TRADE

MAJOR TRADING ITEMS BETWEEN THE UNITED STATES AND SOUTH ASIA
IN MILLIONS OF DOLLARS, JANUARY THROUGH SEPTEMBER, FOR INDIA, PAKISTAN, BANGLADESH

U.S. TO SOUTH ASIA			SOUTH ASIA TO U.S.		
RISING	1993	1994	**RISING**	1993	1994
COTTON INCL. FABRIC	11	59	PETROLEUM, COAL	35	63
IRON, STEEL PRODUCTS	12	22	TOYS, SPORTS	30	47
PRIMARY IRON, STEEL	36	60	EQUIPMENT		
COPPER	24	36	FISH, SEAFOOD	131	189
COMPUTERS AND PARTS	30	45			
INTEGRATED CIRCUITS	14	20			
FALLING	1993	1994	**FALLING**	1993	1994
TURBOJETS, TURBINES	155	52	KNITTED FABRICS	19	11
PETROLEUM, COAL	102	38			
AIRCRAFT AND PARTS	559	336			
MATERIALS-HANDLING	84	52			
EQUIPMENT PARTS					
LARGE ITEMS, LITTLE CHANGE	1993	1994	**LARGE ITEMS, LITTLE CHANGE**	1993	1994
CEREALS	208	163	WOVEN CLOTHING	1,281	1,456
FERTILIZER	205	148	GOLD, JEWELRY	1,129	1,192
ORGANIC CHEMICALS	130	137	KNITTED CLOTHING	377	446

SOURCE: ADAPTED FROM GLOBAL TRADE INFORMATION, COLUMBIA, S.C.

Courtesy of The Journal of Commerce

Positioning Logistics Services

Let's summarize our logistics positioning strategy. The old way was to look separately at inventory levels, cargo movements, transportation linkages, storage facilities, cargo losses, and delivery times, then bemoan the lack of vertical integration within the transportation and distribution industries. An intermediate step was to decide whether it made economic sense to buy portions of these industries and integrate them vertically, or to continue to pay a transaction cost for these services in the market. An improved intermediate step was to contract out logistics services and let independent specialists negotiate the best deals possible.

The new way is to view all parts of the logistics business as a data management problem. Ownership of specific transportation and distribution services is not as important as finding the best on-time service with the least loss of cargo at a reasonable price so that all just-in-time requirements are met; hence, our emphasis on logistics EDI.

Sustainable Competitive Advantage Performance is the real measure of success. Intral's competitive advantage is in doing a cleaner, better job of contracting out logistics services. EDS's advantage is in reengineering the flow of products and information for customers such as Anchor Abrasives. TMM's competitive advantage is in providing intermodal service for cargo.

Are these competitive advantages unique and difficult to imitate? Do the three logistics EDI firms dominate their markets? Intral does now because of its long-term contract with Gillette. Do the three companies have superior access to resources? EDS does now because of its ability to do computer outsourcing to support logistics EDI. Do the three firms restrict the options of competitors? TMM does now because it's a Mexican-owned firm with strong ties to the Mexican government.

Are these competitive advantages sustainable? The answer: Are logistics EDI specialists the key players in logistics EDI? Can they create a virtual logistics system? We will cover this in more detail later.

Summary: Scanning Interactive EDI

Marketers know standardized information protocols are the key to better channel decisions. The near universal use of standardized protocols within the automotive industry keeps transactions costs down for Anchor Abrasives,

OEM suppliers, and the large auto firms. Marketing executives also contract out logistics EDI services to acquire expert knowledge on a fee-for-service basis, and the distribution costs are then shared by Gillette and Intral. Moreover, transportation marketers guide shippers to use ocean container services, such as TMM, as the means through which goods move from place to place. These external market transactions compete with internal vertical integration for the soul of channel management.

National Marketing Decisions

Marketers manage final demand by signaling detailed national information about logistics EDI; see Exhibit 10-7. American manufacturers prefer ANSI X12 and European firms choose UN/EDIFACT. Both add value to bits of information, but only one can be the world's standard for logistics outsourcing. Today, users ask this crucial question about logistics EDI standards: What do I get?

Peter Drucker retells this story: "I was very unpopular in Armonk, New York [IBM headquarters] when I said in the late '60s – before the PC – that the mainframe is past its peak . . . For the first time the people who were getting into information were beginning to ask 'What do I get?' And not 'What can I do?' When that happens, it very soon becomes a biased market . . . There is a war to be fought, but it lies in performance, and not in how one does things."[28]

Exhibit 10-7.
National Marketing Decisions: Logistics EDI
The Marketing Scan

Traditional Frame Analysis for Global Marketing
Firm-Specific 4Ps Analysis and Decision Making Under Uncertainty
Signal national interactive logistics EDI
Succeed from expansion of usage of EDIFACT over ANSI
Grow through rationalization of computer communications
Pay attention to additional uses in ocean transportation

Continued on next page

Exhibit 10–7. *Continued from previous page*

National Marketing Decisions and Marketing Strategy
Just-in-time inventory

Uninterrupted transportation and bulk warehousing services

Foreign trade services including customs assistance

Convergence of logistics and EDI services as a virtual reality

Paperless offices

National Marketing Decisions and Marketing Forecasts
Continuing trend is unrealistic because of information revolution

Amplifying trend builds on routine durable purchases

Doubling trend is realistic because of rapid product diffusion

---

Nontraditional Frame Analysis for Global Marketing

Marketing Management Frame and Marketing Investments
Six-Sigma Questions
What do I get?

How to improve performance?

Which level of quality would you prefer?

How to segment information?

How to add value to bits of information?

Performance-Based Information
All quotes must be accurate

All statistics must show meaningful relationships

All information must be directly accessible

All information must come from artificial intelligence agents

Transaction costs must be reasonable

Marketing Management Frame and Virtual Reality
Create memory offices

Fill in white spaces

Create virtual reality from half-real, half-fictional bits

Make information as if real

Manage spatial data

Reengineer logistics and information into logistics EDI

Carry out paradigm shift with virtual relationships

Improving Performance

Performance is providing "extremely high-quality information, what quality experts would call six-sigma information. (The trendsetter for benchmarking American quality was always Motorola, and until 1989 Motorola was talking about three-sigma quality – three bad parts in a thousand. Six-sigma quality is three bad parts per million.)"[29]

Can logistics EDI deliver this level of quality? Here's an outline for performance-based information. First, all the facts must be true, all the quotes must be accurate, and all the statistics must show meaningful relationships. Second, all information must be directly accessible without intermediaries. Finally, all information must come from artificial intelligence agents roaming databases, downloading interesting stuff, and assembling it for business decision making.

Is segmentation of information the future for logistics EDI? This means an end to simplification by existing batch-based computer and media-based information systems.[30] Then segment the market for extremely high-quality information by wider use of Internet and other online data retrieval systems.

Extending Service

Both the telephone and cable TV companies want to solve the access problem by widening the bandwidth – that is, adding more data lanes to the information highway by laying more fiber-optic wire; hence, the deals by which telephone companies buy cable companies. They are answering the question "What can I do?" – not the question "What do I get?"

Besides failing to answer the right management question, these deal makers miss the entire point of the new world of information technology. "More bits per second is not an intrinsic good. In fact, more bandwidth can have the deleterious effect of swamping people and of allowing machines at the periphery to be dumb."[31] Here is the right question: "Which would you prefer: 500 channels from which you can choose one, or one channel that can be switched to any source on the network?"[32]

Can logistics EDI networks deliver one channel with access to all sources of information about product movements, inventory levels, sailing dates, customs clearances, and shipping deliveries? Will shippers pay the price of these transaction costs?

Marketing Scan: Relationship Marketing

Transaction costs "limit the opportunistic tendencies of outside intermediaries. When the enforcement of contractual arrangements cannot be relied upon in the market, different degrees of forward integration are feasible alternatives."[33] Here are some "white spaces" in which firms such as EDS and Intral can create and dominate virtual logistics EDI networks.

Establishing Memory Offices

Early in this chapter we asked a series of questions about the second P: *Place*. Let's put them into the context of virtual reality. Is logistics EDI the *reality* of products moving through channels of distribution? Is logistics EDI the *fiction* of digital data representing goods ordered, containers shipped, titles transferred, and products sold? Or is logistics EDI the *half-real, half-fiction* convergence of distribution and logistics services with data and information services?

Cargo created out of combining the real and imaginary becomes *as if real*.[34] The text on the computer screen may be thoroughly modern because it is a reality made of bytes, bits, and batches. Yet it is an offense against the fundamental notion of distribution reality (e.g., ships, planes, containers, pallets, boxes, packages, and envelopes). Virtual reality changes both the logistics world itself and our understanding of it. This is a paradigm shift, a new view of channel management, in which virtual reality becomes both the key technological change element and the means to understand such change.

Today's logistics EDI gives marketers a memory office that helps us manipulate whatever data we need to give us the results our customers demand. This is the promise of the new thinking about reengineering business processes from Arthur Andersen Consulting, CSC Index, and, possibly, EDS. It means applying computer simulation to the envelope of logistics services surrounding the positioning and sale of products worldwide.

Creating Virtual Reality

By focusing on the convergence of logistics and EDI as a virtual reality, we avoid making a "category mistake" (chapter 8). Instead, we get answers to these questions: What logistics services do customers want from the telecomputer and EDI industries? Does digital technology drive EDI toward asset specificity and standardization? Do political and business differences increase external uncertainties and force logistics adaptation? Given all the contingencies, how can we make our EDI computer systems as real as possible in our quest for better information about the movement of goods from place to place?

Logistics EDI gives us an improved knowledge of customers integrated with a reorganized means to satisfy them. That's why logistics services are value-added activities. Creating value through logistics is the most important competitive advantage for marketers of the 1990s.[35]

Strategies for Increasing Marketing Effectiveness

Think of marketers who make decisions about freight as our surrogate employees. They are the conduits through which products and information flow from shippers to customers. If they are international freight forwarders, they gather information about and arrange for the following services:[36]

- Transportation services: ocean freight, air freight, surface transport, sea-air, and inland water transport

- Trade services: licenses, visas, and consular formalities; carrier and commercial documentation; letters of credit; customs clearance; cargo tracking/tracing; and shipper export declarations

- Value-added services: packaging, distribution, warehousing, insurance, logistics, project management, management and information services, export market consulting

A successful virtual logistics EDI network depends heavily on the abilities of freight forwarders and other transportation agents.

For example, IBM Netherlands subcontracts its European transportation and distribution services to Nedlloyd, a leading logistics management company. One hundred IBM employees were transferred to Nedlloyd as the latter takes over responsibility for order processing, warehousing, and transportation at IBM.[37] The goal of IBM in using an international freight forwarder is to lower inventory levels and gain uninterrupted service throughout Europe.

Signing up long-term channel participants for virtual logistics EDI networks is the most important issue facing manufacturers and shippers in the 1990s.[38]

Customer satisfaction with freight handling and overall product satisfaction go hand-in-hand. Freight forwarders and other transportation agents determine customers' attitudes and expectations about product availability and delivery times. These intermediaries make or break a firm's efforts to establish business overseas.[39]

Marketing Implementation

Let's close this analysis by asking computer-based logistics EDI to answer this question: Does free trade between the United States and Canada reduce total logistics costs?[40]

Cross-border transportation costs between the two countries remain high, but tariffs have dropped to zero between Canada and the United States. Thus, distance-based cross-border transportation costs play an ever more prominent role in channel management. Here's how one firm reduced total logistics costs.

Gillette asked "What can we do to reduce total logistics costs?" The company used its computer-based logistics EDI system to do an analysis of the impact of US-Canada free trade on its channels of distribution. Gillette decided to close its Canadian plants and ship products from American plants to all points in North America. This is channel management at its best.

Three forecasts. The "continuing trend" forecast is the easiest to make because things go on as before. Interactive logistics EDI doesn't conform to traditional ways of doing business in Europe, the United States, and Japan. Interactive EDI is so new that the "continuing trend" is unrealistic.

The "amplifying trend" forecast assumes computer-driven EDI firms aggressively market their interactive services. In the United States, Europe, and Japan, these routine durable purchases are crucial parts of the their business. This trend will happen because we are at the beginning of a major information revolution with no end in sight.

The "doubling trend" forecast assumes EDI firms convert customers and suppliers' parents to interactive logistics EDI. Product diffusion occurs rapidly because executives want these new interactive logistics EDI services. This information should help marketers put together an effective marketing strategy for interactive logistics EDI.

Summary: Scanning Relationship Marketing

Marketers position logistics EDI services based on services demanded by customers. Successful marketing executives realize they must learn a great deal more about virtual logistics EDI networks before they can offer a total package of services to shippers. Positioning decisions about computer-based logistics EDI systems, wireless technologies to transmit data, and simulators to show users alternative distribution systems are an exciting new business for the future. All service providers who want to manage channels for others must remember their customers' most important question: What do I get?

Inclusive Contexts for Global Marketing

Exhibit 10-8 sums up the inclusive contexts for global marketing in the multimedia industry. We examine reinventing a services marketing category under deregulation, privatization, and liberalization. We also study two types of decision making under uncertainty: culturally based demand analysis and organizationally based industry analysis. These two focuses help us direct our research to answering important questions: How will our customers multiply the use of our services, and how will we make money on our marketing investments? Again, we deal with technology as a driving force in managerial decision making under uncertainty. Our choices determine whether we will be a success at global marketing.

Exhibit 10-8.
Inclusive Contexts for Global Marketing

Market Risk

Govern the market through reinvented business environment

    Deregulation, privatization, liberalization

    Reinvent services marketing category

Unknown competitive possibilities and imperfect information

Political Frame

Firm-Specific 4Ps Analysis (A)

Culturally based decision making under uncertainty

Demand analysis, cultural analysis, age-period cohort analysis

Continued on next page

Exhibit 10-8. *Continued from previous page*

Value creation
  Multiply uses of information
  Reinvent services marketing category
Reengineer user-based information
Cultural Frame

Firm-Specific 4Ps Analysis (B)
Organizationally based decision making under uncertainty
Industry analysis: scale, scope, sequence economies
Transaction costs: marketing bits of information
Organizational incentives
  Share risks and contract out
  Leverage core competencies
  Fill in white spaces
  Create virtual reality network
Teamwork, nonroutine partnerships, networks
Six-sigma question: What do I get?
Virtual reality and paradigm shift
Return on marketing investments
Marketing Management Frame

National Marketing Decisions
Supply analysis
Creative destruction to winnow out winners and losers
Competitive analysis
Segmentation and positioning strategies
Marketing strategy
  Identify customer actions with future logistics payoffs
  Create a new services marketing category
  Classify contract logistics into value-added services
  Reduce transaction costs
  Apply contingency perspective to 4Ps marketing mix
Vision test
Remember trend is not destiny
Technological Frame

Conclusions

Providers of logistics EDI services bring airplanes, ocean vessels, rail cars, and trucks together with data and information so that goods move smoothly among countries at reduced logistics costs. Rapid technological change is occurring, and marketers are groping for the most appropriate logistics strategy.

Let's return to our initial three learning objectives:

1. Discuss the importance of the contingency perspective to a logistics positioning strategy.

    You should have a clear understanding of the many contingencies that affect channel management and of how few of these are covered by the standardization (minimum differentiation) versus adaptation (maximum differentiation) argument.

2. Outline organizational incentive models to help make better decisions about in-house logistics (or vertical integration) and contracted logistics (or market-based transaction costs).

    You should be able to explain why firms choose to contract out their logistics EDI services or provide them in-house as part of their overall channel management. You should redraft your international product positioning plan to include a logistics EDI positioning plan, too.

3. Explain the management decisions taken to exploit virtual logistics EDI networks.

    You should be aware that virtual logistics EDI networks are coming sometime in the future, but not necessarily today or tomorrow. You should introduce changes in logistics EDI management only so long as you can answer your customers' most fundamental six-sigma question: What do I get?

Making the future happen is the work of global marketing executives.

Notes

1. Saul Klein, Gary L. Frazier, and Victor J. Roth, "A Transaction Cost Analysis Model of Channel Integration in International Markets," *Journal of Marketing Research 27:2* (May 1990): 199. Timothy J. Muris, David T. Scheffman, and Pablo T. Spiller, "Strategy and Transaction Costs: The Organization of Distribution in the Carbonated Soft Drink Industry," *Journal of Economics & Management Strategy* 1:1 (Spring 1992): 91-92.

2. The argument presented in this section follows the rules outlined in the Klein, Frazier, and Roth and the Muris, Scheffman, and Spiller articles.

3. Nicholas Negroponte of the Architectural Machine Group at MIT gave us the term memory office. It is described by Stewart Brand, *The Media Lab* (London: Penguin, 1989): 139. Cited by Benjamin Woolley, Virtual Worlds (Oxford, UK: Blackwell Publishers, 1992): 140.

4. Juli Todd, "Maximizing the ASN," *Actionline* (August 1993): 18.

5. Nancy R. Malo, "All Roads Lead to UN/EDIFACT," *Actionline,* August 1993, 20-3.

6. Klein, Frazier, and Roth, 199-200.

7. Adapted from Michael Gerus, "The 16 Rules of EDI," *Actionline,* November 1992, 15-17.

8. This section draws from Joseph B. Fuller, James O'Conor, and Richard Rawlinson, "Tailored Logistics: The Next Advantage," *Harvard Business Review 71:3* (May–June 1993): 87-98.

9. "Making the Middleman an Endangered Species," *Business Week*, June 6, 1994, 114-15.

10. Daniel F. Spulber, "Economic Analysis and Management Strategy: A Survey," *Journal of Economics & Management Strategy 1:3* (Fall 1992): 559-66. L. W. Stern and A.I. El-Ansary, Marketing Channels, 3rd ed. (Englewood Cliffs, NJ: Prentice-Hall, 1988).

11. The ideas in this paragraph come from Eric J. Adams, "Well Connected," *World Trade* 6:10 (November 1993): 46, 48.

12. Daniel F. Spulber, *Regulation and Markets* (Cambridge, MA: MIT Press, 1989).

13. Telephone interview with Joseph McCabe, president and chief executive officer of Intral Corporation, October 27, 1993.

14. William H. Davidow and Michael S. Malone, *The Virtual Corporation* (New York: HarperBusiness, HarperCollins Publishers, 1992): 231-35.

15. Neil Buckley, "Cinderella Industry Finds Its Feet," *Financial Times,* October 5, 1993, 29.

16. Ibid.

17. Phillip Hastings, "Contract Out: Debate Is Renewed," *Financial Times,* October 5, 1993, 30.

18. Claire Gooding, "Information Technology: Focus on Communications," *Financial Times*, October 5, 1993, 31.

19. Ibid.

20. "Telecommunications Survey: New Medium, New Message," *The Economist,* October 23, 1993, 16.

21. Gooding, 31.

22. The EDS case comes from Christopher Lorenz, "Avoiding the IBM Trap," *Financial Times,* October 15, 1993, 12.

23. John Latta, "The Business of Cyberspace," *Virtual Reality Special Report*, July 1992, 28.

24. "Virtual Reality: How a Computer-Generated World Could Change the Real World," *Business Week*, October 5, 1992, 100.

25. Joan O'C. Hamilton, "Going Where No Minds Have Gone Before," *Business Week,* October 5, 1992, 104.

26. Rick Tetzeli, "Cargo that Phones Home," *Fortune,* November 15, 1993, 143.

27. Mary R. Brooks, "International Competitiveness: Assessing and Exploring Competitive Advantage by Ocean Container Carriers," *The Logistics and Transportation Review 29:1* (March 1993): 275-91.

28. Peter Schwartz, "Post-Capitalism," *Wired* (July/August 1993): 97.

29. Michael Crichton, "The Mediasaurus: Today's Mass Media Is Tomorrow's Fossil Fuel," *Wired* (September/October 1993): 57-58.

30. Ibid. 59.

31. Nicholas Negroponte, "Debunking Bandwidth: From Shop Talk to Small Talk," *Wired* (July/August 1993): 101.

32. Ibid.

33. Klein, Frazier, and Roth, 196.

34. Jonathan D. Spence, *The Memory Palace of Matteo Ricci* (London: Faber, 1985): 2, 13. Cited by Benjamin Woolley, *Virtual Worlds* (Oxford, UK: Blackwell Publishers, 1992): 138–40.

35. Fuller, O'Conor, and Rawlinson, 87.

36. Aysegul Ozsomer, Michel Mitri, and S. Tamer Cavusgil, "Selecting International Freight Forwarders," *International Journal of Physical Distribution and Logistics Management* 23:3 (1993): 12.

37. Ibid., 13.

38. Davidow and Malone, 233.

39. Ibid., 234.

40. John C. Taylor and David J. Closs, "Logistics Implications of an Integrated US-Canada Market," *International Journal of Physical Distribution & Logistics Management* 23:1 (1993): 12.

Part Four

Signaling
National Information

Chapter Format

Introduction

Marketing Questions

Environmental Scan: Local Traditions

Initial Analysis of Marketing Opportunities

Clues to Capturing Customers

The Firm-Specific Research Assignment

Competitive Scan: User Friendly Campaigns

Estimates of Market Potential

Similar Market Segments Worldwide

National Marketing Decisions

Marketing Scan: $P + A = B$

Strategies for Increasing Marketing Effectiveness

Marketing Implementation

Conclusions

Cases: Nestle, Coca-Cola, Andy Berlin, Woolward & Partners

Learning Objectives

After reading this chapter, you should be able to:

- Discuss the importance of the contingency perspective to promotion and advertising positioning decisions

- Outline external competitive issues (such as reduced budgets and demands for higher productivity) that are forcing the promotion and advertising industry to reinvent itself

- Explain the management decisions needed to exploit interactive advertising in a global, yet local economy

Promotion Marketing

chapter 11

Introduction

Marketers manage final demand by researching international markets (chapters 3–6),
positioning global brands (chapters 7–10),
and signaling detailed national information
(chapters 11–14). Advertising themes, price
information, selling practices, and value marketing all dispense superior information
about the intensity of consumer demand for
products within nation-states. Here are the
frames for studying local, national, and global
marketing.

Scanning Global Markets

Environmental scan: local traditions.
Advertising indicates attitudes, beliefs,
images, symbols, and presence. Most of these
are intimately tied together by culture, and
marketers err when they make mistakes
about global similarities and real national differences. Although France and the United
States share a common western civilization,
their visual print and TV ads are different
because they reflect old world and new
world values. Although Japan shares a common material culture with the United States,

this common bond is less important than Japan's national culture and its preference for the humorous soft sell in ads. Successful marketers learn how to deal with these different situations around the world.

Competitive scan: user friendly campaigns. Advertising conveys emotional values. Most of these are tied to national cultures, and marketers err when they mistake paradigm shifts in the United States for trends in Europe, East Asia, and Latin America. Clearly, the global firms want more creative and strategic thinking from their advertising agencies both in the United States and Europe, and smaller advertising and different types of service agencies seem to be able to do this job better than the traditional, larger agencies. Moreover, these new competitors are willing to share in both the risks and profits associated with using advertising and promotion to enhance demand, increase sales, and improve returns. Successful marketers learn how to make themselves the best at promotion marketing.

Marketing scan: P + A = B. Advertising is closely tied to the cultural norms of society, and it must change as norms take on new forms during the last part of the 20th century. New products will keep coming to the market in record numbers. In-house marketing teams will spend time and money to position their products within appropriate market segments throughout the world. Sometimes, they will call on outside promotion and advertising experts to help them convey the emotional values of the products to consumers in the United States, Europe, Japan, and elsewhere in the world. As a consequence, a few brands will be truly global in name and fame while the rest will sell well nationally, regionally, and locally. Interactive advertising offers both in-house marketing teams and outside advertising experts the opportunity to tailor products and services to all customers wherever they may be in the world.

Traditional Contexts for Global Marketing

Exhibit 11-1 lists the traditional contexts for global marketing in the case of the promotion and advertising industry. We study a reinvented business environment, pre- and post-first-purchase advertising signals, and marketing strategy. The first reinforces our observation about the changes occurring in the interactive advertising industry. The second reminds us that advertising firms must pay attention to signals about brands. The third prepares us for the hard task of implementing a marketing strategy with continuous future payoffs.

The promotion and advertising case is another symbol of how new industries are being created for a future global economy.

Exhibit 11-1.
Traditional Contexts for Global Marketing

Market Risk
Govern the market through reinvented business environment
Unknown competitive possibilities and imperfect information

Firm-Specific 4Ps Analysis
Decision making under uncertainty
Shift the paradigm
Advertising signals
    Purchase behavior, purchase attitudes, purchase decisions
    Purchase situations, purchase leveraging
Media effectiveness
    Brand opinion or cultural attitudes toward brands
    Brand outlook or private beliefs made public
    Brand choices reflect self-referencing criteria
    Brand associations give meaning to utilitarian concepts
    Brand extensions help capture competitive advantage
Post-first-purchase decisions
    Ads are positive and compare brand favorably with others
    Ads deliver product information consistent with use
    Ads consistently convey positive images
    Ads are tailored to suit emerging consumer demand
    Ads turn ideas into valuable competitive resource
Advertising agencies
    Creeping elegance raises costs
    Local execution of global ads
    One-site, one-sound commercials
    Core media buy, slotting fees, point-of-sale promotions
Teamwork, nonroutine partnerships, relationship marketing

National Marketing Decisions
Marketing opportunities
    Discounting and everyday low prices

Continued on next page

Exhibit 11-1. *Continued from previous page*

Integrated campaigns, double-duty advertising

Contingency perspective

Marketing research

Seismic change of information revolution

Deregulate advertising commissions

Think through pan-European advertising and media buys

Marketing investments, in-house advertising, media offerings

Marketing strategy

Promotion + advertising = brands

Utilitarian versus cultural images

Attitudes toward ads

Brand extensions

Global and national brands

Nontraditional Contexts for Global Marketing

Exhibit 11-2 names the nontraditional contexts for global marketing in the advertising industry. We survey reinventing promotion and advertising, interactive advertising, multidimensional signaling, and six-sigma questions. We are beginning to learn that only by asking the question "What do I get?" will we help ourselves make better marketing investments.

Governing the market. First, let's look at the political frame. Government opens up national markets to rapid technological change through investments in marketing services by global and domestic marketers. Liberalization leads to more accessible markets, especially in interactive advertising. The tempo quickens as marketing executives sell advertising copy, direct marketing, and in-house promotional pieces. Success in governing the market unlocks additional opportunities for relationship marketing.

Exhibit 11-2.
Nontraditional Contexts for Global Marketing

Political Frame

Govern the market through reinvented business environment

Liberalization offers more accessible markets

Reinvent interactive advertising, point-of-sale promotions

Continued on next page

Exhibit 11-2. *Continued from previous page*

Technological Frame
Contingency perspective
Signaling game
Multiplying information about demand
   Expectations of in-house teams
   Promotional expenditures
   Comings and goings of agency clients
Marketing intelligence
   Pooling relationships
   Levels of advertising
   Integrated marketing campaigns
Dissipative advertising or bad signals
Creative ideas, media buys, good signals

Cultural Frame
Worldwide communications
   Learn about brands
   Sift the good from the bad
   Appropriateness of ads' placement
   Judgments about product quality
Multidimensional signaling
   Propaganda, cultural images
   Private views made public
Dominant expectations or period eye
Scale economies in signaling costs

Marketing Management Frame
Marketing investments
Six-sigma questions
   What do I get?
   How to improve performance?
   Which level of quality would you prefer?
   How to segment information?
   How to add value to bits of information?
Price-quality relationships

Marketing decisions under uncertainty. Second, let's study the technological frame. Marketing educators call the multiplying of information about demand a *signaling game.*[1] In-house marketing teams and outside promotion experts pool their information and choose a level of advertising to create demand for global brands and local products. Notwithstanding the best efforts of advertising agencies, demand is never high enough to meet the expectations of in-house teams. The latter indicate their displeasure by terminating existing advertising relationships and inviting other agencies to present their credentials. All this information about demand, promotional expenditures, and the comings and goings of agency clients is common knowledge in the industry. Competitors use such marketing intelligence to make choices about pooling relationships, levels of advertising, promotional practices, and integrated marketing campaigns.

Promotion creates final demand through the constant pooling, separating, and pooling of information among in-house and outside experts. In-house marketing teams assume outside promotion experts have complete information because the latter have given them the impression that this is, indeed, true. When no demand is created (that is, advertising is dissipative), this "bad" signal from ad agencies terminates pooling relationships. When demand is created, the "good" signal from promotion experts does not guarantee their future affiliation with in-house clients. With a little help from competing ad agencies, in-house marketing teams come to believe advertising dollars were wasted by their current agency, and only a new agency will provide them with quality signaling (that is, new creative ideas and media buys).

Hunting for consumers. Third, let's examine the cultural frame. Typically, firms advertise a variety of global and local brands, but all goods within a product line share a common assessment of quality by customers. With the advent of worldwide communications links (chapters 7–10), consumers learn more quickly about product successes and failures anywhere in the world. The task facing in-house marketing teams and outside promotion experts is to help consumers learn about brands, sift the good from the bad, and make better judgments about product quality.

Customers infer product quality from these promotion and advertising signals: the level of advertising expenditures, the appropriateness of the ads' placement, and informed judgments about brands. Moreover, ads must do two cultural things. First, ads must "convey the dominant expectations and conventions that govern the way people see and interpret images at a given time (what the art historian Michael Baxandall calls the *period eye*)."[2] Second, ads must take advantage of the fatal disconnection between pre-1968 and post-1968 age cohort groups (chapters 3–6).

Such marketing intelligence helps in-house marketing teams target products to particular consumer groups. Their customers are those who are most susceptible to choosing global brands over local goods. They make choices based on the upward distortions of advertising expenditures that imply product quality. These advertising signals from in-house teams and outside experts confirm the judgment of final consumers about product quality.

When quality is shared throughout the product line, different brands often signal unique sets of information to final consumers. The Mexicans buy global, largely American brand names (chapter 3). The French and the Germans make purchases based upon branded goods that confirm a safe European place within the changing demographic patterns of western life (chapter 4). The Japanese choose goods that reflect their unique national culture and are in tune with the worldwide cultural attitudes emerging from North America and Europe (chapter 5). And the Chinese seek out products that confirm their drive to be as modern as anyone else in East Asia (chapter 6).

Also, when customers in all markets are aware of the entire product line, firms obtain scale economies in signaling costs. AT&T, BT/MCI, the Baby Bells, and other telcos offer global outsourcing and long-distance services with local connections through wired telephone and wireless cellular companies (chapters 7 and 8). The jump into multimedia by the telecom, cable, and entertainment firms indicates the cost of quality improvement (chapter 9). And the potential of logistics EDI, Internet, and virtual reality forges a new set of fixed costs for collecting and using information throughout the world (chapter 10). Thus, advertising signaling is the crucial task for marketers. It offers a way to measure product quality, a formula to assess costs of quality improvement, and a procedure to structure information.[3]

Segmentation, positioning, and tailoring decisions. Finally, let's look closely at the marketing management frame. Successful marketers gain significant competitive advantages by signaling quality through targeted promotion.

These advertising efforts differ from foreign market to foreign market because national cultures require different levels of product quality, insist on alternative approaches to product improvements, and offer a wide variety of information about the pros and cons of products. Marketing professors call this different mix of promotion activities a contingency perspective (chapter 9).

Firms select competitive advertising strategies in response to the anticipated promotion strategies of rival firms. Actions by firms (e.g., strategies, payoffs, and information) affect consumer demand. Most traditional advertising agencies are losing older clients faster than they are gaining new clients. Smaller agencies and new types of competitors (such as Hollywood talent agencies) with creative and strategic ideas are taking away the business. Some are using interactive advertising to do their promotion jobs differently. They apply the signaling game to the price-quality relationships emerging in the world's media markets.

Organizing global marketing experience. The simultaneous existence of these four different contexts forces marketers to research traditional promotion practices, to position interactive advertising and direct marketing, and to tailor information services to suit local, national, and global tastes. Let's do two things in this chapter. First, we will discuss the use of promotion and advertising to gain market entry under demand uncertainty. Then we will apply this analysis to how in-house teams and external ad agencies signal demand for branded products.

Market Risk Questions

Marketers manage final demand by researching international markets; see Exhibit 11-3. The information age encourages advertisers to fill in all dead spaces with ads - for example, during busy signals on telephone calls and on the tiles of floors in supermarkets.[4] Also, the information age forces ad agencies to perform real work on all jobs so agency personnel stop *creeping elegance* - that is, the incremental but often unnecessary improvements they think up during product design, packaging, in-store displays, and media buys.[5] The environmental, competitive, and marketing scans provide information and insights about the effect of rapid technological change on the promotion positioning strategies of advertising competitors.

Exhibit 11-3.
Market Risk Analysis: Promotion
The Environmental Scan

Traditional Frame Analysis for Global Marketing
Firm-Specific 4Ps Analysis and Advertising Signals
Purchase behavior
Purchase attitudes
Purchase decisions
Purchase situations
Purchase leveraging
Firm-Specific 4Ps Analysis and Media Effectiveness
Brand opinion or cultural attitudes toward brands
Brand outlook is private beliefs made public about brands
Brand choices reflect self-referencing criteria
Brand associations give meaning to utilitarian concepts
Brand extensions help capture sustainable competitive advantage
Firm-Specific 4Ps Analysis and Advertising Agencies
Creeping elegance raises costs
Local execution of global ads
One-site, one-sound commercials
Communications effectiveness
Core media buy, slotting fees, point-of-sale promotions
National Marketing Decisions and Marketing Opportunities
Discounting
Everyday low prices
Integrated campaigns
Communications link
Double-duty advertising
Brand loyalty
Targeting customers
Contingency perspective

Nontraditional Frame Analysis for Global Marketing
Cultural Frame and Signaling National Information
Propaganda
Cultural images
Private views made public
Likability means humor
Period eye

Adding Value to the Selling of Information

In chapter 7, we described the 4Ps scheme used widely by marketing educators. The third P is *Promotion:* Do ads interpret current images? Do promotions tie themselves to the "period eye"? Do brands convey dominant expectations and conventions? Will customers buy products based on advertising global brands?

Advertising Signals   Marketing educators deal with these questions in terms of multidimensional signaling. Here are several signals:[6]

#1. Purchase behavior or brand opinion is the result of cultural attitudes toward the ads about brands. The ads are likable, and this trait is transferred automatically to brands.

#2. Purchase attitude or brand outlook is the fallout of beliefs about brands. The ads make public private views about brands.

#3. Purchase decisions or brand choices reflect cultural image beliefs held by customers. The ads convey dominant social and psychological self-concept impressions.

#4. Purchase situations or brand associations use cultural symbols. The ads give meaning to utilitarian products, store locations, and countries of origin.

#5. Purchase leveraging or brand extension comes from historic presence in the marketplace. The ads turn company names into valuable competitive resources.[7]

Marketing executives look at media effectiveness or "bottom-line" results. These are influenced by ad placements as well as by actual brand-related content. Thus, marketers must target their ads to relevant market segments and insist that advertising experts capture customers in their most natural purchase situations.[8]

Environmental Scan: Local Traditions

Today's advertising signals tell us to combine global commitment with local vision and to make promotion appeals compatible with international and national lifestyles.[9] Which is more important – globalization or localization? Which brands do consumers prefer – global or local brands? The answers are not clear-cut.

Here's what culturally sensitive ad executives believe about localizing promotion and advertising. Messages must use local traditions and symbols of each country to enhance national demand. Also, locally owned advertising agencies do a far better job at meshing ads to national culture than do international agencies headquartered in New York, London, or Tokyo.

Applying the Contingency Perspective to Promotion

For example, although image beliefs are crucial advertising signals in the United States, Europe, and Japan, utilitarian beliefs play a much more important role in eastern Europe and other formerly Communist countries. Consumers in these areas think of ads as propaganda, always misleading, but with some information content.[10] They may watch ads on TV, but they remain unconvinced that the ads convey any meaningful social information. When ads come from western Europe into Poland, the Czech Republic, or Hungary, they need to be customized to give them a truly local feel – that is, more use of Polish and less of German, and more explanation of why brands are worth a premium and why a pecking order exists among brands.

Localizing Promotion

David Newkirk, vice president of Booz-Allen & Hamilton, says this about localization:

> *It's going to be a long time before the media and the way people use media converge, even if the products, the positionings, and the copy strategy all converge. . . McDonalds, Coca-Cola, Pepsi run global campaigns, but they still execute them locally. Take Coca-Cola's new campaign featuring its return to an old bottle shape. In the UK, that campaign is running heavily on posters in bus-shelters, a medium that doesn't exist in the United States. It's different again in France because poster sizes are different there. Such differences in media necessitate that a global advertising message is executed very differently in different countries.*[11]

Globalizing Advertising

Other in-house marketing teams look at Europe in a new way. They are treating Europe as a single market because of the convergence of taste (chapter 4). "The young and the rich have very similar tastes the world over, and that is what's driving the convergences in advertising and media," says Newkirk of Booz-Allen.[12] Nevertheless, Pan-European advertising is still largely a phenomenon of TV, in which 11 of the top 50 companies placing ads are American firms.[13]

One-Site, One-Sound Commercials Bill Britt, the editor of *Euromarketing*, says this about Pan-European advertising: "It's much cheaper to shoot just one commercial and then use it across Europe. It's also cheaper for a company to assign one Euro-marketing manager and to have more junior product managers, rather than full marketing managers at country levels."[14] And John Hegarty, creative director of the London-based independent advertising agency BBH, suggests his client, Levi's jeans, saved about US $3 million by shooting one TV commercial spot for all of Europe.

Cross-Cultural Analysis Thus, some in-house marketing teams and outside promotion experts are guided more by globalization than by localization.[15] The cultural themes, campaigns, content, layouts, and brand names must be the same for all markets to enhance demand worldwide, and international advertising agencies do a far better job at meshing global commitment to local vision.

Let's look carefully at this conclusion. Globalization is a code word for standardization; see Exhibit 11–4. When a decision is made to standardize ad campaigns across nation-states, additional decisions must be made about whether the entire promotion campaign must be standardized, too. Standardization of ads within the EU will not be simple, and adaptations may be required for at least some European countries.[16]

These are questions with no answers:[17] Will the Pan-European ad reflect the French preference for ads portraying children in realistic settings versus the English (and American) preference for ads portraying children in clean and smiling, idealistic conditions? Will the Pan-European ad communicate price information for high-status appeal as is common to do in France but less common in the United Kingdom (and in the United States)? These questions underscore our need to apply the contingency perspective to promotion and advertising.

Initial Analysis of Marketing Opportunities

Let's review the contingency perspective. It gives us a way to resolve the argument among marketers about standardization (minimum differentiation) versus adaptation (maximum differentiation). Also, the contingency perspective pushes us toward a variety of internal and external strategy factors that are the rubrics of competitive marketing:[18]

- If an industry is technology intensive, marketers standardize products and ad programs. If the industry requires customization, marketing executives adapt products and promotion.

- If the product is not culturally specific, marketers standardize the 4Ps. If the industry is culturally specific, marketing executives adapt the 4Ps to suit different countries.

Exhibit 11-4.
English: The World's Second Language.

BROTHER TONGUES

% OF PUPILS IN GENERAL SECONDARY EDUCATION LEARNING ENGLISH, FRENCH OR GERMAN AS A FOREIGN LANGUAGE, 1991–1992

	ENGLISH	FRENCH	GERMAN
HOLLAND	96	65	53
GERMANY	93	23	-
DENMARK	92	8	58
SPAIN	92	10	0.3
FRANCE	84	-	27
BELGIUM (FLEMISH)	68	98	22
ITALY	61	33	3
BELGIUM (FRENCH)	58	1	6
PORTUGAL	55	25	0.4
BRITAIN	-	59	20
IRELAND	-	69	24

SOURCE: EUROSTAT

Courtesy of The Economist

- If competition in the export market is not intense, marketers opt for standardization. If competition is strong abroad, marketing executives opt for adaptation.

- If management lacks international experience, marketers prefer standardization. If management has many years of export work, marketing executives prefer adaptation.

For example, Nestle, a Swiss-owned global multinational firm, has years of experience in positioning, packaging, labeling, and distributing products and promoting brand-named goods worldwide. These products are unique in the minds of customers because the brand names signal significant quality differences. Through promotion, advertising, and integrated marketing campaigns, Nestle has created a pecking order of brands in which print and TV media signal high prices for high quality and low prices for low quality.

Nestle built up its brands of packaged goods in three ways.[19] First, the firm purchased massive amounts of advertising to instill in consumers a favorable attitude about the brands. Second, Nestle promoted the image of its brands to make consumers aware of how the brands meshed with their lifestyles. Finally, the firm pushed its brands to a prominent place on retail shelves, thus making it easy for consumers to buy the products.

Unfortunately, Nestle's competitors are discounting their global and national brands with "everyday low prices," and supermarket retail chains are pushing their private brands at cut-rate prices, too. Nestle's competitors are signaling that high quality comes with lower prices. Their message is substantially different from Nestle's. Should Nestle follow?

Maximizing Communications Effectiveness

Nestle decided to go a different route. The firm chose to use relationship marketing and create a communications link with customers. This is neither standardization or adaptation, but an individualized marketing campaign based on the contingencies faced by the firm in its packaged goods business.

The theme is that Nestle seeks to become a helpful, caring, and trusted companion in the lives of its customers. For example, in its integrated marketing campaign *Le Relais Bebe*, the firm set up rest stops for babies on the main travel routes within France so parents could feed them with Nestle baby foods and change them with Nestle disposable diapers.[20] Also, Nestle provides a toll-free number for new mothers to call for advice on baby nutrition, then follows up with packages of gift coupons every three months for the first 18 months of a baby's life.

Double-Duty Advertising   Nestle chose to do things differently than its competitors. The firm refused to discount and put its marketing dollars into couponing and trade allowances in which price signals are replaced completely by promotion and advertising signals. Also, Nestle refused to use the "everyday low price" strategy in which advertising signals are replaced completely by price signals. Instead, Nestle chose an integrated marketing campaign built on direct, personal communication with consumers that adds value through new ideas about channel management.

This global firm gives three marketing signals to its customers: repositioned products, improved personal services, and quality placements of ads and promotions. All are communicated directly to consumers. Nestle's chief marketing guru, Peter Brabeck, calls this integrated marketing campaign "double-duty" advertising.

Enhancing Brand Management

The Nestle case is a symptom of a much larger problem facing advertising. In the past, the core American media buy was three TV networks and a dose of women's magazines. According to Chris Whittle, one of the new breed of media entrepreneurs, "That's not the way things work anymore."[21]

Because consumers view many brand-named goods as commodities, their loyalty to brands is eroding. For example, in 1975, 77 percent of American consumers bought only well-known brands; this dropped to 62 percent by 1990.[22] Also, consumers are simply tired of the 3,000 marketing messages that bombard them daily.[23] Moreover, most marketers cannot wait for advertising to work; they have to turn their dollars around more quickly. So they pay "slotting fees" to retailers to get shelf space for their branded goods; these fees take money away from traditional advertising.

Hence, print ads in newspapers and magazines and TV network advertising play a diminished role in the selling of goods and services throughout the United States and Europe. Ten years ago, advertising got 43 percent and promotion received 57 percent of all marketing dollars. Today, advertising gets 30 percent and 70 percent goes to slotting fees and other promotions.[24]

How then do firms boost the sales of brands? Nestle chose a direct communications link with its customers. Levi's places its ads on MTV and the Video Jukebox Network. GM uses direct mail to consumers with the income and lifestyles for its new high-quality, high-priced cars. The end result of all this is that print and TV advertising is no longer the only way to carry out a firm's marketing efforts.

Targeting Customers

Let's summarize what we know about the marketing opportunities for advertising and promotion. General demographic data (chapter 4), such as income, sex, education, and age-cohort groups, are less important today than the detailed computerized databases about consumers and their buying habits. These databases permit firms to reach the right people at the right place and at the right time. According to Camillo Pagano, Nestle's worldwide marketing chief, the firm shifted 20 percent of its advertising budget into alternative media so it could target its customers more carefully.[25] This is a significant trend for the future.

Clues to Capturing Customers

Once we move from Europe and the United States to East Asia we know intuitively that we must alter our promotion and advertising images to mesh with the local cultural values predominant in Japan (chapter 5), China (chapter 6), and southeast Asia (chapter 15). Why then do American and European marketing executives fail to follow through on their intuition?

Reordering Advertising Signals

Earlier in this chapter we discussed several advertising signals: likability, private views made public, cultural images, new meaning, and competitive resources. These are discussed in order of their importance to American marketing educators; they reflect the real concerns of western marketing executives. When we apply these advertising signals to Japan, we must change their order – cultural images, private views made public, and likability means humor – and reinvent them within the context of Japanese society.

Cultural Images   *Purchase decisions or brand choices reflect cultural images and beliefs held by customers. The ads convey dominant social and* *psychological self-concept impressions.* The Japanese prefer the soft sell about human emotional sentiments; the tone is very low-key, only suggesting the merits of the product.[26] Only if the product is western do the Japanese like to see Caucasian celebrities, Americanisms, and western settings in their ads. Otherwise, they prefer their own models, language, and social scenes. Japanese advertising lends credence to the claim that promotional adaptation is more useful than standardized messages and media buys in global marketing.

Private Views Made Public Although per capita promotion and advertising expenses in the United States are three times greater than similar costs in Japan, the two countries together spend 70 percent of the world's dollars on TV advertising.[27] However, these facts miss an importance nuance of difference between the United States and Japan.

Purchase attitude or brand outlook is the fallout of beliefs about brands. The ads make public private views about brands. Japanese advertisers prefer to stress company reputation as the more effective way to transfer good "feelings" about brand-named goods to consumers.[28] Brands are part of a product line of goods behind which stands the social position of the firm (i.e., a large extended family of employees, family members, and friends). Foreign firms doing business in Japan are most prone to cultural error when they carry in their marketing baggage the notion that standardization is the key to success in Japan.

Likability Means Humor *Purchase behavior or brand opinion is the result of cultural attitudes toward the ads about brands. The ads are likable, and this trait is transferred automatically to brands.* In chapter 4, we discussed the Japanese culture of *manga*, comic books with a story to tell about the past, present, and future. Likability translates as humor in Japan. For example, humorous things happen to husbands, family members, salarymen, office colleagues, superiors, neighbors, landlords, and other powerful people.[29] Often black humor about disease, funerals, and wars finds its way into *manga*. Anything that is out of control gets a laugh from the Japanese in comic books, in print media, and on TV. Although some of these events are offensive in the United States, they are appropriate for promotion and advertising in Japan.

In summary, these reordered advertising signals confirm the need for a contingency perspective when dealing with global promotion and advertising. In Japan, we face the same reluctance of consumers to buy. Their attitude toward new products is "seen it, done it."[30] They don't want the usual mass-market, me-too brand-named products, and they wait to be convinced that the new niche products from Japan and the West mesh with their culture.

Summary: Scanning Local Traditions

Advertising indicates attitudes, beliefs, images, symbols, and presence. Most of these are intimately tied together by culture, and marketers err when they make mistakes about global similarities and real national differences. Although France and the United States share a common western civilization, their visual print and TV ads are different because they reflect old world and new world values. Although Japan shares a common material culture with the United States, this common bond is less important than Japan's national culture and its preference for the humorous soft sell in ads. Successful marketers learn how to deal with these different situations around the world.

The Firm-Specific Assignment

Marketers manage final demand by positioning promotion within markets committed to coping with local traditions; see Exhibit 11-5. Most advertising occurs after consumers try, use, and repeat their purchases of products. Advertising professionals employ post-first-purchase ads to convince customers to switch brand-named goods. The ads must be consistent with the direct, positive experience of consumers, or the ads must seek to change tentative, negative images into long-term positive attitudes about products.

Exhibit 11-5.
Firm-Specific Analysis: Promotion
The Competitive Scan

Traditional Frame Analysis for Global Marketing
Firm-Specific 4Ps Analysis, Teamwork, Nonroutine Partnerships
Strategic/creative thinking
Integrated marketing campaigns
Measurable results
Continued on next page

Exhibit 11-5. *Continued from previous page*

Bottom-line results

Cost-per-sale

Profit centers

Think tanks

Outsize targets

Futures budgets

One-on-one communication

Aggressive approach

Firm-Specific 4Ps Analysis and Relationship Marketing

Shift the paradigm

Create imagined differences in minds of consumers

Help consumers recognize convincing differences

Discover hidden virtues of products

Share profits

Firm-Specific 4Ps Analysis and Post-First-Purchase Decisions

Ads are positive and compare brand favorably with others

Ads deliver product information consistent with use

Ads consistently convey positive images

National Marketing Decisions and Marketing Research

Pay attention to seismic change of information revolution

Deregulate advertising commissions

Think through pan-European advertising and media buys

Reinvented Advertising Signals

Again, marketing educators deal with these post-first-purchase questions in terms of multidimensional signaling. To reflect post-first-purchase advertising, signals #1 through #3 are restated as signals #6 through #8.[31]

#6.   Purchase behavior or brand opinion is confirmed by post-first-purchase experience. The ads are positive, and they compare one brand favorably to other competing brands.

#7.   Purchase attitude or brand outlook integrates different pieces of information after the post-first-purchase experience. The ads deliver product information consistent with use.

#8. Purchase decisions or brand choices reflect messages first discounted as propaganda from vested interests, then reevaluated differently as customers change their attitudes with trials and use. The ads convey consistently more positive messages about the brand's most favorable attributes.

Some products sell themselves, and advertising simply reinforces positive information. Other products perform poorly. Their overselling by advertising increases the discrepancy between performance and ad claims, eventually turning customers away. Thus marketers must discover positive product attributes and then use these in their post-first-purchase advertising.

Competitive Scan: User Friendly Campaigns

Throughout this chapter and previously in chapter 7, we have pushed the idea that outside experts must work closely with in-house teams. Here's how ad agencies can make relationship marketing happen: "embrace change, do things well, get results, and be user friendly."[32] The most innovative promotion and ad agencies use both strategic and creative thinking to reinvent their clients' business, and they fire clients when the latter don't invest wisely in advertising.

Other suggestions:[33] Execute innovative integrated marketing solutions (not creative executions) because solutions mean measurable results. Measure all image ads and promotion programs. Creativity must be grounded in bottom-line results, such as CPS, (cost per sale). Encourage ad agencies to become think tanks that develop creative concepts and strategies for clients. Reinvent the role of promotion and advertising agencies.[34] Set outsized targets and ask ad experts to think more boldly even when business growth is slowing down. These new ideas should be set down in a futures budget, such as Peter Drucker, the management guru, has outlined.

Local Adaptation Versus Global Standardization

Jon Kramer, the executive vice president of Local Marketing Corporation, sees "a shift back to integrated marketing between in-house and outside teams . . . Database and targeted marketing are crucial to success . . . One-on-one local communication with consumers is more important than regional, national, and international links."[35]

Rick Fizdale, the chairman and chief creative director of Leo Burnett, believes the opposite; he says brand equity can only be safeguarded by showing the same face to all consumers in every country and every medium used throughout the world.[36] Leo Burnett's motto is give lots of service (e.g., creative advertising, PR, direct marketing, in-store promotions, and database marketing), and clients will stay with you forever (United Airlines, Sony, and McDonald's International are some of its clients).

Communicating About Brands

Management guru Peter Drucker, Harvard marketing expert Ted Levitt, research whiz Arthur Nielsen, and the Hollywood folks from Creative Artists Agency told Coca-Cola the bad news.[37] Normal ad agencies advertise brands in the normal way. They shovel money into core buys (i.e., the three TV networks and women's magazines). And they give you "one sight, one sound, one sell."

When Coca-Cola took its ad account away from McCann-Erickson Worldwide and gave it to Michael Ovitz's talent agency, CAA, this move was a paradigm shift for promotion and advertising agencies. It broke the mold for all time. No longer could ad agencies devise big cookie-cutter campaigns for audiences made up of "couch commandos" who zap boring programs and ads off the TV screen. No longer could ad agencies charge their clients costs plus a 15-percent commission – with or without results.

Big companies, such as Coca-Cola and IBM, are willing to go to anyone, anywhere for new ideas. They want 50 ideas pitched in 100 styles to 200 audiences. "The rules are gone. It's kind of like deregulation" of the advertising business, says Jeff Goodby of Goodby Berlin & Silverstein in San Francisco. In-house marketing terms want outside promotion experts who work faster and are fully adaptable to the expanding needs of clients. The latter must concentrate on scrappy clients' underdog business (Volvo), reposition brands (MasterCard becomes "Smart Money"), and use ads to fight back at competitors (MCI versus AT&T). Then, ad agencies will have reinvented themselves for the future.

Estimates of Market Potential

During the 1980s, advertising expenditures in western Europe increased at a compound rate of 11.5 percent a year.[38] National restrictions on television advertising then were eased in Germany, France, and Denmark for all products except tobacco, alcoholic drinks, medicines, drugs, and sanitary products. However, Germany, Denmark, and Belgium continued to restrict promotions, such as in-pack premiums, free mail-ins, purchase premiums, and money-off vouchers. All countries within the European Union limit the extent to which direct marketers can use telemarketing in the promotion and advertising of products. Growth in advertising revenues seem assured as Europe moved into the 1990s (chapter 4), toward the completion of the Single Integrated Market (or 1992), and to the start-up of the European Union (or Maastricht).

Unfortunately, in the 1990s, Europe was saddled with price inflation, higher interest rates, tight money, more unemployment, reduced sales, and lower profits. Multinational firms refused to increase advertising budgets to consolidate or improve market share within Europe. Instead, they insisted advertising agencies do more with less, provide both creative and strategic thinking, and get results. Moreover, these global firms want pan-European messages and consistent corporate images. These trends mean the number of agencies are being cut from many to one for Europe and one for the United States.

Shifting the Paradigm

Both Europeans and Americans suspect advertising does not work, or if it works, advertising does so because one creative person does things differently. According to Karen Stabiner, "A successful advertisement is one that creates an imagined but convincing difference – a difference that does not necessarily reside in the brand itself but lodges persuasively in the customer's brain."[39]

Another creative ad executive is Andy Berlin. In 1992, he came from his own San Francisco agency, Goodby, Berlin & Silverstein, to the New York office of DDB Needham Worldwide, and 15 months later set up another new agency (Berlin Wright Cameron) to handle the account of Volkswagen of America. Throughout his years in advertising, Berlin positioned himself as the risk taker who gets results and for whom controversy just enhances his mystique. The task before him is to get Americans thinking about Volkswagen in a favorable light – to discover VW's true virtues.

According to Berlin, tomorrow's advertising agency must find new ways to do promotion and get into new businesses. He wants to go into joint ventures with his clients and get a share of the sales revenues from the products he promotes; he does not want to earn his living simply from 15-percent commissions for media billings. Also, Berlin wants to dismantle the top-heavy traditional agency and create small, entrepreneurial groups who work as independent contractors with in-house marketing teams.

Here's what Andy Berlin says: "Yesterday, media was three TV networks and women's magazines – the core buy . . . Tomorrow, media will mean hundreds of channels that are themselves retail outlets, connected by toll-free telephone numbers or interactive computers to consumers who never leave their living rooms."[40]

Going for an Aggressive Approach

If we look again at the reinvented advertising signals #6 through #8, we observe the following. Promotions and ads must help consumers discover a product's virtues. Then they must show consumers how to use the brands within the context of their lifestyles. Finally, the ads must be aggressive.[41]

Purchase behavior or brand opinion is confirmed by post-first purchase experience. The ads are positive, and they offer emotional reasons to compare one brand favorably over other competing brands. Humor, a whimsical pitch, an irreverent approach, emotional values, and an offbeat print campaign were used by the upstart San Francisco agency, Woolward & Partners, to maintain Oracle's domination. Then creative differences set in, and according to Iain Woolward, the founder of this high-tech advertising agency, he fired the client.

Purchase attitude or brand outlook is the integration of different pieces of information after the post-first-purchase experience. The ads deliver product information consistent with use in the marketplace. Woolward & Partners also uses images and words to both grab attention and to elicit controversy. For Logitech, a maker of computer input devices, the ads showed a baby boy in diapers saying "Feels Good," and another shot with the baby boy urinating saying "Feels Better." The ad makes the claim that Logitech's mouse is more comfortable to use and move.

Purchase decisions or brand choices reflect messages first discounted as propaganda from vested interests, and then reevaluated differently as customers change their attitudes with use. The ads convey consistently more positive messages by directing attention to the brand's most favorable attributes. Woolward & Partners uses these framing effects to convey to clients and consumers alike the "period eye" seen by its founder, the 44-year-old Iain Woolward. He became an adult after 1968, a Scotsman who came to San Francisco in 1979 as New Age consciousness and the Silicon Valley computer revolution swept across the country. Woolward's ads drive consumers toward new digital data technologies for handling daily lifestyle activities. They debunk the half-truths of established interests and give those who became adults in the 1980s and 1990s the emotional attitudes to break with the past and create new futures. There's tomorrow's interactive culture.

Similar Market Segments Worldwide

Although Latin America is following the lead of North America and pushing advertising agencies to restructure themselves for the coming race to do a better job at serving global firms, most agencies are light years away from the aggressive approach. For example, the Advertising Agencies Association of Argentina is still trying to figure out ways to integrate advertising between that country and Brazil, both members of the Southern Cone Common Market (or Mercosur).

McCann-Erickson Worldwide, Latin America's No. 1 agency network, made Mexico City its headquarters for Mexico and Central America, Caracas for the Andean Pact countries, and Sao Paulo for Mercosur. Local agencies, such as Duailibi, Petit, and Zaragoza Propaganda of Sao Paulo, associate with global agencies, such as DDB Needham with 17 offices in Latin America.

Right now panregional media buying is almost nonexistent, about 3 to 5 percent of the US $11 billion spent in Latin America in major media in 1992. All eyes are on how to put together consistent Latin American strategies without offending local traditions. Paradigm shifts and other new nuances from the United States are for the distant future, not for the present in Latin America.

Summary: Scanning User Friendly Campaigns

Advertising conveys emotional values. Most of these are tied to national cultures, and marketers err when they mistake paradigm shifts in the United

States for trends in Europe, East Asia, and Latin America. Clearly, the global firms want more creative and strategic thinking from their advertising agencies in both the United States and Europe, and smaller advertising and different types of service agencies seem to be able to do this job better than the traditional larger agencies. Moreover, these new competitors are willing to share in both the risks and profits from using advertising and promotion to enhance demand, increase sales, and improve returns. Successful marketers learn how to make themselves the best at promotion marketing.

National Marketing Decisions

Marketers manage final demand by signaling detailed national information about promotion and advertising; see Exhibit 11-6. The US $138 billion worldwide advertising industry is in trouble because agencies have failed to anticipate a key question of clients: What do I get?.

The early 1990s decimated the industry with a severe economic recession, leading to reduced billings, large-scale layoffs, and bankrupt agencies. Also, global firms shifted creative work to smaller high-tech agencies, gave strategic work to Hollywood talent agencies, and used promotion firms to do media buys. Moreover, with the advent of pan-European advertising, fewer hands were needed in the promotion and advertising business as global firms consolidated their European operations and tied them more closely to their North American business.

Exhibit 11-6.
National Marketing Decisions: Promotion
The Marketing Scan

Traditional Frame Analysis for Global Marketing
Firm-Specific 4Ps Analysis and Decision Making Under Uncertainty
Signal national traditions, beliefs, and values
Grow through rationalization of interactive advertising
Pay attention to promotion changes worldwide
Firm-Specific 4Ps Analysis and Post-First-Purchase Decisions
Ads are tailored to suit emerging consumer demand
Ads turn ideas into valuable competitive resource

Continued on next page

Exhibit 11-6. *Continued from previous page*

National Marketing Decisions and Marketing Investments
Inhouse Advertising
Emotional values
Taglines
Campaign concept
Consumer response
Reinvented advertising signals
Media Offerings
Core buys
Interactive buys
Production values
Cleverness
Performance-Based Promotion
Cost-per-sale
Decreasing average cost
Price-quality relationships
National Marketing Decisions and Marketing Strategy
Promotion + advertising = brands
Utilitarian versus cultural images
Attitudes toward ads
Brand extensions
Global and national brands
National Marketing Decisions and Marketing Forecasts
Continuing trend is unrealistic because of information revolution
Amplifying trend builds on aggressive marketing of services
Doubling trend is realistic when agencies do interactive ads

Nontraditional Frame Analysis and Global Marketing
Marketing Management Frame and Marketing Investments
Six Sigma Questions
What do I get?
How to improve performance?
Which level of quality would you prefer?
How to segment information?
How to add value to bits of information?

Forgetting the Old Paradigm

To make matters even worse for traditional advertising agencies, some global firms decided to pull back their use of outside professionals and carry out the creative work in-house. For example, Sony's "electronics unit solicited creative ideas from the company's Hollywood studios, including Columbia Pictures, on how to advertise a point-and-shoot camcorder," the Handycam Snap![42] Sony Pictures provided emotional values, a campaign tag line, and the campaign concept for Sony electronics. Sony Pictures had a fresh angle, and it got a piece of Sony Electronics' promotion and advertising budget. According to Jeffrey S. Brooks, senior vice president of advertising and marketing at Sony Electronics, it wasn't the company's intention to change the relationship between Sony Electronics and Leo Burnett, the Chicago-based advertising agency. "It was to enhance it,"[43] Brooks says.

Reinvented Advertising Signals   When marketing educators think about enhancing demand, their approach is to use multidimensional signals from promotion, advertising, and integrated marketing campaigns. Let's see where this takes us by restating advertising signals #4 and #5 as #9 and #10.

#9. Purchase situations or brand associations are enhanced by paradigm shifts, cross-cultural exchanges, and changes in organizational incentives. New approaches to concepts, taglines, and campaigns tailor utilitarian products, store locations, and countries of origin to suit emerging consumer demand.

#10. Purchase leveraging or brand extension comes from business-to-business advertising about new ideas from the firm. The ads turn company names, traditional and new products, and promotional ideas into valuable competitive resources.

Again, care must be taken in using these advertising signals. Some global firms do a great job in-house, and their promotions reinforce positive information. Others do less well because key executives resist new trends in marketing, advertising, and promotion – for example, the use of interactive multimedia, the paradigm shift, the aggressive approach, and the change in organizational incentives. Thus, marketers must discover positive attributes about products, services, and firms, then use these in their continuing advertising campaigns.

Marketing Scan: P + A = B

Marketing professors tend to support the idea that the level of demand-enhancing advertising increases market demand.[44] Good news about products, services, and firms reinforces the positive properties of advertising and suggests that advertising, in the final analysis, is really worth its cost. Bad news creates dissipative advertising, or an opportunity to alter this information through trial, use, and post-first-purchase advertising.

So we ask these questions about signals from promotion and advertising: How much advertising is enough, or at what level of expenditures is advertising effective? How much is too much? Has the cost per sale of media buys reached its minimum low point, and is the cost per sale of media buys now beginning to increase? Is the unhappiness of global firms with their traditional advertising agencies a reflection of these increasing average costs, and will the newer agencies give the global firms a better return for their money?

Let's begin to develop answers to these questions by formatting them as a multidimensional signaling problem.[45] Our task is to find a powerful single crossing property to explain the signals from advertising costs, price information, selling techniques, and value decisions. We have begun to do this in chapter 10. For example, media buy decisions are based on shifts in executive attitudes about the price-quality relationships offered by promotion and advertising agencies. We will continue to do this in chapters 11 through 13 until we have a wide range of signals about the national information crucial to global marketing.

Scanning for P + A = B

Products plus advertising equals brands or P + A = B. Look at both the utilitarian and image attributes of products as these are promoted through advertising and reflected in brand names.[46] First, we scan to see how we position products (and the envelope of logistics services). Then we add the creative and strategic aspects of advertising (including promotion). And we wind up with brand-named goods. These are the basic ingredients of our marketing scan.

Brand Extensions Brand extensions positively affect advertising efficiency.[47] We need to position a range of products that must be promoted to the proper market segments; if both positioning and advertising are done properly, then we have well-known, easily recognizable brand names. Brand extensions are important elements in our marketing scan. Here is the strongest case for combining promotions with advertising in fully integrated marketing campaigns.

Attitudes About Ads   Attitudes toward ads elicit positive or negative feelings about the brands themselves.[48] These attitudes toward ads (rather than the attitudes toward brands) affect the results of promotion and advertising in terms of future product sales. Here is the strongest case for the aggressive approach. If the ads are humorous and irreverent, if the ads give off emotional values, and if the ads fit into the "period eye," then they will give the brand-named goods an up-to-date character all their own. Attitudes about ads are crucial elements in our marketing scan.

Consumer Responses   Combine information from pre-purchase advertising, trial and use of products, and post-first-purchase advertising to come up with a more carefully drawn picture about brand-named goods.[49] Here is the strongest case for combining traditional media buys with newer, high-tech approaches toward enhancing demand creation through promotion and advertising. Consumer responses from ads (or purchase behavior and purchase decisions) are key aspects of our marketing scan.

Signaling Brand Information

Brands say something about price and quality in the marketplace. A high price may infer high quality. However, when competing products are introduced, lower prices may occur because of consumer responses toward ads, the utilitarian and cultural images held about the brand names, and the overall attitude toward brand-named goods. All these advertising signals fit within the multidimensional signaling game we talked about earlier in the chapter. They will help us understand what is coming in the future.

Strategies for Increasing Marketing Effectiveness

"In a digital, interactive world, it is hard to believe that anyone will sit still for numbing repetitions of intrusive jingles, or for 30-second spots of unrewarding commercial theater."[50] These are yesterday's media buys, the core buy of TV networks and women's magazines, for which traditional advertising agencies got 15 percent, no questions asked.

The big agencies are coming late to the information superhighway, and their crude attempts at doing interactive-type ads fall way behind those of professionals who carry out CD-ROM and interactive-TV technology for a living. Moreover, some of these high-tech interactive companies are simply bypassing traditional agencies and working directly with global advertisers.

Pursuing Interactive Advertising

What's worse for ad agencies is that interactive advertising gives global advertisers the ability to know who is watching ads on a real-time basis. This means actual numbers of viewers, not the estimated audience share or the readership claims made by traditional advertising agencies.

Perhaps, "all media have been making up numbers for advertising for years,"[51] comments Roger Fidler, director of the Knight-Ridder Information Design Laboratory, a research arm of Knight-Ridder, Inc. Recall what Andy Berlin and Iain Woolward said about traditional advertising and what they are doing in terms of production values and cleverness to beat the traditional agencies.

Today, interactive advertising is part of the paradigm shift coming to the world of promotions. How is it done? Who does it? What will be the results? These answers are for the future. Today, just start with Drucker's crucial question (chapter 9): As a global advertiser, what can I do with interactive advertising?

Marketing Implementation

Let's close this analysis by looking once again at the reinvented advertising signals 9 and 10 to see how they can help us enter the new world of interactive advertising.

Purchase situations or brand associations are enhanced by paradigm shifts, cross-cultural exchanges, and changes in organizational incentives. New approaches to concepts, tag lines, and campaigns tailor utilitarian products, store locations, and countries of origin to suit emerging consumer demand. Couch commandos can use their channel changers and surf through the ads until they come across one they will watch.

Right now, they can choose the language of the Coke ad. For example, English and French in Canada (the two official languages), English and Spanish in the United States for the majority Anglo and minority Latino populations, or any other foreign language of interest to them (Japanese, Chinese, etc.). Also, our home TV watchers can choose the product they want to see advertised (Classic Coke, Diet Coke, or Sprite). If they wish, the interactive ad will give them fun facts about the brand and offer them a choice of games to play on their TV screen.

Each time our interactive TV viewers make a choice Coca-Cola counts their number, adds up their choices, and collates the information. These are real-time advertising numbers for the interactive information highway of tomorrow.

Purchase leveraging or brand extension comes from business-to-business advertising about new ideas from the firm. The ads turn company names, traditional and new products, and promotional ideas into valuable competitive resources. Advertising agencies could extend themselves by becoming experts in interactive advertising. They could reinvent themselves into a new kind of creative and strategic information agency for the future. The incentives are in the market for their managements to see, but most don't want any part of an interactive future. Perhaps Andy Berlin and Iain Woolward will pull the advertising community into tomorrow's world. Otherwise, the productivity of traditional advertising will suffer in the United States, in Europe, and throughout the world.

Overcoming Globalization

A second pernicious trend is killing the productivity of advertising. This is the traditional advertisers' own shortsighted global brands strategy and their overemphasis on standardization of image, message, copy, layout, placement, and core buys. Advertising agencies are confusing global "creativity" with what is really relevant to consumers – national culture and local benefits. These traditionalists are failing to build category growth and new brand franchises within intermarket segments throughout the world. This is the essence of the contingency perspective as it pertains to promotion and advertising.

Globalization, standardization, minimum differentiation, least-common-denominator approach, not-invented-here syndrome, and dull campaigns:

This is a global path pocked with the ruts of language and cultural differences. What's to be done about unified global sales pitches? Here are several signals for tomorrow's interactive advertising world:

1. Move with care toward global campaigns, and be sure the new top managers understand how to promote the logic of "think global, act local."

2. Choose carefully among satellite, cable TV, multimedia, print ads, point-of-purchase promotions, and other media buys, and really target global consumers in all countries.

3. Think carefully about savings from unified global sales themes because the costs of failure in lost business could be high.

4. Link the strategy of unified global advertising with the reorganization of the national and regional structures of multinational firms.

Three forecasts. The "continuing trend" forecast is the easiest to make because things go on as before. Interactive promotion and advertising don't conform to traditional ways of doing business in Europe, the United States, and Japan. Interactive promotion and advertising are so new that the "continuing trend" is unrealistic.

The "amplifying trend" forecast assumes that computer-driven agencies aggressively market their interactive services. In the United States, Europe, and Japan, these routine durable purchases are crucial parts of the business. This trend will happen because we are at the beginning of a major information revolution, with no end in sight.

The "doubling trend" forecast assumes advertising agencies convert clients to interactive advertising, or vice versa. Product diffusion occurs rapidly because executives want these new interactive services. This one piece of information should help marketers put together an effective marketing strategy for interactive promotion and advertising.

Summary: Scanning P + A = B

Advertising is closely tied to the cultural norms of society, and it must change as these take on new forms during the last part of the 20th century. New products will keep coming to the market in record numbers. In-house marketing teams will spend time and money to position their products within appropriate market segments throughout the world. Sometimes, they will call on outside promotion and advertising experts to help them convey the emotional values of the products to consumers in the United States, Europe, Japan, and elsewhere in the world. Consequently, a few brands will be truly global in name and fame while the rest will sell well nationally, regionally, and locally. Interactive advertising offers both in-house marketing teams and outside advertising experts the opportunity to tailor products and services to all customers wherever they may reside.

Inclusive Contexts for Global Marketing

Exhibit 11-7 sums up the inclusive contexts for global marketing in the promotion and advertising industry. We examine reinventing the industry. Also, we study two types of decision making under uncertainty: culturally based demand analysis and organizationally based industry analysis. These two focuses help us direct our research to answering important questions: How will our customers multiply the use of our advertising services, and how will we shift the paradigm about what we get from interactive advertising? Again, we deal with technology as a driving force in managerial decision making under uncertainty. Our choices determine whether we will be a success at global marketing.

Exhibit 11-7.
Inclusive Contexts for Global Marketing

Market Risk

Govern the market through reinvented business environment

  Liberalization offers more accessible markets

  Reinvent interactive advertising, point-of-sale promotions

Unknown competitive possibilities and imperfect information

Political Frame

Firm-Specific 4Ps Analysis (A)

Culturally based decision making under uncertainty

Worldwide communications

Continued on next page

Exhibit 11-7. *Continued from previous page*

Multidimensional signaling
  Propaganda, cultural images
  Private views made public
Dominant expectations or period eye
Scale economies in signaling costs
Cultural Frame

Firm-Specific 4Ps Analysis (B)
Organizationally based decision making under uncertainty
Shift the paradigm
  Advertising signals
  Media effectiveness
  Post-first-purchase decisions
Advertising agencies
Teamwork, nonroutine partnerships, relationship marketing
Marketing investments: price-quality relationships
Six-sigma question: What do I get?
Marketing Management Frame

National Marketing Decisions
Contingency perspective
Signaling game
  Multiplying information about demand
  Marketing intelligence
  Marketing opportunities
  Marketing research
Marketing investments, in-house advertising, media offerings
Marketing strategy
  Promotion + advertising = brands
  Utilitarian versus cultural images
  Attitudes toward ads
  Brand extensions
  Global and national brands
Dissipative advertising or bad signals
Creative ideas, media buys, good signals
Technological Frame

Conclusions

Providers of promotion and advertising services bring creative and strategic thinking to their ads and their placement in the media. Rapid technological change is occurring, and marketers are groping for the most appropriate interactive advertising strategy.

Let's return to our initial three learning objectives:

1. Discuss the importance of the contingency perspective to promotion and advertising positioning decisions.

   You should have a clear understanding of the many contingencies that affect promotion marketing, and of how few of these are covered by the standardization (minimum differentiation) versus adaptation (maximum differentiation) argument.

2. Outline external competitive issues (such as reduced budgets and demands for higher productivity) that are forcing the promotion and advertising industry to reinvent itself.

   You should be able to explain why firms are looking for news to promote and advertise their products. You should be able to compare and contrast the approaches taken by traditional agencies versus those proposed by high-tech agencies and the new entertainment competitors.

3. Explain the management decisions needed to exploit interactive advertising in a global, yet local world economy.

   You should be aware that interactive advertising is coming sometime in the future, but not necessarily today or tomorrow. You should introduce changes in promotion and advertising only as long as you can answer your customers' most fundamental question: What do I get?

Making the future happen is the work of global marketing executives.

Notes

1. Svend Albaek and Per Baltzer Overgaard, "Upstream Pricing and Advertising Signal Downstream Demand," *Journal of Economics and Management Strategy* 1:4 (Winter 1992): 677-98.

2. Stephen Greenblatt, "Kindly Visions," *The New Yorker*, October 11, 1993, 115.

3. Kyle Bagwell, "Pricing to Signal Product Line Quality," *Journal of Economics & Management Strategy* 1:1 (Spring 1992): 168.

4. Brent Staples, "Life in the Information Age," *The New York Times,* July 7, 1994, A12.

5. David Kirkpatrick, "Groupware Goes Boom," *Fortune*, December 27, 1993, 102.

6. These advertising signals are adapted from Banwari Mittal, "The Relative Roles of Brand Beliefs and Attitude Toward the Ad as Mediators of Brand Attitude: A Second Look," *Journal of Marketing Research* 27:2 (May 1990): 209-19.

7. Daniel Smith and C. Whan Park, "The Effects of Brand Extensions on Market Share and Advertising Efficiency," *Journal of Marketing Research* 29:3 (August 1992): 296-313.

8. Scott B. MacKenzie and Richard J. Lutz, "An Empirical Examination of the Structural Antecedents of Attitude Toward the Ad in an Advertising Pretesting Context," *Journal of Marketing* 53:2 (April 1989): 63.

9. These conclusions about localization are drawn from Ali Kanso, "International Advertising Strategies: Global Commitment to Local Vision," *Journal of Advertising Research* 32:1 (January-February 1992): 10-14.

10. Dan Michaels and Shailagh Murray, "East Europeans Adjust to Western Ads; Information After Years of Propaganda," *The Wall Street Journal*, July 19, 1993, A5D.

11. Gary Mead, "A Universal Message," *Financial Times*, May 27, 1993, 18.

12. Ibid.

13. Ibid.

14. Ibid.

15. These conclusions about localization are drawn from Ali Kanso, op cit.

16. Bob D. Cutler and Rajshekhar G. Javalgi, "A Cross-Cultural Analysis of the Visual Components of Print Advertising: The United States and the European Community," *Journal of Advertising Research* 32:1 (January-February 1992): 77.

17. Cutler and Javalgi, 78.

18. S. Tamer Cavusgil and Shaoming Zou, "Product and Promotion Adaptation in Export Ventures: An Empirical Investigation," *Journal of International Business Studies* 24:3 (Third Quarter 1993): 483, 500-501.

19. Excerpts from Stan Rapp and Thomas L. Collins, *Beyond MaxiMarketing* (New York: McGraw-Hill, 1994). Cited in "European Prototype Shows Credible Communication with Consumer is Key to Future, Nestle exec says," *Advertising Age*, October 25, 1993, 16.

20. Ibid., 16, S-7.

21. "What Happened to Advertising?" *Business Week* September 23, 1991, 70.

22. Ibid., 68.

23. Ibid.

24. Ibid., 71.

25. Ibid., 69.

26. The conclusions are drawn from Barbara Mueller, "Standardization vs. Specialization: An Examination of Westernization in Japanese Advertising," *Journal of Advertising Research* 32:1 (January-February 1992): 15-24.

27. Carolyn A. Lin, "Cultural Differences in Message Strategies: A Comparison Between American and Japanese TV Commercials," *Journal of Advertising Research* 33:4 (July-August 1993): 40.

28. Ibid., 42.

29. C. Anthony di Benedetto, Mariko Tamate, and Rajan Chandran, "Developing Creative Advertising Strategy for the Japanese Marketplace," *Journal of Advertising Research* 32:1 (January-February 1992): 42-3.

30. Dave Barrager, "Japan Begins to Open the Door to Foreigners, A Little," *Brandweek*, August 2, 1993, 44.

31. Robert E. Smith, "Integrating Information from Advertising and Trial: Processes and Effects on Consumer Response to Product Information," *Journal of Marketing Research* 30:2 (May 1993): 204-19.

32. Eric Clark, "Letter from London," *Promo* 6 (April 1992): 58.

33. "Managing the Promotion Agency of the 1990s," *Promo* 6 (February 1992): 10.

34. R. Craig MacClaren, "No More Business as Usual as Companies Take Bold Moves to Ensure Growth," *Promo* 6 (October 1992): 59.

35. "Managing the Promotion Agency of the 1990s," 10.

36. Ibid.

37. Patricia Sellers, "Do You Need Your Ad Agency?" *Fortune*, November 15, 1993, 147-164.

38. *Europe in the Year 2000* (London: Euromonitor Publications Limited, 1990), 267.

39. Karen Stabiner, "Annals of Madison Avenue: The Berlin Spin," *The New Yorker*, October 11, 1993, 56.

40. Ibid., 49.

41. Burr Snider, "They Fire Clients, Don't They," *Wired* 1:6 (December 1993): 64-7.

42. Kevin Goldman, "Advertising: Sony Unit Turns to Its Hollywood Sister," *The Wall Street Journal*, December 7, 1993, B12.

43. Ibid.

44. Albaek and Overgaard, 677-80.

45. Bagwell, 151-53.

46. Mittal, 209-11, 216-8.

47. Smith and Park, 296-313.

48. MacKenzie and Lutz, 63.

49. Smith, 204-5, 215-7.

50. Timothy K. Smith and Thomas R. King, "Hard Sell: Madison Avenue, Slow to Grasp Interactivity, Could Be Left Behind," *The Wall Street Journal*, December 7, 1993, A1.

51. Ibid., A8.

Chapter Format

Introduction

Marketing Questions

Environmental Scan: Price-Driven Cost Data

Initial Analysis of Marketing Opportunities

Clues to Capturing Customers

The Firm-Specific Research Assignment

Competitive Scan: Higher Price Points

Estimates of Market Potential

Similar Market Segments Worldwide

National Marketing Decisions

Marketing Scan: Product-Development Life Cycle

Strategies for Increasing Marketing Effectiveness

Marketing Implementation

Conclusions

Cases: McKinsey, A.C. Nielsen, J Sainsbury, United Distillers

Learning Objectives

After reading this chapter, you should be able to:

- Discuss the importance of the contingency perspective to a segmented pricing strategy

- Outline the paradigm shift occurring in pricing strategy as price-driven cost strategies build market share, extend product lines toward higher price points, and segment prices

- Explain the management decisions needed to exploit bundled pricing as the means to leverage a firm's competitive advantage

Price Signals

chapter 12

Introduction

Marketers manage final demand by signaling detailed national information about price-cost-quality relationships among branded goods. Price-driven cost strategies dispense superior information about market share, product line extension toward higher price points, bundled prices, segmented pricing, and the intensity of consumer demand for products within nation-states. Here are the frames for studying local, national, and global marketing.

Scanning Global Markets

Environmental scan: price-driven cost data. Pricing indicates the monetary value of products and services. Incumbents set entry price conditions for new entrants. Sometimes new entrants follow the incumbents; at other times new entrants seek higher price points, better access to distribution channels, and faster increases in market share. The global pricing strategy of Japanese firms is an example of the second pricing strategy. Their success comes from understanding the do's and don'ts of pricing, and Drucker's words of wisdom about pricing strategy. In the final analysis, customers make trade-offs between price and quality as long as they are aware of and are willing to take into consideration the real differences among competing products. Although economists have a longer history discussing the theory and practice of pricing, marketers have a great deal more to say about pricing, especially when they make segmented pricing their global pricing strategy.

Competitive scan: higher price points. Segmented pricing is pricing differently to different groups of customers. After entering international markets, all firms worry about revenue leaks, collections, foreign exchange, marketing intelligence, costs, consumer behavior, brand loyalty, and promotions; however, the country of origin plays an important role in how American, British, German, and Japanese firms carry out these pricing tasks during the process of exporting to and selling within overseas markets. In the final analysis, marketers err when they choose cost-based pricing strategies, and they succeed when they select price-driven segmentation strategies. Here, in a nutshell, is the pricing problem faced by marketers throughout the world.

Marketing scan: product-development life cycle. Life-cycle pricing is pricing differently according to the stages of the product-development life cycle. Sometimes, pricing changes market share, and at other times pricing modifies brand share. Lower price points tend to be for mature markets, and higher price points are for growth markets. Sometime, bundled products and services come with higher price points, yet savings are passed on to consumers. Consumer dissonance plays a role in how pricing is accomplished at all stages in the product-development life cycle. Manufacturers want to know which brands are selling, while retailers want to know which product categories are moving merchandise out of their stores. The globalization of brands is leading to global shopping; this leads, in turn, to global pricing strategies. Where it will all end is anybody's guess.

Traditional Contexts for Global Marketing

Exhibit 12-1 lists the traditional contexts for global marketing in the case of segmented pricing strategies. We study a reinvented business environment, price-driven costs, and marketing strategy. The first reinforces our observation about the changes occurring in how governments seek to stabilize prices, rates of inflation, and national currencies. The second reminds us that by driving costs down, prices stay down throughout the product-development life cycle. The third prepares us for the hard task of implementing a marketing strategy with continuous future payoffs as we move down the learning curve. The retailing cases are another symbol of how new industries are being created for a future global economy.

Exhibit 12-1.
Traditional Contexts for Global Marketing

Market Risk

Govern the market through reinvented business environment

    Stabilize prices, wages, and costs

    Maintain low rates of inflation

    Prevent devaluation of national currency

Unknown competitive possibilities and imperfect information

Firm-Specific 4Ps Analysis

Pricing signals

    Best value pricing to minimize overall costs

    Price seeking to maximize expected quality

    Price aversion to minimize individual costs

Price-driven costs

Pricing strategies

    Skimming the cream, cost-plus, target-profit

    Perceived-value, going-rate, price-driven costing

Segmented pricing

    Capture market share, gain higher price points

    Leverage competitive advantage, drive unit costs down

National Marketing Decisions

Pricing opportunities

    Product line pricing, brand bundling, pooled products

    Forex rate forecasting

Value-added information

    Price discounting, packaging data, database management

    Shopping behavior, private- or own-label brands

    Brand loyalty, slotting fees

Consumer behavior: loyals, rotators, deal/price sensitives

Continued on next page

Exhibit 12-1. *Continued from previous page*

Marketing strategy
   Segmented pricing
   Price and market size
   Price and market share
   Life cycle

Marketing investments and six-sigma question: What do I get?

Performance-based retailing
   Move merchandise, calculate sales per square foot
   Set up cost centers, price-cost-quality information

Nontraditional Contexts for Global Marketing

Exhibit 12-2 names the nontraditional contexts for global marketing in segmented pricing strategies. We survey reinventing price stability and national currencies, multidimensional, price-quality relationships, and P + A = B. We are beginning to learn that asking the question "What do I get?" will help us make better marketing investments.

Exhibit 12-2.
Nontraditional Contexts for Global Marketing

Political Frame

Govern the market through reinvented business environment
   Liberalization means end of price controls
   Reinvent price stability and national currency

Technological Frame

Contingency perspective

Signaling game

Multiplying information about prices of competing brands
   Cost-reducing investments
   Product substitutability
   Commitments to sell future products
   Higher investment levels
   Self-interest investments

Price sensitivity (elasticity)

Scale economies in costs of signaling

Continued on next page

Exhibit 12-2. *Continued from previous page*

Cultural Frame
Worldwide communications
- Learn how to undercut prices of incumbents
- Free riders
- Cost linkages across product lines

Marketing Management Frame
What do I get?
Price-quality relationships
- Best-value pricing
- Higher margins
- Price-seeking
- Learning curve
- $P + A = B$
- Premium prices
- Price aversion
- Product-development life cycle

Marketing teams
Game theory: two- and multiple-party games

Governing the market. First, let's look at the political frame. Government reveals weaknesses in national markets by letting foreign competitors undercut traditional prices by domestic firms. The end of price controls leads to more consumers with additional income to spend, especially among those who aspire to a middle-class standard of living. The existence of price stability, the end of price inflation, and the strengthening of the national currency all provide the middle class with reasons to consume, save, and invest; see Exhibit 12–3. Success in governing the market releases additional opportunities for relationship marketing.

Marketing decisions under uncertainty. Second, let's study the technological frame. Marketing educators call the multiplying of information about price-driven cost strategies a *signaling game.*[1] Marketing teams enter new markets with some information about the prices of competing products. Incumbent competitors know their costs and price accordingly, and new

Exhibit 12-3.
US Tariffs on Selected Goods

TARIFF CHANGES FOR CHINA

MANY CHANGES IN TARIFFS FOR IMPORTED GOODS, INCLUDING ITEMS FROM CHINA, WERE
IMPLEMENTED JAN. 1, 1995 UNDER THE GENERAL AGREEMENT ON TARIFFS AND TRADE.

IN THOUSANDS OF DOLLARS	1994 ESTIMATE	TARIFF PRE-URUGUAY	TARIFF POST-URUGUAY	DECLINE
FISH AND CRUSTACEANS	$244,328	.15%	.7%	$195
MINERAL FUELS (COAL AND OIL)	375,520	.71%	.70%	38
INORGANIC CHEMICALS	214,705	.91%	.74%	365
ORGANIC CHEMICALS	270,138	7.18%	3.92%	8,806
PLASTICS AND PLASTIC GOODS	1,293,808	4.80%	4.38%	5,434
LEATHER GOODS OR TRADITIONALLY LEATHER	2,554,428	11%	10.04%	24,523
WOOD PRODUCTS	191,813	4.75%	3.22%	2,935
STRAW PRODUCTS	159,769	7.07%	5.56%	2,413
PAPER	175,897	2.27%	0%	3,993
COTTON THREAD AND FABRIC	163,281	8.85%	8.08%	1,257
CARPETS	162,653	6.53%	2.63%	6,181
KNITTED APPAREL	1,649,606	23.90%	21.57%	38,438
OTHER APPAREL	3,748,841	17.66%	16.10%	58,482
MISCELLANEOUS TEXTILES	594,884	9.12%	7.19%	11,481
FOOTWEAR	5,380,283	10.71%	9.99%	38,738
HATS	208,034	7.53%	5.82%	3,557
FEATHER AND DOWN ARTICLES	543,005	7.82%	7.28%	2,932
CERAMICS	424,997	10.63%	6.48%	17,637
PRECIOUS METALS AND JEWELRY	208,721	2.29%	1.48%	1,273
IRON AND STEEL	423,505	4.01%	1.39%	11,096
TOOLS AND TABLEWARE	284,699	6.39%	4.62%	5,039
MISCELLANEOUS BASE METAL PRODUCTS	244,420	4.91%	2.39%	6,159
MACHINERY	2,291,449	3.56%	1.11%	56,141
ELECTRICAL PRODUCTS	6,151,817	4.51%	1.50%	185,170
RAILWAY GOODS	403,387	3.40%	2.56%	3,388
OPTICAL AND SURGICAL SUPPLIES	675,853	4.69%	1.60%	20,884
CLOCKS	320,327	6.06%	5.62%	1,409
MUSICAL INSTRUMENTS	121,285	5.61%	4.32%	1,565
FURNITURE AND LAMPS	1,607,524	4.50%	1.58%	47,261
TOYS	5,080,576	5.87%	.76%	259,617
MISCELLANEOUS MANUFACTURED GOODS	279,270	6.50%	4.32%	6,088

SOURCE: PRIVATE SECTOR ANALYSIS CIRCULATED IN CONGRESS

entrants go into markets with prices that they expect to offer them profits. This sets up the game.

Although price competition exists among incumbents and new entrants in many different markets worldwide, price signals tend to reflect various combinations of local, regional, or national resources rather than a global marketing effort. Here are several examples:

- Low prices might signal cost-reducing investments, close product substitutability, and commitments to sell future products at low, commodity prices (e.g., long-distance telecommunications).

- Low prices today might signal higher investment levels tomorrow once control is gained over intellectual property (e.g., interactive multimedia), information technologies (eg, logistics EDI), and selling practices (e.g., discount clubs and mega-malls).

- High prices might signal self-interest investments to sell at prices set for high quality of unique products (e.g., high-fashion exports).[2]

Moreover, such price sensitivity (or elasticity) depends on product substitutes[3] and consumer awareness (or dissonance) about market offerings, brand images, and prices.

Hunting for consumers. Third, let's examine the cultural frame. Typically, new entrants respond to entry prices selected by incumbents with a mix of strategies. For example, with the advent of worldwide communications (chapters 6–9), new entrants learn how to undercut the higher prices of incumbents, invest in cost-reduction telecommunications equipment, and price global outsourcing services differently from home telephone services. Or some new entrants prefer to be free riders and not pay attention to how cost linkages differ across product lines (e.g., advertising agencies that charge a flat 15 percent of total billings). Other new entrants delay setting price until they have up-to-date information about how to target local customers from importers, distributors, and retailers. Still other new entrants want to enter all international markets without delay and pitch their global brands at prices suited to all local markets.

Segmentation, positioning, and tailoring decisions. Finally, let's look closely at the marketing management frame. Thus, pricing decisions are based on costs, quality, and brand image. If prices are high because products are imported from a quality source overseas (e.g., high-fashion luxury goods, expensive cars, and executive jets), these goods have an inelastic demand and their production costs are sensitive to high standards of quality. The targeted consumers are those who can pay for these high-cost goods and who want them before mass marketing forces a reduction in prices. To keep a high-quality image, sellers offer customers a set of pooled products, a product line, or a bundle of brands, all reflecting high investment costs and high prices. These price attributes are promoted and continually reinforced through advertising, point-of-purchase selling, and integrated marketing campaigns (chapter 11). Thus, the price limits of the incumbents become the signals of product line quality for new entrants. Marketing professors call this different mix of price activities a contingency perspective (chapters 9-11).

Firms select competitive pricing strategies in anticipation of and in response to pricing strategies of rival firms. Actions by firms (e.g., strategies, payoffs, and information) affect consumer demand. Exporters, database managers, brand marketers, discount retail clubs, and mega-mall retailers all practice price-driven cost strategies.

Organizing global marketing experience. The simultaneous existence of these four different contexts forces marketers to research traditional pricing practices, to offer segmented pricing decisions based on costs, quality, and brand image, and to bundle products and prices based on local, national, and global tastes. Let's do two things in this chapter. First, we will discuss the use of price signals to gain market entry under demand uncertainty. Then we will apply this analysis to how marketing teams make price-driven cost decisions, such as product-line pricing and brand bundling.

Market Risk Questions

Marketers manage final demand by researching international markets; see Exhibit 12-4. The information age encourages marketers to set costs for new products based upon prices acceptable to customers. Through online data services, consumers have as much data about price-quality relationships as do marketing executives. The environmental, competitive, and marketing scans provide information about the effect of computer-based communications on the segmented and bundled pricing strategies of marketers.

Exhibit 12-4.
Market Risk Analysis: Price
The Environmental Scan

Traditional Frame Analysis for Global Marketing

Firm-Specific 4Ps Analysis and Pricing Signals

Pay attention to cost-quality relationships

Find out about brand image

Target consumers

Firm-Specific 4Ps Analysis and Price-Driven Costs
Signals

Best value pricing to minimize overall costs

Price seeking to maximize expected quality

Price aversion to minimize individual costs

Strategies

Skimming the cream

Cost-plus pricing

Target-profit pricing

Perceived-value pricing

Going-rate pricing

Price-driven costing

Negotiated pricing

Segmented Pricing

Capture market share

Gain higher price points

Leverage competitive advantage

Drive unit costs down

Segment prices globally

National Marketing Decisions and Marketing Opportunities

Product-line pricing

Brand bundling

Pooled products

Brand extensions

Forex rate forecasting

Continued on next page

Exhibit 12-4. *Continued from previous page*

Nontraditional Frame Analysis for Global Marketing
Marketing Management Frame and Signaling
What do I get?
Best-value pricing, price-quality combinations, higher margins
Price-seeking, learning curve, P + A = B, premium prices
Price aversion, product-development life cycle, marketing teams

---

Adding Value to Price-Driven Cost Data

In chapter 8, we described the 4Ps scheme used widely by marketing educators. The fourth P is *Price:* Are prices based on costs? Or do prices reflect quality or image, or both? Will customers buy products based on a bundled price strategy? Do firms always anticipate the strategies of competitors? Should firms target prices as the basis for customer choice?

Pricing Signals Marketing educators deal with these questions in terms of multidimensional signaling. Here are several signals:[4]

1. Best-value pricing is choosing the brand with the least overall cost in terms of price and expected quality. Price decisions are based on customers' rational choices.

2. Price-seeking is choosing the highest-priced brand to maximize expected quality. Price decisions are inferred by customers from trade-offs presented by competitors.

3. Price aversion is choosing the lowest-priced brand to minimize costs. Price decisions come from customers' choices to reduce risk, avoid losses, and to minimize expenses.

As marketing executives provide more objective information on quality, customers choose best value pricing. However, when marketers are unable to provide objective information on quality, customers choose price-seeking. Moreover, when marketing executives cannot convince customers about the importance of quality, customers choose price aversion. Customers need good product quality information to make effective price decisions.

Environmental Scan: Price-Driven Cost Data

Today, customers process product quality information in terms of expectations about national economic conditions, purchasing experiences, brand promotions, and consumer characteristics.[5] Will sales rise or fall, and can profits be increased? Is the envelope of logistics services offered by suppliers and distributors suitable? How do repeated promotional activities direct the choice of one set of products over another? Who are the appropriate customers for the products positioned in national and global markets? These, too, are signals.

Applying the Contingency Perspective to Price

A crucial idea from the contingency perspective is the difference between observable and unobservable attributes. This difference exists in pricing, too, when customers make decisions about brand choices. Even under the condition of sufficient customer heterogeneity (chapter 9), the unobservable attributes direct our attention to minimum differentiation in product positioning. When some customers prefer to buy standardized products from sellers with higher prices, price competition is taking place in which the unobservable attributes are more important than the observable attributes.

Marketing Strategy   First, pricing is just one part of an overall marketing strategy to grow market share (chapter 8). New products are added to the product line; additional brand extensions are bundled together; wider distribution of the same branded products occurs; and products are sold throughout the world: all these are ways of diversifying sales, increasing revenue, and growing market share.[6]

Sometimes, new products with special, differentiated attributes demand price skimming until fixed costs are recovered or competitors come into the market with a rival product at a competitive price.[7] If products are added to the product line, the prices of all the products must adhere to the price schedule that customers understand. Do customers have enough information about products to make good choices?

Peter Drucker, the management guru, warns marketing executives not to worship high profit margins and premium pricing.[8] These mistakes over unobservable attributes create opportunities for competitors.

Prices, Costs, and Quality   Second, a pricing strategy includes a cost strategy. Find the unit-cost savings; speed up the product-development life cycle; raise manufacturing productivity; use logistics EDI to outsource components; reposition final products; and reformulate promotional activities: all these are ways to beat the competition.

For example, cost-plus pricing comes from estimating price elasticity, a difficult art at best. On the other hand, target-profit pricing derives from an inability to estimate price elasticity, which is the more typical case. Perceived-value pricing flows from the high value placed on the product by customers who are responding to quality, image, and promotion. Last, going-rate pricing suggests the product is not too different from others in the market. All of these pricing choices are the game that incumbents play in the market.

Peter Drucker makes an important suggestion for pricing strategy. He suggests reversing cost and pricing decisions. Drucker insists marketing executives develop a price-driven cost strategy, based on observable attributes, so that market share is never lost.

Market Segment   Third, adjust the pricing strategy to fit the targeted market segment. Gain customer loyalty; build up brand equity; launch brand extensions; be willing to discount when necessary; keep pricing plans in "sync" with efficient shipping units; measure pricing performance with up-to-date EDI systems; and deliver on the product's promise: all these are ways to command the highest prices possible. Negotiating pricing to suit individual customers on a case-by-case basis makes this pricing strategy work.

Peter Drucker warns against mispricing products by charging what the market will bear. Instead, he suggests pricing new products two or three years down the learning curve so that they are much lower initially than all the competitors' products.

Initial Analysis of Marketing Opportunities

Large Japanese firms pursue a global pricing strategy that includes the following marketing tasks:[9]

- Responding quickly to customer demand to capture market share

- Extending product line toward higher price points

- Leveraging a company's competitive advantage

- Using the experience curve work to drive down unit costs

- Segmenting prices between Japan and the rest of the world

Here's how these concepts drive the export pricing strategy of large Japanese firms.

Buying Market Share

Throughout the run up to the devastating recession of 1992–1993, Japanese firms doubled production volumes over very short periods of time. By improving productivity as volumes went up, these firms gained scale economies that led to substantial cost advantages over foreign firms.

Japanese firms beat out American and European incumbents in new market segments both in the United States and Europe. The western firms cannot bear the costs of trying to get ahead in the product-development life cycle or move faster up the learning curve. The initial penetration prices of Japanese firms were so low that they got huge sales and forced out their local competition (e.g., in watches, cameras, office equipment, and consumer electronics).

Japanese prices abroad reflect their dedication to building market share, improving product quality, lowering costs, and gaining higher profitability in the long run. Japanese firms definitely followed Drucker's advice: *Set up a price-driven cost strategy to capture market share.* Moreover, when prices and costs reflect the need to produce locally overseas, Japanese firms build automotive assembly and other manufacturing plants in the United States and Europe that reflect the acceptable price points in these local markets.

Obtaining Higher Price Points

As Japanese firms became lost-cost producers, they expanded their product lines, developed new models, added line extensions, offered more luxurious items, and sold their products at higher prices (e.g., color TVs, audio equipment, automobiles, computers, and musical instruments). Customers like the ability to trade up, to show off their prosperity with higher value-added goods, and to use more technologically advanced equipment.

Japanese firms definitely follow Drucker's advice: *Premium prices must reflect higher value-added extensions to the product line;* this symbiotic relationship between price and quality must continue indefinitely. Moreover, Japanese firms are able to eliminate cheaper product lines faster than their US and European competitors.

Matching Foreign Market Conditions

Successful Japanese firms price their exports to match demand conditions, levels of income, and distribution margins within each foreign market. For example, when a product is new in Australia, Japanese firms use penetration pricing to gain market share. Because the Germans have more disposable income than Americans, Japanese firms skim the German market to gain share. Given the initial resistance of American-owned wholesalers and retailers to stock foreign goods, Japanese firms offer bigger margins for American companies that take on Japanese products.

Here, too, Japanese firms also follow Drucker's advice: within the worldwide organization, Japanese management *negotiated prices that closely resembled the real economic and business conditions of local markets.* Given the rules regarding dumping (i.e., charging lower prices overseas than in Japan), Japanese firms have to be careful that overseas prices are indeed higher than those in Japan.

Segmenting Prices Globally

Although Japanese firms have a global pricing strategy – namely, to gain market share, drive down unit costs, be first up the learning curve, and leverage competitive advantage worldwide – these firms practice one of the oldest segmentation strategies in the marketing handbook. That is, Japanese firms segment prices country by country and tailor their overall marketing effort to suit the customer demand, income levels, and price-quality expectations of local, regional, and national markets. Pricing is the key tool to gain access to distribution and hence grow market share in the United States, in Europe, and across the globe.

Clues to Capturing Customers

Clearly, many prices are not fixed. Instead, prices depend on the quantity purchased, the power of buyers, transport costs, access to local distribution, and the global pricing strategy of international firms. However, only a few of these attributes are used by buyers and sellers at any given point in time.

Moreover, some attributes are unobservable. Thus, marketers have difficulty in deriving sure measures of price sensitivity, and they don't really know the combinations of trade-offs used by customers to equate quality with the sales price.

Answering the Question *What Do I Get?*

Let's return to the three pricing signals discussed above and match them up with price-quality expectations.

Best-value pricing. If customers practice best-value pricing, a firm's pricing strategy offers many additional price-quality combinations. When the brand name is an observable attribute, then measure the brand image in an after-sale price sensitivity analysis (chapter 11). Moreover, find ways to include the rational choices made from unobservable attributes in the trade-off analysis. For example, Japanese firms give higher margins to US distributors to gain access to the US market.

Price-seeking. If customers practice price-seeking, a firm's pricing strategy is to offer the highest price points possible within the level of quality anticipated by customers. Include a P + A = B analysis in the *ex-ante* (after-sale) price sensitivity analysis. Be sure these trade-offs include product positioning efforts, logistics EDI, and promotion and advertising (chapters 9, 10, and 11). For example, offer premium prices two to three years down the learning curve to capture large market share early in the life cycle of Japanese consumer electronics.

Price aversion. If customers practice price aversion, a firm's pricing strategy is to offer stripped-downed versions of its products because buyers will not pay for more expensive price-quality combinations. Then take these products back to the drawing board, find ways over time to add value, begin a new product-development life cycle, and dash up the learning curve. These examples are the work of marketing teams (chapter 7).

Summary: Scanning Price-Driven Cost Data

Pricing indicates the monetary value of products and services. Incumbents set entry price conditions for new entrants. Sometimes new entrants follow incumbents; at other times new entrants seek higher price points, better access to distribution channels, and faster increases in market share. The global pricing strategy of Japanese firms is and example of the second pricing strategy. Their success comes from understanding the do's an don'ts of pricing and Drucker's words of wisdom about pricing strategy. In the final analysis, customers make trade-offs between price and quality as long as they are aware of and are willing to take into consideration the real differences among competing products. Although economists have a longer history discussing the theory and practice of pricing, marketers have a great deal more to say about pricing, especially when they make segmented pricing their global pricing strategy.

The Firm-Specific Assignment

Marketers manage final demand by positioning price-driven cost strategies within national and global markets; see Exhibit 12–5. Some pricing decisions occur before consumers purchase products. However, skillful pricing experts make many more decisions *ex-ante* (after-sales) to continue the process of building market share. Throughout the product-development life cycle, prices must be consistent with consumers' observable and unobservable attributes about products and services.

Exhibit 12–5.
Firm-Specific Analysis: Price
The Competitive Scan

Traditional Frame Analysis and Global Marketing
Firm-Specific 4Ps Analysis and Managing Price
Industry supply and demand
Product market strategy
Transactions
Firm-Specific 4Ps Analysis and Off-List Discounts
Order size discounts
Payment terms discounts
Off-invoice promotions
Co-op advertising
Revenue leaks

Continued on next page

Exhibit 12-5. *Continued from previous page*

Firm-Specific 4Ps Analysis and Export Pricing
Country of origin
Foreign collections
Foreign exchange
Risk management
Factors and forfaiting
National Marketing Decisions and Marketing Research
Value-Added Information
Price discounting
Packaging data
Database management
Shopping behavior
Private- or own-label brands
Brand loyalty
Slotting fees
Consumer Behavior
Long loyals
Rotators
Deal sensitives
Price sensitives
National Marketing Decisions and Marketing Strategy
Segmented pricing strategy

Managing Price

According to McKinsey & Company, "The . . . most effective way for a company to realize its maximum profit is to get its pricing right. The right price can boost profit faster than increasing volume; the wrong price can shrink it just as quickly . . . Improvements in price typically have three to four times the effect on profitability as . . . increases in volume."[10] McKinsey suggests three levels of price management.

Industry supply and demand. By looking at changing costs, new substitute products, demographic shifts, and the emergence of new competitors, marketers learn about the soundness of the market. Here, Drucker says prices must dictate the costs of production, especially among knowledgeable managers.

Product market strategy. By determining which price and nonprice attributes are important to customers, and then by finding out how much they will pay for these product qualities, marketers gain a greater understanding of price-quality trade-offs. Here *ex-ante* price studies must spell out all possible trade-offs in decisions to buy products.[11]

Transactions. By paying attention to pricing decisions and how low-ranking managers dissipate revenue with ill-advised transactions, marketers learn what to charge as the base price, what terms to offer, what discounts to give, and what incentives are required for each customer. McKinsey offers constructive advice for capturing more revenue through segmented pricing.

Stopping Revenue Leaks

The following are the revenue leaks from the list price: order size discount, competitive discount, payment terms discount, annual volume bonus, off-invoice promotions, co-op advertising, freight, and many more. Nobody within firms really pays attention to them because these off-list discounts are buried in interest expense accounts, company-wide promotions and advertising, and other business transportation expenses.

Ask these questions: Is it necessary to give all these special terms, discounts, promotions, and other price deals? Probably not. Can revenue be improved by closing one or more of these revenue leaks? Definitely yes. How is it possible to make these improvements? Identify a ban of permissible price discounts, offer only a few of these off-invoice discounts, and concentrate on raising revenues from all accounts.

Finally, offer sales personnel incentives for negotiating the transition from over-discounting to improving sales revenues (chapter 13). Salespersons are the front-line troops in making such a monumental change in managing price. Do what the Japanese do: Offer off-list discounts only as part of an overall marketing strategy (chapters 8–11).

Competitive Scan: Higher Price Points

Unfortunately, most American exporters think of pricing after they resolve product, place, and promotion strategies. They are no different from their Canadian and British counterparts. A great deal of North Atlantic export pricing behavior is explained by the need to make minor adaptations for the sake of selling products in a neighboring country. Marketing educators call this the nearest-neighbor approach to export pricing.[12]

Dealing with Country-of-Origin Problems

The pricing strategy of British exporters favors the industry supply-and-demand approach because they are looking for the tone or the soundness of the market. Even so, UK exporters are more prone to give richer discounts off list prices than are American exporters.

On the other hand, German exporters prefer the product-market strategy because they want to match price and quality attributes for their customers abroad. Given the high value added of many of their export products, the Germans are not willing to give more than a minimal off-list discount, and then only to the most valuable overseas clients.

As noted before, Japanese exporters price according to transactions. Their goals are to increase market share and capture higher price points. Price discounts are part of an overall pricing strategy to gain access to local distribution channels in Europe and the United States.

Clearly, the country of origin is a significant factor in the pricing practices of exporters. American, British, and Canadian exporters tend to be reactive setters of prices, and their prices tend to be competitive with those of incumbents. German, Swedish, Dutch, and Italian exporters tend to neutral setters of prices, and they keep their prices steady irrespective of the position on prices taken by incumbents. Japanese, Chinese, and southeast Asian exporters tend to be proactive setters of prices, and their prices are based on the overall marketing strategy, not simply on a global pricing strategy.

Making Sense of Foreign Collections

Do prices include the cost of foreign collections? If collections are slow or difficult, use factors (i.e., middlemen who charge 10 percent of the sales invoice to get your money from foreign debtors). These forfaiting costs are hidden in the prices charged to customers.

Or ask customers to pay their bills through letters of credit issued by international banks. The most secure is an irrevocable letter of credit. When goods are shipped, the bank transfers the payment and charges a 2-percent fee for the LC. These bank charges are also hidden.

Sometimes, give the best customers the ability to pay on open account. From list price they get an order-size discount, a payment-terms discount, a rebate on freight, and other off-invoice discount windfalls. Buyers get off-list discounts to encourage them to pay their bills on a timely basis. It's a good deal for them. The burden of financing and collections is buried in the costs of doing business.

Facing Up to Fluctuating Foreign Exchange Rates

Although movements in foreign exchange rates can have a profound effect on a company's overall competitiveness, successful exporters spend only a minimum of time on currency fluctuations. Their conclusion is that hedging simply doesn't protect the product's profitability, so why spend money covering transactions' exposure (i.e., recorded sales) in the forex markets?

International risk management. Treasury management consultants recommend otherwise. They suggest the economic or future sales exposure is much greater than the transactions exposure, and both types of exposure should be hedged as part of an overall marketing strategy. Moreover, these forex consultants encourage the centralization of the pricing decision as it relates to foreign currency fluctuations. Then all currency exposures are included in one hedging transaction. To make forex management even more complicated, these advisors suggest the construction of a band of risk tolerance around the forward rate, that is, the cost of the currency 30, 60, 90, or 180 days in the future. When the currency moves outside the tolerance band, the parent firm should carry out the hedging transactions with all the options and forwards possible.[13]

Common sense from Peter Drucker. Price targets and higher price points are more important than costs, profit margins, and streams of future revenue. If products are priced correctly, then production costs, the export marketing sales effort, and all international transaction costs are covered, and the firm makes money, too.

Estimates of Market Potential

Let's apply some of these words of wisdom to the pricing strategies practiced by some well-known firms around the world.

Shifting the Paradigm

Two American-owned market research firms compete aggressively to provide marketing information to business clients: A.C. Nielsen (a subsidiary of Dun & Bradstreet) and Information Resources Inc. Both collect data "round the clock from supermarkets, drugstores, and mass merchandisers . . . [R]etailers use the information to stock shelves and adjust prices, and manufacturers use the data to decide on how many of which kinds of products to make, and how to market them."[14] The pricing strategy of these two rivals is to cut price, undercut the other, and claim that their interpretation of the data is superior. The result is profit margins in the teens for both firms, a good sign that could get better.

Price Discounting Prices for these information services are so high that Nielsen can afford to give Kraft a 30 percent discount to take the account away from IRI, and IRI can offer Procter & Gamble a 50 percent discount to take the account away from Nielsen. Both data companies are willing to make deals on prices because they keep adding services that raise profit margins for both of them.

Cut Costs, Build Alliances In the competition to supply data and information, Nielsen teamed up with Electronic Data Systems to drive the costs out of the business of scanning sales data, and, of course, out-compete IRI. Both rely on laser scanners at check-out counters to gather information, and both sell software to help their clients analyze the data. The real task for the future is to "package data in ways that allow manufacturers and retailers to pinpoint how they can increase profits by modifying costly functions like advertising, promotion, and delivery schedules."[15]

Within the United States, IRI has about 55 percent of the US $500 million domestic market. Overseas, Nielsen has about 90 percent of the US $750 million international market, which is heavily centered in Europe. Nielsen competes head on with all the opinion and market research firms that form the Esomar group, headquartered in Amsterdam, the Netherlands.

Nielsen is a 70-year-old company with a variety of old and new methods of gathering data; IRI started out 15 years ago as a database management company. To overcome the competitive disadvantage of older data-collection methods, Nielsen brought in EDS to stitch together all its off-the-shelf software applications, install new networks of PCs, and manage the data processing operations. In short, EDS is reengineering all of Nielsen's key business processes. Over time, EDS is helping Nielsen put together client-server PC networks and multimedia systems and merging laser scanners, computers, telecommunications, and video.

Nielsen is concentrating on developing new software to help customers use information more intelligently. Database marketing is the name of the game. Both Nielsen and IRI are giving ad agencies (chapter 11) a run for their money on data for promotions and advertising. Moreover, EDS, CSC/Index, and Andersen Consulting are also trying to provide crucial information about strategic shopping behavior. Hence, the need to build alliances throughout the consumer intelligence industry.

Consumer Behavior Today, Nielsen and IRI are fully in the business of showing clients how to get more value from the information they are purchasing. According to Leo Burnett, "The Holy Grail of marketing is . . . the link between what advertisers already know about consumers – their age, gender, income – and what they so desperately want to know, namely their buying habits."[16]

With the help of IRI, Leo Burnett has come up with four different behavioral groups, each with its own buying strategy:

> *Long loyals are committed to one brand regardless of price or competition. Rotators, too, care little about price, but for them variety does matter. They regularly switch among a handful of their favorite brands. Similarly, deal sensitives switch among a small set of brands but almost always buy the one that is on special offer. Finally, there are price sensitives, who will purchase whatever product is cheapest . . . Few consumers adopt the same buying strategy for every product category.*

> *Where advertising can be shown to have increased sales of established brands, around 70 percent of growth came not from new users but from those who already buy the product . . . With the right persuasion (for rotators, an alluring advertisement; for deal sensitives, a good deal) they can be induced to buy the brand more often . . . A firm whose brand already appeals to most of the long loyals and rotators in a market will be cutting its own throat if it*

slashes prices low enough to appeal to price sensitives. Conversely, a brand bought mainly by deal and price sensitives might be wise to stop advertising on television and shift spending into price-cutting promotions.[17]

Discount Wars Did J Sainsbury, Britain's largest supermarket chain, not read the reports from IRI and Leo Burnett? Who shops at Sainsbury? Are they long loyals, rotators, deal sensitives, or price sensitives? If they are long loyals or rotators, is Sainsbury cutting its own throat? If they are deal sensitives or price sensitives, is Sainsbury wise in its price-cutting promotions? Does Sainsbury know what the buying strategy is for each of its 300 private-label products? Given that IRI is a weak competitor in the United Kingdom, is it possible that Sainsbury doesn't have the most up-to-date information about consumer behavior?[18]

Sainsbury cut prices on its popular privately owned brand lines, about 10 percent of its annual sales. Rival chains also switched marketing emphasis from quality to low prices. All are sacrificing gross margins to win volume. Will Sainsbury be faced with another UK price war from the newly opened warehouse clubs, such as American-owned Price Costco? Also, will consumers remain loyal to private- or own-label brands? Moreover, will weaker UK chains with many fewer private-label brands, such as Gateway, be squeezed out of the market because the national and global brands aren't selling well anymore?[19]

Brand Loyalty and Disloyalty CEO Arnold Langbo of Kellogg, the breakfast cereal company, doesn't agree with these doomsayers from the United Kingdom.[20] His marketing strategy pushes aggressive advertising and promotions, new products, and higher prices. However, lower-priced, private-label brands (which in the United States are made by Ralston Purina and in the United Kingdom by United Biscuits) are eating into Kellogg's market share, down from 41 percent in 1988 to 37 percent in 1993 in the United States and Canada. In the 1990s, Kellogg's net prices grew by about 1 percent, an all-time low.

John Greeniaus, the president of Nabisco Foods Group, points out that the market share of private-label cereals waxes and wanes according to the rise and fall of disposable income.[21] Can this⊓ be true with the 40- to 50-percent price difference between global brands and private-label cereals? If we recall the last boom period in mid-1980s, Sainsbury and others put their own-label brands on their shelves to improve their profit margins. Today, private-label alternatives have as good a quality as do the national brands. Moreover, once consumers tried the own-label brands, they liked them and didn't go back to global brands.

Today, cereal manufacturers are rolling out a self-destruct promotions strategy. They are paying retailers generous "slotting" fees to get the products on the shelves, and then they are paying consumers in coupons and other promotions to pull the products off the shelves. All these off-list discounts are disguised subsidies, and they reinforce the belief that national brands are no different from private brands.

Promotion Facts   So we come to the last piece in the puzzle about a paradigm shift in pricing strategy.

In 1985, 10 years ago, A.C. Nielsen published a study of 862 packaged-goods promotions, with some staggering results – more than 50 percent of the events studied had zero impact on sales, while only one promotion in 10 generated a 10 percent volume gain. Such promotions have about a 5-percent chance of success, since retailers are offered up to 1,000 deals a week but can only display 50.[22] Marketers knew this a long time ago, but they didn't do much about it. Perhaps the old paradigm is wrong, and a new paradigm for pricing strategy is needed.

Similar Market Segments Worldwide

Segmentation is the guiding principle of marketing. Buyers are segmented by designing marketing strategies more consistent with their diverse cultural preferences. Segmented pricing involves price discrimination – that is, "the offering of different prices for the same product, usually in the form of discounts to more price-sensitive buyers. [It also] involves offering the same prices to all buyers, but with a structure of prices for different points in time, places of purchase, or product types."[23]

Since Ralph Cassady wrote his two classic pieces for the *Journal of Marketing* in 1946, segmenting pricing has been part of the marketing literature.[24] Today, the literature covers negotiating off-list discounts, promotional tie-ins, metering use with coupons, product bundling, channel control, skimming, peak loads, fixed and variable fees, and superstars. Marketers are faced with the practical problem of carrying out a segmented pricing strategy as part of an overall marketing strategy.

Summary: Scanning the Higher Price Points

Segmented pricing is pricing differently to different groups of customers. After entry into international markets, all firms worry about revenue leaks, collections, forex, marketing intelligence, costs, consumer behavior, brand loyalty, and promotions; however, the country of origin plays an important role in how American, British, German, and Japanese firms carry out these pricing tasks during the process of exporting to and selling within overseas markets. In the final analysis, marketers err when they choose cost-based pricing strategies, and they succeed when they select price-driven segmentation strategies. Here, in a nutshell, is the pricing problem faced by marketers throughout the world.

Marketing Decisions

Marketers manage final demand by signaling detailed national information about price-driven cost strategies; see Exhibit 12–6. In the early 1980s, British-owned United Distillers was put together as a holding company for the sale of whiskey worldwide. All its global brands (e.g., Dewars) controlled more than 40 percent of the worldwide whiskey market. Although price decisions were known to affect market size, marketing executives found the sales forces of the subsidiaries paying attention only to the effect of price on brand share. What did United Distillers do to put in place a segmented pricing strategy for its global brands?

Establishing the Price Effect on Market Size

During the last 10 years, pricing became the most important strategy within the marketing mix of United Distillers.[25] Here is a summary of what was accomplished by the firm's marketing executives.

Exhibit 12–6.
National Marketing Decisions: Price
The Marketing Scan

Traditional Frame Analysis for Global Marketing

Firm-Specific 4Ps Analysis and Decision Making Under uncertainty

Signal national price-cost-quality data

Grow through deregulation of interactive data management

Pay attention to price changes worldwide

National Marketing Decisions and Marketing Investments

Six-Sigma Questions

What do I get?

How to improve performance?

Which level of quality would you prefer?

How to segment information?

How to add value to bits of information?

Performance-Based Retailing

Move merchandise

Calculate sales per square foot

Set up cost centers

Provide price-cost-quality information

Do consumer research

National Marketing Decisions and Marketing Strategy

Price and Market Size

Gross domestic product

Disposable income

Retail price inflation

Price and income elasticity

Price and Market Share

Retail audit data

Brand's price elasticity

Brand/price trade-offs

Conjoint measurement

Life Cycle

Across price segments

Bundled products

Continued on next page

Exhibit 12-6. *Continued from previous page*

Bundled price

Consumer dissonance

Downward pricing

Upward pricing

National Marketing Decisions and Marketing Forecasts

Continuing trend is realistic because of segmented pricing

Amplifying trend builds on aggressive marketing of information

Doubling trend is realistic because of wider diffusion of data

---

Price and market size. First, these marketers recognized that the ability of consumers to afford goods affects market size. In the case of whiskey, market volume goes up as gross domestic product and disposable income grow faster than retail price inflation. Throughout North America and Europe, whiskey faces mature markets; this is the tone of the market. Thus, small changes in price elasticity must be accompanied by large changes in income elasticity before the market size grows.

Price and market share. Second, these marketing researchers used retail audit data to estimate a brand's price elasticity (i.e., the effect of a price change assuming all other brands in the market remained the same), then they simulated the effect of different pricing strategies across a range of brands.[26] With these results, the marketers did brand/price trade-offs. These swaps gave them two important results: the ability to predict the effect of price on demand for each brand, and the means to identify and quantify market segments, in terms of brand loyalty.

From the research work at United Distillers, let's answer the "What can I do?" question: How to maintain price premiums, obtain higher price points, and maximize a price advantage to build brand equity? Within the family of brands sold by United Distillers, few consumers adopt the same buying strategy for medium-priced, expensive, and deluxe brands. For example, the medium-priced brands are more likely to be mixed with soda. This product category is more sensitive to price.[27]

From this work let's also answer the "What can I do differently?" question: If prices are lowered on more expensive brands, do volume increases make up the difference in sales revenue? If competitors lower prices on expensive brands, should their lead be followed, or should prices be kept high with the expectation that sales revenue from expensive brands will not be affected by the price changes from competitors?[28] This product category is more sensitive to deals, not price.

Economic performance. Although more whiskey is bought as economies grow, the sale of brown whiskey is in decline throughout North America and Europe. Consumers prefer white spirits (vodka and gin), wine and beer, nonalcoholic drinks, colas, juices, and flavored water. Clearly, those countries that are growing and prospering in East Asia and Latin America will be major markets for whiskey in the future.

Using Price to Segment Markets

Pricing strategy is a crucial part of an overall marketing strategy. New marketing research techniques provide important information about how prices affect market size and market share. Brands of whiskey have different price elasticities among long loyals, rotators, deal sensitives, and price sensitives, and their price elasticities change when marketers reposition expensive brands as medium-priced brands.

In the case of United Distillers, when two brands were repositioned with lower prices in 1989, their share of the market jumped by 10 percent, and their value of sales increased by 7 percent in 1990. Downward positioning through price decreases worked well in segmenting the whiskey market for the firm. The results from upward positioning through higher price points are unknown. Intuition about diffusion and the life cycle suggest United Distillers will not be as successful in repositioning expensive brands into deluxe brands.

Marketing Scan: Product-Development Life Cycle

Price plays a crucial role in the adoption of innovations and in the selection of low- and higher-priced durable goods.[29] Also, as prices are adjusted for inflation and income changes, new product adoption goes even more smoothly. Moreover, price affects diffusion within the life cycle differently because adoption is different from one product category to another.

Also, price elasticities don't increase over the life cycle. This conclusion helped United Distillers in the decision about whether to use upward pricing in positioning its deluxe whiskey brands. Because whiskey is in the mature phase of its life cycle, long-term, committed, loyal customers want downward pricing. Moreover, rotators will substitute other whiskey brands, and deal sensitives will switch from whiskey to other drinks.

Scanning for Life Cycle Transitions

Although United Distillers accepts the cost of maintaining separate brands within all price segments (i.e., medium-priced, expensive, deluxe), the firm is seeking to transport its equity in some brands across price segments. Downward positioning through lower price points is comfortable with the firm's loyal customers, and they have increased the volume of their purchases within the medium-priced segment.

Higher Price Points and the Growth Phase of the Life Cycle

On the other hand, higher price points sit very well for customers of consumer electronic goods, white-line appliances, and other durable goods in which innovation and change are the hallmark of new products. Customers tend to equate upward pricing with higher quality, more after-market support, and better value. Moreover, these consumers know that the life cycle for these products never reaches maturity within their time horizon of strategy shopping behavior. When they form families, they will stock up on these goods and replace them with newer models as products wear out or as technology makes them obsolete.

Bundled products. Yet there is a price-quality trick to all of this. After many years of shopping experience, consumers know now to buy the top end of lower-priced goods, rather than the bottom end of the higher-priced goods. They believe the price-quality correlation is better for them with the former rather than the latter.

For example, compare a bargain PC at US $1,399 (Compaq Computer Presario 425) versus a premium PC at US $2,448 (Compaq Computer Deskpro XE). Both are bundled products with an Intel 486 chip, 4 or 8MB of RAM, 200MB or 570MB hard disk, a 14-inch VGA monitor, and Microsoft Windows. Note that the bargain computer has more hard-disk capacity and comes with a fax modem; the bargain computer is a better buy than the premium computer.[30]

In short, by moving from lower price points to higher price points, and by moving from the introduction to the growth phase of the life cycle, product and price bundling become more important to customers. They see more savings in the bundle than on individual items, and they act accordingly in their shopping behavior.

Bundled price. A mixed bundling pricing strategy is more profitable than other selling alternatives.[31] Sellers must offer buyers savings on both individual and bundled items, but a larger proportion of the savings must be offered on the bundle rather than on individual items. Consumers are first looking for price savings on the bundle, then nonprice savings on the bundle (i.e., after-market support), and almost as an afterthought are they looking for price savings on the individual items, too.

Coping with Consumer Dissonance

Consumers are willing to cope with one brand name in two or more price segments when the following conditions are met: The individual and bundled product meet the performance expectations of customers, and the bundled product offers extra features that measure up to its bundled price. Consumers do not want to feel shortchanged when they pay for the extras.[32]

When no tangible extras exist, such as in the case of whiskey, advertising must be used to convince consumers that the higher-priced product is better than the lower-priced product with the same brand name. However, when United Distillers positions its whiskey as the international choice for the English and the Scots, others nationalities, such as the Thais and the Japanese, believe whiskey has higher quality and better value because the product connotes an international lifestyle.

A lower-priced, domestic product makes consumers unhappy with their national lifestyle and envious of those who can enjoy global products. A higher-priced, international product makes consumers happy with their lifestyle. If for some reason the national government raised tariffs on the imported whiskey so that the local price was too high for current customers, they would opt out of the brand rather than trade down to lower price points and become unhappy with their reduced lifestyle.

As always, the task for marketers is to maintain brand equity through market segmentation by product positioning, distribution services, promotion and advertising, and pricing. Trying to change consumer values about products, brands, and prices is almost impossible once the product-development life cycle moves from the growth phase to maturity. The diffusion of products across many price segments leads consumers to accept certain price points as the crucial indicator of price-quality relationships. These don't change once the product is well established in the marketplace.

Strategies for Increasing Marketing Effectiveness

While manufacturers invest in brands, retailers sell product categories of national and private-label brand names, and all compete for customer loyalty on the basis of price.[33] Is there loyalty between manufacturers and retailers? What role will manufacturers play in redesigning the retail business? Who can help retailers sell in clear market niches?[34]

Wal-Mart showed the way in turning retailing away from selling and toward moving merchandise. The firm integrated the entire process from manufacturer to customer with real-time information about customer purchases.

Aldi, a German food discounter, cut its assortment of goods to those regularly bought by households, designed internally, and sold under its own private label. Its sales per square foot of shelf space – a retailer's basic capital and cost center – have doubled over the last 10 years.

Ikea keeps its prices low by forcing customers to do the final assembly of its finished furniture. Yet when customers are in the Ikea stores, they typically spend between one and two hours longer than they do in rival furniture outlets.[35] Ikea gives them subsidized meals and children's play areas while they touch the exhibits of furniture. When Ikea first came to the United States, it tried to sell beds only in European sizes, which standard American mattresses and sheets don't fit; this is a classic outsider's marketing mistake.[36] Today, Ikea simply orders American-made beds for its American stores.

Providing Information

In the new world of retailing, service means providing information to customers. Modern retailers dispense painless shopping, a means to get away from the chore of buying food, clothes, drinks, appliances, and other things to maintain a lifestyle. Throughout the world, catalogue and home television sales are growing in volume so customers don't have to go to stores to shop.

And just around the corner is the virtual-reality concept of shopping for merchandise through interactive computers and EDI systems. All of these changes in retailing call for new ways to segment pricing as part of an integrated marketing strategy.

Underselling Competitors   When Wal-Mart and Price Costco joined their Mexican partners (CIFRA and Comercial Mexicana) in invading the Mexican retail business, they began underselling the department stores (e.g., Sears and Liverpool), specialty shops (for clothing and computers), and the street vendors, kiosk operators, and other members of the informal economy.[37] With the beginning of NAFTA in January 1994, the two discounters act as wholesalers to many smaller, family-owned stores that sell all types of merchandise. Moreover, through the two discounters, Mexicans obtain the quality, spare parts, service, and warranties that previously were not available from the informal economy of Mexico.

Many Mexican customers at the Mexico City and Monterrey stores don't think the price breaks are as good as those found in the discounters' stores in the United States. Also, some Mexican customers find the discounters' prices only slightly lower than those at traditional Mexican retail outlets. However, most of these customers like the ability to buy in bulk, the guarantee of quality, service, and the policy of no questions asked about returns. Sam's Clubs in Mexico trade under the name Club Aurrera, a well-known supermarket chain owned by CIFRA, and they specialize in selling products in bulk to other Mexican retail merchants. In fact, the Polanco Club Aurrera sells more per square meter than the most successful Sam's Club in the United States.[38]

Today, Liverpool, Mexico's up-market retail chain, has a joint venture to build 100 K-mart stores in Mexico; Gigante, Mexico's second largest retailer, has a joint venture with Fleming, the largest US wholesaler. All the American partners provide their Mexican partners with the skills to build a national distribution system within Mexico. Even Sears, which has been in Mexico since 1947, completely overhauled itself within Mexico and is now catering to the top 10 percent of the Mexican consumer market. "Tell me a success story" is Sears' new motto for customer service within Mexico.[39]

According to Peter Drucker, retailing – rather than manufacturing or finance – may be where the action is today in the United States, the United Kingdom, and in Mexico.

Marketing Implementation

Advertising, price signals, brands, and consumer research are the topics of chapters 10 and 11. The discussion started with game theory, moved on to pricing theory, added consumer behavior, paradigm shifts, brand extensions, price and income elasticity, then ended with segmented pricing. These concepts are applied to advertising agencies, database management firms, whiskey distillers, and retail stores. All of them depend to a large extent on American-style consumer research.

Debunking American Research Culture

However, when Sara Lee started trying to sell Hanes and L'eggs pantyhose (called tights by the British) to Marks & Spencer, a giant of British retailing, Sara Lee got a nasty cultural shock from Marks & Spencer. Sara Lee's product development path is classic American marketing: "design, test with consumers, redesign, retest, sell in a test market area, redesign some more, study the results, and then go national."[40]

Marks & Spencer said no with this reason: "The best research tool is the cash register." Its idea of consumer research is to design the best possible product, offer it at the lowest possible price, and wait to see if customers buy. This cash-register research works well because Marks & Spencer controls 40 percent of the underwear market, 20 percent of the hosiery market, and owns all the stores, too.

Eventually, Sara Lee used the Howard Marlboro Group, a New York-based in-store marketing firm, to adapt L'eggs packaging and point-of-sale displays to the traditions of the St Michael line, the brand name used by Marks & Spencer. "L'eggs for St Michael" are sold at price points established by Marks & Spencer for the British market rather than those more commonly used in the United States.

Shopping 'Til You Drop

Although Marks & Spencer continues to promote L'eggs and other American products, Harrods, another London-based department store, stopped promoting and advertising American goods. Too many British and other Europeans are taking their vacations at Gurnee Mills (north of Chicago), the Mall of America (Minneapolis), or Sawgrass Mills (near Fort Lauderdale).[41] These are all huge indoor discount shopping malls, with friendly sales personnel, merchandise unavailable back home, at prices far cheaper than those in Canada, Britain, Switzerland, and Tokyo.

Bundled Product/Service Attributes   Pricing theory tells us that the overseas trip, the discount mall, the merchandise in the stores, and the in-store shopping experience are bundled together. Notice the bundled price for the whole shopping trip (including transportation) gives foreign consumers a great savings, and the price deals on individual merchandise give them smaller savings, too.

Moreover, some of these foreign customers used to come to the United States for vacations and to shop on New York's Fifth Avenue, Chicago's Miracle Mile, or Los Angeles's Rodeo Drive. They paid more for the vacation and the merchandise they acquired because they bought them individually. Now they buy them together, and the total price is lower. That's successful product bundling.

Pricing Global Brands at a Discount

Foreign shopping visitors to the United States are getting global brands at a discount. They now make up 5 percent of all shoppers in these giant malls. The farther they come from overseas the more they spend in the malls. On a long-term basis, such global strategic shopping in the United States puts pressure on local retailers, such as Marks & Spencer and Harrods, to price their products at American price points. This change in pricing strategy is already noticeable at Simpson Sears of Canada, Sam's Club or Club Aurrera, Price Costco (in the United States, Mexico, and the United Kingdom), and J Sainsbury in the United Kingdom.

Global brands drive us toward global shopping, and both drive us toward global pricing. As always, Peter Drucker saw it first. Retailing is where the action is today.

Three forecasts. The "continuing trend" forecast is the easiest to make because things go on as before. Segmented pricing and an emphasis on higher price points conform to traditional ways of doing business in Europe and the United States. These make the "continuing trend" forecast realistic.

The "amplifying trend" forecast assumes computer-driven data collection firms aggressively market their information services. These routine purchases of research services are crucial to the success of exporters, consultants, retailers, and others. This trend will develop because we are at the beginning of a major information revolution, with no end in sight.

The "doubling trend" forecast assumes information and marketing research firms convert clients to interactive data management. Product diffusion occurs rapidly because executives want these new interactive services. This one piece of information should help marketers put together an effective marketing strategy for interactive segmented and bundled pricing.

Summary: Scanning the Product-Development Life Cycle

Life-cycle pricing is pricing differently according to the stages in the product-development life cycle. Sometimes, pricing changes market share; at other times pricing modifies brand share. Lower price points tend to be for mature markets, and higher price points are for growth markets. Sometimes, bundled products and services come with higher price points, yet savings are passed on to consumers. Consumer dissonance plays a role in how pricing is accomplished at all stages in the product-development life cycle. Manufacturers want to know which brands are selling while retailers want to know which product categories are moving merchandise out of their stores. The globalization of brands is leading to global shopping which, in turn, leads to global pricing strategies. Where it will all end is anybody's guess.

Inclusive Contexts for Global Marketing

Exhibit 12-7 sums up the inclusive contexts for global marketing through segmented pricing strategies. We examine reinventing price stability. We also study two types of decision making under uncertainty: culturally based demand analysis and organizationally based industry analysis. These two focuses help us direct our research to answering important questions: How will our customers pay for multiplying the uses of information, and how will we shift the paradigm about what we get to a price-driven cost strategy? Again, we deal with technology as a driving force in managerial decision making under uncertainty. Our choices determine whether we will be a success at global marketing.

Exhibit 12-7.
Inclusive Contexts for Global Marketing

Market Risk

Govern the market through reinvented business environment

Liberalization means end of price and wage controls

Reinvent price stability and national currency

Unknown competitive possibilities and imperfect information

Political Frame

Firm-Specific 4Ps Analysis (A)

Culturally based decision making under uncertainty

Worldwide communications

Learn how to undercut prices of incumbents

Free riders

Cost linkages across product lines

Multidimensional signaling

Propaganda, cultural images

Private views made public

Dominant expectations or period eye

Scale economies in signaling costs

Cultural Frame

Firm-Specific 4Ps Analysis (B)

Organizationally based decision making under uncertainty

Shift the paradigm

Pricing signals

Price-driven costs: What do I get?

Pricing strategies

Segmented pricing

Price-quality relationships: P + A = B

Marketing teams

Game theory: two- and multiple-party games

Marketing Management Frame

Continued on next page

Exhibit 12-7. *Continued from previous page*

National Marketing Decisions
Contingency perspective
Signaling game
Multiplying information about prices of competing brands
   Pricing opportunities
   Value-added information
   Consumer behavior: loyals, rotators, deal/price sensitives
   Price sensitivity (elasticity)
Marketing strategy: segmented pricing
Marketing investments and six-sigma question: What do I get?
Performance-based retailing
Technological Frame

Copyright © Douglas F. Lamont. All rights reserved.

Conclusions

Segmenting pricing through price discrimination is a game played by incumbents and new firms locally, nationally, and internationally. Bundling products, services, and pricing is an important strategy for firms that wish to attract new customers.

Let's return to our initial three learning objectives:

1.   Discuss the importance of the contingency perspective to a segmented pricing strategy.

   You should have a clear understanding of the many contingencies that affect pricing and how few of these are covered by the standardization (minimum differentiation) versus adaptation (maximum differentiation) argument.

2.   Outline the paradigm shift occurring in pricing strategy as price-driven cost strategies build market share, extend product lines toward higher price points, and segment prices.

   You should be able to explain why firms must target prices first and then cost out the manufacturing and distribution of products. You should be able to compare and contrast the approaches taken by advertising agencies, whiskey manufacturers, supermarkets, discount clubs, and mega-malls.

3. Explain the management decisions needed to exploit bundled pricing as the means to leverage a firm's competitive advantage.

   You should be aware that new forms of bundled pricing, such as foreigners shopping at US mega-malls, is shaping the future of a global pricing strategy. You should introduce changes in pricing only as long as you can answer your customers' most fundamental questions: What can I do?; What can I do differently?

Making the future happen is the work of global marketing executives.

Notes

1. Kyle Bagwell, "A Model of Competitive Limit Pricing," *Journal of Economics & Management Strategy* 1:4 (Winter 1992): 585–606.

2. Thomas Nagle, "Economic Foundations for Pricing," *Journal of Business* 57:1, pt.2 (January 1984): S9.

3. Ibid., S10.

4. Gerard J. Tellis and Gary J. Gaeth, "Best Value, Price-Seeking, and Price Aversion: The Impact of Information and Learning on Consumer Choices," *Journal of Marketing* 54:2 (April 1990): 34–45.

5. Manohar U. Kalwani, Chi Kin Yim, Heikki J. Rinne, and Yoshi Sugita, "A Price Expectations Model of Customer Brand Choice," *Journal of Marketing Research* 27:3 (August 1990): 251–62.

6. Allan J. MaGrath, "Ten Timeless Truths About Pricing," *Journal of Business and Industrial Marketing* 6:3–4 (Summer/Fall 1991): 15–23.

7. Hugh M. Cannon and Fred W. Morgan, "A Strategic Pricing Framework," *Journal of Business and Industrial Marketing* 6:3–4 (Summer/Fall 1991): 59–70.

8. Peter Drucker, "The Five Deadly Business Sins," *The Wall Street Journal* October 21, 1993, A18.

9. Some of these ideas come from Kenneth A. Grossberg, "The Ins and Outs of Japanese Pricing Strategy," *Journal of Pricing Management* 1:3 (Summer 1990): 6–12.

10. Michael V. Marn and Robert L. Rosiello, "Managing Price, Gaining Profit," *Harvard Business Review* 70:5 (September–October 1992): 84-94.

11. Dirk Huisman, "Ex-ante Measurement of Price-Sensitivities in the Case of Multi-Attribute Products," *Marketing and Research Today* 20:1 (March 1992): 24-32.

12. Sharon V. Thach and Catherine N. Axim, "Pricing and Financing Practices of Industrial Exporting Firms," *International Marketing Review* 8:1 (1991): 32-46.

13. Fred Cohen and Rhonda Price, "Competitive Pricing Strategies for Exporters," *Journal of Pricing Management* 2:2 (Spring 1991): 37-9.

14. Gabriella Stern and Richard Gibson, "Data Raids: Rivals Duel Bitterly for Job of Supplying Market Information," *The Wall Street Journal* November 15, 1993, A1, A9.

15. Barnaby J. Feder, "Scanning Sales with an Eye on Rival," *The New York Times* December 2, 1993, C1, C2.

16. "Consumer Behavior: Strategic Shopping," *The Economist* September 26, 1992, 82, 87.

17. Ibid.

18. Guy de Jonquieres, "Sainsbury Unveils Discount War and Grocery Slowdown," *Financial Times,* November 4, 1993, 16.

19. Guy de Jonquieres and Neil Buckley, "It's Hell in the Aisles," *Financial Times* November 7, 1993, 8.

20. Andrew E. Serwer, "Kellogg: What Price Brand Loyalty," *Fortune,* January 10, 1994, 103-4.

21. "Indigestion: A Survey of the Food Industry," *The Economist,* December 4, 1993, p7-8, 11.

22. John C. Yokom, "Facts: The Final Frontier of Promotion," *Promo,* November 14, 1988, 28.

23. Nagle, S14.

24. Ralph Cassady, "Some Economic Aspects of Price Discrimination Under Nonperfect Market Conditions," *Journal of Marketing* 11 (July 1946): 7-20. "Techniques and Purposes of Price Discrimination," *Journal of Marketing*, 11 (July 1946): 135-50.

25. Clive Sims, Adam Phillips, and Trevor Richards, " Developing a Global Pricing Strategy," *Marketing and Research Today* 20:1 (March 1992): 3-14.

26. Ibid., 4.

27. Ibid., 6.

28. Ibid., 8.

29. Philip M. Parker, "Price Elasticity Dynamics over the Adoption Life Cycle," *Journal of Marketing Research* 29:3 (August 1992): 358-67.

30. Stratford Sherman, "How I Bought My Computer," *Fortune* January 10, 1994, 79.

31. Manjit S. Yadav and Kent B. Monroe, "How Buyers Perceive Savings in a Bundle Price: An Examination of a Bundle's Transactions Value," *Journal of Marketing Research* 30:3 (August 1993): 350-578.

32. Devangana Bhat and Sakina Pittalwala, "Transporting Brand Equity Across Price Segments," *Marketing and Research Today* 21:2 (May 1993): 97-101.

33. Leonard M. Rudy, "Stretching 'Fickle' Loyalty to Its Limits," *Promo,* October 1992, 18.

34. Peter Drucker, "The Retail Revolution," *The Wall Street Journal* July 15, 1993, A14.

35. John Thornhill, "Hard Sell on High Street," *Financial Times* May 16-17, 1992, 9.

36. Richard W. Stevenson, "Ikea's New Realities: Recession and Aging Consumers," *The New York Times,* April 25, 1993, F4.

37. Louis Uchitelle, "U.S. Discounters Invade Mexico," *The New York Times* March 12, 1993, D1, D2.

38. Damian Fraser, "Retailing Revolution South of the Border," *Financial Times* January 19, 1993, 21.

39. Matt Moffett, "US Firms Yell Ole to Future in Mexico," *The Wall Street Journal* March 8, 1993, B1, B5.

40. Michael Wahl, "Pushing Yankee Products in Lord Rayner's Court," *Brandweek* 34:28 (July 12, 1993): 26-29.

41. Barnaby J. Feder, "US Malls Luring Foreign Shoppers," *The New York Times*, December 13, 1993, C1, C3.

Chapter Format

Introduction

Marketing Questions

Environmental Scan: Customer Loyalty

Initial Analysis of Marketing Opportunities

Clues to Capturing Customers

The Firm-Specific Assignment

Competitive Scan: Customer Expectations

Estimates of Market Potential

Similar Market Segments Worldwide

National Marketing Decisions

Marketing Scan: Customer Satisfaction

Strategies for Increasing Marketing Effectiveness

Marketing Implementation

Conclusions

Cases: Wal-Mart, BT, Microsoft, NTT

Learning Objectives

After reading this chapter, you should be able to:

- Discuss the importance of the contingency perspective to a customer-oriented sales strategy

- Outline customer-oriented sales force behavior as the basis for using customer expectations to build customer loyalty

- Explain the sales decisions needed to enhance personal selling, catalogue sales, and direct marketing

Sales Force Behavior

chapter 13

Introduction

Marketers manage final demand by signaling detailed national information about sales force behavior. Customer-driven sales strategies disseminate excellent information about price-quality relationships of the entire product line, and they assist customers in making purchase decisions. Here are the frames for studying local, national, and global marketing.

Scanning Global Markets

Environmental scan: customer loyalty. Selling practices convey attitudes toward quality, value, customer satisfaction, personal service, and feedback from customers, sales personnel, and competitors. Most of these come about by the sales force developing a customer orientation, building customer loyalty, and committing to the success of a high-quality product line. Although some sales details can be written (e.g., the franchise agreement), many situations force sales personnel to accept noncontractable randomness. This is especially true in Japan where culture, tradition, and business practice all overturn many assumptions about sales force behavior. Successful sales and marketing people learn how to deal with these different selling opportunities throughout the world.

Competitive scan: customer expectations. Excellent sales force behavior matches product performance with the expectations of customers. Sometimes, sales personnel use computer-based data to complete sales; more of this sales automation will come about as vidkids replace their parents, the MTV generation, in the work force. Nevertheless, almost all sales people use their eyes and ears to help customers answer this question: What do I get in terms of quality, value, satisfaction, and personal service? These four observable attributes show up in studies about building customer loyalty in the United States and Canada, Europe, and Japan. Successful marketers learn how to make themselves the best at selling.

Marketing scan: customer satisfaction. Customer-oriented sales strategies are built on customer loyalty, expectations, and satisfaction. In the Japanese computer and telecommunications industries, these strategies must take into consideration how government bureaucracies govern the market, direct key decisions, and lead in the hunt for tomorrow's customers. When Japanese and American firms join together in alliances, partnerships, and joint ventures, trust must be built to make relationship selling effective in both Japan and the United States. Both personal selling and direct marketing can be used to build ongoing cooperation, design joint sales strategies, and enhance the selling effort. Although the globalization of selling is coming, many sales activities must be done locally because national culture is more important to customers than the global, largely American freedom lifestyle.

Traditional Contexts for Global Marketing

Exhibit 13–1 lists the traditional contexts for global marketing in the case of sales force behavior. We study a reinvented business environment, relationship selling, and marketing strategy. The first reinforces our observation about the changes occurring in how governments seek to strengthen competitive behavior among investors and business persons. The second reminds us that an effective sales force is still the most potent weapon in the quest for sales. The third prepares us for the hard task of implementing a marketing strategy with continuous future payoffs as we move down the learning curve.

Exhibit 13-1.
Traditional Contexts for Global Marketing

Market Risk

Govern the market through reinvented business environment

Unknown competitive possibilities and imperfect information

Firm-Specific 4Ps Analysis

Signaling sales behavior

Quality

Value

Customer satisfaction

Personal service

Sales feedback panels

Relationship selling

Reliability with products performing as anticipated

Consistency with offerings made by competitors

On-time delivery

Dependable after-market services

Customer problems resolved immediately

Account sensitivity and guidance

Service department excellence

Credible sales approach

National Marketing Decisions

Marketing research

Computer-based sales information

Sales force behavior

Marketing strategy

Final demand

Customer satisfaction

Sales effectiveness

Selling partnerships

Enhanced selling

Nontraditional Contexts for Global Marketing

Exhibit 13-2 names the nontraditional contexts for global marketing as these pertain to sales force behavior. We survey local incentive packages (see

Exhibit 13-4) and multimarkets, pre- and post-entry decisions, perceptions, and information about personal selling and franchising. We are beginning to learn that by asking the question "What do I get?" we help ourselves make better marketing investments.

Governing the market.[1] First, let's look at the political frame. Governments compete with one another for investments by foreign firms in local markets. Information about local incentive packages (i.e., power and transportation, telecom services, government purchases, and forgiveness of taxes) is incomplete because some investors succeed and others do less well in getting commitments from local governments. Also, some competitors are evaluating several nation-states, hoping to determine the markets in which country risk is lowest and where market entry would be most profitable.

Exhibit 13-2.
Nontraditional Contexts for Global Marketing

Political Frame

Govern the market through reinvented business environment

Local incentive packages for investments

Multimarket context

Technological Frame

Contingency perspective

Signaling game

Multiplying information about pre- and post-entry

Pretend costs are higher in high-quality product line

Reduce initial monopoly prices in face of competition

Target product line to loyal customers

Price sensitivity (inelasticity)

Scale economies in costs of signaling

Cultural Frame

Alter customer perceptions about uniqueness and desirability

Enhance positive features

Create a positive image

Increase product differentiation

Value-added nonprice features

Continued on next page

Exhibit 13-2. *Continued from previous page*

Marketing Management Frame

Personal selling

Information about franchises

Use exclusivity clauses to forgo opportunistic behavior

Give franchisee monopoly in downstream retail market

Offer franchisee most favored customer clause

Prepare for multimarket inconsistency problems

Brace for noncontractable randomness

Signaling "What do I get?"

Sales force makes comparisons about observable attributes

Sales force builds long-term customer loyalty

Anticipated selling strategies of rival firms

Game theory: two- and multiple-party games

Competition goes on at two levels. The first is between national governments, as each attempts to price incentives in a manner that deflects foreign direct investments away from the others' markets. The second is between investors in different markets, as each attempts to price products in a manner that deflects entry away from the others' markets.

If competition for investments cuts across several world markets concurrently (i.e., Mexico, Poland, and southern China), foreign investors tend to select higher-cost technology and higher future prices. Investment and marketing teams want to produce a higher-quality product that is unique for sale in *all* major markets of the world, and they want the highest possible profits from their expanded financial commitment.

In global marketing, executives make initial investment and ongoing sales decisions based on incomplete information within a multimarket context. Marketing teams try to compare government incentives, post-entry market growth, and additional sales to near and distant trading partners. Although marketers might end up with a set of mixed strategies, the strategy of entering the highest-priced markets is the optimal entry strategy. Once done, new investors can expect competitors to join in as free riders in which the competitors use observable (price) decisions as the basis for their unobservable (investment) decisions. If the sales force has a customer orientation, foreign firms prosper overseas by providing price information and after-market service to governments, suppliers, clients, and customers as they make their purchase decisions. The behavior of sales personnel makes or breaks government plans for economic success and business decisions for maximizing profits.

Marketing decisions under uncertainty. Second, let's study the technological frame. Marketing educators call the multiplying of information about pre-entry and post-entry product line quality a *signaling game.*[2] Sales personnel increase market share by "pretending" costs are higher in the high-quality product line, then reducing initial monopoly prices under the pressure of competition, and finally targeting the product line to loyal customers. Competitors use promotion and advertising (chapter 11), price-driven cost strategies (chapter 12), selling practices (Chapter 13), and value and quality judgments (chapter 14) to offer the entire high-quality product line to particular consumer groups. These marketing strategies set up the game.

Exhibit 13-3.
Industry Growth Worldwide

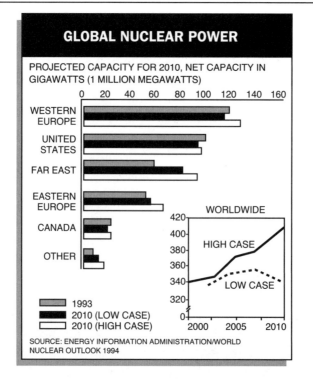

Courtesy of The Journal of Commerce

Some global consumers (e.g., Mexicans who live American lifestyles, committed Europeans among younger age-period cohort groups, and accomplished North Atlantic, trans-Pacific, and East Asian overseas Chinese) know about quality-product-price relationships from their previous purchase decisions in more mature American, European, and Japanese markets. They cannot be fooled by local monopolists in northern Mexico, eastern Europe, and coastal China. Over time, the prices of high-quality local products fall. Their absolute decline is the greatest for local goods whose cost is most sensitive to an end of tariffs under free trade and the subsequent import of comparable goods from trading partners within NAFTA and the EU, or among competitors from East Asia. Moreover, the prices of all high-quality goods fall with the absolute decline being greatest for goods whose cost is most sensitive to product quality and whose demand is most inelastic with respect to own price.

In short, selling executives widely advertise quality and price and sell the entire product line to all culturally bilingual consumers (e.g., both Mexicans and Americans, Czechs and Germans, and Chinese and Japanese). Marketers also gain scale economies in the costs of signaling advertising incentives, price-driven cost strategies, selling practices, and value and quality judgments. Most importantly, marketers acquire the opportunity to target a specific group of global customers (within and among nation-states) that might be buyers for the full high-quality product line.

Hunting for consumers. Third, let's examine the cultural frame. Typically, the sales force tells customers about the high-quality attributes of the product line. Sales personnel try to alter customer perceptions about uniqueness and desirability. At first, if successful, the sales force positions the product, enhances positive features, creates a positive image, influences consumers to buy the product, and, most importantly, increases product differentiation.[3] Over time, if very successful, the sales force reduces search costs for customers and, most importantly, increases product standardization in the minds of customers.[4] In both situations, the assignment of sales personnel is always the same: to "close" the sale – namely, use value-added, nonprice features to sell the high-quality product line and then, if necessary, use price comparisons to continue selling the same product line.

Segmentation, positioning, and tailoring decisions. Finally, let's look closely at the marketing management frame. Thus, selling decisions are based on assisting customers in making purchase decisions. This requires customer orientation in sales force behavior.[5] Such selling practices differ from foreign market to foreign market because national cultures require different levels of marketing communication, personnel selling, and direct marketing. Marketing professors call this different mix of selling activities a contingency perspective (chapter 8).

Firms select competitive sales force strategies in response to the anticipated selling strategies of rival firms. Actions by firms affect consumer demand. Most successful sales personal work more closely with their customers than with their firms so that their signals about price-quality relationships make or break the selling effort of firms.

Organizing global marketing experience. The simultaneous existence of these four different contexts forces marketers to research traditional selling practices, to pursue customer-oriented selling efforts, and to tailor sales force behavior based on local, national, and global tastes. Let's do two things in this chapter. First, we will discuss how the sales force maintains market share under demand uncertainty. Then we will apply this analysis to how marketing teams make selling decisions to retain customer loyalty.

Market Risk Questions

Marketers manage final demand by researching international markets; see Exhibit 13–4. The information age encourages marketers to develop links among quality, expectations, customer satisfaction, and profitability. Through customer orientation by sales force personnel, consumers have as much data about price-quality relationships as do marketing executives. The environmental, competitive, and marketing scans provide information about the effect of sales force behavior on the selling practices of marketers.

Adding Value to Selling Practices

In chapters 8–12, we described the 4Ps scheme used widely by marketing educators. The four Ps are product, place, promotion, and price. How does the sales force deliver a high-quality product line? What does this behavior mean in terms of customer satisfaction and loyalty? Do customer-oriented selling practices increase profitability?

Exhibit 13-4.
Market Risk Analysis: Sales Force Behavior
The Environmental Scan

Traditional Frame Analysis for Global Marketing
Firm-Specific 4Ps Analysis and Signaling Sales Behavior
Quality
  Gap between delivered and desired fitness for use and reliability
  Product line's superiority over competing offerings
Value
  Quality relative to price or benefits received relative to costs
Customer Satisfaction
  Evaluation of first-purchase decisions
  Cumulative judgments about price and after-market services
  Subsequent purchases
  Past, present, and future experiences
Personal Service
  Build relationships through gift-giving, entertaining, meetings
  Use *gomen nasai* (I'm sorry) letters to cement relationships
  Stress salaries over commissions
Sales Feedback Panels
  Assess the needs of customers
  Monitor changes in attitudes of customers
  Follow new initiatives of competitors
  Prepare formal reports on findings
National Marketing Decisions and Marketing Opportunities
  Stress sales force behavior
  Pay attention to observable and unobservable attributes
  Answer six-sigma questions
  Build customer loyalty
  Make "close" on sale

Nontraditional Frame Analysis for Global Marketing
Marketing Management Frame and Information About Franchises
  Use exclusivity clauses to forgo future opportunistic behavior
  Give franchisee monopoly in downstream retail market
  Offer franchisee most favored customer clause
  Prepare for multimarket inconsistency problems
  Brace for noncontractable randomness

Continued on next page

Exhibit 13-4. *Continued from previous page*

Marketing Management Frame and Signaling "What do I get?"
   Sales force makes comparisons about observable attributes
   Sales force builds long-term customer loyalty

Sales Behavior Signals Marketing educators deal with these questions in terms of multidimensional signaling. Here are several signals:[6]

1. Quality is the gap between delivered and desired fitness for use and reliability.

2. Quality is the collective judgment of customers about a product line's superiority over competing offerings.

3. Value is the perceived quality relative to price or benefits received relative to costs incurred.

4. Customer satisfaction is the evaluation of first-purchase decisions and the cumulative judgments about price, after market services, and subsequent purchases.

5. Customer satisfaction is based on all past experiences, present experience, and the anticipation of future experiences.

As marketing executives provide more objective information on quality and value, customers increase their satisfaction with the high-quality product line. The latter become more loyal customers. They tend to tolerate price increases and are more willing to pay for the benefits they receive. Loyal customers also will buy more frequently and in greater volume over time. Moreover, they give marketing executives more degrees of freedom in correcting mistakes. Thus, marketers must encourage the sales force to develop a customer orientation.

Environmental Scan: Customer Loyalty

Today, global customers have expectations about the quality of American, European, and Japanese goods. Mexicans, Hungarians, and Chinese have accumulated knowledge about the ability of foreign firms to deliver quality for a price. Also, those who enjoy or aspire to the global, largely American lifestyle sometimes accumulate information about quality from advertising, direct marketing, and sales personnel before initial or repeat purchases. Moreover, Mexicans expect substantial benefits from joining NAFTA; Hungarians see their future happiness tied to the EU; and the Chinese along the coast anticipate living East Asian, overseas Chinese lifestyles in the near future. All these are part of their collective customer satisfaction with global brands widely distributed throughout the world. They too ask the six-sigma question: What do I get? And they add more questions: When do I get it? Why must I wait so long? Can't you do something to speed up delivery?

Applying the Contingency Perspective to Selling

An important idea from the contingency perspective is the difference between observable and unobservable attributes. This difference exists in selling, too, when customers update expectations even though they have imperfect information about price-quality relationships in the multimarkets of the world. Many customers, especially those who became adults in the 1950s, 1960s, and 1970s, are shocked at the rate of change in computer-based communications; they don't know how to rate product-line quality and value and their own expectations about the future of telecom services. Advertising, direct marketing, and point-of-purchase promotion do not answer all questions. These customers need informed sales personnel to walk them through the benefits of these new technologies and build up their expectations about future satisfaction. Here then is the key role of the sales force in the diffusion of information about improvments in the quality of the product line and strengthening customer loyalty.

Answering the Six-Sigma Question

What do I get? Keep this question in mind because customers rarely have clear and stable preferences in mind before they go about their purchase decisions. Instead, they make their choice based on the specific tasks required of the product. If firms change the set of alternatives before customers, then customers make different purchase decisions. Sales force personnel can influence these choices by pointing out the benefits of new American products over traditional Mexican products, and of better-quality Japanese goods over competing European and American goods. The sales force is expert in making comparisons based on observable price-quality relationships. Promotion and advertising personnel are adept in raising unobservable issues in the purchase decision. However, it still remains for the sales force to make the "close" on the sale. Sales personnel do this by staying close to their customers and answering the six-sigma question: What do I get?

Building Customer Loyalty

Answering this question is easier said than done. Customers have difficulty in determining their preferences. They also change their preferences when offered competing alternatives. Moreover, their preferences are even less reliable in predicting future choices of totally new technologies, such as wireless, multimedia, and other computer-based communications. Because these unobservable attributes influence choice in purchase decisions, the sales force must take them into consideration when employing positioning, promotion, and pricing strategies. If successful, the sales force builds long-term loyalty among customers.

Exclusivity Clauses Customers have an irrational fear that sellers might alter products or services in such a way to erode the value of goods already bought. This is especially true in selling franchises. Wal-Mart in Mexico, Benetton in Europe, Kentucky Fried Chicken in Japan, and McDonald's in China: the franchisor convinces the franchisee that no competing franchises will be set up after the franchisee sinks nonrecoverable start-up costs. The franchisor signs an exclusivity clause agreeing to forgo future opportunistic behavior and giving the franchisee a monopoly in the downstream retail market – that is, no competing franchises within a limited geographic area.[7] Is this enough protection to guarantee customer loyalty?

Most Favored Customer Clauses Unfortunately, demand and supply are not constant over time, and sometimes the exclusivity clause does not work as well as other legal arrangements, such as a most favored customer clause. If the first franchisee obtains an MFC clause from the franchisor (that is, give the first one the same price breaks that others get in the future), future franchisees cannot get a better deal in terms of price or goods delivered from the franchisor.[8] This MFC clause strengthens the loyalty of the first franchisee to the franchisor and the franchise business.

Multimarket Inconsistency Problems Under a free-trade regime, neither an exclusivity nor an MFC clause overcomes the tendency of citizens in one country to cross the border to shop in a neighboring country. For example, in the Wal-Mart case, the US stores are company owned, and the Mexican stores are franchises sold to a joint venture partnership, or Wal-Mart and CIFRA (see chapter 2). Prices are higher in Mexico because locally produced goods cost more than similar goods manufactured in the United States. Also, the costs of transportation and distribution within Mexico are higher, and these add an extra burden to the sale of imported American goods within the Wal-Mart stores in Mexico. Thus, Mexican consumers find it worthwhile to drive from northern Mexico (and even from Mexico City) to the United States to buy household goods and consumer electronics.

Similarly, in regions seeking free trade with neighbors, the Czechs, Poles, and Russians prefer to buy their sweaters and sportswear from Benetton stores within the EU where prices are lower. Finally, Japanese consumers avoid local franchisees by combining vacations with shopping to buy all types of high-quality goods anyplace but Japan, where local prices are high.

What do I get? When do I get it? Why must I wait so long? Can't you do something to speed up delivery? Today, customers use computer-based telecommunications to find out where products are located and then go shopping abroad to meet their needs. These customers are more loyal to global brands than to local sites for completing their purchase decisions. This is a crucial unobservable attribute, and one that sales personnel must deal with in their drive for long-term customer loyalty.

Noncontractable Randomness Again, demand and supply are not constant over time. Global shopping (see chapter 12) for durable goods minimizes the usefulness of exclusivity and MFC clauses within multimarkets that are joined together under free-trade agreements. Global shopping requires new approaches to selling practices and a change in sales force behavior. Most marketing teams are simply unaware of this emerging global marketing problem, and little has been done to change behavior among exporters, importers, distributors, sales agents, wholesalers, and retailers – all those in the front lines of global shopping.

Is Wal-Mart in Mexico ready for other franchisors seeking market position, too? All of them compete against one another for government incentives to invest locally and for capable national partners to give them good local cultural information. Hence, noncontractable randomness exists in the Mexican market as Price-Costco, K-mart, and others take on Wal-Mart in Mexico City or as McDonald's, Mr. Donut, and Pizza Hut take on KFC in Tokyo.

Exclusivity clauses are of little help in protecting against noncontractable randomness and maintaining customer loyalty. Sometimes, MFC clauses offer help in overcoming noncontractable randomness and strengthening customer loyalty. When national markets become hot, such as Mexico and countries in East Asia, customers have more money and will spend it wherever they can get the best deals. Stress in customer orientation must be placed on promoting global brands so that loyal customers will buy these products anyplace in the world.

Initial Analysis of Marketing Opportunities

Selling is different in Japan (see chapter 5).[9] All personal service happens before a sale is closed – constant gift giving, extravagant entertaining, and marathon meetings. All these are designed to build relationships. Sales personnel (i.e., *sarariiman*, salarymen, or white-collar office workers) are paid a flat salary for relationship building.

To them, business is war.[10] They work 200 hours more per year than their US counterparts, they have an ethic of strong corporate loyalty, and some literally die from overwork. These corporate warriors obey their company's orders by proceeding alone (sometimes overseas) to new posts. After an eight-hour work day, salarymen denote two or three more hours' service as unpaid overtime. Sundays are for family time, but many salarymen are out on the golf course on Sunday, strengthening business relationships with customers.

The sales force in Japan represents its accounts. If anything goes wrong, the sales people must do everything possible to fix it. They do so through *gomen nasai* (I'm sorry) letters, more gift giving, and additional entertainment, and they do so by cutting costs and being sure products never break down. Selling is all about service, and lifetime customers are always right.

Here are some observations about selling in Japan:[11]

1. Golf, expensive restaurants, and hostess clubs are sales entertainment activities.

2. Sales reps keep their key account even when they move up the corporate ladder.

3. Selling rules are highly ritualized.

4. Sales reps need formal introductions.

5. Sales reps practice face saving.

6. Sales reps practice space saving by not bringing extra items to meetings.

7. Sales reps give gifts to their bosses during the midsummer and year-end gift seasons. They give chocolate gifts of obligation (rather than romance) to women employees on Valentine's Day, and they accept their return chocolate gifts of obligation on White Day. They make sure that gifts are gifts, not bribes.

8. Sales reps work to continually improve products, add value, cut costs, and improve quality to maintain lifetime customers. This is service.

All of these thoughts show the interest in stability among sales personnel within Japan.

Changing Selling Behavior

Yet some changes are coming in Japan, too. Masanori Suzuki, an 18-year veteran of IBM, founded Japan Database in 1988.[12] He hired one sales person on a commission basis, Daniel Wong (overseas Chinese in lifestyle, English out of Hong Kong in nationality), to sell UTP data-grade cabling for networks and computer systems to foreign multinationals in Japan. Wong provides his clients with service in English while the other Japanese sales persons provide their clients with service in Japanese. While Wong works on commission, all other Japanese sales persons work on a flat salary.

Other examples of changing selling behavior include the following:[13]

■ Keyence, an Osaka-based maker of laser-based factory automation controls, compensates its sale force based on performance, not tenure.

There are no more obligatory drinking parties after work and golf outings at Keyence.

- Mabuchi Motor, a Tokyo-based supplier of small electric motors found in VCRs, offers only low-cost, standardized products. It refused to make the endless customer-specific modifications urged by the industry and kept its costs way down. There is no customer orientation at Mabuci Motor.

- Aoyama Trading, a Hiroshima-based discount retailer, developed better skills at forecasting styles and sales, dropped suits by expensive garment makers, and opened up a cut-rate shop in Tokyo's high-fashion Ginza district. There is no maintenance of genteel customs at Aoyama.

These are all small companies. They are not members of any *keiretsu*, the groups of vertically and horizontally related larger companies common in Japan. However, to stay alive they have to compete, and the best way they know is to change selling behavior.

Learning About Selling from *The Laughing Salesman*

The Laughing Salesman is a "black humor" *manga* about a smiling salesman who sets up people for unexpected consequences under the guise of helping them overcome their problems.[14] He was created in 1969 by Fujiko Fujio, a master of the art of *manga*, to offer comic book readers an insight into the life of salarymen. *The Laughing Salesman*'s accounts are customers weighed down by life, troubled by their jobs, and facing competition from younger, more aggressive trans-Pacific Japanese. They weren't doing well before the boom of the bubble economy of the 1970s and 1980s, and they are doing even less well today with the hard recession of the 1990s. These salarymen read this *manga* as an escape from their problems. Now women are fans of *The Laughing Salesman* because they see their husbands as business warriors fallen as casualties in the current restructuring of the Japanese economy. These salarymen wanted to be good corporate warriors and, in the end, their desire to excel is the root of their unhappiness. They see the new world ahead of them in an episode called "Part-Time Jobs: The Inside Line" (or "Top Secret Information on Part-Time Jobs"). *The Laughing*

Salesman tries to help them, but he cannot change them from salarymen into sales reps paid by commissions. There's the black humor in this *manga*.

Clues to Capturing Customers

Once we move from North America or Europe to Japan we know intuitively that we must alter our selling practices to mesh with local cultural values. Why then do marketing executives fail to use this same intuition when we move from low technology to computer-based, high technology in the telecom services industry? Are classic sales and marketing techniques suitable in this new age?

Answering the Question *What Do I get?*

Let's review the classic practices. We start by assessing the needs of customers. Then we identify the product concepts that deliver the benefits to satisfy these needs. We do more marketing research by collecting statistical data. Then we build prototype products. We do more consumer research by collecting cultural information. Then we carry out positioning, pricing, packaging, and promotion strategies. At last, we make sales.

Marks & Spencer modified this classic approach to sales and marketing by suggesting L'eggs would survive or fail based on sales at the cash register. Many Japanese companies start with new research and development, modify the results, improve the quality, drive costs down, and finally gain significant market share. Sometimes their new products shape customer expectations.

In the telecommunications industry, many new products are coming through research and development; customers are unfamiliar with the new technology, are unprepared for using the new technology, and resist using the new technology. Thus, telecom services companies must take the initiative and decide what their customers might need in the future.

At British Telecommunications (BT), the sales force monitors changes in the attitudes and perceptions of customers and new initiatives taken by competitors.[15] The sales force plays an important market intelligence role that has been formalized by placing sales persons into Sales Feedback Panels and requesting that the panels prepare a formal research report on their findings about the future.

Win-Win Sales Marketing Strategy

Here are the recommendations from the Sales Feedback Panels about creating a win-win marketing strategy:

- Turn wide-ranging strategic statements about the role different technologies might play into specific tactics that can be executed by the sales force.

- Be sure customers who call for service are taken care of as quickly as possible.

- Give sales persons the chance to tailor promotion and advertising, direct mail, and other marketing communications products to fit each and every loyal customer.

These panels showed that the sales force is able to see the big picture facing BT and to give detailed suggestions about has to achieve the firm's long-term objectives. Also, these sales panels strengthened the customer orientation of the sales force. Finally, these feedback panels turned research results into sales – that is, what we can do to sell new computer-based telecommunications equipment and services.

Summary: Scanning Customer Loyalty

Selling practices convey attitudes toward quality, value, customer satisfaction, personal service, and feedback from customers, sales personnel, and competitors. Most of these come about by the sales force developing a customer orientation, building customer loyalty, and committing to the success of a high-quality product line. Although some sales details can be written (e.g., the franchise agreement), many situations force sales personnel to accept noncontractable randomness. This is especially true in Japan where culture, tradition, and business practice all overturn many assumptions about sales force behavior. Successful sales and marketing people learn how to deal with these different selling opportunities throughout the world.

The Firm-Specific Assignment

Marketers manage final demand by positioning customer-oriented sales and service strategies within national and global markets; see Exhibit 13–5. Remember Drucker's most important six-sigma question: What do I get?

Customers ask the question this way: How are my needs and expectations being met from the products and services offered in the marketplace? Wal-Mart customers want lowest prices, brand-named goods packaged in bulk sizes, good in-store merchandising, instant service, and parking. American customers of Wal-Mart get all five observable attributes, but Mexican customers obtain only four out of the five because prices are not the lowest within the joint US-Mexico market.

No matter what the front-line workers do in the Mexican Wal-Mart stores – that is, no matter how friendly the greeters are who welcome customers; no matter how helpful are the sales floor personnel who field questions; and no matter how quickly cashiers ring up purchases – Mexican customers believe they are receiving less value than Wal-Mart shoppers in the United States. Thus, marketers who execute the CIFRA-Wal-Mart sales strategies must work on pricing so that Mexican customers make their repeat purchases in Mexico. This sales effort will give Mexicans increased customer satisfaction with their shopping experience within the Mexican-based Wal-Mart stores.

Exhibit 13-5.
Firm-Specific Analysis: Sales Force Behavio
The Competitive Scan

Traditional Frame Analysis and Global Marketing
Firm-Specific 4Ps Analysis and Relationship Selling
What Do I Get in Terms of Quality?
Reliability with products performing as anticipated
Consistency with offerings made by competitors
On-time delivery with sales personnel taking care of emergencies
What Do I Get in Terms of Value?
Dependable after market services
Customer problems resolved immediately
What Do I Get in Terms of Customer Satisfaction?
Business expertise and image
Dedication to the customer
Account sensitivity and guidance
Product performance and quality
Service department excellence
Confirmation of capabilities

Continued on next page

Exhibit 13-5. *Continued from previous page*

What Do I Get in Terms of Personal Service?
Credible sales approach

Improved communications

Promises are always kept

National Marketing Decisions and Marketing Research
Computer-Based Sales Information
Rumors become insights and tomorrow's facts

Download end-of-day activity data

Upload leads, price lists, status reports

Human eyes process visual data

Sales Force Behavior
Negotiate partnership contracts

Match product performance with customer expectations

Sell custom applications for commercial use

Package products for resale by retail shops

Deal with noncontractable randomness

Promote multimarket sales

Copyright © Douglas F. Lamont. All rights reserved.

Competitive Scan: Customer Expectations

According to Learning International, "Companies unable to match performance with customers' expectations will be surpassed by more responsive competitors."[16] Learning International suggests the following six clues to answering the question: What do I get that satisfies me as the buyer?[17]

Business expertise and image. Customers want the expertise of sales personnel and the firm.

Dedication to the customer. Customers want sales personnel to solve marketing problems and be their partners.

Account sensitivity and guidance. Customers want sales personnel who can take care of pricing problems.

Product performance and quality. Customers want high-quality products.

Service department excellence. Customers want reliable logistics and after-market service personnel.

Confirmation of capabilities. Customers want to confirm their impressions with references.

By far, the most important factor is the first: Customers want the expertise of sales personnel, their knowledge of other suppliers and competitors, and their own personal insights about whether the deal is a good value over the long run. In short, salespeople based in North America are crucial consultants to their US and Canadian customers.

Improving Sales Performance

Are these same skills required for Europe and Japan? Within the EU, sales personnel have three ways to build customer loyalty, improve their performance, and get the greatest payback possible.[18]

First, they must address the quality concerns of customers in terms of reliability, consistency, and on-time delivery. Second, they must get on top of after-market services, make them dependable, and improve their ability to solve customer problems immediately. Third, they must improve credibility of the sales approach by forging stronger personal ties and improving communications about products and services.

On the other hand, within Japan, customers expect products and services to be of the highest quality and to perform as anticipated.[19] Also, customers require sales personnel to be informed about their competition and to meet the emergency needs of their customers. Finally, the most important issue for Japanese customers is that sales personnel keep their promises.

Tapping into Information from Sales Personnel

Sales people in the United States, Europe, and Japan see their customers and competitors day in and day out, each week and month of the year. They know the rumors. These insights may become tomorrow's facts. Usually, sales personnel may have a wealth of information, but they keep it to themselves because they are never asked about it or they don't have the computer tools to download activity data at the end of the sales day.

If selling practices are going to be brought into the new world of interactive connectivity, the sales force must be able to upload their leads, price lists, engineering and configuration lists, product availability, status reports on previous orders, and e-mail messages from a central server system located at the company's headquarters. This sales automation system also must provide credit checks and inventory files, track sales calls, and schedule appointments for the future.

As the vidkids of the Nintendo generation replace the MTV/PC generation in the workplace, these new sales personnel will simply be more comfortable with the convergence of media technologies.[20] Interactive on-line technology is as routine for the vidkids as dialing (or auto-dialing) the phone is for their MTV parents. The vidkids-turned-sales-people use their computers to interact with their customers and to gather information about future prospects.

Because the sales force represents the single biggest marketing cost in major corporations, there's a tremendous drive today among senior executives to improve the odds of sales persons coming back with orders.[21] Hence, an expanding market of about US $2 billion for sales force automation and software tools has developed, and the need for consultants to reengineer the sales process among major companies is recognized.

But do be careful. One pair of human eyes processes more visual data in one day than all the world's computers combined.[22] Don't let the sales force become glued to the computer screen, only to forget about cold calls, sales acumen, cultural nuances, personal selling, and the "close" on the sale. These are what customers expect from their sales personnel.

Estimates of Market Potential

Let's see how Microsoft matched performance with customer expectations in Japan.[23] According to Cindy Durkin, the marketing manager of the Far East Region for Microsoft, Japan has five different, incompatible hardware architecture platforms (versus only two in the United States). All of them are proprietary systems. Thus five different versions of applications software, keyboard layout, monitor design, and printer support exist in Japan.

As early as 1977, Microsoft formed an alliance with Kuzuhiko Nishi, the founder of ASCII Corporation, now Japan's largest software and computer magazine publishing firm. Through an excluse contract, Microsoft provided MS-DOS (and later Windows) and ASCII licensed the software, languages, and operating systems.

Since the original partnership contract did not include a most favored customer clause, 10 years later Microsoft set up its own subsidiary in Tokyo to expand its business into desktop applications without the help of ASCII Corporation. The new software had to support the input and output of 7,000 pictorial characters (so called double-byte character sets). It had to read, store, and sort kanji and kana characters (see chapter 4). Moreover, the new software had to include an option to write vertically, from right to left, in addition to English style from left to right. This is localization, adaptation, and maximum differentiation suitable only for one national market, Japan.

Today, about 20 percent of the PCs in Japan have Microsoft Windows installed versus about 70 percent in the United States. Also, only about 500 Windows applications are localized for Japan versus 5,000 in the United States. Besides the technical difficulties of changing the rest to double-byte character sets, most commercial applications in Japan remain proprietary.

Here's what Microsoft wants to do with its software. The firm wants to create a sales force that sells custom applications for commercial use. The firm also wants to package its software for resale by computer shops and other retailers. Moreover, the firm wants to offer its software by direct marketing and telemarketing. These goals will be a major test of Microsoft's sales force in Japan. We can anticipate a substantial amount of noncontractable randomness to develop as Microsoft and its competitors seek sales in price-sensitive customer markets.

Multimarket Software Sales

Already, 120 Japanese software products are available in the United States including system software (such as PC-based Microsoft Windows 3.1J, and Mac-based Apple JLK), word processors (such as Microsoft Word for Windows 5.0J, WordPerfect J for DOS, and WordPerfect 2.2J for Mac), desktop publishing, utilities, illustrations, machine translation, fonts, and many other applications.[24] When these are sold through authorized resellers, the resellers must give extensive user support because not all files are compatible with familiar, English-language versions of the same programs. Apple did this. However, Microsoft did not give in-house support when it introduced Windows 3.1J in the United States, and this limited the ability of its American sales force and US resellers to provide personal service to US-based Japanese firms. This lack of after-market services in the United States will come to haunt Microsoft both in the United States and Japan as potential Japanese customers decide Microsoft is unwilling to match its performance with the expectations of its customers.

Similar Market Segments Worldwide

486 DOS-based PC equipment from the United States works on 115–120 volts at 60 hertz. However, similar equipment in Kansai and the western areas of Japan operates on 100 volts at 60 hertz, and in Tokyo and the eastern areas of Japan it operates at 50 hertz.[25] Computers can handle this disparity, but laser printers and scanners cannot handle the differences. Although American-made computers can be used in Japan, printers must be bought in Japan for use in Japan.

Japanese electrical plugs are the two-prong, ungrounded variety; special adapter plugs must be imported from the United States before American PCs can run in Japan. Finally, PCs, software, utilities, adapter plugs, and everything else are more expensive in Japan than in the United States. However, this difference is narrowed somewhat by the costs of transporting and insuring computers shipped from the United States to Japan.

Given the chance of incompatibility between American and Japanese software, files, and utilities and the availability of online services in both countries, the time has come for Japanese sales persons (such as Tomoko Zenman, who is one of the few women in Japan selling PCs via telemarketing for Dell Computer Corp.[26]) to offer bundled hardware and software products and after-market services. For example, CompuServe has an agreement with the Nissho Iwai Corporation and Fujitsu Limited to offer the former's online service, called NiftyServe, in Japan.[27] It offers the Comics Forum for consumers of *manga*, the PR & Marketing Special Interest Group, the Travel Special Interest Group, and the Foreign Language Education Forum among its 300 forums. NiftyServe can run on IBMs or compatibles, and on Macs, and it can use DOS/V and WordPerfect, and KanjiTalk and System 7.

Summary: Scanning Customer Expectations

Excellent sales force behavior matches product performance with the expectations of customers. Sometimes, sales personnel use computer-based data to complete sales; more of this sales automation will come about as vidkids replace their parents, the MTV generation, in the work force. Nevertheless, almost all sales people use their eyes and ears to help customers answer this question: What do I get in terms of quality, value, satisfaction, and personal service? These four observable attributes show up in studies about building customer loyalty in the United States and Canada, Europe, and Japan. Successful marketers learn how to make themselves the best at selling.

Exhibit 13–6.
National Marketing Decisions: Sales Force
The Marketing Scan

Traditional Frame Analysis for Global Marketing

Firm-Specific 4Ps Analysis and Decision Making Under Uncertainty

Signal national sales information

Grow through relationship selling

Pay attention to personal selling changes worldwide

National Marketing Decisions and Marketing Strategy

Final Demand

Govern the market

Make decisions under uncertainty

Hunt for consumers

Relationship Selling Builds Customer Satisfaction

Complex and customized services

Many unsophisticated buyers

Dynamic and uncertain future

Sales Effectiveness

Account penetration

Cross-selling

Retention

Selling Partnerships

Ongoing cooperation

Mutual disclosure

Design of sales strategies

Training sales personnel

Long-term horizons

Enhanced Selling

Continued on next page

Exhibit 13-6. *Continued from previous page*

Catalogue sales

Tele-marketing

Direct marketing

National Marketing Decisions and Marketing Forecasts

Continuing trend is realistic because of customer orientation

Amplifying trend builds on automating sales data

Doubling trend presumes selling partnership grows sales

National Marketing Decisions

Marketers manage final demand by signaling detailed national information about customer-oriented sales strategies – that is, unless the government steps in to regulate the market. Here is the Internet situation in Japan.

Governing the market.[28] The freewheeling, democratic style of the Internet (i.e., the global, largely American culture in computer communications) runs smack into the desire of Japan's Ministry of Posts and Telecommunications (P&T) to establish standards, some of which are against the wishes of Japanese users of Internet. Even in 1994, Japan still lagged in logging on to the Net. Japan has five networks for every 100 in the United States. Outbound Net traffic from Japan is about "42,000 Mbytes, roughly the same as that from Taiwan, a country with one-sixth of Japan's population, and less than half that from Australia, the Pacific Rim's most aggressive network user."[29] Japanese firms that claim they can provide network services are not given operating licenses by the Ministry. On the other hand, P&T permits foreign firms, such as InterCon Systems and AT&T, to send Internet packets out of Tokyo and down Trans-Pacific Cable No. 4 to San Jose, California. Their clients include TWICS, Japan's first public access Internet provider, a for-profit firm whose subscribers are foreigners based in Japan.

Making marketing decisions under uncertainty.[30] The Ministry of International Trade and Industry, which governs the market for computers, and the Ministry of Posts and Telecommunications, which governs the market for communications, are fighting among themselves for who has control over computer-based communications, Internet, the proposed information superhighway, and the new social infrastructure for Japan. Since computers are no longer stand-alone devices, and since they can be connected to central servers and other computers in a telephone-based network, MITI believes it has primary responsibility for governing the computer communications market.

Post and Telecommunications disagrees, but it has lost power with the partial privatization of Nippon Telegraph and Telephone Corp. (NTT). P&T wants to lay fiber-optic cables to all Japanese homes and offices and control the whole network within Japan. NTT also wants to build the Net and finance the construction by raising the cost of local phone calls. The Ministry of Finance agrees because it could then sell off the 66 percent of NTT that the government still owns.

Hunting for consumers.[31] NTT is changing, too. In the past, the firm presented its customers with a network interface and told them to adapt their systems accordingly. Today, customers tell NTT what network standards they need, and the firm must accommodate them. This is a customer-oriented approach toward investing in and selling telecom services within Japan.

NTT is also trying to deregulate its telephone tariffs. Its leased lines cost five to eight times more than those in the United States. NTT competes with Japan's new common carriers – DDI Corp., Japan Telecom, and Teleway Japan – for leased-line sales. The Ministry of Posts and Telecommunications is reluctant to let NTT drop its prices too fast because P&T fears the negative impact on the new common carriers.

Moreover, Tokyo Electric Power Co. is laying a fiber network alongside its power transmission lines. The Power Co. is a partner in the Tokyo Telecommunications Network Co., which will provide interactive telecom services through regional power companies and cable TV operators in competition with NTT.

Finally, NTT is forming alliances to develop multimedia services, such as Japan's Softbank (a provider of video on demand over NTT's data communication lines), America's General Magic, and even with Microsoft. The deal with Microsoft will give NTT access to Japanese software applications both in Japan and the United States and the opportunity to compete in North America, too.

Marketing Scan: Customer Satisfaction

Clearly, the emergence of a partially privatized NTT as a partner with Microsoft has major implications for relationship marketing throughout the world. These two firms are in the process of making long-term commitments to reduce transaction costs, lower the uncertainty of future benefits, and obtain advantages not available in short-term exchanges between buyer and seller. According to marketing educators, relationship selling occurs when the following occur:[32]

1. The service is complex, customized, and delivered over a continuous stream of transactions.

2. Many buyers are relatively unsophisticated about the service.

3. The environment is dynamic and uncertain in ways that affect future needs (demand) and offerings (supply).

Both partners are customers of one another, and they both demand satisfaction from the other. This is the essence of relationship selling.

Scanning for Sales Force Behavior

The management of NTT and Microsoft, and especially their sales and marketing teams, must contribute to customer loyalty, expectations, and satisfaction. Also, their work together must be characterized by sales effectiveness (e.g., account penetration, cross-selling, retention), ongoing cooperation, mutual disclosure, design of sales strategies, and training sales personnel to function effectively in selling telecom services.

Long-term planning and delivery horizons face customers as those in Japan wait for MITI, P&T, and Finance to settle their turf wars over computer communications. Also, a great deal of uncertainty confronts customers as those in Japan and the United States wait for network providers and users, software developers, and many others in the multimedia business to develop protocols for computer-telephone interfaces, after-market services, and reseller opportunities through franchises, telemarketing, and direct marketing.

Do Microsoft and NTT trust one another? Do their joint customers trust them to provide a high-quality product line? Does everyone involved trust all sales persons to behave in a manner consistent with the long-term interests of customers? Do all the past, present, and future interactions match performance with customer expectations? Do customers gain satisfaction from the partners, their sales force, their products and services, and all other aspects of the selling relationship?

Coping with Future Purchases

NTT and Microsoft will continue to deepen their relationship as long as future benefits exceed current and future costs. They will stay in the partnership as long as each anticipates higher levels of satisfaction. Moreover, the partners will stay in the alliance as long as they face higher costs of switching to alternative services. Building long-term relationships is something the Japanese do very well, and it is something that far-sighted American firms are learning how to do, too.

Here are some potential problems facing the two partners. NTT is a Japanese firm, and Microsoft is an American firm. Their national cultures are different; however, they both share the trans-Pacific business culture, which tends to dominate sales and marketing from the American Northwest, British Columbia, and Alaska to South Korea and Japan. Also, NTT is a partially privatized firm and is just learning to be customer-oriented while Microsoft has always put its customers first. Moreover, NTT uses salarymen while Microsoft gives commissions to sales people, resellers, direct marketers, and others.

Nevertheless, both firms are crucial players in the fast-expanding computer-based telecom services industry. They have key expertise, and when joined together their technologies enhance each other for the benefit of their customers. These observable attributes facilitate their attraction for one another. In summary, relationship selling (high contact, mutual disclosure, and cooperative intentions) breeds relationship quality about products and services in the minds of customers, and relationship marketing in the work of alliance partners.

Strategies for Increasing Marketing Effectiveness

Sales and marketing teams, sales force behavior, and sales persons' effectiveness all promote customer loyalty, effectiveness, and satisfaction. These are all forms of personal selling – one-on-one cold calls, status reports, and the "close" on the sale. Along with helping clients make purchase decisions, sales persons provide product literature, quote prices, negotiate terms, and check on delivery. Although a great deal of the data are automated through servers connected to PCs in a computer-based network, segmentation, positioning, and targeting offerings remains an art of salarymen, manufacturers' representatives, and other commissioned sales agents. The sales force remains the eyes and ears of the firm.

Enhancing Selling

Sometimes a direct marketing approach helps enhance the selling effort. A great deal of the data available to the sales force can be refined and used for mailing catalogues and other product information. These help the telemarketing sales force offer additional services, do a better job of segmentation, deliver specialized assortments, and increase the total amount of money spent by customers.

English-language catalogues can be used with a few modifications in the United States, Canada, the United Kingdom, and Australia. Pictures in American catalogues must be reshot with Mexican and Latin American models before the direct marketing effort can be successful in the Spanish-speaking countries to the south of the United States. Direct marketing advertising copy works best when it uses the local language rather than a business language, such as English (see chapter 11). Although a global, largely American culture exists, Mexicans, French, Germans, Japanese, and Chinese prefer both personal selling and direct marketing to be in their native language and reflect their own national cultures (see chapters 3–6). Careful marketers will use a CETSCALE approach in doing their marketing research about what is ethnocentrist and what is nonethnocentrist within countries where they plan to send business letters, direct mail pieces, and printed catalogues (see chapter 3).

With all printed pieces, sales and marketing personnel must "think globally, but act locally." Generally, firms that already sell outside their home country are willing to try direct and telemarketing overseas. Direct marketing tends to be an additional tool for sales and marketing personnel rather than the primary means of selling products and services internationally.[33]

Marketing Implementation

Since the beginning of the free trade in North American (first in 1989 between the United States and Canada, then in 1994 between these countries and Mexico), 94 percent of all small Canadian exporters use direct marketing in trying to sell their products within the United States.[34] Their printed materials are already in English because three-quarters of Canada uses English as the first language. Why do Canadian exporters use direct marketing? They lack an installed based of sales persons within the United States and chose an alternative way to make their presence known to American customers.

Also, 80 percent of small Mexican exporters use direct marketing in trying to sell their products within the United States Their materials must be translated from Spanish to English, which adds to their costs of selling within the United States. They, too, use direct marketing in lieu of a well-established sales force in the United States.

Moreover, 75 percent of small American exporters use direct marketing in trying to sell their products in Canada and Mexico. Usually, American firms don't bother to translate their printed materials to French (for Canada) and Spanish, and this failure impedes their ability to make direct marketing as effective a sales tool as possible in global marketing.

Global selling is closely bound to national culture. Therefore, the sales force must always ask the crucial six-sigma question: What do I get?

Three forecasts. The "continuing trend" forecast is the easiest to make because things go on as before. Customer-oriented selling and an emphasis on loyalty, expectations, and satisfaction stress appropriate sales force behavior. These make the "continuing trend" forecast realistic.

The "amplifying trend" forecast assumes computer-driven data assists sales persons to expand their selling efforts and "close" more sales. If the sales personnel have high-quality products, if they offer high-quality logistics services, if they promote their products and services correctly, and if the prices are right, then this trend will develop because we are at the beginning of a major revolution in sales automation.

The "doubling trend" forecast assumes sales and marketing teams from different companies join together to create new product offerings that expand the total market, segment the market further, and target many new customers. Customer satisfaction with all the new products continues to grow because the sales force and their telemarketing associates convince customers to buy these new goods. This one assumption should give marketers pause before they put together a marketing strategy based on unrealistic numbers. Selling is still an art – even when two or more partners are involved in the partnership.

Summary: Scanning for Customer Satisfaction

Customer-oriented sales strategies are built on customer loyalty, expectations, and satisfaction. In the Japanese computer and telecommunications industries, these strategies must take into consideration how government bureaucracies govern the market, direct key decisions, and lead in the hunt for tomorrow's customers. When Japanese and American firms join together in alliances, partnerships, and joint ventures, trust must be built to make relationship selling effective in both Japan and the United States. Both personal selling and direct marketing can be used to build ongoing cooperation, design joint sales strategies, and enhance the selling effort. Although the globalization of selling is coming, many sales activities must be done locally because national culture is more important to customers than the global, largely American freedom lifestyle.

Inclusive Contexts for Global Marketing

Exhibit 13-7 sums up the inclusive contexts for global marketing as these pertain to sales force behavior. We examine reinventing incentive packages. We also study two types of decision making under uncertainty: culturally based demand analysis and organizationally based industry analysis. These two focuses help us direct our research to answering important questions: How will our customers react to multidimensional signaling, and how will we shift the paradigm about what we get to a customer-oriented selling strategy? Again, we deal with technology as a driving force in managerial decision making under uncertainty. Our choices determine whether we will be a success at global marketing.

Exhibit 13–7.
Inclusive Contexts for Global Marketing

Market Risk

Govern the market through reinvented business environment

   Local incentive packages for investments

   Multimarket context

Unknown competitive possibilities and imperfect information

Political Frame

Firm-Specific 4Ps Analysis (A)

Culturally based decision making under uncertainty

Multiplying information about pre- and post-entry

   Pretend costs are higher in high-quality product line

   Reduce initial monopoly prices in face of competition

   Target product line to loyal customers

Price sensitivity (inelasticity)

Scale economies in costs of signaling

Cultural Frame

Firm-Specific 4Ps Analysis (B)

Organizationally based decision making under uncertainty

Shift the paradigm

Signaling sales behavior

   Sales feedback panels

   Relationship selling

Personal selling

Information about franchises

   Use exclusivity clauses to forgo opportunistic behavior

   Give franchisee monopoly in downstream retail market

   Offer franchisee most favored customer clause

   Prepare for multimarket inconsistency problems

   Brace for noncontractable randomness

Signaling "What do I get?"

Anticipated selling strategies of rival firms

Game theory: two- and multiple-party games

Marketing Management Frame:

Continued on next page

Exhibit 13-7. *Continued from previous page*

National Marketing Decisions
Contingency perspective
Signaling game
Multiplying information about pre- and post-entry
Marketing research
  Computer-based sales information
  Sales force behavior
Marketing strategy
Scale economies in costs of signaling
Technological Frame

Copyright © Douglas F. Lamont. All rights reserved.

Conclusions

Selling through salarymen, sales persons, manufacturers' representatives, and commissioned agents is the game played by incumbents and new firms locally, nationally, and internationally. Customer-oriented selling is an important strategy for firms that wish to attract new customers who seek high-quality goods.

Let's return to our initial three learning objectives:

1. Discuss the importance of the contingency perspective to a customer-oriented sales strategy.

    You should have a clear understanding of the many contingencies that affect sales force behavior and purchase decisions, and of how few of these are covered by the standardization (minimum differentiation) versus adaptation (maximum differentiation) argument.

2. Outline customer-oriented sales force behavior as the basis for using customer expectations to build customer loyalty.

    You should be able to explain why firms put their customers first in designing a sales strategy. You should be able to compare and contrast the approaches taken by retail discounters, software firms, and telecom services companies.

3. Explain the sales decisions needed to enhance personal selling, catalogue sales, and direct marketing.

You should be aware that automating sales does not end the need for sales persons to pay attention to the cultural demands of selling worldwide. Many people are both ethnocentrist and nonethnocentrist at the same time, and their choice depends on the product, its quality, and the firms making the offering. You should introduce changes in selling only as long as you can answer your customers' most fundamental question: What do I get?

Making the "close" on sales is the work of global marketing executives.

Notes

1. The microeconomics discussion draws heavily from Kyle Bagwell, "A Model of Competitive Limit Pricing," *Journal of Economics & Management Strategy* 1:4 (Winter 1992): 585-606. The macroeconomics application to country risk, governing the market, and international business decisions is my own.

2. Kyle Bagwell, "Pricing to Signal Product Line Quality," *Journal of Economics & Management Strategy* 1:1 (Spring 1992): 151-74.

3. Joe S. Bain, *Barriers to New Competition* (Cambridge, MA: Harvard University Press, 1956). Cited in William Boulding, Eunkyu Lee, and Richard Staelin, "Mastering the Mix: Do Advertising, Promotion, and Sales Force Activities Lead to Differentiation?," *Journal of Marketing Research* 31:2 (May 1994): 159.

4. Philip Nelson, "Advertising as Information," *Journal of Political Economy* 82 (July-August 1974): 729-54. Cited in Boulding, Lee, and Staelin, 159-60.

5. Judy A. Siguaw, Gene Brown, and Robert E. Widing, "The Influence of the Market Orientation of the Firm on Sales Force Behavior and Attitudes," *Journal of Marketing Research* 31:1 (February 1994): 106-16.

6. Eugene W. Anderson, Claes Fornell, and Donald R. Lehmann, "Customer Satisfaction, Market Share, and Profitability: Findings from Sweden," *Journal of Marketing* 58:3 (July 1994): 53-66.

7. Patrick DeGraba and Andrew Postlewaite, "Exclusivity Clauses and Best Price Policies in Input Markets," *Journal of Economics & Management Strategy* 1:3 (Fall 1992): 423–54.

8. Ibid.

9. Some of the information in the following paragraphs comes from Paula Champa, "How to Sell in Japan," *Selling* 1:5 (December 1993): 39–47.

10. Mark Schilling, "Kigyo Senshi: The Corporate Warrior," *Mangajin* 18 (June 1992): 6–9.

11. Champa, 46.

12. Champa, 42, 44.

13. Walt Shill, "Lessons of the Japanese Mavericks," *The Wall Street Journal,* November 1, 1993, A18.

14. Frederik Schodt, "Fujiko Fujio (A) creator of *The Laughing Salesman,*" Part 1, *Mangajin* 36 (June 1994): 28–32, 78. Part 2, *Mangajin* 37 (August 1994): 28–32, 56.

15. David Brant, "The Role of the Salesforce in Strategic Marketing," *ESOMAR* (October 1978):159–69.

16. *Profiles in Customer Loyalty*, (Stamford, CT: Learning International, 1989), 4.

17. Ibid.

18. *Achieving Customer Loyalty in Europe*, (Stamford, CT: Learning International, 1992), 4.

19. *Customer Satisfaction in Japan*, (Stamford, CT: Fuji Xerox Learning Institute and Learning International, 1992), 1.

20. Thomas Forbes, "How to Get Up to Speed on the Selling Superhighway," *Selling* 1:9 (May 1994): 47–53.

21. "Taking a Laptop on a Call," *Business Week,* October 25, 1993, 124.

22. Jack Falvey, "The Hottest Thing in Sales Since the Electric Fork," *The Wall Street Journal,* January 10, 1994, A12. Falvey is quoting George Gilder.

23. "Microsoft in Japan," *Mangajin* 23 (February 1993): 22–23, 26.

24.   Douglas Horn, "No More Excuses! It's Time to Teach Your Computer Japanese,"
      Mangajin 29 (September 1993): 12, 85.

25.   Douglas Horn, " Computer Q&A," *Mangajin* 31 (November 1993):
      20-21, 75

26.   Champa, 44-45.

27.   Brett Pawlowski, "CompuServe and Japan," *Mangajin* 18 (June 1992): 21.

28.   Bob Johnstone, "Wiring Japan," *Wired* 2:2 (February 1994): 38, 40, 42.

29.   Ibid.

30.   Ibid.

31.   Bob Johnstone, "Turf Wars," *Wired* 2:6 (June 1994): 64-66, 68-69.

32.   Lawrence A. Crosby, Kenneth R. Evans, and Deborah Cowles, "Relationship
      Quality in Services Selling: An Interpersonal Influence Perspective," *Journal of
      Marketing* 54:3 (July 1990): 69.

33.   Martin T. Topol and Elaine Sherman, "Trends and Challenges of Expanding
      Internationally via Direct Marketing," *Journal of Direct Marketing* 8:1 (Winter
      1994): 32-43.

34.   Lisa D. Spiller and Alexandra J. Campbell, "The Use of International Direct
      Marketing by Small Businesses in Canada, Mexico, and the United States," *Journal
      of Direct Marketing* 8:1 (Winter 1994): 7-16.

Chapter Format

Introduction

Marketing Questions

Environmental Scan: Value Added per Employee

Initial Analysis of Marketing Opportunities

Clues to Capturing Customers

The Firm-Specific Assignment

Competitive Scan: Activity Response Forecasting

Estimates of Market Potential

Similar Market Segments Worldwide

National Marketing Decisions

Marketing Scan: Value-Focused Thinking

Strategies for Increasing Marketing Effectiveness

Marketing Implementation

Conclusions

Cases: Ford, Nissan, BMW-Rover, Honda, Mercedes, Fiat, Toyota

Learning Objectives

After reading this chapter, you should be able to:

- Discuss the importance of making changes on a grand scale to increase marketing opportunities

- Outline a value marketing strategy as the basis for carrying out relationship marketing between two merging firms

- Explain the value marketing decisions needed to portray individual firms as car makers to watch in world auto markets.

Value Marketing

chapter 14

Introduction

Marketers manage final demand by understanding that value marketing strategies depend on making changes on a grand scale. Marketers must contend with relationship public policy, relationship production, relationship selling, and relationship marketing. Here are the frames for studying local, national, and global marketing.

Scanning Global Markets

Environmental scan: value added per employee. Value marketing conveys attitudes toward relationship public policy, relationship production, relationship selling, and relationship marketing. Most of these results come about by management making changes on a grand scale, dismantling hierarchy, adding value per employee, and committing their firms to customer orientation. Successful marketers learn how to promote global answers to the question: What do I get?

Competitive scan: activity response forecasting. Shifts in the competitive climate (e.g., long-term recessions and significant changes in exchange rates) create demand uncertainty. Traditional quick-response programs, such as just-in-time, don't give solutions in matching unpredictable demand with preprogrammed supply. Firms must think on a grand scale, use both historical data and expert judgment to forecast future sales revenues and other marketing activity, and learn how to manage risk better. What do I get? Develop a value marketing strategy; pay attention to relationship public policy, production, selling, and marketing; and forecast cross-border success among firms with different nationalities. Successful marketers learn how to make better value marketing decisions.

Marketing scan: value-focused thinking. Marketers keep on the lookout for decision opportunities to create a value marketing strategy. They ask three questions: What is the context of the decision? What is the object of the decision? What is the direction of preference or impact of the decision? Marketing executives must combine strategy and means objectives to produce potential decision opportunities. For the world auto industry these are divided into forecasts for mature industrial markets (such as Japan, the United States, and Europe) and for emerging markets (such as Mexico, Brazil, Poland, Turkey, and China). To get going on all these markets is the order of the day for firms that want to become the world's largest, most important car makers.

Traditional Contexts for Global Marketing

Exhibit 14–1 lists the traditional contexts for global marketing in the case of value marketing. We study relationship public policy, value-focused thinking, and marketing strategy. The first reinforces our observation about the changes occurring in how governments seek to bring about competitive behavior among sales and marketing persons. The second reminds us that an effective business team must think broadly, grandly, and with vision. The third prepares us for the hard task of implementing a marketing strategy with continuous future payoffs as we move down the learning curve.

Nontraditional Contexts for Global Marketing

Exhibit 14–2 names the nontraditional contexts for global marketing as these pertain to value marketing. We survey local incentive packages and multi-markets, pre- and post-entry decisions, perceptions, and information about personal selling and franchising. We learn that asking the question "What do I get?" helps us make better marketing investments.

Exhibit 14–1.
Traditional Contexts for Global Marketing

Market Risk
Relationship public policy

Decisions to gain international market share

Demand uncertainty in international markets

Activity response forecasts

Foreign exchange rate forecasting (forex)

Reinvented business environment

National champions

Deregulation, privatization, liberalization

Firm-Specific 4ps Analysis
Decision making under uncertainty: value-focused thinking

Relationship production

Double or triple value added per employee

Make changes on a grand scale (or ambition)

Work on project management basis

Sum of new products developed to fulfill unmet market needs

Relationship selling

Promote worldwide with local campaigns

Sum of sales to customers where they see gains in values

Relationship marketing

Develop globalization strategy with worldwide connections

Answer the question: What can I do?

Sum of partnerships with customers, suppliers, and customers

Deal with overcapacity, declining sales, weakened finances

Remember who are weak and strong within industry

Relationship management

Review national assumptions about management

Find out status of managers and technical personnel

National Marketing Decisions
Marketing opportunities

Pay attention to changes in consumer interests

Place decision making in hands of customers

Compare performance against competitors' (benchmarking)

Design strategies to get down the learning curve first

Continued on next page

Exhibit 14–1. *Continued from previous page*

Marketing research

Determine whether firms have complementary operations

Look for parent firms with experience in handling takeovers

Ask about dispersal of highly skilled activities

Measure how well the parent firm is handling the acquisition

Marketing strategy

Achieve scale economies in distribution, sourcing, and R&D

Cream off the best in acquisitions

Make deals reshaping a world industry

Think on a grand scale

Governing the market.[1] First, let's look at the political frame. Japan matters. It promotes change through public policy. Its bureaucrats seek to dominate the markets of consumer-friendly technologies. This is one of the main realities facing global marketing. Others discussed in this book are as follows:

- The global, largely American fast food, entertainment, sports, and business culture as the second-culture worldwide

- The emergence of multimarkets for computer-based wired and wireless telecommunications and multimedia services

- The promotion of price-driven cost strategies to answer the crucial six-sigma question: What do I get?

Among Japanese, there is little debate about the importance of public policy. Government ministries (such as MITI, P&T, and Finance) practice convoy protection (*gosō-sendanteki gyōsei*) as the objective of their administrative control over industries, firms, and consumers.

Positive bureaucratic appraisal extends to allowing discount retailing, negotiating export restraints among auto assemblers, setting standards for digital telephone service, and all other forms of industrial policy. Japan is a capitalist development state in competition for international market share with free-trade, capitalist regulatory nation-states, such as the United States, Canada, the United Kingdom, and many countries in Europe.

During the last 15 years, Japan became the world's premier manufacturing, financial, and commercial power. This nation-state emerged into the first rank of economic powers. Japan gained this strength with the help, direction, and control of its public bureaucrats. Japan's public policy is called governing the market, a prototype of nationalist economics for most countries in East Asia.

Most western executives made initial investment and ongoing marketing decisions in Japan and East Asia with little understanding of the role played by bureaucrats in forming public policy. The westerners did not spend the years required to build relationships with key bureaucrats and industrial leaders: Their behavior was incorrect for Japan. Also, western business persons failed to develop a customer-oriented marketing strategy. They did not sell Japanese bureaucrats and managers on the merits of their products and services for Japanese customers. These westerners did not know that rational choices of gains and losses really had no meaning to Japanese bureaucrats whose world view is, indeed, different. Moreover, these successful "Fortune 500" executives (in the United States and the EU) simply forgot the art of creating value in the minds of their Japanese customers.

Exhibit 14–2.
Nontraditional Contexts for Global Marketing

Political Frame
Govern the market through reinvented business environment
  Dominate markets of consumer-friendly technologies
  Carry out positive bureaucratic appraisal
  Compare results between capitalist development nation-states
    and free-trade, capitalist regulatory nation-states

Technological Frame
Contingency perspective
Signaling game
Scale economies in costs of signaling

Cultural Frame
Eternal marketing ideas
  Knowledge and relationships
  Skills and customers
Products and markets

Continued on next page

Exhibit 14–2. *Continued from previous page*

Reinventing value
Coproducing value with customers
Reconfiguring how value is created in the future

Marketing Management Frame
Decision making under uncertainty
   Global marketing cultures
   Rational choice theory
   Public and industrial policies
Process
   Uncover hidden objectives
   Create alternatives
   Identify opportunities
   Guide strategic thinking
   Elaborate interconnecting decisions
   Guide information collection
   Facilitate involvement of stakeholders
   Improve communication
   Evaluate alternatives
Three key questions
   What is the context of the decision?
   What is the object of the decision?
   What is the impact of the decision?
Value-focused thinking
   Recognize and identify decision opportunities
   Create better alternatives for decision problems
   Develop an enduring set of guiding principles

Marketing decisions under uncertainty.[2] Second, let's study the technological frame. Marketing educators call the multiplying of faithful national economic, cultural, and political risk information a *signaling game*. (See chapters 3–6 for a comprehensive discussion of country risk.) Those who are the best scholars reject rational choice theory because it seeks to replace the concept of national "culture" with some form of core interests to which all nations, peoples, and cultures subscribe. Marketing educators do recognize the importance of the global, largely American culture, the trans-Pacific business culture, and the East Asian overseas Chinese culture. However, those who are the best researchers avoid overgeneralizing these "global marketing" cultures (i.e., their global brands, global advertising, global retailing, and global selling) as the world's single norm.

Marketing executives know that national institutions develop over long periods of time. Because nations are ancient, their institutions are infused with centuries of social and historical meaning. For example, the Ministry of International Trade and Industry, the Ministry of Posts and Telecommunications, the Ministry of Finance, and many government bureaucracies form the ideological history of Japan. Their internal life as social organizations is the path through which all economic, business, investment, and marketing decisions must pass.

Sometimes, institutions make mistakes in their competition with one another. For example, Japanese customers for Internet services are ready and waiting for public-access providers. Japanese customers have calculated their future benefits and determined what is in their best interests. They wait for MITI, P&T, and Finance to settle their turf wars and make changes in Japan's computer-based telecommunications policy.

Most western business executives don't know what is really going on within Japan's bureaucracy – that is, "coalition complexity, disputed preferences, incomplete information, transaction costs, contradictory motivations, economic limitations, the weight and drag of previous institutional arrangements, opposition parties, international factors, and social and cultural limitations."[3] This leads marketers to misunderstand what it takes to be successful within Japan, to compete against Japanese firms in North America and Europe, and to deal with Japanese economic power in the rest of Asia.

Hunting for consumers.[4] Third, let's examine the cultural frame. Some things seem eternal in global marketing: knowledge and relationships, skills and customers, and products and markets. All of them take place within an institutional framework set by the public policy of nation-states. For example, Japanese bureaucrats permit the Tokyo Electric Power Co. to lay fiber-optic cable to compete with NTT and other telecom service firms. This is an invasion from an unrelated sector, the power industry, that changes the commanding positions within the bureaucracy and the competitive rules for Japanese firms. The power company is reinventing value, coproducing value with its customers, and reconfiguring the way in which value is created in the future. This is innovation within the social life of Japanese government ministries, and such change works best when it meshes skills with customers.

Segmentation, positioning, and tailoring decisions. Finally, let's look closely at the marketing management frame. Under public policy regimes of both capitalist development and free-trade, regulatory capitalist nation-states, marketers create value for customers. Marketing educators deal with these questions in terms of multidimensional signaling. Here are several signals:[5]

1.   Relationship public policy is the sum of decisions made to gain international market share by bureaucrats in capitalist development and free-trade, regulatory capitalist nation-states.

2.   Relationship production is the sum of new products developed on an ongoing basis to fulfill unmet market needs.

3.   Relationship selling is the sum of sales made to customers where they see gains in values important to them (e.g., lower retail prices, public access networks for interactive connectivity, and a high-quality product line).

4.   Relationship marketing is the sum of alliances, partnerships, joint ventures, and wholly owned investments made with existing or new partners from traditional and nontraditional competitors, suppliers, and customers.

5.   Customer orientation is placing decision making directly in the hands of customers.

6.   Customer orientation is designing effective interactive strategy prospectively to get down the learning curve before domestic and foreign competitors.

Value marketing takes place within a set of institutions created by nation-states to serve their own nationalist economies, the competitive position of their firms, and the marketing needs of their consumers.

Organizing global marketing experience. The simultaneous existence of these four different contexts forces marketers to research value-focused thinking, to pursue value marketing decisions, and to carry out relationship marketing within local, national, and global markets. Let's do two things in this chapter. First, we will discuss how marketers make value marketing decisions under different regimes of public policy. Then we will apply this analysis to how marketing teams create effective marketing strategy.

Market Risk Questions

Marketers manage final demand by researching international markets; see Exhibit 14–3. The age of globalization requires marketers to be careful about overgeneralizations about "global marketing" cultures. Through positive bureaucratic appraisal, marketers and their suppliers and customers determine whether government will keep their commitments to long-term economic reforms, preserve the foreign exchange value of the currency, and practice the rule of law for business contracts. The environmental, competitive, and marketing scans provide information about the effect of value decisions on the total marketing effort.

Exhibit 14–3.
Market Risk Analysis: Value Marketing
The Environmental Scan

Traditional Frame Analysis for Global Marketing
Market Risk and Business Environment
Look for stability, predictability, and no harsh surprises
Sum of decisions to gain international market share
Firm-Specific 4Ps Analysis and Relationship Production
Double or triple value added per employee
Translate added value into additional revenue
Improve return on quality
Make changes on a grand scale (ambition)
Work on project management basis
Gain commitment from senior management
Sum of new products developed to fulfill unmet market needs
Firm-Specific 4Ps Analysis and Relationship Selling
Promote worldwide with local campaigns
Sum of sales made to customers where they see gains in values
Firm-Specific 4Ps Analysis and Relationship Marketing
Develop globalization strategy with worldwide connections
Answer the question: What can I do?

Continued on next page

Exhibit 14–3. *Continued from previous page*

Sum of partnerships with customers, suppliers, and customers
National Marketing Decisions and Marketing Opportunities
Pay attention to changes in consumer interests
Place decision-making in hands of customers
Compare performance against competitors (benchmarking)
Design strategies to get down the learning curve first

Nontraditional Frame Analysis for Global Marketing
Political Frame and Reinvented Business Environment
Consumer-friendly technologies
Positive bureaucratic appraisal
Capitalist development nation-state and free-trade, capitalist
regulatory nation-states
***Marketing Management Frame and Decision Making
Under Uncertainty***
Avoid overgeneralization about "global marketing" cultures
Reject rational choice theory
Govern the market by setting public and industrial policies

Copyright © Douglas F. Lamont. All rights reserved.

Defining the Offering

Value marketing is about configuring offerings that firms make to customers. Offerings are shaped by the following:

- The institutional framework of market transactions (Aka govern the market, public policy, or country risk) (see chapters 3-8)

- The 4Ps or product positioning, interactive channel management, the aggressive approach to promotion and advertising, and price-driven cost strategies (see chapters 9–12)

- Customer-oriented teamwork and relationship sales and marketing behavior (see chapters 8 and 13)

- Reconfiguring marketing strategies, shifting responsibilities for final products, and providing a wide selection of value-creation activities (see chapters 9 and 14)

Today, new entrants in the telecom services and multimedia industries are offering new technologies (i.e., wireless and radio communications, interactive connectivity, and digitalized information) while incumbent tele-phone and cable TV firms seek to change direction in the face of shifting val-ues by bureaucrats, suppliers, and customers. Newcomers have no commitment to old ways of defining the business, shaping the interface between firms and customers, and creating value in the marketplace.[6] These new competitors push for fundamental change in how business is done in the future. This reinvention of value is at the heart of effective relationship marketing.

Environmental Scan: Value Added Per Employee

Relationship production is the sum of new products developed on an ongo-ing basis to fulfill unmet market needs. Firms within alliances measure the success of stable relationships by the value added per employee. VAE "is sales minus costs of materials, supplies, and work done by outside contractors. Labor and administrative costs are not subtracted from sales to arrive at value added"[7] per employee. To become a master at staying on top of relationship production, put new hires in teams and encourage them to work with sup-pliers and customers (i.e., horizontal integration) on product development, logistics EDI, interactive advertising, segmented pricing, and customer-ori-ented selling. Choose suppliers based on their technology, quality, and after-market service. Compare results (AKA benchmarking) in terms of VAE, time to market, and customer satisfaction with the most successful firms around the world.

Answering the Six-Sigma Question

What do I get? Keep this in mind because buyers of parts and equipment are becoming more demanding in their purchase decisions. In automotive OEM sales, suppliers must earn Ford's Total Quality Excellence Award and similar quality awards from GM, Chrysler, Nissan, Toyota, and Honda.[8] Half of the auto suppliers who won these awards are the American subsidiaries of Japanese auto suppliers, such as Nippondenso Co., the world's largest auto-parts maker. Most of the rest are big American companies, such as Goodyear and the Universal Joint Division of Dana Corp. Then come the small firms, such as Anchor Abrasives (nut-inserted discs; see chapter 10), Perstorp Components (noise insulation sheets), Plumley (sealants, gaskets, and other rubber products), Manchester Stamping (door latches and other small metal stampings), Gates Power Drive Products (pulleys and brackets), and Automotive Industries (sun visors, door panels, and armrests). These firms earn quality awards because their senior management stays close to its customers and answers the six-sigma question: What do I get?

Translating Added Value into Additional Revenue

What do I get in terms of additional revenue? What is the financial impact of quality improvements? An increase in sales? More pretax revenues? Higher after-tax returns on capital invested? What is the return on assets (i.e., after-tax income divided by total assets)? At AT&T, new quality initiatives must yield at least a 30-percent drop in defects and a 10-percent return on investment before they are funded by the firm. This is how AT&T measures its return on quality (ROQ).[9]

ROQ works well as a quantitative measure when firms also decide to sell more high-quality products at cut-rate prices to existing customers. Together, these joint efforts build market share faster and more cheaply than efforts to compete for new customers. There's money to be made in customer loyalty, expectations, and customer satisfaction.

Dismantling Hierarchy

We make value marketing decisions to accomplish the following goals: increase value added per employee, raise the return on assets, and improve the return on quality. They are best attained through horizontal corporations (AKA as process-managed or team-managed firms) where we organize around process, let customers drive performance, reward teams for results, and maximize supplier contacts (see chapters 7–10 and 13). New product development, sales and fulfillment, and customer support: these three processes are key building blocks for tomorrow's corporations.

Unfortunately, these adjustments to vertical organizations, functional departments, and strategic business units don't always work out. Although most business firms are not as old as nations, both share an institutional bias against rapid change. Moreover, although American firms may favor revolutionary reform (AKA as reengineering), the European or Japanese business environment might prefer evolutionary or slower revisions in their moves toward flatter organizations. All seem to be going through *discontinuous change*[10] rather than the seamless variety suggested by management consultants.

The horizontal corporation is still so young that we have few hints of its second-order effects on relationship public policy, relationship production, relationship selling, and relationship marketing. Right now, we are thinking about how to do better in old businesses. Our task in making value marketing decisions is to think about tomorrow, then ask how to do better in new businesses, with new products, and with different customers.

Making Changes on a Grand Scale

Let's call this ambition.[11] We aspire to double or even triple the value added per employee; this means moving faster up the product-development life cycle, making massive improvements in on-time deliveries, halving after -market service calls, doubling ROQ, and so on. Even if we don't quite make our VAE goal, we will have significantly improved our value marketing effort with these value marketing changes.

For example, as Mexican firms learn to compete against American and Japanese firms that are investing in Mexico, they are slashing layers of management, becoming more responsive to customers, and improving productivity. "According to a McKinsey Global Institute study, productivity in Mexican telecommunications increased by 24.1 percent between 1985 and 1993, in steel mills by 42.3 percent over the same period, and in the food industry by 12.5 percent in the five years to 1992."[12] Even so, absolute productivity levels in banking, steel, and food are still between 30 to 40 percent of the levels in the United States, and more must done even more quickly so that Mexican firms can catch up to American firms. The former's unique family-owned business culture, which was based on closed borders and non-price competition, now must give way to a professionally managed corporate culture that prefers NAFTA's open borders, horizontal team management, price-driven cost competition, and customer-oriented sales behavior.

For example, foreign-owned firms in Mexico, such as Ford in Hermosillo (see chapter 3) and Nissan (with its US $1.2 billion plant in Aguascalientes), have productivity levels close to sister plants in the United States and Japan. Ford's improvements in Mexico have the complete support of senior management, while Nissan gives its Mexican workers clear aims and breaks down its projects into manageable parts.[13] Such project management pushes training, teamwork, product quality, less hierarchy, and more corporate communications about value added per Mexican employee. These are, indeed, changes on a grand scale, as shown in Exhibit 14–4.

Exhibit 14-4.
NAFTA Partners' Investments

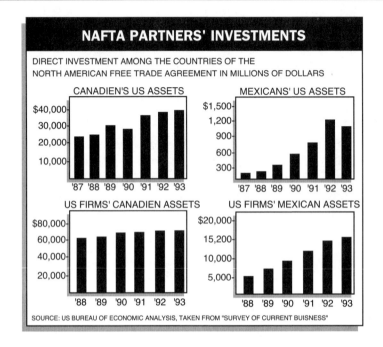

NAFTA PARTNERS' INVESTMENTS

DIRECT INVESTMENT AMONG THE COUNTRIES OF THE
NORTH AMERICAN FREE TRADE AGREEMENT IN MILLIONS OF DOLLARS

CANADIEN'S US ASSETS

$40,000
30,000
20,000
10,000

'87 '88 '89 '90 '91 '92 '93

MEXICANS' US ASSETS

$1,500
1,200
900
600
300

'87 '88 '89 '90 '91 '92 '93

US FIRMS' CANADIEN ASSETS

$80,000
60,000
40,000
20,000

'88 '89 '90 '91 '92 '93

US FIRMS' MEXICAN ASSETS

$20,000
15,200
10,000
5,000

'88 '89 '90 '91 '92 '93

SOURCE: US BUREAU OF ECONOMIC ANALYSIS, TAKEN FROM "SURVEY OF CURRENT BUISNESS"

Courtesy of Journal of Commerce

Initial Analysis of Marketing Opportunities

Senior management support, project management, and ambition: these are the attributes of value marketing at the Ford Motor Company. Ford's goal is to become a truly global company. According to Ford's senior economist, Martin Zimmerman, "nation-states are no longer the main markets. They are being replaced by regional trading areas, which means production and distribution within each area must be reorganized . . . on a more global basis."[14]

Relationship Public Policy

Since 1979, through Ford's 25-percent stake in Mazda, Ford made Mazda a player in the United States and Mexico, and Mazda made Ford a player in Japan. Both practice relationship public policy and help bureaucrats in Michigan (US), Sonora (Mexico), and Japan make decisions to gain international market share. Zimmerman defines relationship public policy as follows:[15]

> *Is there a commitment to long-lived economic reform, and therefore little chance that abrupt policy changes will wipe out an investment's strategic value? ... Ford wants stability.*

> *Is the regulatory system predictable? ... Ford doesn't like constant rule changes affecting foreign investment, exchange controls, or contract law.*

> *Does the country manage its own affairs with reasonable skill, maintaining the value of its currency and preserving political stability? Ford wants to avoid harsh surprises once big sums are committed.*

Relationship Production

During the late 1980s and early 1990s, Ford spent US $6 billion in the research and development, production, manufacturing, and assembly of its new world car, the Mondeo in Europe or the Contour in North America (including Mexico). The firm's senior management employed relationship production and logistics EDI to gain market share in the EU and within NAFTA. For this work, Ford obtained three new models, two new engines, two new gear boxes, and nine new or revamped factories.[16] Today, Ford can assembly 800,000 Mondeos or Contours per year on both sides of the North Atlantic.

Also in 1994, the firm merged its North American operations with Ford Europe into a single operating unit. The task is to cut costs of platform and engine development, reduce the time taken in model change-overs, and produce a wider variety of cars and trucks for diverse markets around the world.[17] Moreover, Ford uses its single operating unit to scour the world looking to buy more common parts from fewer suppliers at lower prices through logistics EDI (see chapter 10). Finally, all of this is done through teams of engineers and marketers whose chief assignment is to speed up new-vehicle development, carry over more parts from one model to another, and expand the use of computer simulations so that purchasing becomes customer-oriented, too.[18]

Now Ford is conceiving a new, 21st century Escort for *both* Ford and Mazda of Japan (in which Ford holds a 25-percent stake).[19] Ford plans to use its large-car expertise and Mazda prepares to contribute its experience with niche products, such as minivans or multipurpose vehicles. For Ford and Mazda, relationship production is the sum of the new products they develop on an ongoing basis to fulfill unmet market needs.

Relationship Selling

Relationship selling is the sum of sales made to customers where they see gains in values important to them (e.g., lower retail prices, public access networks for interactive connectivity, and a high-quality product line). In Europe, the Mondeo is a smash hit, achieving sales of 470,000 cars and leadership of the midsized segment. In the United States, $100 million is being spent on a major advertising campaign to introduce the Contour (and its sister, the Mercury Mystique).[20]

Relationship Marketing

Relationship marketing is the sum of alliances, partnerships, joint ventures, and wholly owned investments made with existing or new partners from traditional and nontraditional competitors, suppliers, and customers; see Exhibit 14–5. Ford plans to use the Mondeo/Contour project as its cash cow for expanding production and sales in East and South Asia.[21] By 1994, Ford had four car-parts joint ventures in China and one major investment in India, but GM and the Japanese auto firms also are seeking international market share in Asia. Sometime in the future, Ford will connect its 270 suppliers worldwide, merge its Asian and Latin American businesses into a single operating unit, and then pull in Mazda, too. This is an ambitious globalization strategy that depends completely on raising the value added per employee within Ford, among its worldwide suppliers, and within Mazda.

Clues to Capturing Customers

Senior management support, project management, and ambition: these are the attributes of value marketing at Nissan, too. It also practices relationship public policy. For example, Nissan built a US $1.2 billion state-of-the-art auto-assembly plant in Aguascalientes, Mexico. It got the cooperation of the state's governor to build a business-friendly environment (i.e., no strikes, telephone service, water and sewer connections, buses to transport workers, and close ties to the ruling party's political machine). There Nissan employs relationship production by bringing its Japanese suppliers, such as Nippondenso

Exhibit 14-5.
US Exports

SOLID EXPORTS

1993 TOP DESTINATIONS OF U.S. SECONDARY
WOOD PRODUCTS - MILLED AND FINISHED ITEMS
SUCH AS CABINETS, FURNITURE AND MUSICAL INSTRUMENTS

CANADA	$650
MEXICO	$164
JAPAN	$90
GERMANY	$81
U.K.	$42
SOUTH KOREA	$22
NETHERLANDS	$14
TAIWAN	$11
HONG KONG	$8
OTHER	$280

TOTAL: 1.36 BILLION

Courtesy of Journal of Commerce

and Taichi-S, to Aguascalientes, applies relationship selling through local distributors within Mexico, and implements relationship marketing with TMM, a Mexican ocean shipping line, to bring parts from Japan and export Sentras to other countries within Latin America.

Customer Orientation

Nissan is doing this in Mexico even when its sales in both the United States and Japan are being attacked by imports from the United States and Europe. Luxury cars (such as Cadillac Sevilles, BMWs, and Volvo Estates), US-made Honda Accord wagons and coupes, German-made GM Opels, and Fords (some of which are assembled at Mazda's plant in Japan) are selling more widely among Japanese consumers.[22]

These customers have a growing interest in different styles and want to buy value for money. Ford's left-hand-drive Mustang is sexy here; it offers air bags that cost much more in Japanese-made cars; and its Japan-delivered price is about US $7,000 less than domestic-built sports cars. The Mustang is "an American cultural icon at a discount price"; it directly attacks Nissan's Z cars and Toyota's Supra.[23] Ford is importing the right-hand drive Probe, Laser, and Mondeo models and selling its imports through Autorama dealerships, the retail chain it owns with Mazda. Through customer orientation Ford is placing decision making directly in the hands of Japanese customers.

Today, Japanese consumers perceive American cars to have the same quality as do Japanese cars. Also, the fuel consumption of American cars is comparable with that of Japanese cars. Moreover, the Japanese auto firms have been slow to respond to changes in market fashions, such as the demand for sports cars, station wagons, and Jeeps. Finally, distributors within Japan have been so hard hit by the recession that they are willing to sell imported cars just to stay in business. For example, even Tokyo Nissan Auto Sales now sells Fords.[24] Through customer orientation, American auto companies are designing effective interactive strategy to get down the learning curve before their Japanese competitors react with new vigor.

Answering the Question *What Do I Get?*

Of course, such aggressive relationship selling by Ford and other foreign auto companies couldn't have come at a worse time for Nissan and other Japanese auto companies. Recession in Japan, plus a higher yen (in terms of the US dollar), saw domestic demand for Nissan cars drop by 7 percent and domestic production drop by 12 percent.[25] Exports to Europe dropped by 30 percent, and exports to other overseas markets declined by a similar amount.

Restructuring, cost cutting, reducing the variety of models, pressuring suppliers to lower prices, selling unused land, and reengineering are not the answers for Nissan in Japan. Although US operations are profitable in dollar terms and Mexican operations are profitable in peso terms, both have a limited impact on Nissan's bottom line.[26] The United Kingdom has excess inventories, Spain is bleeding red ink, and Europe is a disaster for Nissan.

Perhaps Nissan needs to follow Ford's example (or carry out benchmarking). That is, Nissan may need to reorganize its Japan and US operations into a single operating unit and build a world car with a global, largely American style enhanced by Japanese quality. What do I get? Nissan needs to apply value marketing to its long-term turnaround efforts; this means more focus on customer orientation and on relationship selling and marketing. Nissan needs to make changes on a grand scale.

Summary: Scanning Value Added per Employee

Value marketing conveys attitudes toward relationship public policy, relationship production, relationship selling, and relationship marketing. Most of these results come about by management dismantling hierarchy, adding value per employee, making changes on a grand scale, and committing to customer orientation. Successful marketers learn how to promote global answers to the question: What do I get?

The Firm-Specific Assignment

Marketers manage final demand by positioning customer-oriented value marketing strategies within national and global markets; see Exhibit 14–6. Sometimes, the competitive climate shifts, especially when firms face a deep recession or a fundamental change in exchange rates.

Exhibit 14–6.
Firm-Specific Analysis: Value Marketing
The Competitive Scan

Traditional Frame Analysis and Global Marketing
Market Risk and Relationship Public Policy
Research demand uncertainty in international markets
Study global flows: activity response forecasts
Collect past data and expert judgment about demand and supply
Use care in exchange rate forecasting
Learn to manage risks
Recall long economic history of national champions
Recognize more recent pattern of privatization
Serve both local public and foreign private interests
Firm-Specific 4Ps Analysis for Relationship Production
Study licensing agreements
Examine location of higher value-added activities
Pay attention to headquarters effect

Continued on next page

Exhibit 14-6. *Continued from previous page*

> ### Firm-Specific 4Ps Analysis and Relationship Marketing
> Deal with overcapacity, declining sales, weakened finances
> Remember who are weak and strong within industry
> ### Firm-Specific 4Ps Analysis and Relationship Management
> Review national assumptions about management
> Find out status of managers and technical personnel
> ### National Marketing Decisions and Marketing Research
> Study national differences
> Determine whether firms have complementary operations
> Look for parent firms with experience in handling takeovers
> Ask about dispersal of highly skilled activities
> Review strategy behind merger
> Measure how well the parent firm is handling the acquisition
> ### National Marketing Decisions and Marketing Strategy
> Achieve scale economies in distribution, sourcing, and R&D
> Cream off the best in acquisitions
> Make deals reshaping a world industry
> Think on a grand scale

Facing Demand Uncertainty

In 1994, Japan found itself still in a deep recession. Consumers bought less. Firms cancelled overtime, reduced work, cut wages, transferred employees, and retired breadwinners. The length and depth of the recession surprised many Japanese companies. They had made a bad forecast about the economy and its future recovery.

Also in 1994, the Japanese yen rose in terms of the US dollar. Some firms were surprised. For example, Nissan "assumed an exchange rate of roughly 120 yen to the dollar. But the dollar is currently fetching . . . [less than 100] yen, which has undercut the value of Nissan's US earnings when repatriated to Japan."[27] The high yen made Nissan's exports too expensive in the United States. Thus, potential export profits dissolved into substantial real losses, all because Nissan had made an inaccurate yen-dollar forecast.

Moreover, Nissan was unable to cut its costs fast enough in Japan. The firm had too many plants, models, suppliers, and employees. Even though

Japanese consumers are buying American-made station wagons, coupes, and Jeeps, Nissan built up an inventory of unwanted cars and lost many potential sales. All of this adds substantially to Nissan's cost of doing business.

Typical Japanese-style techniques, such as just-in-time inventory (JIT), cannot resolve Nissan's problem. Such quick-response programs place in the computer a production schedule based on the original, inaccurate sales forecast. Suppliers' long lead times constrain Nissan's ability to make changes quickly in its production schedule. Thus, we must try to figure out what forecasters can and cannot predict well, offer marketers the opportunity to postpone decisions about their most unpredictable items, and wait for market signals to help us make better forecasts about demand uncertainty.

Competitive Scan: Activity Response Forecasting

Think on a grand scale about the future. Employ historical data and expert judgment, and divide products into two categories:[28]

1. Demand is predictable. Produce items with predictable demand in advance or at off-peak times. Match supply with known demand for items with long lifetimes and steady sales. Most cars sold in Japan are those with engines smaller than 2,000 cc. Nissan could keep a few of its factories running full time to make the most popular and least expensive Japanese cars. Nissan should never be out of these autos.

2. Demand is unpredictable. Reserve greater factory capacity for making items with unpredictable demand closer to the time when they will roll out for the selling season. Make smaller amounts to see how these goods fare. Use this information to determine which products to make more of during the initial selling period, and which to cut prices on to get rid of unwanted inventory. A few cars sold in Japan are sports cars, utility vehicles, and others with larger engines. Nissan could retool one of its assembly lines as demand grew among Japanese. Nissan would have to back-order some of these autos until supply caught up with demand.

Given that demand for most new items is unpredictable and new products are being introduced more quickly, firms need to pay attention to the variety of their offerings, their ability to supply these offerings on a timely basis, and the actual demand for items with predictable and unpredictable demand.

For example, auto companies have a hard time predicting which colors will be hot each year. Sometimes they overproduce some colors and underproduce others, generating an unwanted inventory of unsold cars. Nissan could ask its customers to choose their favorite colors, paint the cars, and deliver them weeks later to customers. These expert choices give Nissan historical data for use in future decisions about car paints. In short, market uncertainty becomes a manageable risk for Nissan.

Improving Exchange Rate Forecasting

Firms in industries with significant research and development intensity react to currency appreciation with increased R&D spending.[29] The firms manufacture instruments, electric and electronic equipment, chemicals, and transportation equipment, and they tend to invest more than 3 percent of sales revenue in R&D. These firms are known in the trade as high-tech.

Although Ford spent US $6 billion to bring the Mondeo/Contour model to European and North American markets, it did not invest these R&D funds based on the appreciation (or depreciation) of the German mark, the British pound sterling, or the US dollar. Changes in real exchange rates did not speed up or slow down the development of a world car or the initiation of a single operating unit for both Europe and North America.

Instead, Ford made these investments to improve its international competitiveness vis-à-vis General Motors, Chrysler, Nissan, Toyota, Honda, Fiat, Renault, and Volvo. Ford wanted to get down the learning curve before its competitors, and it wanted to do so on a grand scale. Thus, Ford committed its senior management to reengineering, benchmarking, and value marketing and forced its worldwide supplier network and its Japanese partner, Mazda, to join in the rush to become more competitive. In short, change in exchange rates was a manageable risk for Ford.

Implementing Value Marketing Thinking

Does Ford have such an overwhelming lead in R&D that it is difficult for Nissan and the others to catch up? No. The auto industry is not as high-tech as some other industries. Nissan could catch up.

Is the technological gap between the two firms too large? No. Nissan needs to work on implementing new technological developments as rapidly as possible. After all, Toyota and Honda also face the uncertainty of demand outlined by Ford, and they are making money.

Does Ford's import share of the Japanese market determine Nissan's behavior in Japan? No. Nissan and the other Japanese auto companies dominate over 90 percent of the domestic Japanese market. Ford, GM, and Chrysler sell cars in small niche markets.

Should Nissan react with more aggressive price cuts, increases in productivity, and quality improvements? Yes. Nissan needs to practice activity response forecasting, react quickly to demand uncertainty, and make definitive changes in its domestic and international competitiveness. Then Nissan must develop a long-term strategy for implementing value marketing within Japan and in export markets.

If these things are done, market uncertainty and changes in exchange rates become manageable risks for Nissan just as they are for Ford.

Estimates of Market Potential

Let's see how Germany's BMW played the game of value marketing on a grand scale when it grabbed Britain's Rover Group (MG, Rover, and Land Rover) from the clutches of its Japanese partner, Honda. Before the deal, BMW manufactured premium products in the upper niches of the auto market, where margins are fattest, gained scale economies with its output of about one million cars per year, and looked like a global player by competing successfully in the world's toughest auto market, the United States.[30] After the deal, Fiat, Renault, Peugeot, and Volkswagen – all Europe's national champions who are not global players, especially in the United States – wondered which of them would close its doors because BMW now has a 7-percent share of the European market, GM and Ford have very large subsidiaries in Europe, and Toyota and Nissan are ramping up large-scale production in the United Kingdom.

Value Marketing Strategy

BMW identified likely European targets that could extend its car range and achieve scale economies in distribution, component sourcing, and R&D.[31]

Then BMW surprised its rivals by "creaming-off" the best when it purchased the profitable Rover Group. Even more important, BMW outflanked its German arch rival, Mercedes-Benz, in the following ways:[32]

- BMW becomes one of the world's leading players in four-wheel-drive, all-terrain vehicles through Land Rover.

- BMW moves into small cars (that is, it goes down market with the Rover) without diluting its highly prized brand image.

- BMW gains access to a low-cost European production base and control of the European car maker that has learned most about Japanese production and engineering methods.

- BMW establishes a presence in some of the fastest-growing auto markets in East Asia and Latin America.

This strategy allows BMW to join a long list of German firms with major investments in the United Kingdom (e.g., Siemens, Hoechst, BASF, Bosch, Weidmuller, Mercedes-Benz, Wella, Linde, Continental, Bayer, and Schering).[33] BMW's takeover of Rover is on par with the reorganization of Ford into a single operating unit. These are deals that fundamentally reshaped the world automobile industry. They show ambition on a grand scale by the senior management of BMW and Ford.

Relationship Public Policy

The BMW deal ends British-owned volume car production, something that goes back to the 1880s and that gave rise to the economic literature on key industries as national champions. The mines, steel, autos, oil and natural gas, telephones, radio and TV broadcasting: all were national champions until the 1980s when privatization, deregulation, liberalization, and free trade came into sight as the only path toward successful market reform.

The BMW takeover of Rover ends the capacity of British bureaucrats to pursue a positive appraisal of UK public policy within the auto industry. "The car group has been financially abused on an amazing scale over the past 30 years: pushed by the British government into unworkable mergers, then nationalized, eventually denationalized into transitory British ownership when an American deal seemed too politically controversial, but finally sold to a German company for a quick turnaround profit."[34] Now it's up to BMW management and British bureaucrats to develop the habit of relationship public policy so both foreign private and local public interests are served by BMW's foreign direct investment in the United Kingdom.

Relationship Production

Takeovers and mergers in the auto industry are littered with failure, and BMW has no previous experience with mergers and acquisitions. Moreover, Honda retains a stranglehold over some of Rover's key models with tight licensing agreements that place strict limits on the use Rover makes of Honda's technology. Honda could insist that BMW-Rover reengineer everything and remove all Honda technology from Rover cars, or Honda could accept reality and see its technology pass to BMW.

In reality, most of the higher value-added activities of Honda and Toyota take place in Japan, of Ford and GM in the United States, and of BMW and Mercedes-Benz in Germany. "Nissan's European technical center is an exception, doing design and development work which is integrated closely with the company's UK and Spanish plants."[35] The net result is that the home country benefits from the "headquarters effect," that is, a high concentration of technical skills and senior management. Britain can anticipate that BMW will rationalize its R&D activity at home in Bavaria, Germany.

Relationship Marketing

While both Toyota and Nissan made wholly owned investments in the United Kingdom, Honda took the low-cost option and built its European strategy around collaboration with Rover. Honda's 20-percent share of Rover was the cement in its relationship with Rover. When BMW captured Rover Honda lost face in Japan; Honda then began to sever its equity link with BMW-Rover.[36]

Similar to Nissan, Honda has serious overcapacity in Japan with three years of declining sales and weakened finances. Also in the United States, Honda's best-selling model, the Accord, is no longer a best seller and sales are declining here, too. Moreover, in Europe, Honda is weaker than its Japanese rivals. The end of the special relationship between Honda and Rover could not have come at a worse time for Honda.

Similar Market Segments Worldwide

What does BMW get from its takeover of Rover? That's the six-sigma question. BMW acquires small-car capability, the Land Rover all-terrain vehicle, and markets in East Asia and Latin America. Those are the positive benefits.

However, there are some negative results, too. BMW gets a wide gulf in the nature of marketing management between German and British managers.[37] German managers consider their technical skills and their expert knowledge to be the most important part of their jobs. British managers see themselves as executives rather than technical personnel. There's the making of a long-term status problem. BMW's German managers must work with British technical shop workers who are not managers when Rover seeks to resolve technical problems. British managers also change jobs frequently, while German managers stay for decades in their same jobs and functional areas. The two countries provide different career systems and different ways of doing business.

On the other hand, Rover's British managers have been working with Japanese managers for more than five years. Rover's managers have picked up the Japanese penchant for the technical content of jobs and the higher position of technical specialists in the organizational structure. These views are closer to German managerial attitudes, and they should make for a smoother transition of Rover executives into BMW-Rover technical managers.

Forecasting Cross-Border Success

Although differences in nationality loom large in approaches to managerial practice, success in cross-border mergers depends on other factors as well.[38]

First, both firms must have complementary operations. This offers few opportunities for arguing over rationalization of capacity or where to cut and who should be let go. BMW produces high-priced quality cars in which brand image is all important. Rover manufactures smaller cars and the all-terrain Land Rover. BMW-Rover has complementary operations in Europe and clean slates in the United States, Latin America, and East Asia.

Second, the new parent firm has experience in handling takeovers and mergers and acquisitions. BMW has no experience in implementing cross-border mergers.

Third, the new parent firm is willing to disperse highly skilled activities and managerial decision making to its new foreign subsidiary. BMW will depend on Honda-trained Rover technical operations personnel, but it will be inclined to keep most of the higher value-added activities at home in Bavaria.

Lando Zappei, the Munich-based head of Booz-Allen Acquisition Services, says the keys to success in a cross-border acquisition are the strategy behind it and whether the merger is handled well. Zappei believes how well the merger is handled is most important. Philippe Haspeslagh, a Belgian-born acquisitions expert at Insead, the international business school outside Paris, puts a lot more stress on a firm's experience with mergers. If Zappei is correct, the BMW-Rover merger has a 50-50 chance of success; if Haspeslagh is right, the BMW-Rover acquisition might not work out at all.

The two firms start with different national approaches to mergers, technical support, and managerial effort. BMW also brings to the table a huge deficit in M&A experience. To improve the chances of success, BMW must work at organizational learning, deal with demand uncertainty, practice activity response forecasting, and improve the ability of BMW-Rover to manage market risks in Europe, North America, and elsewhere in the world.

Summary: Scanning for Activity Response Forecasting

Shifts in the competitive climate (e.g., long-term recessions and significant changes in exchange rates) create demand uncertainty. Traditional quick-response programs, such as just-in-time, don't give solutions in matching unpredictable demand with preprogrammed supply. Firms must think on a grand scale, use both historical data and expert judgment to forecast future sales revenues and other marketing activity, and learn how to manage risk better. What do I get? Develop a value marketing strategy; pay attention to relationship public policy, production, selling, and marketing; and forecast cross-border success among firms with different nationalities. Successful marketers learn how to make better value marketing decisions.

Marketing Decisions

Marketers manage final demand by signaling detailed national information about customer-oriented value marketing decisions – that is, unless we make inaccurate forecasts about the predictability of demand for or the supply of goods and services; see Exhibit 14-7. Here is the situation for European auto firms.

Exhibit 14-7.
Marketing Decisions: Value Marketing
The Marketing Scan

Traditional Frame Analysis for Global Marketing

Firm-Specific 4Ps Analysis and Decision Making Under Uncertainty
Signal national value-focused thinking
Grow through relationship marketing
Pay attention to the predictability of demand

National Marketing Decisions and Marketing Forecasts
Continuing trend is realistic because of value-focused thinking
Amplifying trend takes advantage of all decision opportunities
Doubling trend firms compete for international market share

Nontraditional Frame Analysis for Global Marketing

Marketing Management Frame and Marketing Strategy Process
Uncover hidden objectives
Create alternatives
Identify opportunities
Guide strategic thinking
Elaborate interconnecting decisions
Guide information collection
Facilitate involvement of stakeholders
Improve communication
Evaluate alternatives

Three Key Questions
What is the context of the decision?
What is the object of the decision?
What is the direction of preference or impact of the decision?

Value-Focused Thinking
Recognize and identify decision opportunities
Create better alternatives for decision problems
Develop an enduring set of guiding principles

In one stroke, BMW reduces its reliance on its home market in Germany, where labor and manufacturing costs are among the world's highest, and gets cheap labor to assemble small cars. Although German firms enjoy a reputation for high-quality industrial craftsmanship and engineering, they can't compete because of high German labor costs. Labor costs in Germany are double the equivalent costs in Britain, and they make it prohibitive to assemble small and luxury cars in Germany.[39]

Mercedes-Benz, BMW's domestic rival, follows a different course of action.[40] The product strategy of Mercedes-Benz is to take its luxury brand name into new sectors of the international automobile market, that is, into small cars and four-wheel drive sport/utility and multipurpose vehicles. The location strategy of Mercedes-Benz is to manufacture at low-cost centers outside Germany, such as the United States, Mexico, and southeast Asia. The jobs strategy of Mercedes-Benz is to shed a fifth of its workforce by 1995. These three decisions reflect management's attempt to restructure Mercedes-Benz in light of changes in the world's automobile industry.

Marketing Scan: Value-Focused Thinking

Even in the late 1980s Mercedes-Benz was looking for ways to make better value marketing decisions. It purchased Freightliner trucks in the United States and opened a Mexican operation now making 12,000 buses and trucks per year. Mercedes-Benz believes regional trading blocs, such as NAFTA, are the crucial opportunity for improving international competitiveness. The firm builds vans and gear boxes in Argentina and trucks in Brazil for sale throughout the southern cone countries of South America or the regional trading bloc called Mercosur (or Mercosul in Portuguese).

Elsewhere, Mercedes has 30 percent of the market for trucks in Europe, 0.1 percent in China, and about 1 percent in southeast Asia.[41] The firm practices "a think global and act local" manufacturing strategy. For example, buses produced in Beijing are built on a chassis made in Brazil, and those assembled in Shanghai use a Turkish model. About 50 percent of all parts are made within local domestic factories because Mercedes, unlike Ford, does not believe in the world car and the world truck. Management thinks the world car concept is myth.

Scanning for Value Marketing Decisions

Here are the decision opportunities open to the senior management at Ford, Nissan, BMW, Honda, Mercedes-Benz, and other auto firms as they set marketing strategy.

First, marketers think about values. Follow this process: uncover hidden objectives, create alternatives, identify opportunities, guide strategic thinking, elaborate interconnecting decisions, guide information collection, facilitate involvement of stakeholders, improve communication, and evaluate alternatives. Then ask the following three key questions:[42]

What is the context of a decision? For Ford, BMW, and Mercedes-Benz the context of their individual decisions is the restructuring of the auto industry worldwide. For Nissan and Honda the context of their individual decisions is Japan's long-term recession and the appreciation of the yen vis-à-vis the US dollar.

What is the object of the decision? Again, for the first three auto companies the object of their individual decisions is manufacturing capacity in North America and Europe. For Nissan the object of its individual decision is its financial losses in the United Kingdom and Spain. For Honda the object of its individual decision is finding another low-cost way to participate in the European auto market.

What is the direction of preference or impact of the decision? Finally, Ford wants to build a world car for both Europe and North America. It's leading the auto industry.

BMW needs small cars and utility vehicles in its product line for the North Atlantic area. It wants to avoid using its high-quality brand name on Rover cars.

Mercedes-Benz prefers cars and trucks with local content. It wants to use its high-quality brand name for its new, smaller cars.

Nissan needs cars that meet customer needs in Japan, the United States, and Europe because it must stop its slide in sales revenues or face substantial shrinkage in cash flow.

Honda wants to replicate its success in the United States in Europe, but without paying the huge investment costs required of a crucial player in Europe.

Decision opportunities. All these are the strategic objectives of the auto firms, which provide fundamental guidance for senior management, teams of middle managers, and everyone else in the organization. Then add means objectives – for example, BMW cuts prices in the United States to maintain market share against luxury imports from Japan. Finally, combine strategic and means objectives to produce potential decision opportunities. After deciding to go ahead with increasing manufacturing capacity in North America and cutting prices in the United States, BMW negotiates with the state of South Carolina to build a new plant in the United States.

Value-focused thinking. Such thinking helps in three ways: to recognize and identify decision opportunities, to create better alternatives for decision problems, and to develop an enduring set of guiding principles for the firm.[43]

Strategies for Increasing Marketing Effectiveness

Italy's Fiat, France's Renault, Germany's Volkswagen, and Japan's Nissan are the casualties of the 1993–94 slump in the European car market. Perhaps the European-owned auto firms need a new value marketing strategy.

Here is the Fiat story.[44] It is Italy's national champion. The firm received fat government subsidies for building new car assembly factories in southern Italy and for laying off workers elsewhere in Italy. Nevertheless, Fiat's share of the European market slipped from 15 to 11 percent. Even though Fiat is better sheltered from Japanese competition than the others because of strict Italian import controls, its share of its home market dropped from 53 to 45 percent. Fiat's numbers were not good.

Moreover, Fiat was too dependent one market, Italy; one man, its chairman, the 72-year-old Giovanni Agnelli; and on one small-car model (first the Uno and now the Punto). Both models were successful, but their margins are thin so Fiat cannot build up a strong cash position. Unfortunately, Fiat's larger, higher-margin cars, such as the sporty Alfa Romeo and Lancia, were designed only for the Italian market and now are out of date.

After many years of delay, in 1996 Fiat finally will introduce new models designed for the wider European market rather than simply the smaller, less competitive Italian market. However, Fiat will still have too many older plants scattered throughout Italy, and they will keep Fiat productivity below the European average for the rest of the 1990s.

Fiat has two factories in Poland, where it controls 50 percent of the market. Fiat has one factory in Brazil, where it controls 20 percent of the market. Its joint venture in Turkey controls one-half of the national market. Fiat exports about 15 percent of its Italian production to other countries in the EU and elsewhere in the world.

Enhancing Value Marketing

What's the context of Fiat's decisions? To stop the slide in sales and to turn itself around quickly, especially before the EU demands that Italy give up import controls and let Japanese models made in Britain into Italy.

What's the object of Fiat's decisions? To increase margins, cash flow, and profits, or find a joint venture partner or buyer that can do a better job with Fiat's Italian, Polish, and Brazilian assets.

What's the direction of preference or impact of Fiat's decision? To quickly move down the learning curve toward world competition before the other auto companies realize Fiat lost the race some 5 to 10 years before.

Time may be working against Fiat. It stuck with Italy as its national champion long after BMW and Mercedes-Benz moved to become European companies, and long after these firms, as well as Ford, GM, Nissan, Honda, and Toyota, moved to become world auto firms. Fiat missed several decision opportunities, especially the attempt by Ford in the 1980s to add Fiat to the its world network, similar to Ford's relationship with Mazda.

To increase marketing effectiveness, Fiat must recognize and identify decision opportunities, create better alternatives for solving decision problems, and develop an enduring set of guiding principles for the firm. Fiat must get on with the job of doing value-focused thinking as the first step in crafting a value marketing strategy. Only then might it pull out of its slump.

Marketing Implementation

Toyota is a good example of how to pull out a slump. In the late 1980s, Toyota cars, similar to other Japanese cars, were overengineered and too expensive. They did not meet the expectations of consumers. Toyota and its suppliers were forced to get back to basics so that they could weather the long recession and the appreciation of the yen without having to share new models as Nissan, Mazda, and Honda are doing to survive.[45] Unlike its domestic competitors, Toyota did not have to close one factory or lay off its workers. Instead, in 1994 Toyota started selling a sport-utility vehicle and spiffed-up versions of its small cars in Japan. Moreover, at its Georgetown, Kentucky plant, Toyota begin producing a luxury model for sale in the United States that is priced between the Camry and the Lexus. Now Toyota sells more cars in the United States than it imports from Japan, and all its models are scheduled for "ground-up" redesign during the mid-1990s.

Today, Toyota is leaner, meaner, richer, and tougher. Although its grand scale "Global 10" program of capturing one-tenth of the world auto market has been shelved, Toyota will sell at least 6 million cars by the year 2000. The firm keeps its costs down by seeking savings through relentless manufacturing-and-design frugality. It wants again to create "value for money" cars for its customers as it did in the early 1980s. Toyota also wants to be Japan's only full-line car manufacturer, matching demand with a diversity of supply. Finally, the firm wants to be the American car killer in Japan and the United States, and the German and American car killer in Europe.

Three forecasts. The "continuing trend" forecast is the easiest to make because things go on as before. Two world-class firms, Ford and Toyota, compete for international market share in Japan, the United States, and Europe. BMW rivals Mercedes-Benz in Europe, and the two of them are against Ford and Toyota in the United States. Nissan and Honda are in trouble in both Japan and Europe, but they are holding their own in the United States. Fiat, Renault, and Volkswagen survive in Europe, and Chrysler and GM survive in the United States, but their value-focused thinking does not extend to world-class competition across the board everywhere in the world. These value-focused judgments make the "continuing trend" forecast realistic.

The "amplifying trend" forecast assumes Nissan or Honda, or both of them, will pull out of their slump in Japan, and GM will rekindle its efforts to compete for international market share. We don't know whether these three auto firms will make a success of the decision opportunities presented to them, but we anticipate one or all of them will make an effort to compete for a position in the world car race.

The "doubling trend" forecast assumes that all the European firms will get in the race for world car status, too. This is unrealistic because they are tired national champions rather than aggressive competitors in the world auto industry. This one assumption should give marketers pause before they put together a marketing strategy based on unrealistic numbers. Value marketing is still an art, even when very large firms are involved in investments, exports and imports, and joint ventures.

Carmakers to Watch

Here are some surprises in the emerging markets of the developing countries.[46]

Mexico. By shifting low-volume production of larger models back to the United States, Ford freed capacity in its Mexican plants to turn out more low-priced compacts for the Mexican and US markets. Cars destined for the Mexican market come without many high-tech extras because these push prices up to the point that fewer than 15 percent of all Mexican consumers could afford these compact cars. Nevertheless, one of every five Ford cars sold in Mexico comes with air bags, and the Nissan Sentra made in Tennessee, US, and as the Tsuru in Aguascalientes, Mexico have the same technological specifications. All new cars sold in Mexico City must meet stringent antipollution guidelines, even the Opel Corse, renamed the Chevy, which is made in GM's plant in Zaragoza, Spain.

Brazil. When Fiat replaced its ancient lineup with up-to-date cars, its share soared from 12 to 24 percent.

> *Also Fiat of Brazil, already the Italian auto maker's largest subsidiary, is investing US $1 billion in expanding the plant here – four times the parent company's total investment planned at all other Fiat plants around the world ... With its rapid growth, Fiat has drawn 53 car-parts manufacturers to the [Minas Gerais] region. It now employs 18,000 people here, and a similar number work in nearby auto-parts factories. The company is in the process of raising the Minas Gerais-originated content of its cars, from 25 percent in 1989 to 60 percent in 1996."[47]*

GM is aggressively starting the same process, and its share is already 26 percent. Both produce engines for Brazil that run on gasohol and leaded gas.

GM's Brazilian unit designs and builds a small pickup truck for the Mideast, Asia, and Latin America. Moreover, the VW division of Autolatina, a Brazilian joint venture owned 51 percent by VW and 49 percent by Ford, is working with VW's Shanghai group to engineer and develop a new version of the VW Santana for China.

In 1993, Brazilian production rose to 1.39 million units.[48] Brazil overtook Italy and Mexico to became the tenth largest auto producer in the world. Thus, in the 1990s, car assemblers in Mexico and Brazil are battling for market share in Latin America.

Poland. Rapidly building on its early market entry, Fiat now uses one of its two local plants as the sole source of the Nuova Cinquecento city car for all of Europe.

Turkey. Toyota's new assembly plant, due to start production in 1995, leads a wave of Japanese and Korean car makers moving in this market. Until Turkey's free-trade and customs agreement with the European Union is put into effect, Turkish-made cars are for domestic consumption and for sale within Central Asia rather than for export to Europe. Fiat and some German firms are in a good position to become crucial players in the eastern European markets. Other foreign investors may become also-rans in the Commonwealth of Independent States, the former Soviet Union.

China. Through two separate joint ventures, Volkswagen is rapidly expanding local assembly capacity of the VW Santanas while building a nation wide service network. VW also produces engines for China that run on gasohol and leaded gas.

The rest of the world. Moreover, more Czechs buy new cars than Swedes do, and Brazil and Argentina outrank Spain. According to DRI/McGraw-Hill, by 1998 auto markets in South Korea, Taiwan, and Thailand combined will rival Britain and France. All of this suggests that the competitive map of the world auto industry is being redrawn and some players (e.g., Fiat and VW) might gain strength from their successes in Brazil and China. These emerging markets want tomorrow's new models. Get going on Mexico, Brazil, and Latin America. Get going on East Asia, and especially China. Get going on the Czech Republic, Hungary, and eastern Europe. Get going on Turkey and the Middle East. That's the order of the day for all world-class car makers.

Summary: Scanning for Value-Focused Thinking

Marketers are on the lookout for decision-opportunities to create a value marketing strategy. They ask three questions: What is the context of the decision? What is the object of the decision? What is the direction of preference or impact of the decision? Marketing executives must combine strategy and means objectives to produce potential decision opportunities. For the world auto industry these are divided into forecasts for mature industrial markets (such as Japan, the United States, and Europe) and for emerging markets (such as Mexico, Brazil, Poland, Turkey, and China). To get going on all these markets is the order of the day for firms that want to become the world's largest, most important car makers.

Inclusive Contexts for Global Marketing

Exhibit 14–8 sums up the inclusive contexts for global marketing as these pertain to value marketing. We examine competition between capitalist development nation states and free trade, regulatory nation-states. We also study two types of decision making under uncertainty: culturally based demand analysis and organizationally based industry analysis. These two focuses help us direct our research to answering important questions: How will our customers react to multidimensional signaling, and how will we shift the paradigm to value-focused marketing thinking? Again, we deal with technology as a driving force in managerial decision making under uncertainty. Our choices determine whether we will be a success at global marketing.

Exhibit 14–8.
Inclusive Contexts for Global Marketing

Market Risk
Relationship public policy
    Decisions to gain international market share
    Demand uncertainty in international markets
    Activity response forecasts
Foreign exchange rate forecasting (forex)
Reinvented business environment
    National champions
    Deregulation, privatization, liberalization
Continued on next page

Exhibit 14-8. *Continued from previous page*

Positive bureaucratic appraisal
Capitalist development nation-states
Free trade, capitalist regulatory nation-states
Political Frame

Firm-Specific 4Ps Analysis (A)
Culturally based decision making under uncertainty
Eternal marketing ideas
Knowledge and relationships
Skills and customers
Products and markets
Scale economies in costs of signaling
Cultural Frame

Firm-Specific 4Ps Analysis (B)
Organizationally based decision making under uncertainty
Shift the paradigm
Relationship production
Relationship selling
Relationship marketing
Relationship management
Process, three key questions, value-focused thinking
Game theory: two- and multiple-party games
Marketing Management Frame

National Marketing Decisions
Opportunities, research, strategy
Contingency perspective
Signaling game
Scale economies in costs of signaling
Reinventing value
Technological Frame

Conclusions

Value marketing decisions are crucial to gaining international market share. Competitors must be expert in practicing relationship public policy, relationship production, relationship selling, and relationship marketing. By answering the six-sigma question (What do I get?), marketers are ready to take advantage of crucial decision opportunities. These make some auto firms world-class competitors, and others the also-rans of the world auto industry.

Let's return to our initial three learning objectives:

1. Discuss the importance of making changes on a grand scale to increase marketing opportunities.

    You should have a clear understanding of why marketing executives pursue grand scale opportunities to make the transition from national firms to world-class, value-added competitors.

2. Outline a value marketing strategy as the basis for carrying out relationship marketing between two merging firms.

    You should be able to deal with demand uncertainty and learn how to manage risk.

3. Explain the value marketing decisions needed to portray individual firm as car makers to watch in world auto markets.

    You should be aware that successful marketers turn decision opportunities into higher sales revenues, increases in market share, improved cash flow, and additional profits.

Doing value-focused thinking is the work of global marketing executives.

Notes

1. David Williams, Japan: *Beyond the End of History* (London: Routledge, 1994).

2. Chalmers Johnson and E. B. Keehn, "A Disaster in the Making: Rational Choice and Asian Studies," *The National Interest* 36 (Summer 1994): 14–22.

3. Ibid., 17.

4. Richard Normann and Rafael Ramirez, "From Value Chain to Value Constellation: Designing Interactive Strategy," *Harvard Business Review* 71:4 (July–August 1993): 65–77.

5. "Strategy and the Art of Reinventing Value," Harvard Business Review 71:5 (September–October 1993): 39–51. Numbers 2 through 6 are adapted from the article.

6. See the comments of Kees van der Heijden in "Strategy and the Art of Reinventing Value," *Harvard Business Review* 71:5 (September–October 1993): 40, 42.

7. "Quality," *Business Week*, November 30, 1992, p. 66.

8. Ibid., 70–71

9. Ibid., 56

10. Thomas A. Stewart, "Welcome to the Revolution," *Fortune*, December 13, 1993, 72.

11. "State of Re-engineering Report 1994," (Cambridge, Massachusetts: CSC Index, 1994). Cited by "Re-engineering reviewed," *The Economist*, July 2, 1994, 66.

12. Damian Fraser, "Mexico's open door Lets in Winds of Change," *Financial Times*, July 12, 1994, 5.

13. 1994). Cited by "Re-engineering reviewed," *The Economist* July 2, 1994, 66.

14. Robert Keatley, "Ford Reorganizes to Stay Competitive and Reach New Markets in the World," *The Wall Street Journal*, July 22, 1994, A4A.

15. Ibid.

16. "The World Car: Enter the McFord," *The Economist*, July 23, 1994, 69.

17. James Bennet, "Ford Revamps with Eye on the Globe," *The New York Times*, April 22, 1994, C1–C2.

18. Neal Templin, "Ford's Trotman Gambles on Global Restructuring Plan," *The Wall Street Journal*, April 22, 1994, B3.

19. John Griffiths, "Ford Motor Chief Senses a Sea Change," *Financial Times*, April 11, 1994, 18.

20. "The World Car: Enter the McFord," 69.

21. Ibid.

22. Michiyo Nakamoto, "Japanese Buying More Foreign Cars," *Financial Times*, May 24, 1994, 6.

23. Valerie Reitman, "Mustang Leads Ford's Charge on Japan," *The Wall Street Journal*, June 9, 1994, B1, B8.

24. Michiyo Nakamoto, "Drive into the Rising Sun," *Financial Times*, June 17, 1994, 16.

25. Michiyo Nakamoto, "Dismal Year for Japan's Carmakers," *Financial Times*, June 1, 1994, 22.

26. Jathon Sapsford, "Nissan Finds the Road is Rough Despite Cost Cutting," *The Wall Street Journal*, April 7, 1994, 4.

27. Ibid.

28. Marshall L. Fisher, Janice H. Hammong, Walter R. Obermeyer, and Ananth Raman, "Making Supply Meet Demand in an Uncertain World," *Harvard Business Review* 72:3 (May-June 1994): 83-94.

29. Joachim Zietz and Bichaka Fayissa, "The Impact of Exchange Rate Changes on Investment in Research and Development," *The Quarterly Review of Economics and Finance* 34:2 (Summer 1994): 195-211.

30. "Then There Were Seven," *The Economist*, February 5, 1994, 19-20, 22.

31. Simon Davies, "BAe Flies Away from Rover with a Sack-Full of Cash," *Financial Times*, February 1, 1994, 19.

32. David Marsh, "Foothold in a Low-Cost Manufacturing Base," *Financial Times*, February 1, 1994, 21.

34. Barry Riley, "Why Rover Has Had to Lead a Dog's Life," *Financial Times*, February 2, 1994, 13.

35. Christopher Lorenz, "Nationality Should Still Count," *Financial Times*, February 11, 1994, 11.

36. Kevin Done, "Honda Climbs Out of the Front Seat," *Financial Times*, February 22, 1994, 19.

37. Christopher Lorenz, "Styles of Execution," *Financial Times*, February 23, 1994, 9.

38. Christopher Lorenz, "Nationality Still Matters," *Financial Times*, April 27, 1994, 9.

39. Richard W. Stevenson, BMW Will Buy Rover of Britain," *The New York Times*, February 1, 1994, C1, C4.

40. Kevin Done, David Waller, and Paul Betts, "German Giant Driven Off Course," *Financial Times*, September 20, 1993, 15.

41. Christopher Parkes, "Driven to 'Think Global and Act Local'", *Financial Times*, January 20, 1994, 3.

42. Ralph L. Keeney, "Creativity in Decision Making with Value-Focused Thinking," *Sloan Management Review* 35:4 (Summer 1994): 33–41.

43. Ibid. 41.

44. "Fiat's Long Road to the Altar," *The Economist*, January 29, 1994, 65–66.

45. "Toyota Retooled," *Business Week*, April 4, 1994, 54–55, 57.

46. "New Worlds to Conquer," *Business Week*, February 28, 1994, 50–52.

47. James Brooke, "Inland Region of Brazil Grows Like Few Others," *The New York Times*, August 11, 1994, C1–C2.

48. Thomas Kamm, "Pedal to the Metal: Brazil Swiftly Becomes Major Auto Producer As Trade Policy Shifts," *The Wall Street Journal*, April 20, 1994, A1.

Chapter Format

Introduction

Country Risk Questions

Environmental Scan: Continuing Trend Forecasts

Initial Analysis of Marketing Opportunities

Clues to Capturing Customers

The Firm-Specific Assignment

Competitive Scan: Amplifying Trend Forecasts

Estimates of Market Potential

Similar Market Segments Worldwide

National Marketing Decisions

Marketing Scan: Doubling Trend Forecasts

Strategies for Increasing Marketing Effectiveness

Marketing Implementation

Conclusions

Cases: Telecommunications, packaged brand-named foods

Learning Objectives

After reading this chapter, you should be able to:

- Discuss the liberalization, deregulation, and privatization contexts for telecommunications within the "hot" countries

- Outline the use of environmental, competitive, and marketing scans in selling "hot" products with global brand names

- Explain the importance of finding "hot" market segments among affluent young business executives throughout the world

Marketing Forecasts

chapter 15

Introduction

Marketers manage final demand by researching international markets (chapters 2–5), positioning global brands (chapters 6–9), and signaling detailed national information (chapters 10–13). Here are our forecasts for global marketing in the mid-1990s.

Scanning Global Markets

Environmental scan: continuing trend forecasts. The ability of Mexico, Chile, Brazil, Finland, Poland, the Czech Republic, Hungary, Korea, China, Thailand, Malaysia, Turkey, Palestine-Israel, South Africa, and Ghana to deliver an increasing number of telephone lines to middle-class customers is a test of whether these "tigers" and "tiger" cubs are "hot" countries. Notwithstanding the current state of liberalization, deregulation, and privatization in the Americas, Europe, Asia, the Middle East, and Africa, marketing executives foresee higher levels of imitation, rapid rates of product diffusion, and the positive impact of the demonstration effect. Successful global marketers learn how to sell all types of telecommunications services throughout the world.

Competitive scan: amplifying trend forecasts. The willingness of consumers in Mexico, Chile, Brazil, Finland, Poland, the Czech Republic, Hungary, Korea, China, India, Thailand, Malaysia, Turkey, Palestine-Israel, South Africa, and Ghana to purchase cordless telephones, wireless services, fast foods, consumer electronics, textiles and clothing, Christmas tree decorations, stone and tropical fruit, and many other brand-named goods depends on their disposable income. Local people earn their living through exports to the developed and "hot" countries, especially to those where the links are based on free trade. Several Latin American and central European countries, the overseas Chinese Confucian world of East Asia, the Indian Hindu world of South Asia, and South Africa have moved quickly down the road of integrating their economies with the global, largely American economy. Their westernized youth are buying into the global consumer culture, and some of them will convince their parents to accept the freedom culture, too.

Marketing scan: doubling trend forecasts. The willingness of foreign marketers to do business in Mexico, Chile, Brazil, Finland, Poland, the Czech Republic, Hungary, Korea, China, India, Thailand, Malaysia, Turkey, Palestine-Israel, South Africa, and Ghana depends on the opportunities offered by these nation-states. Some are "hot" countries. Local business executives become an important market segment for the purchases of wireless telephones, multimedia entertainment, automobiles, fast foods, breakfast cereals, and many other global, largely American products. Successful marketers learn how to sell all types of goods to all kinds of people in every possible market situation in the world.

Continuing Trend Forecasts

- Wired telephone capacity will grow where high levels of installed capacity already exist because older age-period cohort groups use their high levels of disposable income to continue purchasing traditional, landline telephones.

- Wireless telecommunications capacity will explode all over the world including those areas in which there are high levels of installed wired capacity because younger age-period cohort groups, including all the newest waves of business executives, will spend their more limited disposable income on universal, interactive, computer-based, multimedia telephones.

Amplifying Trend Forecasts

- Brand-named goods will grow sales everywhere as long as individual goods conform to local cultural traditions and government public policies because TV demonstrates the value of global brands over local goods to both youth and their parents.

- Fast foods, consumer electronics, wireless telephones, and many other "hot" global, largely American products will explode all over the world because vidkids, young adults, and new parents are shifting their allegiances from traditional, national, or ethnocentric lifestyles to modern, universal, or nonethnocentric lifestyles.

Doubling Trend Forecasts

- "Hot" countries (Mexico and China) provide three types of business opportunities: initial market entry, expansion of the national market, and global rationalization. These are the best places to anticipate a doubling of sales in the entry and growth phases of the product-development life cycle, especially when goods are targeted to youth and their parents.

- Medium-risk countries (Brazil and India) propose only two business opportunities: initial market entry and expansion of the national market. These are the best places to anticipate an amplification of sales to young, technologically sophisticated business executives, but not to expect the same burst of sales to older traditionalists who still control family wealth.

- High-risk countries (Vietnam and Ghana) dangle only one type of business opportunity in front of marketers: initial market entry. These are the best places to await a continuation of export sales to westernized young and old alike so long as they are middle class, have some disposable income, work with western firms, and are favorites of government.

Global marketing exists within traditional (Exhibit 15-1) and nontraditional (Exhibit 15-2) frames of reference. These provide the framework for collecting, sorting, and analyzing information about global markets. They help us make forecasts about the future of global industries, firms, and products. These frames are the essence of global marketing.

Exhibit 15–1.
Traditional Contexts for Global Marketing

Country Risk
Reinvent nation-states through economic reforms

Audits: nation-states

  Low-risk industrial and "hot" countries

  Medium- and high-risk countries

Audits: global and cultural lifestyles

  Global, largely American lifestyle

  Asian perspective toward consumption

  Humbling feedback from failures of secularism

  Clumsy vetting of age-period cohort groups

Audits: national market segments

  Compute the rough size of the middle class

  Determine how many have high levels of disposable income

  Calculate the real size of the market segments

  Break down segments into market niches

Firm-Specific 4Ps Analysis
Decision making under uncertainty

Audits: consumer income

  Demonstration effect

  Disposable personal income

Audits: brand-named products

  Wired interactive multimedia in industrial countries

  Wireless services in "hot" countries

  Global brand names in medium-risk countries

  Well-received export goods in high-risk countries

Audits: marketing's 4Ps

  Product positioning of packaged brand-named goods

  Local sourcing and channel management

  Integrated promotion and TV advertising

  Price-driven cost strategies

  Selling quality, after-market services, and relationships

Continued on next page

Exhibit 15–1. *Continued from previous page*

National Marketing Decisions

Signaling information

Audits: investment choices

Mexican acculturation

Asian conversions

New vistas from the Middle East and Africa

Slower product diffusion among ethnocentrists

Audits: marketing strategy

Time effect of product diffusion

Do local consumers encourage initial market entry?

Does government favor expansion of the national market?

Do foreign firms believe in global rationalization?

Sales to young, sophisticated business executives

Copyright © Douglas F. Lamont. All rights reserved.

Nontraditional Contexts for Global Marketing

Exhibit 15-2 names the nontraditional contexts for global marketing as these pertain to our marketing forecasts. These audits tell us about what to expect in the future. They are all drawn from our analysis in chapters 1–14. Let's close by reminding ourselves that we are looking for signals from the market about how we can improve our value-focused thinking.

Governing the market. First, let's look one last time at the political frame. The "hot" countries are reinventing their economic relationships with neighboring countries – for example, Mexico and Chile with the United States under NAFTA, Finland and the Czech Republic with Europe under the European Union, and China and southeast Asia with Japan under the East Asian Economic Consensus framework. Most "hot" countries are ending decades of state control over the domestic economy and are carrying out programs of liberalization, deregulation, and privatization to compete in the global economy. Moreover, some "hot" countries follow Japan as capitalist development nation-states, while others copy the United States or Europe as free-trade, capitalist regulatory nation-states. All "hot" countries want to minimize country risk so that economic growth, inflation, unemployment, capital formation, and foreign exchange reserves approximate those in the industrial countries. Never again do the "hot" countries want to slip back into being medium-risk or, even worse, high-risk countries.

Exhibit 15-2.
Nontraditional Contexts for Global Marketing

Political Frame

Govern the market through reinvented business environment

Audits of country, market, financial, and business risks

Technological Frame

Contingency perspective

Signaling game

  Product-development life cycle

  EDI logistics

  Interactive advertising

  Price-driven cost strategies

  Customer-oriented sales behavior

  Value-focused marketing

Cultural Frame

Recongfiguring how value is created in the future

  Global consumers

  Quality-product-price relationships

  Demonstration effect

Cultural attributes unknown to marketers

Marketing Management Frame

Value-focused thinking

  What is the context of the decision?

  What is the object of the decision?

  What is the impact of the decisions?

Differentiation of cultural attributes

Free-trade regional groups

Marketing decisions under uncertainty. Second, let's study the technological frame. Interactive computer-based multimedia wireless technology is simply outpacing the development of a 4Ps marketing strategy. This problem is crossing over into fast foods, discount retailing, packaged food marketing, automobiles, and many other industries. Hence, marketers struggle with speeding up the product-development life cycle and implementing EDI logistics, interactive advertising, price-driven cost strategies, customer-oriented sales force behavior, and value-focused thinking in the industrial, "hot," and medium-risk countries. Marketers call the dispensing of information about national economic, cultural, and political risk a *signaling game*. From these signals come choices about where, what, how, and with whom to invest in all markets of the world.

Hunting for consumers. Third, let's examine the cultural frame. Some global consumers (e.g., Mexicans who live American lifestyles, committed Europeans among younger age-period cohort groups, and accomplished North Atlantic, trans-Pacific, and East Asian overseas Chinese peoples) know about quality-product-price relationships from their previous purchase decisions in more mature American, European, and Japanese markets or from TV. This demonstration effect forces the prices of high-quality local products to fall over time.

A second culture exists worldwide. It's the global, largely American, fast-food, entertainment, sports, and business culture. Stir into that pot traditional Mexican and Latin American sensibilities, and add European and North Atlantic ideas about age-period cohort groups. Then fast-forward to Japanese convictions and overseas Chinese judgments about America's freedom lifestyle. Finally, mix in Indian Hindu cultural preferences, Muslim religious values, and African sensibilities, and we have the world as we know it today in the mid-1990s: "Think globally, but act locally."

Unfortunately, many marketers are guilty of clumsy vetting when they do cultural research, particularly on Japan, China, India, the Middle East, the Muslim countries, and sub-Saharan Africa. They fail to situate these countries and societies in their historical contexts – for example, partially closed, partially open societies, different rates of industrialization, and leads and lags in the study of American and European material success.

Segmentation, positioning, and tailoring decisions. Finally, let's look closely at the marketing management frame. Marketers have difficulty predicting consumer choices as tastes (or the unobservable attributes) become more heterogeneous among the industrial, "hot," medium-risk, and high-risk countries. Even though marketing executives offer global brands (i.e., standardized products), consumers everywhere impose differentiations of their own based on cultural attributes unknown to marketers. The demonstration effect convinces people to buy goods but does not show them how they might use them locally. All these decisions take place within a set of regional trading institutions created by nation-states to serve their own nationalist economies, the competitive position of their firms, and the marketing needs of their consumers. Hence, marketing needs to be both global and local.

Organizing global marketing experience. The simultaneous existence of these four different contexts forces marketers to research value-focused thinking, to pursue value marketing decisions, and to carry out relationship marketing within local, national, and global markets. Let's do two things in this chapter. First, we will discuss how marketers look at global-local marketing within "hot," medium, and high-risk countries. Then we will apply country, firm-specific, and national analysis to how marketing executives create effective marketing strategy for crucial global products.

Country Risk Questions

Marketers manage final demand by researching international markets; see Exhibit 15-3. For example, NAFTA and the EU offer executives a long-term planning horizon. These business persons learn how to deal with political risk in Mexico, the differences in national character between France and Germany, and the continuing cultural distance between Japan and the Chinese-speaking countries in East Asia. American, Japanese, and European executives compete for global market share by making choices about which countries are "hot" or places where economic growth will increase faster than the average worldwide.

Exhibit 15-3.
Country Risk Analysis
The Environmental Scan

Traditional Frame Analysis for Global Marketing
Country Risk and Marketing Audit
Reinvent nation-states through economic reforms
Compete for market share through investments in "hot" countries
Study trends in cross-border consumption within free-trade areas
Find similar market segments within "tigers" and "tiger" cubs
Low-Risk Industrial Countries
US, Canada, European Union, Japan, Singapore
Continued on next page

Exhibit 15-3. *Continued from previous page*

Low-Risk "Hot" Countries

Mexico joins NAFTA, Chile commits to free trade with the US
Finland and Poland join the EU and assist central Europe
Czech Republic and Hungary join the EU and aid the Balkans
Korea, Taiwan are "tigers"; Thailand, Malaysia are "tiger" cubs

Medium-Risk Countries

Brazil, Argentina, and others within Mercosur
Baltic countries under Finland's umbrella
Indonesia within ASEAN; China and India
Turkey outside the EU, Israel-Palestine-Jordan, Morocco
South Africa, Namibia, Botswana, Zimbabwe

High-Risk Countries

Andean Pact, Central American, Caribbean countries
Russia, Ukraine, other CIS countries
The Philippines, Burma, Vietnam, Indochina
Iran, Pakistan, and South Asian countries
Egypt and North African countries
East, West, and central African countries

Firm-Specific 4Ps Analysis and Marketing Opportunities

Pay attention to demonstration effect
Measure availability of disposable personal income

National Marketing Decisions and Continuing Trend Forecasts

Spread wired interactive multimedia in industrial countries
Grow competing wireless services in "hot" countries
Cultivate global brand names in medium-risk countries
Sow well-received export goods in high-risk countries

"Hot" Countries

Today, marketers see northern and central Mexico as direct competitors with South Korea, southern and coastal China, Thailand, and Malaysia. These are the five best investment opportunities for building world-scale telecommunications systems, auto-assembly plants, discount retail stores, fast food franchises, and many other key industries. Marketers call these five "hot" countries "tigers" or "tiger" cubs.

Moreover, American, Japanese, and European investors view Chile, Brazil, Finland, Poland, the Czech Republic, Turkey, Israel-Palestine-Jordan, India, and South Africa as "tiger" cubs. These countries are ramping up to compete for scarce capital, managerial talent, and value marketing services. As a result, American, Japanese, and European investors can choose among the industrial countries (Europe, the United States, and Japan), the five "hot" countries (Mexico, China, and East Asia), and the higher-risk "tiger" cubs (South America, central and eastern Europe, the Middle East, South Asia, and southern Africa) for their investments, exports and imports, and domestic sales. This is our mid-1990s country risk analysis.

Coping with Risk in Latin America

Mexico used to be Latin American in terms of language, culture, politics, and economics. Although Mexico still speaks Spanish, Mexico is merging its economy with that of the United States. As a consequence, Mexico is the "hot" country within the hemisphere, the one to watch to see whether free-market economics is indeed the wave of the future for Latin America.

Chile Far to the south, Chile studies the Mexican example and ponders its own economic future. Free trade with Mexico and the United States (or through NAFTA) guarantees unimpeded access to North America for Chilean food products. Today, journeys to Philadelphia take less than 15 days and to Rotterdam 22 days on fast refrigerator ships for peaches, nectarines, plums, apricots, and grapes.[1] Chile is now the southern hemisphere's dominant fruit exporter, followed by New Zealand (kiwi fruit), Argentina, South Africa, and Australia.

As a member of NAFTA, Chile would receive Japanese, Korean, and other Asian manufacturing investments, whose reason for being there is to export goods free of American tariffs to the United States These goods from Chile would compete directly for US market share with similar products from northern and central Mexico. A NAFTA relationship could make Chile a "hot" country, too.

The alternative is for Chile to be the fifth member of Mercosur, the common market of southern South America. This means finding markets for Chilean products across the Andes and redirecting trade away from North America toward South America. Transportation costs are higher and disposable personal income is lower in southern South America. Thus, a decision for a Mercosur relationship takes Chile off the list of "hot" countries.

Brazil and Mercosur Notwithstanding the world's view of what's hot and what's not, Brazilian business executives from the city-state of São Paulo (whose gross regional output is equal to the gross domestic product of Mexico) and from Brazil's three southern states of Paraná, Santa Catarina, and Rio Grande do Sul are investing heavily in the other Mercosur countries of Argentina, Paraguay, and Uruguay. These Brazilians are taking advantage of Mercosur's large internal market of about 200 million people and Mercosur's rules that give preference to local business investments over foreign. Brazilian executives are increasing inter-regional trade with the expectation that Brazil and Argentina will be each other's best trading partner, similar to the relationship of the United States and Canada.

Nevertheless, Brazil is not a "hot" country in the minds of global investors. Its central government lacks the ability to control price inflation, the money supply, and the value of the national currency; it is unable to privatize the state sector and deregulate the private sector. Brazil remains the single most important example within Latin America of how not to govern the market. Moreover, lessons learned in Mexico and Chile must still be applied within Brazil – but Brazil does not have the United States in its corner and a NAFTA relationship in its future.

Other Countries in the Americas The same can be said about other countries in Latin America. Venezuela, Colombia, Ecuador, Peru, and Bolivia are all members of the Andean Pact, an agreement to lower the barriers for trade and investment among the five countries and to set common rules for investment by firms from nonmember countries. Venezuela and Colombia have free-trade agreements with Mexico, and these three countries offer special deals for the countries of Central America (Guatemala, El Salvador, Honduras, Nicaragua, Costa Rica, and Panama). Moreover, the countries within the Caribbean have a limited preferential trading relationship with the United States called the Caribbean Basin Initiative (CBI).

Chile, Mercosur, Andean Pact, and CBI countries all seek free-trade access to the US market. Some believe the United States will extend NAFTA to include all countries within the western hemisphere. Most observers don't expect this to happen any time soon. Thus, most countries in Latin America have interesting possibilities for trade and investment, but only Mexico and perhaps Chile are truly "hot" countries for global marketers.

Managing Risk in Europe

Europe is a very large free-trade area. It is also a common market in goods, services, capital, and labor. Moreover, Europe is an emerging political entity in which the member nation-states pool their economic sovereignty for the common good.

When new members join, business executives study a country's economics to see whether it is destined to be the new "hot" country within Europe. Northern Italy played this role in the 1960s and early 1970s, and Spain earned this title in the 1980s.

What of the future? Upon accession, Finland might take on this role in the 1990s because it has special talents for helping the Baltic and Slavic countries of central Europe become more market oriented. Later on in the decade, the Czech Republic or Hungary might become a "hot" country as the European Union gropes for solutions to the economic problems faced by the Balkans.

Struggling with Risk in Asia

At the moment, Japan uses price-driven cost strategies to manufacture products within Asia to gain market share all over the world. Korea seeks to emulate Japan. Should the two Koreas be joined economically a new country of 70 million people would be a direct competitor of Japan in mainland China, southeast Asia, and North and South America. Also, should the Association of Southeast Asian Nations (ASEAN) become another NAFTA, Thailand, Malaysia, Singapore, Indonesia, The Philippines, Brunei, and Vietnam could meld themselves into a market of about 250 million people. Most of these East Asian countries are labeled "tigers" or "tiger" cubs by world investors. Finally, the South Asian countries, especially India, are struggling with how to govern the market with the successes of Japan and without the failures of Brazil. India wants to add value to its exports of mango juice, dates and figs, tomato paste, exotic fruits, ocean fish, and processed foods so that it can compete directly with Chile and other countries in the southern hemisphere.

Contending with Risk in the Middle East

Turkey, which straddles both Europe and Asia, wants to be a full member of the European Union. The country competes with Russia and Iran for influence in Central Asia. Turkey outside of the European Union is not a "hot" country, but Turkey inside the Union could be a "hot" country for trade and investment. It has a large internal market and strong links to other Turkish-speaking peoples throughout Central Asia and China.

Should the Israel-Palestine-Jordan-Syria peace initiatives continue, a new burst of economic activity will come to the Middle East region. Even though the trans-Jordanian region needs major investments in infrastructure, the Arab and Israeli populations consume at high levels, have overseas savings to draw on, and are more prosperous than other peoples in the region. Both Turkey and Palestine-Israel bring more to European trade and investment than do Ukraine, Rumania, Belarus, and even Russia.

Dealing with Risk in Sub-Saharan Africa

Once the United States copes with Mexico and Latin America, Europe manages recovery in eastern Europe and the Balkans, and Japan struggles with market reform in China and the new markets of southeast Asia, what amount of international capital and managerial talent are left for South Asia, the Middle East, Arab North Africa, and sub-Saharan Africa? Not a great deal. The really "hot" countries (Mexico, Korea, China, Malaysia, and Thailand) get the bulk of the world's resources. The rest are also-rans in the great game of global business.

South Africa Within sub-Saharan Africa, only the reformed South Africa merits very close attention. It has capital, a pool of managerial talent, and a black middle class. South Africa has accountants who know their trade, sophisticated banks, and a bureaucracy that collects the taxes and delivers the mail. Unfortunately, thanks to union successes, labor in South Africa costs twice as much as in Brazil or Mexico, and eight times as much as in China. However, productivity is low because black workers are products of an apartheid education system that deliberately schooled them for menial work.[2] According to Kyoji Yoshino, Japan's economics attache in Pretoria, "Many Japanese companies invest in Southeast Asia because labor cost is cheaper than South Africa, skills are higher, and sometimes the loyalty to the company is more excellent."[3]

Ghana Many global marketers are unwilling to invest in Africa for fear of losing everything to government incompetence, tribal warfare, and endemic poverty. In the World Bank's ranking of sub-Saharan African countries by their macroeconomic policies, only Ghana saw its growth rate, consumption, and goods available in the market rise modestly.[4] Exchange rates are realigned, triple-digit inflation is tamed (to roughly 20 percent a year), and hotel guests in Accra, the capital, chat on cordless telephones. Still Ghana has a 40 percent functional literacy rate, too low to be successful economically, and many urban areas are without power for days at a time.[5] In deals made with Ghanian residents of the United States and the United Kingdom, Ghana exports textiles, pineapples, and shrimp and imports software, textile looms, pesticides, and boats.[6] These trade deals start Ghana down the road toward moving from a high-risk to a medium-risk country.

Thus, country risk is the highest in sub-Saharan Africa (except South Africa), lower in the Middle East and South Asia, still lower in eastern Europe and Latin America, even lower in Mexico and the East Asian countries, and the lowest in North America, Europe, and Japan. Global investors do these risk analyses to grow sales, increase market share, and make money.

Environmental Scan: Continuing Trend Forecasts

Let's assume things will remain the same. For example, Europe, the United States, and Japan grow their economies between 2 and 3 percent annually. The people consume at high levels, save at lower levels, and demand more and better goods from global marketers. Theirs is a European, Euro-American, North American, Ameri-Asian, trans-Pacific, or overseas Chinese lifestyle.

Global business executives and younger age-period cohort groups in the developed countries, the "tigers," and the "tiger" cubs prefer similar goods in casual fashions, fast foods, entertainment, consumer electronics, and many other products. Thus the freedom lifestyle (i.e., McDonald's, Coca-Cola, Levi's or Pepes, and Disney) captures the same number of people in two key market segments: business persons and young adults.

Paying Attention to Cultural Signals

This cultural information forms the basis of the following continuing trend forecasts:

- Chile, Argentina, and southern Brazil share consumers who are recent immigrants to the Americas from southern and central Europe. All three find young adults choosing the freedom lifestyle. However, middle-aged parents in Chile and Argentina tend to be more conservative than those in Brazil.

- Central and eastern Europe, the Balkans, and Russia share a history of central planning, state control, and no markets. Business entrepreneurs are the first to choose the freedom lifestyle because they now have money to spend on nondurable and durable goods. Others might join them in the future.

- East Asia selects parts of the freedom lifestyle that fit into the traditions of Japan, China, and the overseas Chinese cultures of Southeast Asia. Both business executives and young adults are the most aggressive in consuming westernized products.

- The Middle East also selects parts of the freedom lifestyle that fit into the religious traditions of Islam. Male business executives are free to consume products from the freedom lifestyle, while women are more restricted in their purchases by custom, tradition, and religion. Both men and women reject Levi's and Pepes jeans, certain foods and drinks, and western advertising themes as being against the teachings of Islam.

- Southern Africa is blending European individuality with African group culture into an emerging Euro-African lifestyle. Its cross-cultural ingredients are unclear because the political changes are so recent. We don't know to what extent the freedom lifestyle will capture young adults and newly married parents.

- India is different. Although many Indians live in Europe and the United States, they have not had the same impact on India as the overseas Chinese have had on China. Again, the cross-cultural ingredients are unclear because the economic changes made by the Indian government are so new. We don't know whether the freedom lifestyle will be an acceptable alternative among young adults.

Initial Analysis of Marketing Opportunities

Successful marketers ask the following marketing questions: Who uses the product? How to increase market share? How to provide value? What customer signals show changes in local markets? With answers to these questions, marketing executives know rates of product diffusion for wired and wireless telephone services throughout the world. This helps them make their continuing trend forecasts.

Obtaining Information

The wired telephone conforms to traditional lifestyles in Europe, the United States, and Japan. All three have high levels of installed capacity, and additional wired telephones are installed as customers need more lines. Also, as population grows more lines are appended to the telecom networks.

Wireless Telecommunications Where installed wired capacity is low (e.g., Mexico, Brazil, China, southeast Asia, eastern Europe, and elsewhere in the world), the wired telephone does not conform to the changes we anticipate in the global, largely American lifestyle. Most affluent Mexicans, Brazilians, overseas Chinese, Thais, Poles, Czechs, and others prefer wireless telephones as the only real alternative to the lack of installed wired telephone capacity.

The widespread use of wireless telephones among affluent professionals who carry out their business in the five "hot" countries provides Americans with a demonstration of the utility of wireless communications. In this case, the global, largely American lifestyle for telecommunications services will be transformed by market events both inside and outside the United States. This impact of the demonstration effect on continuing trends in telecommunications is especially important in positioning wireless telephones for use by the younger, upper-income, business executives in North America and Europe.

Interactive Services Countries that are far from centers of economic power (e.g., Chile and Australia) tend to be major users of interactive telecommunications, such as Internet. Again, the demonstration effect alters our analysis of continuing trends in interactive services within the industrial countries of the world. Personal communications through Internet, interactive logistics EDI, and interactive promotion and advertising will slowly change the way we do business in Europe, the United States, and Japan.

Forecasting Continuing Trends

Continuing trend forecasts for wired telephones are realistic in the three industrial countries of the world, but they are unrealistic for wired telephones elsewhere in the world. Also continuing trend forecasts for wireless telephones and interactive services are not helpful to marketers because the global, largely American freedom lifestyle is beginning to shift from wired to wireless telecommunications. Even where there is widespread installed capacity, the costs of wireless telecommunications are coming down while more people become familiar with and are able to use wireless telephones. The demonstration effect of Mexicans and overseas Chinese, as well as users in the United States and Europe, will accelerate the acceptance of wireless telephones and interactive services throughout the industrial countries. Thus, we must disaggregate our continuing trend forecasts so that they are used only where they are applicable in today's global markets.

Clues to Capturing Customers

If they conduct their research well, marketers come up with acceptable continuing trend forecasts for wired telecommunications services within Europe, the United States, and Japan. If we do the same type of continuing trend analysis for wireless, cellular, multimedia, and interactive services in the industrial countries, the "tigers," and the "tiger" cubs, we will underestimate the potential market. Thus, continuing trend forecasts for wireless and interactive telecommunications are unrealistic in the United States and Mexico, Japan and Korea, and Germany and Poland.

Segmented Pricing

Given the appropriateness of continuing trend analyses for wired telecommunications and the inappropriateness of these analyses for wireless telecommunications, marketers must use segmented pricing to differentiate traditional from nontraditional services. Marketers also can charge higher price points for wireless, cellular, multimedia, and interactive services throughout the world. More importantly, prices can be substantially higher in the "tigers" and "tiger" cubs because wireless services are bought by the elite who have high levels of disposable income.

Sensing the Global Free-for-All

"Fax machines in Sri Lanka, cellular phones in the Brazilian rain forest, satellite dishes in Russia, videophones in Manhattan – they're all part of a telecommunications revolution that, with blinding speed, is changing the way the world works."[7]

The biggest potential prizes in the Americas are Mexico and Brazil – Latin America's two most populous countries with low penetration of phone lines. Wireless cellular competition is already in place, and long-distance competition begins in 1996 in Mexico. Neither is the case in Brazil.

Currently, 11 of the 12 wired and long-distance markets within the Europe are closed to competition. Only Britain is open to foreign competition, and it is the single European country that can meet the Europe's mandate for voice-line competition by 1998. Some of the future "hot" countries within Europe, such as Finland, are fully open to competition, while Poland, the Czech Republic, and Hungary are somewhat open to foreign investors.

The biggest potential prizes in Asia are China and India – the world's two most populous countries, with the lowest penetration of phone lines. China wants to add 80 million lines over 10 years, and India wants to add 40 million lines by the year 2000. China is beginning to open up to foreign competition, while India still remains closed to new investors. All of the "hot" countries within East Asia are more or less open to foreign competition, whereas the "tiger" cubs in the Middle East and southern Africa are still closed to competition.

Most of the world still awaits liberalization, deregulation, and privatization in the telecommunications industry. Yet year by year, all telecommunications services are being opened to competition. No one knows what the global telecommunications industry will look like five years from now. What we know is as follows: "With high-capacity cables, digital switches, and satellites, a multinational corporation – or a tiny garment factory – can conduct business anywhere, anytime, searching out customers and suppliers around the world."[8]

Summary: Scanning Continuing Trends

The ability of Mexico, Chile, Brazil, Finland, Poland, the Czech Republic, Hungary, Korea, China, Thailand, Malaysia, Turkey, Palestine-Israel, South Africa, and Ghana to deliver an increasing number of telephone lines to middle-class customers is a test of whether these "tigers" and "tiger" cubs are "hot" countries. Notwithstanding the current state of liberalization, deregulation, and privatization in the Americas, Europe, Asia, the Middle East, and Africa, marketing executives foresee higher levels of imitation, rapid rates of product diffusion, and the positive impact of the demonstration effect. Successful global marketers learn how to sell all types of telecommunications services throughout the world.

The Firm-Specific Assignment

Marketers manage final demand by positioning global products; see Exhibit 15-4. The demonstration effect offers executives product-development life cycles that lead in some countries and lag in other countries. No one product life cycle exists for all countries. Today, however, the global market is open to all nation-states who are as good at global business as are the industrial and "hot" countries.

Exhibit 15-4.
Firm-Specific Analysis
The Competitive Scan

Traditional Frame Analysis for Global Marketing
Country Risk and Marketing Audit
"Hot" Products and Life Cycle
Promote global, largely American lifestyle
Champion "old world" nuance to global middle-class lifestyle
Boost Asian perspective toward consumption
Cater to the idea of "I buy, therefore I am"
Cultural Context
Accept universality-of-freedom lifestyle
Pay attention to age-period cohort groups
Avoid humbling feedback from failures of secularism

Continued on next page

Exhibit 15-4. *Continued from previous page*

Try to avoid clumsy vetting of product information
Help Muslims participate in global business culture
Firm-Specific Analysis and Marketing's 4Ps
Product positioning of packaged brand-named goods
Local sourcing and channel management
Integrated promotion and TV advertising
Price-driven cost strategies
Selling through quality, after-market services, and relationships
National Marketing Decisions and Marketing Research
Coping with Mexican acculturation
Managing Asian conversions
Dealing with new vistas from the Middle East and Africa
Accepting slower product diffusion among ethnocentrists
National Marketing Decisions and Amplifying Trend Forecasts
Spread brand-named goods everywhere
Grow special niche goods to meet cultural and religious needs
Cultivate governments and work within public policies
Sow demonstration effect from TV in the value of global brands
Harvest fast foods, consumer electronics, wireless telephones
Plant "hot" products among vidkids, young adults, new parents
Graft nonethnocentric lifestyles on older cultures

"Hot" Products

Some products, similar to telecommunications services, do well everywhere. These usually go under the title global brands.

American examples include Ford, Levi's, Coca-Cola, McDonald's, Subway, Disney, and Microsoft. They promote the global, largely American lifestyle.

European illustrations of the Euro-American leisure lifestyle include BMW, Pepes, Benetton, St. Michaels, Nescafe, Souchard, Electrolux-Zanussi, Bayer, and Nokia. They champion an "old world" nuance to the global, middle-class lifestyle.

Japanese examples of the trans-Pacific freedom lifestyle include Accord, Walkman, Panasonic-National, Obligation, Eve's Seduction, Fuji film, and NEC. They boost an Asian, largely Japanese perspective toward consumption and global competition.

Coping with Mexican Acculturation

Today, global brands are being modified by the emergence of "hot" countries into competition with the industrial countries. Here are two Mexican examples:

■ As Americans buy more *salsa piquante* (or hot sauce) than ketchup as the condiment of choice, Mexican snack foods from Sabritas are finding their way into snack food chips from Frito Lay. (Both firms are owned by Pepsi Cola.)

■ GM produces a four-cylinder, gas-saver, subcompact car in Spain (called the Opel Corsa) that sells well in Mexico under the brand name Chevy, a name Mexicans instantly recognize because they are familiar with larger, four-door American-made cars called Chevrolet. In 1996, the Chevy will be produced in GM's plant in Ramos Arizpe, Mexico.[9]

The reverse is going on as well. Mexicans buy Bart Simpson piñatas rather than traditional burros, Domino's Pizza rather than tacos as snack food at the bull fights, and Gloria Trevi's Madonna-like pop songs rather than traditional mariachi music. Free trade with the United States means accepting the global, largely American lifestyle. According to Guadalupe Loaeza, the author of "Compro Luego Existo" ("I Buy, Therefore I Am"), within 10 years Mexicans will be asking themselves "Who are we?" Mexicans, Mexican-Americans, Americans?[10]

Managing Asian Conversions

In Japan, McDonald's sells Chinese *dim sum* food called McChao, locally owned firms (such as DomDom, MosBurger, Lotteria, Love, Bikkuri Donkey, and First Kitchen) fry burgers, and Suntory sells US submarine sandwiches. According to Fred Deluca, the founder and president of Subway, which has about 6,300 franchised outlets internationally, "the subs served in Tokyo are exactly the same as would be bought in a New York store."[11] Jotaro Fujii, president of Subway Japan, wants the submarine sandwich to displace the *obento*, a lacquered box with a pile of pickled vegetables, salted salmon, dried seaweed, and slice of bamboo shoot, with rice and fermented bean soup. Hamburgers, submarines, and other fast foods cater to changing Japanese tastes for fast-food, largely American lunches.

Korea Korean firms (such as Samsung, Gold Star, Daewoo, Kia, and others) make air conditioners, white-line appliances, consumer electronics, and many other goods in competition with Japanese products. These are additional brand names whose prices are lower because they come to market after the public accepts the new technology. This is one reason why Japanese firms tend to employ price-driven cost strategies to get down the learning curve as fast as possible before their products are copied by others in Asia.

Overseas Chinese Overseas Chinese firms from Taiwan, Hong Kong, Thailand, Malaysia, Indonesia, and Australia produce Christmas tree decorations, textiles and clothing, and other low-value products in Mexico, Guatemala, the Dominican Republic, and elsewhere within the CBI for sale in the United States under brand names long established and owned by American firms. The overseas Chinese firms are bound by close family connections rather than independent MBA-type management. In this, they are different from American, European, and Japanese multinational firms.

India and Overseas Indians From Bombay, India the family-owned firm of Shyam Ahuja sells flat woven rugs (or dhuries) under its own brand name through 80 up-market stores from New York to Tokyo, Hong Kong, London, Sydney, and Mexico City. The designs are based on themes and colors (e.g., bold reds) from American and Mexican Indians or the first nations of North America.[12]

Overseas Indian firms from the United States and Canada produce software in India, and textiles for clothing in Mexico and the Caribbean for sale in the United States under their own brand names and those owned by American firms. Overseas Indian firms are also tied closely to family relationships. Both overseas Chinese and overseas Indian firms are doing the same in Europe, and they are trying to enter the Japanese and other East Asian markets, too. These two types of family-based firms may be the prototypes for business firms from both "hot" and medium-risk countries.

Dealing with New Vistas

Down the road, competition will come from business executives from South Asia, central Europe, the Middle East, and southern Africa. They, too, want to grow sales, increase market share, and make money in the industrial, "hot," and middle-risk countries of the world with their IBM-compatible computers, rubber gloves, oil, and many other global products. Global brand names (such as Coca-Cola, BMW, and Walkman) sell in all countries throughout the world. In many cases, the cola drinks are bottled, the autos are distributed, and the sound systems are sold by local people – the overseas Chinese, overseas Indians, and others. They are partners with multinational firms in selling global products locally.

Competitive Scan: Amplifying Trend Forecasts

If we assume marketers will more aggressively market their "hot" products not only in the industrial countries, the "tigers," and the "tiger" cubs, but also in other nation-states, we prepare amplifying trend forecasts for the Muslim countries of North Africa, the Middle East and West Asia, Central Asia, South Asia, and Southeast Asia. These are more complicated forecasts.

Understanding Real Cultural Differences

Islam defines itself as popular and accessible, a religion. Islamic identity is raised up over the rejected ancient Greek philosophies and the modern global, largely American culture. These two rejections lead to significant consequences in the way Islamic societies consume such products as jeans.

Along with westerners, Muslims share the concept of individual responsibility for one's acts (of personal behavior, of consumption). In this both peoples differ profoundly from those who live in the overseas Chinese Confucian world of East Asia or the Indian Hindu world of South Asia.

Since most American, European, Japanese, overseas Chinese, overseas Indian, Mexican, Korean, and other global business executives are not Muslims, they have a knowledge vacuum about the 1.2 billion believers in Islam. All of them work and live within the world of "consumerism – junk food, clothes, leisure, rock music, television programs, pop heroes, media celebrities. It also has a sacred pilgrimage place. Disneyland is like the Vatican for the Catholics, [Mecca] for the Muslims, and Amristar for the Sikhs. . . [but] Disneyland can be replicated" for Latin Americans, the Japanese, Europeans, and all who accept the modern American consumer culture.[13]

Paying Attention to Cultural Signals

Let's look at just one cultural signal that many western marketers fail to notice when they do business in Muslim societies – who wears jeans.[14] Although jeans are part of the global, largely American culture, in Muslim countries they are worn only by westernized youth in westernized settings, such as discos, coffee bars, and shopping malls. Jeans have not caught on among most people in the Muslim countries worldwide.

Islam stresses modesty among both men and women, and people appear immodest wearing jeans. Islam also requires a sitting prayer position, and jeans are too tight to wear during prayer. Moreover, many Muslims (particularly in African and Asian countries) eat their heavy meal at lunch time, and baggy trousers and loose fitting robes require no change of clothes to rest in during the stupor of the midday heat. The problem for global marketers is to help Muslim consumers participate in the global business culture without losing their commitment to the Prophet, the Koran, and Islam.

Trendsetting in India

As marketers learn more about real cultural differences, these executives study both the global and national context of an industry. For example, packaged breakfast cereals are displacing traditional breakfasts in many parts of the world. Within India, Kellogg, the US cereal company, is trying to change the breakfast habits of 150 million middle-class consumers.[15] They eat hot local food with bread rather than packaged cereals. Although India is the world's fourth largest wheat-growing country, it has no tradition of consuming wheat-based cereals and pasta; both are essentially western products. Pizza Hut, another US firm, is introducing pizza to India's cities.[16]

TV is making everyone in India brand conscious. "If you don't stock what people see on television, you lose customers. It's a real nuisance," says Pooyransh Saini who owns an 8-by-6-foot store in the village of Kotputli in the northwestern state of Rajasthan.[17] Surf, Unilever's detergent, rather than the local brand, 555; Godrej refrigerators rather than the partner's name, GE; Kellogg cereals; Pizza Hut; Kentucky Fried Chicken; Coca-Cola; Colgate; Cadbury's; Nestle: all are examples of brand awareness, shopping attitudes, purchasing behavior, and trendsetting in today's India.

Global Brand Marketing

The Swiss firm, Nestle, is a global brand franchise machine that lives mostly on local brands. Nestle rejects "the one-world, one-brand school of marketing. The company prefers brands to be local . . . only technology goes global."[18] Nestle is the largest branded food company in Mexico, Brazil, Chile, and Thailand, and it's on the way to becoming the leader in Vietnam and China, too. Some of its brand names are as follows: Nescafe instant coffee, Carnation powdered milk, Perrier bottled water, Stouffer's microwave dinners, Findus frozen foods, Bear Brand condensed milk, KitKat candy, and Milo powdered chocolate drink.

Estimates of Market Potential

Today, a great deal of marketing research done on "hot" global products concerns the following questions:

1. Is the self-expression found in juniors the birth of a youth culture?

    Latin America. Yes in Mexico, Chile, Brazil, Venezuela. Perhaps in Ecuador, Argentina, Colombia. No in Peru, Central America, the Caribbean.

    Central Europe, the Balkans, and the Caucasus. Yes in Finland, Poland, the Czech Republic, Hungary. Perhaps in the Baltic countries. No in Russia, Belarus, Ukraine, Rumania, Bulgaria, Turkey, Georgia, Armenia, CIS countries in Central Asia.

    East, Southeast, and South Asia. Yes in Korea, Hong Kong, Taiwan, Thailand, The Philippines, Australia, New Zealand. Perhaps in Singapore, southern and coastal China. No in Indonesia, Vietnam, India.

    Muslim North Africa, Middle East, and West Asia. Yes in Israel. No in all other countries.

    Southern Africa. Perhaps in South Africa. No in all other countries.

2. Do the youth harmonize their individual, independent self-expression within the whole of local societies?

    Yes. Even in Mexico, which has moved the fastest into the orbit of the global, largely American cultural lifestyle, the youth still maintain traditional commitments to extended families, local cultural institutions, and consumption practices. These are even more true with the youth in East and South Asia, the Muslim world, and sub-Saharan Africa.

Although some things are changing within India, Turkey, and South Africa, many parts of the youth culture from Europe and the United States are not appropriate in marketing goods in these parts of the world. Here's what we do know. Product diffusion occurs slowly because most people tend to be ethnocentrists who favor traditional consumption habits. Marketers will find customer markets in China and India, the Middle East, and sub-Saharan Africa, but they will have to work at translating these potential preferences into actual sales.

Similar Market Segments Worldwide

Although sales will continue to grow in the traditional industrial markets, increased food consumption per capita is over and operating margins for the food multinationals (Nestle, Heinz, Kellogg, Hershey, and others) are down near single digits. None of them will go out of business, but they all must redouble their efforts to grow product sales in the "hot" and middle-risk countries. The amplifying trend forecasts assume more younger Mexicans, Chileans, Brazilians, Finns, Czechs, Koreans, Thais, Indians, and others will purchase packaged foods. This will happen.

However, the amplifying trend forecasts do not assume the adult working males, working women, parents, and older people in China and India will purchase these western goods. This could happen, as it has in Japan and Thailand, but centuries of tradition are ready to do battle against the global, largely American cultural preference for processed packaged food.

Summary: Scanning Amplifying Trends

The willingness of consumers in Mexico, Chile, Brazil, Finland, Poland, the Czech Republic, Hungary, Korea, China, India, Thailand, Malaysia, Turkey, Palestine-Israel, South Africa, and Ghana to purchase cordless telephones, wireless services, fast foods, consumer electronics, textiles and clothing, Christmas tree decorations, stone and tropical fruit, and many other brand-named goods depends on their disposable income. Local people earn their living through exports to the developed and "hot" countries, especially to those where the links are based on free trade. Several Latin American and central European countries, the overseas Chinese Confucian world of East Asia, the Indian Hindu world of South Asia, and South Africa have moved quickly down the road of integrating their economies with the global, largely American economy. Their westernized youth are buying into the global consumer culture, and some of them will convince their parents to accept the freedom culture, too.

National Marketing Decisions

Marketers manage final demand by signaling detailed national information; see Exhibit 15-5. Here's how they view the nation-states of the world.

Exhibit 15-5.
National Marketing Analysis
The Marketing Scan

Traditional Frame Analysis for Global Marketing
Country Risk and Marketing Audit
Compute the rough size of the middle class
Determine how many have high levels of disposable income
Calculate the real size of the market segments
Break down segments into market niches
Firm-Specific 4Ps Analysis and Decision Making Under Uncertainty
Signal national information about "hot" countries
Gain from export opportunities
Succeed from investment openings
Grow through global rationalization within national markets
National Marketing Decisions and Marketing Strategy
Pay attention to demonstration effect
Be sure incomes are high enough to support sales efforts
Know importance of time effect of product diffusion
National Marketing Decisions and Doubling Trend Forecasts
Compare business opportunities in "hot" countries
Do local consumers encourage initial market entry?
Does government favor expansion of the national market?
Do foreign firms believe in global rationalization?

Continued on next page

Exhibit 15-5. *Continued from previous page*

Anticipate sales to young, sophisticated business executives

Grow sales to older age-period cohort groups

Nontraditional Frame Analysis for Global Marketing

Marketing Management Frame and Value-Focused Thinking

What is the context of the decision?

Young adopt new ideas and technologies quickly

Older people who are traditionalists take longer to change

What is the Object of the Decision?

Imagine Mexico as America

Envision central Europe as the real Europe

Visualize China as Japan

Pretend Muslims interact well with freedom lifestyle

What is the Direction of Preference or Impact of the Decisions?

Invest in "hot" countries first

Sell "hot" product first

Cater to "hot" market segments

Identify potential decision opportunities

Develop an enduring set of guiding principles

"Hot" countries (Mexico, the Czech Republic, and China) offer marketing executives three types of business opportunities: initial market entry, expansion of the national market, and global rationalization. With lots of work and the help of neighbors, these countries will become prosperous players in regional free trade and the larger global economy. Their good fortune is for them to lose – that is, a return to bad government, poor economic policy, and closed borders. Nevertheless, it's a mistake not to take advantage of these low-risk countries when they are "hot" and ready to do business with the world.

On the other hand, medium-risk countries (Brazil, Turkey, India, and South Africa) propose only two business opportunities: initial market entry and expansion of the national market. Through exports by foreign trade experts, direct sales by importers, and local distribution through manufacturers' representatives, wholesalers, and retailers, these countries might become affluent customers in North-South and East-West trade. Once these nation-states open up their national markets to free trade, they, too, might become "hot" countries in the future. However, it's a mistake to plan exports and investments based on the expectation that some time in the future these medium-risk countries will become the newest "tigers" in the global economy.

Finally, the high-risk countries (Vietnam and Ghana) dangle only one type of business opportunity in front of marketers: initial market entry. Imports can be sold locally provided enough foreign exchange exists from exports. However, exports from these countries depend on local sources of supply, uninterrupted electrical power and truck transport, swift processing of customs documents, available wharf and cargo space at ports, shipping routes by liner conferences, and efficient payments by local and foreign banks. Since these nation-states tend to suffer under bad governments, miserable macroeconomic policy, and protectionist trade efforts, no chance exists within any planning period to turn these high-risk countries into "tiger" cubs.

Although the global economy is open to all nation-states, no new dawn is coming for high-risk countries, no transformation is starting for every medium-risk country, and not all "hot" countries will change into industrial nations. This is our mid-1990s country risk analysis.

"Hot" Market Segments

Some market segments are important to marketers throughout the world. These are the middle class (20 million in Mexico and 150 million in India). These are the people with high levels of disposable income (8 million in Mexico and 60 million in India). Moreover, these are the Mexicans who will buy Bart Simpson *piñatas* for their children's birthday parties, and the Indians who will try Kellogg cereals for breakfast. Finally, these are the local business elite who need cordless and wireless phones in Mexico City, São Paulo, Shanghai, Bangalore, Warsaw, Budapest, Cairo, Johannesburg, Accra, and elsewhere in the world. Add them up, and the market segment for wireless telecommunications services among countries is very large indeed. Here, too, are the potential customers for automobiles, consumer electronics, packaged foods, and all the brand-named goods offered in the world's markets by multinational firms.

Marketing Scan: Doubling Trend Forecast

Let's review our continuing and amplifying trend forecasts because they feed into our doubling trend forecasts.

Continuing Trend Forecasts

Wired telephone capacity will grow where high levels of installed capacity already exist. Wireless telecommunications capacity will explode all over the world, including those areas in which there are high levels of installed capacity. Since these products are for the affluent middle class with high levels of disposable income, their growth in sales mirrors what will happen with other world-class goods, such as automobiles, discount retail stores, fast foods, and breakfast cereals. As the technology becomes more widely available, younger age-period cohort groups will make purchases for their families, and older age-period cohort groups will join in the consumption of wireless telephones, multimedia, interactive services, and other demands of the information revolution. Leads and lags in product diffusion will show up among countries because of the demonstration effect, government policies toward information, and the import capacity of the national economy. The sale of goods that threaten governments and their view of social peace, such as palm-sized satellite receivers, will slow, but not go away altogether. Thus, our trends in global markets will continue.

Amplifying Trend Forecasts

Brand-named goods will grow sales everywhere, but individual goods must conform to local cultural, religious, and social traditions. Fast foods, consumer electronics, wireless telephones, and many other "hot" global products will explode all over the world. Since these products are for both the affluent middle class and those who will feel prosperous through the use of credit and debit cards, their growth in sales will outpace records achieved during previous periods of worldwide economic growth. Younger age-period cohort groups will try to be westernized consumers with a preference for jeans, hamburgers, music videos, sports fashions, and the freedom lifestyle. Older age-period cohort groups may resist because they are traditionalists, nationalists, and ethnocentrists, but they, too, will join in the freedom lifestyle or eventually be replaced by their children in the work force. How fast the older groups go over to the freedom lifestyle of the younger groups will vary from country to country, but all groups will be affected by TV's demonstration of what is possible in today's world. Thus, we can make amplifying trend forecasts.

Doubling Trend Forecasts

Here we assume that all age-period cohort groups convert to the global, largely American lifestyle. This is the most likely forecast, especially in northern and central Mexico. With NAFTA in place, product diffusion occurs more rapidly among nonethnocentrists and less rapidly among ethnocentrists; however, power distance, inequality of incomes, and the lack of disposable income retard product diffusion, especially in southern Mexico.

Within Europe, we assume older people will convert to the freedom lifestyle and the purchase of sports and leisure wear. This, too, is our most likely forecast. Remember the following: product diffusion occurs more rapidly in western Europe and more slowly in eastern Europe. Power distance, the inequality of incomes, and the lack of disposable income are problems throughout eastern Europe, Russia, and the CIS countries.

If we assume we can convert older Japanese to the freedom lifestyle, we are making a least likely forecast. Product diffusion occurs slowly in Japan and only when goods are vetted through many years of cultural adaptation by juniors, young adults, baby boomers, and older Japanese.

Again, if we assume we can convert older Chinese to the overseas Chinese lifestyle, we are making a least likely forecast. Product diffusion occurs slowly in China because power distance, inequality in incomes, and the lack of disposable income all exist in mainland China.

Nevertheless, buyers do exist among the young business elite throughout the world for the brand-named goods offered by multinational firms. The task for marketers is to find them and make the "close" on the sale.

Strategies for Increasing Marketing Effectiveness

Suppose older age-period cohort groups are willing to adopt new technology, change patterns of consumption, and give up past behavior. Perhaps they are willing to make these changes at the same rate as younger age-period cohort groups. This would have to be for something special – such as the transistor radio, TV, or wireless telephone.

Or imagine Mexico and Latin America as the United States, and central and eastern Europe as Europe. According to the proponents of cultural bilingualism, local national cultures are converging with the popular Euro-American culture. Then visualize China and Southeast Asia as Japan, whose national cultures react differently to attempts to transplant the emerging trans-Pacific culture. Finally, pretend Indian Hindus, Muslims, and Africans will find positive ways to interact with the global, largely American consumer culture. All of them will buy those special goods listed above because their utility has been shown to be high in the industrial and "hot" countries of the world.

Interpreting Demographic Information

If we can make these assumptions, then we are ready to go forward with our doubling trend forecasts. Within the industrial countries, installed telephone capacity will limit the rate of product diffusion of wireless service among older people. Within the "hot" countries, the lack of disposable income also will limit the rate of product diffusion of wireless services among older age-period cohort groups.

Using the Diffusion Model

However, if we define the older age-period cohort group as highly successful business executives, then we can anticipate interactive wireless telephone sales to double year after year for the indefinite future. This is the most likely forecast for the United Kingdom, Europe, the United States, and Japan, and among the overseas Chinese, Muslim, and African executives of the world. Product diffusion occurs rapidly because high-income business executives want these new interactive wireless services now – today, not tomorrow. Sales personnel must pay special attention to this market segment.

A group of business executives will want to get into postlinear interactive multimedia entertainment. If we further define our older age-period cohort group as highly successful young adult, married males, then they are our potential customers for interactive multimedia in the United States. Product diffusion occurs rapidly because high-income married males want these new interactive multimedia services for business and personal use. Sales personnel must pay special attention to this market niche.

In summary, the country effect (or national culture) has little influence on the rate of product diffusion for wireless, interactive, and multimedia computer-based telecommunications products. More important is the time effect (or the time between first innovation in the country of origin and wider distribution in other countries). The time effect is being shortened day by day by the demonstration effect of the worldwide information revolution.

Marketing Implementation

If done well, marketers come up with acceptable doubling trend forecasts for all important industries. For packaged brand-named cereals the country effect (i.e., national culture, traditional society, and religious conservatism) is more important than the time effect. For discount retailing both the country and time effect tend to be equally important. For automobiles the time effect is more important than the country effect. Given real cultural differences throughout the world, sales and marketing teams from different countries must join together to create new product offerings that expand the total global market, segment the market by important demographic information, and target new middle-class customers with high levels of disposable income. We must be careful before we put together a marketing strategy based on unrealistic numbers. Value marketing is still an art even when very large firms are involved in all markets of the world.

Summary: Scanning Doubling Trends

The willingness of foreign marketers to do business in Mexico, Chile, Brazil, Finland, Poland, the Czech Republic, Hungary, Korea, China, India, Thailand, Malaysia, Turkey, Palestine-Israel, South Africa, and Ghana depends on the opportunities offered by these nation-states. Some are "hot" countries. Local business executives become an important market segment for the purchases of wireless telephones, multimedia entertainment, automobiles, fast foods, breakfast cereals, and many other global, largely American products. Successful marketers learn how to sell all types of goods to all kinds of people in every possible market situation in the world.

Inclusive Contexts for Global Marketing

Exhibit 15–6 sums up the inclusive contexts for global marketing. We do our audits and make our forecasts from the information we collect through the traditional and nontraditional frames of reference. Again, we examine competition between capitalist development nation-states and free-trade, regulatory nation-states. We also study two types of decision making under uncertainty: culturally based demand analysis and organizationally based industry analysis. Our intention is to shift the paradigm to a new approach global marketing.

Exhibit 15–6.
Inclusive Contexts for Global Marketing

Country Risk
Reinvent nation-states through economic reforms
Audits: nation-states, lifestyles, segments, business risk
Political Frame:

Firm-Specific 4Ps Analysis (A)
Culturally based decision making under uncertainty
External marketing ideas
Recongfiguring how value is created in the future
   Global consumers
   Quality-product-price relationships
   Demonstration effect
Cultural attributes unknown to marketers
Scale economies in costs of signaling
Audits: consumer income, brand-named products, marketing's 4Ps
Cultural Frame

Firm-Specific 4Ps Analysis (B)
Organizationally based decision making under uncertainty
Shift the paradigm
   Relationship production
   Relationship selling
   Relationship marketing
   Relationship management
Process, three key questions, value-focused thinking
Continued on next page

Exhibit 15–6. *Continued from previous page*

Value-focused thinking
  What is context of decision?
  What is the object of the decision?
  What is the impact of the decisions?
Differentiation of cultural attributes
Game theory: two- and multiple-party games
Audits: teamwork, learning organization, relationship marketing
Marketing Management Frame

National Marketing Decisions
Contingency perspective
Signaling game
  Product-development life cycle
  EDI logistics
  Interactive advertising
  Price-driven cost strategies
  Customer-oriented sales behavior
  Value-focused marketing
  Audits: technologies, investment choices, marketing strategy
Technological Frame

Conclusions

Global marketing thrives under the following banner: "Think globally, act locally." The primary contexts of global marketing include country risk, firm-specific analysis, and national marketing strategies. With good hard and soft information about "hot" countries, "hot" products, and "hot" market segments we can make continuing, amplifying, and doubling forecasts about future sales in national markets.

Let's return to our initial three learning objectives:

1.   Discuss the liberalization, deregulation, and privatization contexts for telecommunications within the "hot" countries.

You should have a clear understanding of why the information revolution sweeping through the computer-based telecommunications industry is a paradigm for all other industries worldwide. It affects their risk analysis, product planning, logistics EDI, interactive promotion, price-driven cost strategies, sales force behavior, and value marketing decisions in ways not well understood today

2.   Outline the use of the environmental, competitive, and marketing scans in selling "hot" products with global brand names.

You should be able to scan the "hot," medium-risk, and high-risk countries, compare their business opportunities, and make value-based marketing decisions. You should be able to apply these environmental, competitive, and marketing scans to the telecommunications, packaged foods, discount retailing, and automobile industries.

3.   Explain the importance of finding "hot" market segments among affluent young business executives throughout the world.

You should be aware that disposable personal income and the demonstration effect from TV affects the leads and lags in global sales. You should be able to use continuing, amplifying, and doubling marketing forecasts to enhance sales in the most appropriate market segments and niches of the world.

Making global marketing a triumph is the work of global marketing executives.

Notes

1.   David Dodwell, "Exports Add Savour to Chile's Fruit Cocktail," *Financial Times*, November 18, 1992, 30.

2.   Bill Keller, "The Revolution Won, Workers Are Still Unhappy," *The New York Times*, July 23, 1994, 2.

3. Bill Keller, "In Mandela's South Africa, Foreign Investors Are Few," *The New York Times*, August 3, 1994, C2.

4. Thomas L. Friedman, "Africa's Economies: Reforms Pay Off," *The New York Times*, March 13, 1994, 4.

5. Tim Carrington, "Ray of Hope: Amid Africa's Agony, One Nation, Ghana, Shows Modest Gains," *The Wall Street Journal*, January 26, 1994, A1, A5.

6. Thomas J. Lueck, "Small City in New Jersey Goes After Global Trade with Help of Residents," *The New York Times*, January 27, 1994, A13.

7. "The Global Free-for-All," *Business Week*, September 26, 1994, 118–26.

8. Ibid., 118.

9. Anthony DePalma, "G.M. Coloring Mexico with Chevys," *The New York Times*, May 12, 1994, D1, D6.

10. Tim Padgett, "The Gringos Are Coming!" *Newsweek*, November 30, 1992, 55.

11. Robert Thomson, "Eating Seaweed and Submarines," *Financial Times*, April 2, 1992, 10.

12. David Housego, "Showman on a Magic Carpet Ride Abroad," *Financial Times*, April 2, 1992, 10.

13. Akbar S. Ahmed, *Postmodernism and Islam* (London: Routledge, 1992), 99.

14. This section is adapted from chapter 5 of Ahmed, *Postmodernism and Islam*.

15. Naazneen Karmali, "Kellogg Tackles Indian Food Habits," *Financial Times*, September 16, 1994, 18.

16. Shiraz Sidhva, "India Takes on Wheat Giants," *Financial Times*, September 15, 1994, 26.

17. Rahul Jacob, "India Gets Moving," *Fortune*, September 5, 1994, 102.

18. Carla Rapoport, "Nestle's Brand Building Machine," *Fortune*, September 19, 1994, 148.

Index

U